BY Michael C. D. Macdonald

SIMON AND SCHUSTER
NEW YORK

# AMERICA'S CITIES

*A REPORT
ON THE MYTH
OF URBAN
RENAISSANCE*

Copyright © 1984 by Michael C. D. Macdonald
All rights reserved, including the right of reproduction in whole or in part in any form. Published by Simon and Schuster, A Division of Simon & Schuster, Inc., Simon & Schuster Building, Rockefeller Center, 1230 Avenue of the Americas, New York, New York 10020. SIMON AND SCHUSTER and colophon are registered trademarks of Simon & Schuster, Inc.
Designed by Irving Perkins and Associates.
Manufactured in the United States of America
10 9 8 7 6 5 4 3 2 1
Library of Congress Cataloging in Publication Data
Macdonald, Michael C. D.
America's cities.
Bibliography: p.
Includes index.
1. Cities and towns—United States. 2. Urban renewal—United States. 3. Urban economics. I. Title.
HT123.M284  1984      307.7′6′0973      84-5426
ISBN 0-671-43913-8

We have made every effort to trace the ownership of all copyrighted material and to secure permission from copyright holders. In the event of any question arising as to the use of any material, we will be pleased to make the necessary corrections in future printings. Thanks are due to the following authors, publishers, publications, and agents for permission to use the material indicated.

Simon & Schuster, Inc.: *Revolt of the Haves* by Robert Kuttner, copyright © 1980. *Everybody Else's Money* by Michael M. Thomas, copyright © 1982. *The World Challenge* by Jean-Jacques Servan-Schreiber, copyright © 1981.

Random House, Inc.: *The Streets Were Paved with Gold* by Ken Auletta, copyright © 1979. *The Death and Life of Great American Cities* by Jane Jacobs, copyright © 1961.

The Julian Bach Literary Agency, Inc.: *Cities in a Race with Time* by Jeanne R. Lowe, copyright © 1967.

Editorial Research Reports: *American Regionalism,* copyright © 1980.

The Encyclopedia Britannica, 11th edition (1910–11).

*(continued at back of book)*

# ACKNOWLEDGMENTS

ANYONE WRITING ABOUT America's cities owes a few obvious debts. An early and common one is to John Gunther's *Inside U.S.A.* of 1947, still a fresh adventure today. The best overall source is the regional series on our fifty states from Neal R. Peirce, starting with his *The Megastates of America* in 1972 and concluding with his and John Keefe's *The Great Lakes States of America* in 1980. These nine books are thorough, and also fun to read. A third basic debt is to Jeanne R. Lowe's *Cities in a Race with Time,* this work of 1967 remaining, in my opinion, the best book about American cities. While I have used it here only for the section on Philadelphia, it has long been a model for analysis, thoroughness and opinionated fairness.

Beyond these sources and recent works like Joel Garreau's *The Nine Nations of North America,* let me note a few journalistic sources. *The New York Times, Washington Post* and *The Wall Street Journal* are the best dailies, while *U.S. News & World Report* proved the most reliable weekly source for urban issues. *U.S. News* has a mild business bias, and so, inevitably, does another good weekly for urban issues, *Business Week.* Cities are economies before they are anything else, so it is also not surprising that the best magazine series on our cities was one of twenty city profiles in *Nation's Business* in 1975 and 1976.

Among the people and institutions that helped with ideas or research, let me note a few here. The Tricentennial Commission of Philadelphia sent me several of its excellent reports. Representative Robert Edgar (D–Pa.), who chairs the Northeast-Midwest Congressional Coalition, sent many of the superb studies put out by that group since 1976. State Senator Donald E. Lukens (R-Ohio) sent some useful data on Ohio budgets in the 1980s.

## 6 · ACKNOWLEDGMENTS

Also helpful were Professors Barry Bluestone, Marilyn Gittell, Norman Krumholz, Richard P. Nathan and Richard Wade, and Andrew Mott of the Center for Community Change. I am especially grateful to Professor Arthur M. Schlesinger, Jr., for his friendly encouragement early on. I am also indebted to Jeffrey Hall of the New York City office of the Census Bureau, to the FBI for sending its Crime Reports, and especially to Samuel N. Ehrenhalt, Regional Commissioner for the Bureau of Labor Statistics in New York, a lively economist whose insights into urban economies were very helpful. I also owe a long-term debt to Meyer M. Kailo, one of New York City's finest civil servants over four decades in health, housing and transit, who taught me how to analyze urban issues and organize material.

A few more debts over the years. Daniel Wolf at *The Village Voice* first encouraged my writing, while Jack Newfield and David Schneiderman at that paper have been helpful in recent years, as has my fine editor there, Ross Wetzsteon. I must thank a few close personal friends whose friendship and support have been helpful over the past few years: Mel Arrighi and Patricia Bosworth, Cornelia Foss, Kim Ginsberg and Lenny Green. In politics, I owe my earliest debt—as do thousands more—to the late Allard K. Lowenstein. I am also grateful for having known the late Dr. George A. Wiley, the founder and leader of the National Welfare Rights Organization, whose many fine grassroots leaders included Joyce Burson, Beulah Sanders, Johnnie Tillmon and Jeanette Washington. Above all, I owe a great deal to the insights of my friend Herman Badillo, former Bronx Borough president, U.S. representative and deputy mayor of New York. He is one liberal who has stayed the course, and America's poor have had few champions as bright and untiring. I know no smarter analyst of urban economic and social issues, and few with such a deft and nasty wit, the latter helpful in lightening the gloom of defending cities!

Finally my thanks to my agent and editors. Peter Matson's belief in this first book was what every new author needs, and his advice on the text was always frank and invaluable. My editor, Alice Mayhew, took a chance on a neophyte, and urged a stronger focus on the Sunbelt cities. I am very grateful for that crucial suggestion, and for numerous others she has made. In the text editing, she was assisted by a bright and sympathetic young editor, David Masello, and I am in his debt as well.

*To*
*My father, Dwight Macdonald,*
*and*
*My mother, Nancy Macdonald,*
*with love*

# CONTENTS

# INTRODUCTION

AS THEY WATCHED the organist at Radio City Music Hall, the tiny Italian turned to the tall descendant of Gouverneur Morris. "That's how the city must be run," said Mayor Fiorello La Guardia to City Council President Newbold Morris. "Like the organist, you must keep both hands on the keyboard and both feet on the pedals—*and never let go.*" That ideal of government is gone today. More than 70 percent of America lives in metropolitan areas, but our cities are dying because too many people have ignored them. Federal neglect, state tax revolts and passive mayors are among the forces shrinking cities today. This book will examine twenty-two cities, twelve in the Sunbelt states of the South and West, ten in the Snowbelt states of the Northeast and Midwest. Most of them are deep in a downward spiral of service cuts, taxpayer flight and revenue loss.

This spiral is usually seen as limited to aging Snowbelt cities like Detroit, Philadelphia, St. Louis or New York, but it is also a force that empties out southern cities like Atlanta, Birmingham, Miami and New Orleans, while it threatens western boomtowns like Houston and Los Angeles. No major American city is truly safe from the downward spiral. All the shiny new office towers, luxury hotels or pedestrian malls downtown cannot hide the growing abandonment behind Potemkin village façades. The urban "renaissance" depicted in national magazines in the late 1970s never really happened. The urban disaster described by the Kerner Commission in 1968 and the Eisenhower Commission in 1969 has gotten worse, as federal neglect and citizen apathy take an inevitable toll.

The federal neglect can be seen by noting the fate of Harry Truman's Fair Deal of 1948, which had pledged civil rights, de-

11

cent housing, full employment and national health insurance. Civil rights has since been realized in law if not custom, but the other three goals cost money. Absent the will to raise money for the job, America remains the only major industrial democracy without three basic benefits:

• By 1968, the Kaiser Commission was reporting on a severe national housing crisis. Today, we have even more cancerous slums, like the South Bronx, the Third Ward of Houston, Roxbury in Boston or Watts in Los Angeles.

• Full employment was defined as 4 percent joblessness by Richard Nixon in 1971. It is defined today as 6.5 percent, and some think 8 percent will soon be deemed "full" employment in a nation unwilling to train, retrain or relocate workers in federal programs long used in Europe and Japan.

• National health insurance took big strides with Medicare and Medicaid under Lyndon Johnson, with Richard Nixon expanding nutrition supplements like food stamps, school lunches, and the Women, Infants and Children (WIC) feeding grants. But some 34 million Americans still had no health insurance of any kind in 1983, in the wake of Reagan cuts to the working poor and normal lack of coverage.

Citizen apathy is symbolized by the tax revolt. This book will see its destructive path in even liberal states like California, Minnesota and New York, where it imposes new fiscal burdens on strapped and shrinking cities. Rather than close loopholes for the rich, the tax revolt feeds them instead. Middle-class voters backed Proposition 13 in California, then it gave two of every three dollars in tax relief to corporations and realtors. Nationally, the "people's tax cut" of Ronald Reagan meant that those who earned under $22,900 a year lost $30.7 billion in federal benefits, while those earning more gained $223.6 billion in tax relief.

Beyond this perverse redistribution of wealth from the poor to the rich, citizen apathy grew on many fronts. Where 62 percent of America voted for a President in 1960, only 52 percent did by 1980. Narcotics were obscure in 1960, but Americans were spending an estimated $81 billion for drugs in 1981. Where employee theft was $16 billion in 1970, it was up to $76 billion by 1981. Where 8 percent of America evaded taxes in 1973, an estimated 25 percent did in 1981, for a federal revenue loss of nearly $90 billion.

This book will examine the grim effects of federal, state and local neglect that surrounds America's growing urban crisis. It will go past the publicized pockets of gentrified neighborhoods or the new waterfront malls to see the real economic and social facts of our fading urban life. While some of the twenty-two cities examined here are stable and a few more can be saved, most of them are very troubled or even past the point of no return. Some of the profiles will be brief, but nearly half of them will be extensive, with the last chapter devoted to the growing service crisis and economic problems of New York City. Various kinds of cities will be seen, from diversified Snowbelt paragons like Milwaukee, Minneapolis and Wichita to troubled company towns like Birmingham, Detroit and Las Vegas, the latter in a tailspin as legal betting spreads to forty-seven states and Atlantic City gets the East Coast action. Vegas is a minor, artificial city, but gambling is very much a part of our nation, so the brassy pleasure dome is detailed. Las Vegas also has had our highest alcoholism, suicide, and/or child-abuse rates.

Beyond our gambling craze, this book covers much social and economic ground in its twenty-two city profiles. We shall detail the crisis of rubber and steel in Ohio, of autos in Detroit, and of machine tools in Milwaukee. We shall see why Denver may be the Sunbelt's most stable city, and why Houston is its most overrated boomtown. To see a service crisis in detail, we shall look at crime, housing, health and subways in New York, and see how much of that city's fiscal and service crisis is based on tax breaks for realtors and, to a lesser extent, inflated deals for municipal unions. To keep data to a minimum, I generally use statistics from the 1980 census year as a benchmark, although frequent exceptions are made.

Readers can also find out why we may lose our high-tech lead to Japan in the 1990s. They can learn how New Bedford diversified from whales to mills in the 1840s, and how Wichita went beyond making small planes to a broad-based economy that is often five points under our national unemployment rates. They can visit Minneapolis and witness a unique European enclave of deep cultural and social resources, and see how St. Louis went from being the only city to hold a World's Fair and an Olympics in one year to a Carthage that lost 47 percent of its people after 1950. Readers can also discover Kansas City as the home of our best small art museum, our first and best shopping mall, and the next largest number of fountains outside Rome. They can watch Newark go from a booming factory town in 1950, when it had more residents than Dallas, Denver, Phoenix, San Antonio, San Diego or San Jose—six of the Sunbelt's ten biggest cities in 1980 —to an abandoned, burned-out shell today.

Sunbelt cities are hardly immune to the urban crisis. Atlanta, Birmingham, Miami and New Orleans are the four worst examples among the ten major Sunbelt cities to lose at least 5 percent of their people in the 1970s. Atlanta, for example, is still "the city too busy to hate," but 42 percent of its white residents left in the 1970s. Even Houston has become a gilded El Dorado for jobless Snowbelt factory workers, with a service crisis erupting in 1981, followed by recession in 1982. Few big Sunbelt cities are truly stable.

This book will not abandon all hope for our cities, but it will seek to reveal their truth. This writer's liberal bias will be fairminded, hopefully. When a black mayor like Coleman Young or Maynard Jackson uses racist rhetoric to fend off critics, I shall run the quotes that the media like to forget. When an old liberal like Governor Hugh Carey of New York freezes welfare grants for six years while cutting back taxes for the rich in a prelude to Reaganomics, I shall highlight the details. When Ronald Reagan turns from hurting cities, his positive acts shall be noted. His belated but welcome war on drugs will be described, as will his innovation as California governor: indexing welfare grants to inflation, something that liberal governors still will not do. I shall try to limit myself to a few basic prejudices in this book: cities must be saved, poor people must be helped, economies must be revived with massive federal programs to employ, train, retrain or relocate unskilled workers in a postindustrial scene.

Regarding the selection of the cities in this book, I never intended a thorough survey of all major American cities. Instead, I often looked for certain types, sometimes omitting similar cities. While many of our big cities are profiled, so are some medium-sized ones to illustrate things like company towns, diversified economies or regional problems. As a result, at least four major cities are not covered here. Let me briefly note, then, why Boston, Chicago, San Diego and Washington are not among the twenty-two city profiles.

San Diego is mainly a military company town, and I have included a more interesting example in San Antonio, "Mother-in-law of the Army." Washington was omitted as a unique government city (only Las Vegas has a higher share of service workers). It was also excluded on grounds of familiarity. As a reader of the *Washington Post,* I could have given the District a thorough review. Given space limits, however, only one city would get such a "roof to cellar" appraisal. Having always lived in our biggest and most important city, I inevitably chose New York for that full treatment. Boston was omitted on similar grounds. The story of its service crisis following the 1980 Proposition 2½ tax cuts is a compelling cautionary tale, but only one city would get a thorough profile of its service crisis, and that was New York.

Omitting Chicago from this book was most difficult; rising from the ashes of its 1871 fire, it has dominated our industrial heartland ever since. With machinery and steel in the lead, the Chicago–Gary nexus was long our biggest factory area, only yielding to Los Angeles–Long Beach in 1980. The city of big shoulders was also broad-based in its diverse economy, with forty-four front offices from the *Fortune* 500 in 1971, the world's busiest commodities market, and retailing giants like Montgomery Ward and Sears, the latter erecting the world's tallest building in the Loop. The world's busiest airport is out at O'Hare, and one of our busiest ports is the inland one on Lake Michigan. Because architecture is one of many leitmotifs in this book, Chicago would seem a logical profile, since Sullivan, Wright and Mies were the local geniuses who led our premodern, modern and Miesian schools of urban design.

Or there is political drama: the Mafia-picked congressmen from the First Ward; the vote stealing and the municipal union peace kept by often inflated wages; the infamous machine, its 35,000 members once outnumbering even the 31,500 Chicago-area workers at Sears. And over all this there had loomed Richard Daley, mayor of Chicago and chairman of the Cook County Democratic Central Committee, with Neal R. Peirce writing in 1971 how "holding these two jobs is a bit like being Premier of the U.S.S.R. and First Secretary of the Communist Party at the same time." There were Daley's tax breaks for business powers in the Loop, and his service neglect for blacks in the South and West sides. There were the most segregated neighborhoods of any major American city. There were the police given Daley's alleged order to "shoot to kill" arsonists and "shoot to maim" looters during the riots after the death of Martin Luther King. There was the gimmick of separate park, school and transit budgets to muddy the fiscal and service-delivery waters. All around this polarized, confused and inequitable mess there was the myth of "the city that works," propagated by America's media in the wake of a police riot at the 1968 Democratic Convention.

The post-Daley era has relaxed the controls and destroyed the myths of the city that worked. Chicago's mass-transit system turned out to be aging, badly maintained and broke. The public schools went bust, the city squandered tax breaks downtown, and the famous union peace was broken by strikes. In the 1970s 11.9 percent of Chicago's people left the city, about 500,000 of them white. A Chicago that had been roughly 45 percent black or Hispanic in 1970 was a 55 percent minority city in 1980. By 1981, only twenty-five Fortune 500 offices were left.

Then came the election of 1983. Real issues like Harold Washington's crusade against the machine, or a city in economic and social crisis, were swept aside. At stage center was a lurid media carnival, which focused on charges of "racism" from both sides.

The 1983 election results, however, were pleasantly anticlimactic. An 82 percent turnout of voters confirmed new black power, and a lot of white interest in civics as well. History may yet term this election a catharsis, a final flurry of wild swings before two fighters fell with grudging respect into each other's arms at the bell. Or perhaps the 500,000 white emigrants will be joined by even bigger hordes. In any event, the best man seemed to have won. In defeat, Bernard Epton was a whining loser who abandoned the scene by flying to Florida, while the victorious Harold Washington was a gracious host at a unity breakfast. Perhaps he would join neighboring mayors Richard Hatcher of Gary and Henry Maier of Milwaukee—long America's two most militant mayors—to form a Great Lakes triumvirate to plead the urban cause in Washington. (Maier's leadership over more than twenty years will be seen in the Milwaukee section; Hatcher was the only mayor blackballed from Reagan briefings due to his activism as head of the U.S. Conference of Mayors.)

As fascinating and important as Chicago is, it was omitted from this book on two main grounds. The lesser reason was the weak coverage given Chicago in national papers like *The New York Times, Washington Post* and *The Wall Street Journal*. Why such thin reportage, apart from the 1983 election? Is it because Chicago is too much like New York, an eternal "second city" in eastern press eyes? Or does it reflect unconscious liberal animus against the Daley era at the *Post* and *Times*? Whatever the cause, this weak Chicago coverage made for sketchy research on current issues, an incentive for omission from a book that was not a thorough survey of all big cities. The basic reason for omission, however, was Chicago's strong resemblance to New York. Apart from Chicago's segregation, poor services and party machine, the two cities have similar economies in their double life as factory and front-office towns. Their service crisis, fiscal problems and economic decline also have elements in common, and both took an 11 percent census loss in the 1970s.

The Sunbelt section opens with a regional overview. This has been a violent area since the era of western mining camps and southern slavery, and the flood of rootless migrants after 1950 had led to the Sunbelt having nine of our ten most violent metro areas in 1980. The overview also examines the limits of western mineral wealth and water supplies. Chapter 2 explores the recent myth of the New South, in reality the home of rural shacks in the Mississippi Delta, severe white poverty in Appalachia and a welfare grant in oil-rich Texas that was last raised in 1969. Chapter 3 is on southern cities, starting with violent Miami and shrinking Atlanta, ending with brief notes on troubled Birmingham and New Orleans. Chapter 4 is on Texas cities. There are the Houston and Dallas service crises, with Dallas still run by a group of 200 corporate leaders since the late 1930s. There is San Antonio, where there is the fourth lowest average hourly wage among our 209 metro areas. Chapter 5 proceeds west to the Rocky Mountain cities. Denver is the most stable Sunbelt city, Las Vegas is a foundering company town, and Phoenix is a bloated sprawl, and a big, vile slum for one in six Phoenicians with polluted air in a former health spa. Chapter 6 is about California, once called "west of the West" by Teddy Roosevelt. We look first at crime and tax revolt in this rootless, volatile state, and then look briefly at San Francisco and thoroughly at Los Angeles, a boomtown deserted by some 300,000 white residents during the 1970s. A 60-mile radius from downtown L.A. encompasses the twelfth biggest GNP on earth, but also the most virulent teen-age gangs on earth.

Part II on the Snowbelt starts with Chapter 7's look at three common problems for aging cities of the region: tax and service cuts, the crime wave after 1977, and the collapse of heavy industry, as well as the automation of service jobs. Chapter 8 examines the bright side, the story of how Kansas City, Milwaukee, Minneapolis and Wichita diversified their economies well in advance of the current crisis for smokestack industries. All four of these Snowbelt paragons tend to have low crime and unemployment rates. Chapter 9 looks at the troubled but salvageable cities of Baltimore and Philadelphia. The national press has hailed Baltimore's revived waterfront, and in the city of brotherly love, the calm Philadelphia mayoral primary between a black, W. Wilson Goode, and Frank Rizzo. But both cities took big census and factory losses in the 1970s, and have major economic and social problems. The chapter also looks at three cities past the point of no return: Detroit, St. Louis and Newark. Chapter 10 is a full portrait of New York City. Still the world's capital of commerce, communications and culture, it lost 11 percent of its people in the 1970s, saw median family income plunge, and has had fiscal and service crisis since 1975. Its economic future is bright for 600,000 daily commuters with Manhattan office jobs, but dim for millions of unskilled residents in a city that lost 550,000 of 1 million factory jobs after 1950. New York City has had a major office and construction boom in Manhattan since 1980, including mega-projects like the South Street Seaport, the $292 million Portman hotel near Times Square and the giant Convention Center scheduled to open by 1986. But meanwhile, housing abandonment and middle-class exodus spread northward in the Bronx and southward in Brooklyn, two boroughs where half the city lives. Even Manhattan is being rapidly turned into the home of the very rich or very poor, and while commuter jobs grow in Midtown and Wall Street offices, the ongoing loss of factory jobs means the city's unemployment rate is often a point or two above the national average.

# PART I
# THE SUNBELT

# CHAPTER 1 |

# SUNBELT IN SUNSET

DURING THE 1970s, the Sunbelt states grew spectacularly in people, jobs and wealth. The 1980 census saw them pick up seventeen seats in Congress from the older Snowbelt states. The Sunbelt is half the nation, yet it created 70 percent of all new jobs. High tech expanded in Silicon Valleys as aging factories closed around the Great Lakes. With all our big military bases and most of our defense plants, the Sunbelt states will benefit mainly from the Reagan binge on defense. Finally, they have almost all our oil and natural gas, most of our coal, and in 1979, southern and western states produced 81 percent of our mineral wealth.

Yet the Sunbelt heads for its sunset, due to an urban crisis that knows no regional bounds. In the South and West today, too many poor people, too much crime, too few services, too many taxpayers leaving town all reflect the old downward spiral of the Snowbelt cities. The Sunbelt states had 90 percent of our census growth in the 1970s, yet big cities like Atlanta, Birmingham, Denver, Louisville, New Orleans, Norfolk, Oakland, Portland, San Francisco and Seattle lost at least 5 percent of their residents in the decade. Regional crises like growing water shortages out West and too many unskilled workers down South plus Sunbelt violence that is as old as slavery or Sutter's gold has resulted in a witches' brew for a troubled paradise today.

Part of the Sunbelt sunset is external. The overall crisis of American cities described by the Kerner Commission in 1968 and the Eisenhower Commission in 1969, and ignored by Washington ever since, figures here. Until Washington funds sizable aid and job programs for the older cities of the Snowbelt and Sunbelt alike, the downward spiral of joblessness, decay, crime, service cuts and taxpayer flight will continue.

Some of the Sunbelt urban crisis, however, is internal and self-imposed. For example, the oil states of Louisiana, Oklahoma and Texas often have huge state treasury surpluses from severance taxes on oil and natural-gas exports. But Louisiana hasn't rushed any special aid to New Orleans, called the poorest of our fifty big cities in a 1977 survey, and Oklahoma has no Marshall Plan for the sizable census of blacks in a run-down North Tulsa slum. While Texas had more than $500 million in surplus revenues for 1982, it hasn't raised its punitive welfare grant since 1969. Where Texas gave welfare aid to only one of every three children living below the poverty line in 1975, New York gave welfare aid to almost all state residents living in poverty.

Even liberal California caused many of its problems. The 1978 tax revolt has wrecked local and state revenues, with continuous fiscal crisis since 1981, and endless service cuts for cities in a very rich state. This endangers the poor and elderly, encourages middle-class exodus from dying cities, and threatens the state economy. California was the fifth biggest spender for education among the states before the Proposition 13 deluge of tax cuts, but was forty-fourth by 1980. This meant that San Jose State had a third of its engineering faculty spots unfilled and had to turn away half its student applicants. With fewer trained workers to staff Silicon Valley next door, the Valley's biggest employer opened a new factory for up to 6,000 workers in Austin, Texas. Arizona, Idaho and Oregon have also lured jobs out of the Valley, an unthinkable feat a few years ago when California was a full-service state.

## Sunbelt Violence

Crime and the Sunbelt are a familiar team. The Colt .45 was invented in Paterson, New Jersey, but the "great equalizer" settled the West and enforced racism down South. The violent mining camps of the 1850s, the water-hole feuds, the massacre of Indians, the poisoned well of slavery, then Reconstruction and finally Jim Crow—these are among the foundations of Sunbelt violence. Compounding these today are the nervous mobility and rootlessness of the region.

Florida had 1.9 million net migrants in the 1970s, and also had six of the ten most violent metro areas in America for 1980. Texas gained more than a million migrants in the 1970s; Dallas and Houston had half as many cops as Chicago and almost twice as much crime. California, with 1.3 million net migrants in the 1970s, has long been our most rootless state, as the final stop for opportunity seekers like the Midwest migrants of the 1920s or the Okies of the Depression. California has gone from crackpot cults and funny-money crusades in the 1930s to survivalist arsenals and tax revolts today.

During the early 1970s, Snowbelt cities often dominated the murder, rape and robbery data, but then Sunbelt cities took over. In 1972 and 1975, Detroit took five of six first places for the worst rate in these three violent crimes. In 1980, Miami had 65 murders per 100,000 residents, against 50 for runner-up Detroit. Miami was also first with 2,029 robberies per 100,000 residents, against 1,422 for second-place New York. Newark had the most rapes, but the next three cities were Atlanta, Denver and Dallas. And 1981 saw more of this as Miami led the nation in murder and assault, and was second only to Newark for robberies.

In 1980, FBI reports showed that nine of the ten most violent metro areas were in the Sunbelt, the exception being the casino town of Atlantic City. Handgun sales in Miami quadrupled from 1979 to 1981. Estimating that sadomasochism accounts for 10 percent of all of San Francisco murders, the Coroner's Office wisely gave preventive counseling to Bay Area gays prone to that one facet of gay life. Even Hawaii saw the Japanese *Yakuza* moving in on Honolulu the way Mafia hoods did in Vegas after "Bugsy" Siegel opened the Flamingo Hotel in 1947. One more example of unusual Sunbelt violence is that, with the exception of the Tylenol Killer, John Wayne Gacy in Chicago, and the Son of Sam killer in New York, almost all of the psychotic mass killers of the past dozen years have been from the Sunbelt states: Juan V. Corona, Charles Manson, the Zodiac Killer, Wayne B. Williams, Theodore Bundy, the Freeway Killer, the Reverend Jim Jones and his more than 900 victims, the Hillside Strangler, and Elmer Wayne Henley. All of our major assassination attempts have been by Sunbelt residents as well: the killers of John and Robert Kennedy and Martin Luther King, and the three failed assassins of Gerald Ford and Ronald Reagan.*

## Biting Uncle's Hand

Minorities are now the majority in Atlanta, Birmingham, Los Angeles, Miami, New Orleans and San Antonio, and should soon dominate Dallas, Houston and San Francisco. Cities with high minority shares inevitably have more poverty and needs, and are thus more dependent on federal aid. For all the Sunbelt attacks on Washington, the region's cities cannot survive without its help. A 1980 Princeton study showed that if all federal aid was removed, local taxes would have to be hiked 31 percent in Houston, 40 percent in Tulsa, 42 percent in Los Angeles and 66 percent in Phoenix.

Ninety billion dollars in federal water projects was essential for oasis cities like Los Angeles, Phoenix and San Diego, and the rich fields of the Imperial Valley in California and the Salt River Valley of Arizona. Special federal welfare formulas after 1938 helped bust southern states. Seventy-eight percent of the military payroll and 58 percent of the prime contracts were in Sunbelt states in 1979. All of this means a huge "imbalance of payments" between Washington and the two regions. Between 1975 and 1979, Snowbelt states sent Washington $165 million more in taxes than they received in federal aid, while Sunbelt states sent Washington $112 billion *less* in taxes than they got back in aid.

Yet the Sunbelt has long been a source of virulent attacks on Washington. Barry Goldwater, George Wallace, Jimmy Carter and Ronald Reagan all ran against Washington in their presidential campaigns. Without generous federal aid that gave the South and West an industrial base, the region would have been mainly a colonial source of raw materials for export to and processing by the Snowbelt industrial states.

Federal aid breaks for the South and West continue today. The

---

* The two worst prison fires in recent years have been in Sunbelt states, with forty-two inmates killed in the Maury County jail in Tennessee in 1977 and twenty-seven prisoners killed in the Biloxi county jail in Mississippi in 1982. In both cases, toxic fumes from burning polyurethane mattresses killed the victims. Federal court orders banning polyurethane from jails had been issued some time before.

big ticket is defense. *The Unprotected Flank,* a Northeast-Midwest Congressional Coalition study of Pentagon spending, revealed in 1980 that:

- The Sunbelt with 52 percent of our people got 58 percent of the prime defense contracts and 84 percent of all Pentagon construction funds.
- The Sunbelt had 75 percent of all our military bases, including all of the major combat divisions.
- The Sunbelt had 78 percent of the defense payroll. While Snowbelt states lost 36,000 defense jobs after 1950, Sunbelt states gained 516,000.

The growth of Sunbelt defense jobs began during World War II, when states like California, Georgia and Texas became arsenals of democracy. After World War II, Sunbelt committee chairmen in Congress helped transfer military bases from Snowbelt states. Today all but one of the active combat divisions in America are south of the 37th parallel. Having thirteen divisions in the Sunbelt makes little sense for several reasons. Such deployment hinders access to the NATO theater and hampers our ability to send up to 350,000 troops to Europe within two weeks. And there is the matter of climate. As Neal R. Peirce has observed in the *Washington Post:* "Today not a single major combat division is located in the Frost Belt where it might learn wintertime fighting skills or test the weapons to be used in a snowy European, Afghanistanian or Korean theater of war."

While Northeast ports are the main link to Europe, 40 percent of all naval base closings after 1965 were in that area, under a "tidewater strategy" aimed at closing all of the region's military ports. Philadelphia and Portsmouth, New Hampshire, bases were spared after much political pressure, but the huge Boston Naval Shipyard and Quonset Point in Rhode Island were closed. *The Unprotected Flank* also notes that putting all bases and most defense plants in the Sunbelt makes Soviet targeting easier. Sixty percent of all Pentagon emergency production plants are in the Snowbelt, but "current Pentagon spending patterns, however, rather than maintaining this necessary industrial base, are working to weaken it by draining defense dollars out of the region."

A generation of high-precision weapons has shifted most prime defense contracts to new factories in the South and West. At the start of that generation, Eisenhower's defense secretary and former GM president Charles E. Wilson made the famous claim that "what's good for the country is good for General Motors." But as journalist William Sweet observed in 1980, Wilson's Pentagon tour was "not especially good for General Motors or the industrial Midwest." Recent congressional studies show that Snowbelt states still get most of the subcontractor dollars, but the region's industrial tailspin threatens that minor lead. The Sunbelt has the big aerospace plants and NASA facilities for prime contracts. It is also the region that dominates in high tech. There is Silicon Valley in California, the Silicon Prairie of the Dallas-Fort Worth metroplex, the Research Triangle of North Carolina, and Arizona, which is our third biggest high-tech state.

Beyond the prime contracts and high-tech subcontractors is the vast military payroll. In 1979, Snowbelt states got $6.9 billion in Pentagon personnel outlays, while the Sunbelt got $25.3 billion. This is the result of so many combat divisions being located in one region, with the "volunteer army" adding tens of billions to Sunbelt payrolls after 1973, because of the extra pay needed to recruit, retain and retire a mercenary corps.

Additional federal aid breaks for the Sunbelt include welfare/Medicaid payments for the South, and huge water projects for the West, essential for growth in farming, industry mining, and population in a very arid region.

The welfare breaks go back to 1938, when FDR called the South "the nation's No. 1 economic problem," and got Congress to give it special aid. Today Snowbelt states like Illinois and New York get 50 cents from Washington for every Medicaid dollar spent, while South Carolina gets 72 cents, Alabama 73 cents, and Mississippi 78 cents. What makes this federal favoritism even more galling is that the South got rich after 1940 by driving 4.7 million poor blacks up north, partly by keeping welfare payments so low and restricted.

As a result of this huge shift of the poor, the Snowbelt recently had 750,000 more welfare clients than the Sunbelt. Further, it gave more humane levels of aid to more eligible clients. Yet despite taking in the South's poor, Snowbelt states averaged 52 cents in federal reimbursement per Medicaid dollar versus 59 cents in southern states.

Then there were the West's water projects. The dry region deserves more help in this area, but the federal aid is inordinate. For example, Arizona gets $66.90 per capita in federal water-project aid a year, while New York gets 15 cents.

What Uncle Sam gave, he could in theory take away. Out of a mixture of guilt about being helped and the fear of being abandoned, Sunbelt leaders lash out at federal saviors. As Bernard De Voto once put it about the West's attacks on Washington, "get out and give us more money." The sooner these attacks end, the better for both regions, as Sunbelt and Snowbelt unite to demand a thorough federal program to save all cities.

## Energy

Western states have nearly all our oil and natural gas, and these are the tip of the vast mineral iceberg. The big potential resource is synfuel, in a region with 50 percent of our coal and 95 percent of our oil-shale reserves. One coalfield in Montana, Wyoming and North Dakota could power America for 100 years. Unit coal trains a mile long are a common sight in Rocky Mountain states. Liquefied as synfuel, the coal reserves could yield 500 billion barrels, or four times the proved Saudi fields. Oil-shale deposits are even bigger. Colorado, Utah and Wyoming reserves could produce at least 600 billion more barrels of synfuel. There could be enough synfuel for 175 years of freedom from OPEC, enough time to perfect a cheap photovoltaic cell to harness the sun forever.

The immense wealth of the West in coal, oil, oil shale, copper, uranium and other minerals is reflected in the fact that only six mineral-rich states had 40 percent of our state treasury surpluses in 1980. Mineral wealth plus the western strengths of aerospace, agriculture, defense and high tech made this *the* region for job and census growth in the 1970s. Between 1969 and 1976, eight of the ten states creating the highest share of new jobs were out West.* Twelve of the fourteen states growing more than 20 per-

---

* Canada has a similar shift, with the western mineral wealth of Alberta luring migrants from the eastern provinces. Most of Canada lives in Ontario and Quebec, the industrial heartland just north of our Midwest factory belt, but the 1970s saw oil-rich Alberta grow five times faster than Ontario and seven times faster than Quebec. As Montreal grew 1 percent and Toronto 7 percent, Alberta's capital, Edmonton, grew 18 percent and its oil center of Calgary by 26 percent.

cent in the 1970s were there, the West getting twelve of the Sunbelt's seventeen new seats in Congress in 1982. Until 1985 anyway, the West also holds the Executive Branch, with a President from Los Angeles, a Vice President from Houston.

A major break for western energy states was the lifting of Richard Nixon's sensible freeze of domestic oil and natural-gas prices, the last vestige of his wage-price controls of 1971. The deregulation of oil prices by Jimmy Carter and Congress in 1979 meant a huge revenue boost for the western states. Projected state treasury windfalls from the severance taxes imposed on exported oil by 1990 included: California, $22 billion; Texas, $33 billion; Alaska, $37 billion.* And that was just oil. Natural-gas and coal reserves elsewhere add billions more in western severance taxes each year.

Meanwhile, the Snowbelt suffers. It has longer winters, less fuel-efficient factories, and 75 percent of our fuel-heated homes. Where New England used oil for 79 percent of its energy, America used it for 49 percent. The Snowbelt's high need for diesel and heating oil meant that 1979 price decontrol did for its states what OPEC had long been doing to nations like Brazil, India, the Sudan and Turkey—all paying half their export earnings for oil by 1980. Sunbelt states got tax windfalls; Snowbelt states paid the bills. Yet in 1981, Ronald Reagan not only cut the windfall-profit tax for Sunbelt oil states, but he also cut federal fuel-aid grants for the Snowbelt working poor. For 1982, one consumer group projected that 1.5 million homes might be without heat that winter as recession, fuel costs and Reagan cuts moved in. Long before this, our annual death rate from cold-related causes had already gone from 350 a year in the 1960s to more than 700 by 1978.

America desperately needs a fair energy policy, one that mixes price controls, conservation, low-income energy grants and long-range development of renewable resources like solar power. None of these elements, however, were in the current Reagan

---

* Few will move to Alaska's harsh tundra as the oil benefits grow, but the state's awesome revenue windfall illustrates the story. Alaska earned so much in extra oil severance taxes from the 1979 price decontrol that it ended its income tax, rebated two years of taxes, and sent every resident a check of up to $1,050 for 1981. As writer Michael J. McManus observed in 1981, "Next year, Alaska estimates it will get $3.9 billion—enough to write a check for $10,000 for every man, woman and child in the state. And in a few years, Alaska thinks it will be getting $10 billion a year—or $100,000 per family of four!"

policy. In contrast, Canadian policy keeps Alberta's oil fixed at 75 percent of the OPEC price. Ottawa also demands a fair share of oil tax revenues from the big producer province that has 85 percent of Canada's petroleum.

In 1982, however, the West's oil boom collapsed. Small oil producers were trapped between rising costs and falling OPEC prices. A world glut cut prices 10 percent, interest rates were 16 percent, and the independents were caught short. So many failed to meet loans that on July 5 the fourth largest bank in oil-rich Oklahoma failed. The Penn Square Bank failure was one of the biggest in our history, its losses including $250 million for Chase Manhattan and $1 billion for Continental Illinois. Tulsa's jobless rate doubled in a year, as the oil-rig count fell by 40 percent. The summer of 1982 found people sleeping under Tulsa bridges or in their cars, with the welfare department seeing a record 1,024 people on one August day.

By the middle of 1982, drilling was down 29 percent. Many oil tracts were on the market, with sellers "coming back to us at prices they literally laughed at" in 1981, according to one Denver oilman. In 1981, there had been so many rigs in the field that oil companies invested $150 million in drilling in Idaho, which had had 160 consecutive dry holes since the first Potato State well of 1903. Oil and gas drilling had been so deep in the Overthrust Belt of Utah, the Tuscaloosa Trend of Louisiana and the Anadarko Basin of Oklahoma that some wells were five miles deep, where temperatures reach 500 degrees and pressures are 30,000 pounds per square inch. A drill-casing producer noted that "down there, it's pretty much the way Hades is described in the Bible." But by 1982, a falling rig count saw the head of Hughes Tool ask, "What's wrong with 1982 being the second best year in drilling history?" He had a point. Oil and gas taxes, royalties and leases, are a third of Louisiana revenues, and while the 1982 glut cost the state $80 million in taxes, a $556 million profit was still left.

The problem ahead for oil is the exhaustion of our reserves around the year 2020.* In his television debate with Jimmy Carter

---

* The year 2020 has also been projected as the year the Ogallala aquifer feeding the Great Plains runs dry. Based on earthquake cycles, 2020 may also be the outer time limit for a "great quake" to hit Los Angeles and/or San Francisco. The median retirement peak for the baby-boom census cohort should also be roughly 2020, which will mean a huge strain on Social Security funds and health resources.

in 1980, Ronald Reagan claimed there was more in our wells "than has been taken out in 120 years that they have been drilled." In 1981 a Rand Corporation study suggested otherwise. Looking at specific oil fields rather than projecting from abstract models, Rand cut old estimates in half, which could mean twenty to forty years left at current drilling rates. The General Accounting Office warned Congress in 1981 to act soon to "help assure that potentially severe economic dislocations in the southwest's basic industry are anticipated in time to take mitigating action and, thus, preclude the need for huge federal aid expenditures in what could become a distressed area." It's hard to see Texas, Louisiana and Oklahoma as a mineral dust bowl, but the depletion of oil reserves looms ahead. With 2 million wells drilled in 1981, we have sunk four times the wells of the rest of the non-Communist world, and few virgin fields remain. The 11.3 million barrels produced daily in 1970 were down to 10.1 million by 1980. New recovery techniques and deep wells can only delay the depletion for a few years.

Then there is coal. Once the "fuel of last resort," coal was revived in the 1970s, as Jimmy Carter pushed oil-to-coal conversion to cut the OPEC noose. With low sulfur content, western coal was attractive, but drawbacks like "acid rain" and other pollution, and more black lung for miners, remain. Over the long term, too much burning of coal could mean too much carbon dioxide in the atmosphere. This would cause a "greenhouse effect," warming the planet, with possible climatic chaos everywhere.*

Meanwhile, western coal production took off. Wyoming production went from 7 million tons in 1970 to 103 million by 1981. Exports grew strongly. If enough railways could be built and ports deep-dredged, 45 million metric tons of steam coal shipped in 1980 could go to 460 million by the year 2000. Australia and South Africa dominate markets today, but our larger reserves could make America "the Saudi Arabia of coal." A big customer could be Japan, with Rocky Mountain states a logical supplier for the Pacific Basin.

---

* Brookhaven National Laboratory suggests that up to 2 percent of all deaths in America and Canada may be due partly to sulfur dioxide smoke particulates from sources like the Ohio Valley smokestacks. That would be 40,000 annual deaths in the two nations. Without coal to fire power plants, electricity to prolong lives elsewhere would be impossible. Once cheap solar power is found, however, coal will be quickly retired.

There are 1.3 trillion tons of coal out West, about a 1,500 years' supply. Not only are there serious environmental problems to consider, but also the coal is far from its markets. This leads to things like the mile-long "unit coal train" with 100 hopper cars. Thirty-five of these monstrous centipedes lumbered through the Colorado city of Littleton each day in 1981, and there may be eighty a day by 1990. (The city of 28,000 asked voters to back a tax to put the trains in a trough, local bumper stickers lamenting "Trains, Trains and more Trains.")

Another way to ship Rockies coal to faraway markets is through slurry pipelines, which combine a mix of powdered coal and water sent from strip mines to power plants. A decade ago a 1,036-mile slurry line was proposed from a Wyoming mine to an Arkansas power plant, moving about 25 percent of Wyoming's current output. Wyoming is a high-growth state: third for census growth in the 1970s, first for job growth in 1980. But the slurry line would have used 6.5 billion gallons of water a year, and farmers were so opposed that Governor Ed Herschler was elected in 1974 mainly by opposing the pipeline. Joel Garreau in the *Washington Post* noted slurry drawbacks for the West, and added, "There's got to be a better way, right? Well, there are synfuels. Of course, synfuels from coal cost about twice what Saudi sweet does. Tar and ash byproducts contain some of the most potent carcinogens known to man. And a coal synfuel plant requires as much as 10 billion gallons of water a year."

There was synfuel pollution of water in 1980 in Stroudsburg, Pennsylvania. A synfuel plant from the 1880s had produced "town gas" from coal for street lighting—one of 11,000 such American plants in the 1920s, before western pipelines with cheap natural gas closed them down. Late in 1980, tar blobs rose in a Stroudsburg creek whose course had been changed after a 1955 flood that killed 500 people. Now the creek flowed over huge tar lagoons that held 8 million gallons of gasified waste. When that waste leaked out, the creek was closed. It could cost $150 million to clean up all the cancer-causing tar below. Coal synfuel plants also had problems. A federal agency warned Ronald Reagan that liquefaction could cause cancer, poisoning, respiratory illness and chemical burns among the workers involved.*

---

* Nazi Germany used the Lurgi process to maintain oil supplies in World War II. South Africa, which uses the process today, took in Polish technicians fleeing from the martial-law regime in 1981. The rationale was that these white technicians could expand the industry, giving blacks more service jobs.

But the big synfuel ticket is oil-shale rock. The English used it for heat in the seventeenth century, and in the nineteenth century the Ute Indians taught our western pioneers about "the rock that burns." By the 1850s, some fifty American companies used shale heat. Then on August 27, 1859, the mining tools of E. L. Drake dropped into a crevice sixty-nine feet below the ground at Titusville, Pennsylvania, and the oil rush was on. Only lately have some 600 billion barrels' worth of shale deposits in Colorado, Utah and Wyoming been considered for synfuel production.

Synfuel's latest revival followed the OPEC price shock of 1979. As oil prices doubled overnight, Jimmy Carter and Congress hastily launched a Synthetic Fuels Corporation backed by $88 billion in loan guarantees. Synfuel was suddenly an Eighth Wonder, with Exxon projecting a national output of 15 million barrels a day by 2015. That would meet all our needs, while employing 860,000 people, almost as many as the 1.1 million Americans in mining today. Add those people who would service new synfuel cities and that could mean 8 million more people, most of them in the water-scarce West.

All the shale mining would leave a lot of debris. As shale rock is crushed, cooked, cooled and liquefied, it expands 25 percent in a "popcorn effect." A shale industry meeting Jimmy Carter's goals would produce enough annual waste to match all the earth moved in building the Panama Canal. As a former Energy Department official has noted, "These are not nice plants. These are big, dirty plants." Joel Garreau projects that all the shale cooking over 100 years would mean up to a

> trillion tons of tailings left over. That's literally mountains of waste, off which dust will blow, clouding the air for hundreds of miles. The minerals that will leach off the tailings when the rains hit will make the Colorado River, from which millions get their drinking water, even more unpalatable than it is now.

Garreau warns that the resulting acid rain could sterilize "land downwind . . . downwind is the Great Plains. . . ." A federal study of 1981 warned that production and use of synfuel would mean 2.3 times the emission of carbon dioxide than from conventional fuels—one more push toward the possible "greenhouse effect." The plants would also release exotic pollutants like arsenic, cadmium, benzene and mercury. Shale-oil workers might be more prone than oil drillers to skin cancer.

There were also political problems. Ronald Reagan insisted that companies pay 40 percent of front-end costs for plants backed by federal loan guarantees. That drove small synfuel firms from the field. He also slowed down Synthetic Fuels Corporation approvals, choosing a former opponent of the SFC as its head. Oklahoma oil tycoon Edward Noble swore, "I'm not here to drill holes in the bottom of the boat," but by early 1982, the *Washington Post* noted how SFC's "goal has shifted from massive production to making a political point." Jimmy Carter's short-term goals were cut by at least 60 percent; the idea now was to show the Saudis the synfuel flag.

One canceled project was a coal synfuel plant in Morgantown, West Virginia. Its cost had doubled to $1.5 billion, and a congressional staffer noted that "for 2 billion you could weatherize all of New England." This would have been an unusual joint venture with Germany and Japan. Japan had planned to use the technology later in Australian and Chinese mines. This would have been the biggest international energy project in history, and its defeat represented a second loss in synfuel for seventy-nine-year-old Senator Jennings Randolph. In 1943, he had flown from Morgantown to Washington in a plane powered by synfuel to dramatize its use. FDR had signed Randolph's synfuel bill, hailing it as insurance for domestic oil supplies after World War II. An article had observed back then that "Congress is determined that this country shall not repeat the error it made in rubber by waiting for a crisis before developing a synthetic industry."* A decade later, Eisenhower killed synfuel on the grounds that we had enough oil, and that private industry, not government, should be responsible for developing synfuel resources. Three decades later, Reagan canceled the West Virginia project.

Also hobbling synfuel was conservation at home, extravagance abroad. America cut oil imports nearly in half after 1977 with things like more fuel-efficient cars, homes or planes. Prince Feisal flooded oil markets after 1980 to keep OPEC prices stable, and to keep synfuel expensive. One expert told *The Wall Street*

---

* America had to improvise a synthetic-rubber industry, mainly in Houston, when the Japanese seized our rubber resources in the Far East. Meanwhile, Germany had synthetic rubber and synfuel ready for World War II.

*Journal* of Feisal's "sting," which created doubts "about a continuing rise in oil prices," making synfuel a bad bet.

The final blow for synfuel was the end of the Colony project in Colorado. It was owned by the Tosco Corporation and Exxon, and was to be the biggest SFC project, its 50,000 daily barrels by 1985 to be 1 percent of our oil imports. Through room-and-pillar excavation, some 9,000 miles would be bored into the mine—ten times the length of the New York City subway system. There would be the $800 million new town of Battlement Mesa, with shopping centers, parks, seven public schools, a golf course and ten sites for churches. The town would be a far cry from the trailer parks of recent western boomtowns, the "metal ghettos," whose crime, bars and prostitutes had updated the old mining camp. Reagan set aside a $1.1 billion SFC loan guarantee along with $400 million for a nearby project from Union Oil of California.*

With 25,000 people by 1990, this would have been the biggest town between Denver and Grand Junction. There were projections that the Colony and other Colorado synfuel plants would cut imports by 3 percent, create 75,000 new jobs, and add 500,000 residents to the West Slope area by 1995. By early 1982, property prices were tripling at the Colony project, and the first traffic light had been installed. The press was starting to run synfuel slump stories, but the big Colony project kept growing. On Friday, April 30, new hires were added to 2,100 workers at the huge site. Then on Sunday, Exxon suddenly pulled the plug, citing the oil glut and the doubling of Colony costs to $6 billion. A month later, only 3,000 cleared acres dotted by red fireplugs remained. By 1983, only two synfuel pilots proceeded: the 10,000-barrel-a-day project of Union Oil in Colorado, and a $2.1 billion coal-gasification plant in North Dakota.

Meanwhile, the safer and surer paths of conservation and alternative energy remain. For example, there is the biomass conversion of waste or plants to energy, long used in Europe. After a decade of talk in America about burning trash for energy, our cities are still reluctant to use their huge "garbage goldmines."

---

* The Union project had as its goal 10,000 daily barrels of synfuel by 1983. Another project in the area, proposed by Occidental and Tenneco, was to cook the shale in vast underground "retorts" blasted out by dynamite. The goal was a new retort every three days, each thirty stories high and half as wide as a football field. Three hundred thousand pounds of explosives would be needed every day.

Only Hawaii has truly explored the options. Relying on imported oil for 92 percent of its energy, it had no choice. Through biomass, the island of Hawaii is halfway to self-sufficiency. In 1980, sugar-cane waste, burned in generators, generated 140 million kilowatt hours. Eucalyptus trees, hay, wood chips and even the shells of macadamia nuts have also been used. Other exotic sources include using the interaction of warm and cold sea currents in "ocean thermal conversion," and a 6,450-foot-deep hole in the Kilauea volcano, draining steam power from the hottest well on earth at 660 degrees. Finally, Hawaii has 14,000 solar panels for heating water, the biggest such census of reflectors in America.

Solar is an obvious natural for the Sunbelt states, and Israel has pioneered solar ponds that would be useful in the western states. Heavy with salt, the ponds retain solar heat so well that research ponds have boiled. The hot water is used for space heating or for generation, then returned to the renewable pond. Ormat Turbines of Israel has a solar pond in the Dead Sea, and was hired by Southern California Edison to start one in the Salton Sea. Ormat's president looks beyond his Dead Sea to our Great Salt Lake. Since a solar pond of half a square mile can power 3,500 homes, the 1,750 square miles of the Great Salt Lake could, in theory, light up 12.25 million homes—or almost all of California.

Photovoltaic cells are prohibitive today at $10,000 per peak kilowatt. It will take years to push this awesome price down. The Japanese have invested heavily in this alchemist's stone for OPEC dependents. The cells would liberate Third World nations that hand over half their export earnings to the OPEC extortionists. In America, however, Ronald Reagan proposed to cut our renewable-energy funds 67 percent in 1982, while doubling aid to nuclear power—despite Three Mile Island, the Washington Public Power Supply System's fiscal debacle in the state of Washington, and a 1980 Gallup poll showing that nuclear power ranked last and solar first among seven energy choices. Reagan has left PVC development to the private sector. ARCO has balanced a $261 million loss in mineral mining for 1981 with a smarter investment of $250 million in PVC research through 1985. That is only a minor first step. Only a big fiscal push from Washington can prevent Japan from capturing a major high-tech front. He who controls a cheap PVC can make Prometheus look like a piker, but solar power ranks even lower than synfuel in the odd energy priorities of Washington today.

The threat of a third OPEC price shock remains. Despite the sharp price drops after 1982, it can happen again. Warning of this in his book *Global Insecurity,* Daniel Yergin recalled how the first two shocks cost industrial nations some $1.2 trillion in lost growth. About the still-slow recovery from the 1979 shock, he observed that "it's as if the economy was getting up off the floor after being knocked down in 1972, only to be kicked before it could get back on its feet again." The third shock would be a "long count" at best. As our oil reserves drop steadily each year on the way to total depletion by 2020, the OPEC extortions can only grow. A start on an environmentally safe synfuel program, more stress on conservation incentives and education, and major federal aid for renewable energy like solar ponds and PVCs are parts of Yergin's proposed program. The western states, for all their great mineral wealth, can no longer do the job alone.

## Water

Old western water wars are reviving off new pressures in our fastest-growing region. Rapidly expanding oasis cities and too much irrigation are draining aquifers and overdrawing the Colorado River, "the Nile of the West." Many western cities face severe water crisis.

In 1966 an obscure young congressman from Fort Worth wrote a book titled *The Coming Water Famine,* in which he warned that America

> is running out of its most indispensable commodity. That commodity is clear, usable water. And unless we learn very quickly how to trap it, conserve it, share it, purify it and keep it unpolluted—and in some cases move it from one place to another— we soon are going to be in desperate straits.

Fifteen years later, Representative Jim Wright was the House Majority Leader, and his prophecies were being realized. The 1981 drought dramatized how growth and irrigation waste were lowering western water tables and depleting its surface water supplies. The drought's peak in June saw a rash of cover stories on the growing crisis. "Water: Will We Have Enough to Go

Around?" asked *U.S. News & World Report*. "Are We Running Out of Water?" wondered *Life;* "Wringing America Dry" declared *The Progressive;* while *Science 81*'s cover for June showed a rancher, a miner, a homeowner, an Indian and a soldier lined up next to a rusty hand pump in the desert, with the West's $64,000 question as the headline: "Rationing the Colorado: Who Gets the Last Drop?"

The 1981 drought, like the far worse one of 1976–77, is now past. But basic problems remain in a region where 50 percent of our land gets 25 percent of our snow and rain, and where Los Angeles with twelve inches of rain is barely above the desert average of ten inches. This is the arid region derided in 1852 by Daniel Webster to his Senate peers: "What do we want with this worthless area—this region of savages and wild beasts, of shifting sands and whirlpools of dust, of cactus and prairie dogs? To what use could we ever hope to put the great deserts and these endless mountain ranges?" But this was before $90 billion worth of federal water projects were opened, most of them in the West: huge dams like Hoover, Shasta and Grand Coulee; the Moffat Tunnel, which burrows twenty-three miles through the Rockies to send water from the Western Slope of Colorado to the Eastern Slope, where 80 percent of the state lives; and the mammoth California Aqueduct, which a state official claimed in the 1960s would soon "take its place with the Great Wall of China and become one of only two man-made things on earth the moon visitors are expected to be able to see with the naked eye."

The Colorado River supplies much of the West with about 15 million acre-feet of water a year. Each foot is contested by seven states, several Indian tribes and Mexico. There has been nearly continuous litigation since the 1922 Colorado River Compact portioned out the annual flow. Unfortunately, the Compact was signed in an unusually wet era. Lesser annual flows since 1922 have added to the endless legal roil, with George Will comparing the overbooked river to "a corporation in which the stockholders own 150% of the stock."

Thirteen and a half million Southern Californians face a water crisis after 1985, when half their share of the Colorado River goes to Arizona under a Supreme Court decree. Seventy percent of California lives in the arid south while 70 percent of state water is up north. To draw on that surplus after 1985, a $5 billion canal was voted on in 1982. Its defeat meant less rampant growth out West at last.*

As our fastest-growing state in the 1970s, Nevada is also one of our driest states. Carson City's manager noted a doubled census since 1970 and sighed in 1981 that "when I came here in 1978, I was told at that time that we had five years before we reached capacity. But now we find we have enough for 500 more dwelling units. We are, for practical purposes, out of water. . . ." Nearby Reno was the tenth fastest growing metro area in the 1970s, expanding 60 percent. Its city manager reviews each housing project since "one new development could wipe out our available water." The Paiute Indians own Lake Pyramid, which feeds Reno. They make money from recreation permits on the thirty-mile lake, and want more water in it, which would mean wiser water use by Reno and surrounding farms. When farmers wouldn't line open irrigation ditches and Reno wouldn't meter water use, the chairman of a Paiute council asked at a California legislative hearing in 1969: "Can you not leave one people alone? Can you not honor one promise? Can you not respect even one lake, and one stream, one nearly extinct breed of the fish and one natural pelican rookery, and one natural lake—the greatest of the lakes left from the days of the great glaciers?"

The main threat to the arid West is all the census and job growth after 1970. The 30 million Southwest residents could double by the year 2000. On top of this growth may be a return to an earlier Dry Age. Arizona tree-ring studies show that 1900 to 1960 —when the big western water systems were built—was an unusually wet time out West. In contrast, the previous 200 years had been very dry. The droughts of 1965, 1976–77 and 1981 may have been signs of a returning Dry Age.

Even if the recent droughts are not part of a new trend, the growth of a still-arid region must either slow down or costly new systems must be built to ship in water from increasingly remote

---

* Other California dreams to tap the humid Northwest included the building of an aqueduct across Nevada to tap into the Snake River of Idaho, and a huge funnel in the Pacific Ocean near Portland to trap water emerging from the Columbia River for shipment to the arid south. The grandest fantasy was for a 500-mile reservoir to be set in the Rocky Mountain Trench in British Columbia to trap the massive Yukon River flow. From this giant reservoir three huge canals would flow to twenty-two western states, three northern states in Mexico, seven provinces in Canada, and refresh the Great Lakes, the Missouri and Mississippi rivers, and add more hydropower to Niagara Falls.

sources. Otherwise, vast crops will be lost in America's major farm area. Neither option seems real. The end of western growth is predictable, even without a new Dry Age. A national policy might even emerge to revive the already-built Snowbelt cities as a humid "Waterbelt" comes back to full, productive life.

Beyond these examples are three broad problem areas for the West and water: the Ogallala aquifer feeding the Great Plains, industrial migrants, and a possible revival of synfuel, with its huge water demands.

In the fall of 1966, Venice was sinking because it had overdrawn its ground-water supplies. Today, new aqueducts bring in drinking water from the Alps, so the sinking of the Venice aquifer has stopped, but the decline of the vast Ogallala aquifer feeding the Great Plains has not received nearly the same media attention. The landscape of Canaletto, Guardi and Turner fell eight inches in a century—the Ogallala fell 700 *feet* in parts of the West in just thirty years. It feeds hundreds of millions of acres of the Great Plains, the crops which feed much of America and part of the Third World. Within forty years, the Ogallala may run dry.

The Ogallala is a huge underground lake formed by receding waters in the Ice Age, its volume roughly equal to Lake Huron. This vast formation of water-laden sand, silt and gravel lies under 225,000 square miles of the Great Plains, stretching from Texas to Colorado and Nebraska. The big aquifer supplies 2 million people and is the main spring for a semiarid region producing 13 percent of our corn, 16 percent of our wheat, 25 percent of our cotton, 38 percent of our grain sorghum and 40 percent of our grain-fed beef.

In the 1930s, the big lake under the Dust Bowl had only 600 wells drawing on its vast reserve. Since 1950, however, irrigation has grown sixfold on the Great Plains, and more than 150,000 wells now mine the Ogallala. Within twenty years, the aquifer may be so low in parts that only expensive pumping will be able to tap the deep water beds. John Boslough in *Science 81* has predicted the possible "end of most High Plains irrigation by the end of the century. That will mean economic hardship for the region and serious food shortages for the nation and possibly for the rest of the world."

Nebraska only began mining the Ogallala in the 1970s, so water is near the surface there and the aquifer bed is often 1,000 feet thick. But thirty years of heavy mining in Kansas and Texas have meant water that is often 500 feet below ground, with a water bed only 200 feet thick in places. While the Ogallala drops a few inches yearly in Nebraska, it sinks from two to five feet in Kansas and Texas.

Replenishing the underground lake is a difficult task. From twelve to twenty-two inches of rain or snow fall annually on the Great Plains, and at most just three inches seep down to recharge the big aquifer. Speeding up the process by pumping imported water into the ground would mean a vast new network of canals, pumps and reservoirs. One congressional proposal was to ship in water from the Missouri or the Arkansas River. This would cost anywhere from $6 billion to $25 billion, depending on water volume moved and distances covered. It would take nine years to design and fifteen to build.

If a third OPEC price shock arrives and makes synfuel competitive again, huge water demands to cook, cool and liquefy shale reserves would occur out West. As columnist James Wieghart pointed out in 1980, "The fight for water rights, which is as old as the West itself, will take on a new intensity as Exxon and Gulf join the farmers, ranchers and sheepherders and the city folks in the battle for that scarce, but vital commodity."

A Colorado study shows that there is enough state water for energy development over twenty years, provided that $2.5 billion in dams and reservoirs are built to store and ship new surface water needed for synfuel. Writing in the *Washington Post*, Joanne Omang notes a federal study projecting national water supplies for "26 oil shale plants and eight coal conversion plants, each drinking 50,000 to 2 million barrels of water a day, depending on the process. It also assumes that all water not now under contract is captured and that new reservoirs, pipes and pumps are built."

Environmentalist Jonathan Lash warns that rather than build all those new water systems, synfuel firms would simply buy up "existing water rights and displace agricultural users as they have in the past." At the peak of the synfuel boom in 1981, water rights to Colorado land rose to $1,700 an acre.

Another strain on western water is a new internal migration. Reversing the path of 9 million Southerners who went north to man factories after 1945, new migrants from the Snowbelt are moving south and west today. As cyclical layoffs became permanent job losses in Snowbelt factory towns, these high-tech

Okies took off. There was also a growing flight from Mexico, a nation that was creating only one job for every two new job-seekers at a time of 40 percent unemployment. Some see the arid West doubling its population by the year 2000.

Yet a 1980 Presidential Commission chaired by former Columbia president William McGill told Jimmy Carter, in essence, to let Snowbelt cities die by encouraging their people to go south and west. Even Jack Kemp and HUD secretary Samuel Pierce denounced the McGill Report for neglecting a region in need of federal aid. Sunbelt wariness about the new migrations was noted in 1980 by governors Jay Rockefeller of West Virginia and Richard Lamm of Colorado, who wrote in *The New York Times* about

> the common misconception that this migration pattern is "good" for the South and West. In fact, the Sun Belt states are already struggling to absorb rates that are from three to four times the national average. . . . It costs Colorado approximately $6,000 per person a year to provide necessary government and social services. Where is the West going to get the water to support all of the new growth? Where will it find the tax resources to duplicate all the municipal services for people who have just abandoned their own in another part of the country?

Meanwhile, it still rains fifty-nine inches a year in New York City for every seven inches in Phoenix. Russell Baker has observed in 1981, "a great deal of Sun Belt territory is already having trouble finding water to support its present population. The hordes from Blizzard Country are not going to bring the Great Lakes with them."

# CHAPTER 2

# THE MYTH OF THE NEW SOUTH

THE MYTH BEGAN on November 3, 1970, when southern voters sent George Wallace and racism a stunning message, by electing four liberal governors. Jimmy Carter in Georgia, Reubin Askew in Florida, Dale Bumpers in Arkansas and John West in South Carolina were hailed by the media as a "new breed." The four new governors reflected the apparent maturity of a region that John Gunther called the "problem child of the nation" in 1947. Standing on the capital steps in Atlanta, with black leaders on the podium behind him, Jimmy Carter memorably declared in his inaugural speech of 1971: "I say to you quite frankly that the time for racial discrimination is over. Our people have already made this major and difficult decision."

The next week, *Time* put Carter on a "New South" cover. The runner-up for the cover had been Reubin Askew of Florida, who would keynote the Democratic Convention of 1972, and be a presidential candidate in 1984. The Class of 1970 down South was a "new breed" indeed. Strom Thurmond hired a black aide in 1971. While continuing to vote very conservatively, he gave visible endorsement to the idea of racial equality. George Wallace, whose 1963 inaugural speech had pledged "segregation now, segregation tomorrow, segregation forever," declared in his 1975 inaugural speech that "the people in government in this state are concerned with all our citizens, whether they be black or white. It shall continue this way."

The political advance reflected economic growth. *Congres-*

*sional Quarterly* took a drive down IS 85 to illustrate the region's boom in 1980. It began at the Research Triangle of Raleigh, Durham and Chapel Hill, with high-tech think tanks linked to North Carolina State, Duke and the University of North Carolina. Next the IS 85 route passed by Greensboro, home of Burlington, our biggest textile firm, and High Point, one of our major furniture centers. After that came Winston-Salem and tobacco, then Charlotte, second only to Atlanta as a distribution hub for the South. In South Carolina, IS 85 passed through Spartanburg and Greenville, two more textile centers, and finally ended in Atlanta, the terminal for most southern roads and rails, and capital of the New South.

Devastated by the Civil War, then divided by Reconstruction, the South remained underdeveloped through World War I. It slowly diversified in the 1920s, mainly in low-wage industries like apparel, food, furniture, lumber, textiles, tobacco, manned by nonunion labor in often terrible working conditions. *Congressional Quarterly* recalls that by the 1930s, low taxes and cheap labor had lured so many northern textile mills that the South had more cotton spindles in operation than the North.

World War II was a catalyst. Southern committee chairmen in Congress began shifting military bases from the Snowbelt. Washington spent billions expanding strategic industries like munitions, airplanes, chemicals, ship-building, adding 100,000 factory jobs. The South also mechanized its farms, with surplus black laborers all but forced north by a mix of racism, slow growth and punitive welfare grants.

Meanwhile, industry developed: $9.8 billion in value added to raw material by manufacturing in 1938 became $65 billion by 1958. The 1960s saw gains in high-wage sectors like electronics, petrochemicals and rubber. *Congressional Quarterly* recalls that even farms diversified, going beyond commodity crops with volatile prices like cotton and tobacco to more profitable sectors like livestock and poultry. The huge southeastern timber preserves began to rival those of the Pacific Northwest. Aerospace, once concentrated in California and Washington, saw southern inroads in Georgia and Texas, NASA outposts at Cape Canaveral, Huntsville and Houston, and major regional airlines going national, like Braniff of Dallas, Eastern of Miami and Delta of Atlanta.

The 1970s economic boom was complemented by social

change. For example, there was the rapid growth of black elected officials in the South, from 250 in 1968 to 2,332 by 1979. As the 1980s began, minority mayors ruled all major southern cities save Dallas and Houston, with Maynard Jackson in Atlanta, Richard Arrington in Birmingham, Ernest Morial in New Orleans, Henry Marsh in Richmond, Maurice Ferre in Miami and Henry Cisneros in San Antonio. Black voting blocs were now so big in some southern states that in Georgia, where 66 percent of all whites were registered in 1979, 75 percent of the blacks were.

The economic, social and political progress suggested that the New South had finally arrived. Ninety years after Henry W. Grady, editor of the Atlanta *Constitution,* coined the phrase at a meeting in New York City, the media in 1976 blended our Bicentennial and Jimmy Carter's candidacy for President into a New South binge. Whole issues or series in *Time, Newsweek, The Saturday Review, The New York Times* and *The Wall Street Journal* focused on the New South. Journalism professor Gene Burd of the University of Texas was the first to label the media explosion the "Sunbelt Bliss Blitz." Burd recalled how the *Times* series helped launch a "press shift" of praise for the Sunbelt in 1976. He characterized the Bliss Blitz of '76 as a mix of carny and chauvinism, where

> geography, meteorology, geology, and sociology are mixed indiscriminately by journalists in a blast of bombast, saccharine sales pitches, and simplistic and optimistic epigrams, which are constant, repetitive, alliterative, and combine the poetic civic ideology of the chamber of commerce with the self-fulfilling prophecy of the press.

An odd example of the Bliss Blitz was a mini-essay for a special *Time* New South issue by the distinguished author of *Origins of the New South.* In the essay, C. Vann Woodward reiterated the popular myth among white and black southerners that the civil rights crusade was part of what Jimmy Carter claimed was a special relationship between the races down south, a unique bond between black and white unknown elsewhere. This revision is refuted by the current fact of very low welfare grants and very high barriers to welfare eligibility in all Southern states.

Against such facts, Woodward in *Time* proclaimed that "the old grounds for Northern moral superiority" had been pulverized by the Boston busing brouhaha of 1974, that "a new type of

Southern patriot took delight in pointing a finger at Boston, that oldest moral critic and accuser of the South." But rage over busing is mainly based on class, not racial, divisions, a distinction brushed aside by Woodward when he says:

> Self-righteousness withered along the Massachusetts-Michigan axis. Northern morale was further lowered by Viet Nam and Watergate, devastating blows at the widely held myths of invincibility, success and innocence. Those myths were never shared by the South anyway. In their present state of disenchantment and demoralization, Northerners are apprehensively looking south for leadership.

The war was escalated by a southern President with strong backing from a South rich in military bases and contractors like Brown & Root of Houston, prominent among four firms which built over $1 billion in Vietnam bases. Watergate revolved around the President of "Southern Strategy" fame. Those "apprehensively looking for leadership" on such issues wouldn't find it in a militaristic South, but in Massachusetts, which led the antiwar effort as the only state for McGovern in 1972, and supplied two main martyrs of the Watergate probe, Archibald Cox and Elliot Richardson. In fairness to Woodward, he later described the New South's condition in blunt terms as being still "much the poorest of the country's regions. The old Southern distinction of being a people of poverty among a people of plenty lingers on. There is little prospect of closing that gap overnight."

Beyond the Bliss Blitz of '76 lurked "the nation's No. 1 economic problem" of 1938. Blacks inevitably dominated a depressed scene. The South's share of American blacks had dropped from 80 percent in 1940 to 53 percent, as millions went north for a better life. But many blacks had remained, often living in wretched conditions reminiscent of a Brazilian *favela*. Debunking "The Myth of the 'New South' " for *Ebony* in 1979, Ron Harris noted how the suburban homes of a few mobile blacks in Memphis or Charlotte "appear unimportant when compared to the substandard structures—many with outside toilets and no running water—that house half the Black families in Mississippi, Arkansas and South Carolina." Harris contrasted the publicized advances of blacks in Atlanta with the town of Moultrie, where half the blacks were poor, and 87 percent of those over twenty-five were school dropouts. He added that what New South promoters "fail to mention is that Atlanta is not a typical Southern city—Moultrie is." He concluded that

> despite all of the talk about the new "right-thinking" South, about "racial change," about the increased number of black elected officials and "smooth integration of schools" and "more black employment"—despite this, to be black in the South is, for the majority of black people, still to be poor, undereducated and isolated from the white community; to live in substandard, segregated housing; to be underrepresented on juries; to be shut out from employment in all but the lowest-paying, most menial jobs.

There were also some very poor whites. Blacks were three times more likely to be poor and Great Society programs cut Appalachian poverty in half, but in 1978, only three of 397 Appalachian counties had per capita incomes above the national median, and many squalid shacks remained in mountain hollows. All told, eight southern states in 1975 had poverty shares that were at least 50 percent above those of non-South states:

### THE POOR AS A SHARE OF ALL PEOPLE

| | | | |
|---|---|---|---|
| Mississippi | 26% | Kentucky | 18% |
| Arkansas | 19 | South Carolina | 17 |
| Louisiana | 19 | Tennessee | 16 |
| Georgia | 18 | Texas | 15 |
| | *U.S.A.* | *10%* | |

The South also had six of the ten poorest states for per capita income in 1980, including the four lowest income states of all: Mississippi #50, Arkansas #49, Alabama #48, South Carolina #47, Tennessee #42 and Kentucky #40. Indeed the South, with 31 percent of our people, didn't have one state among our top twenty income earners. Texas with its East Texas oil fields was #21, Oklahoma with its Anadarko field was #31, Louisiana with its Tuscaloosa Trend was #35 among states for income.*

---

* The South, however, is rich compared to Indian reservations and Puerto Rico. Even the mineral-rich Navajos—with 50 percent of our uranium and 25 percent of our coal—had 40 percent unemployment in 1981. Where 14 percent of America was poor, more than 80 percent of the Navajo nation was, and this is America's richest tribe. A quarter of its homes have no running water and half have no

Nor was progress reflected by all those minority mayors in big cities like Atlanta, Birmingham, Miami, New Orleans, Richmond and San Antonio. All the cities save Richmond were deep in the downward spiral of service crisis. These mayors preside over emptying ruins, and only massive federal aid can arrest the decay. As Jesse Jackson showed America in 1983, a mix of racial gerrymandering, annexation, at-large districts, intimidation and double registration requirements had diluted and discouraged black voting down South. Thus while blacks were 36 percent of Mississippi's voters, 30 percent of North Carolina's, 26 percent of Alabama's and 22 percent of South Carolina's, all 29 Congressmen from those states were white. Black candidate Robert Clark almost won a Delta district in 1982, but the closest Mississippi blacks got to Congress that year was through Katie Hall, elected to a Gary, Indiana, seat. She grew up in the Delta, but left the day after graduating from college, for opportunity up north.

Even the southern establishment questions the myth of the New South, as seen in the final report of the 1980 Commission on the Future of the South. Convened every six years to examine the region, this blue-ribbon group was chaired by F. David Mathews, HEW secretary for President Ford. Other members included U.S. Senator David Boren (D–Okla), and Ronald Reagan's choice as head of the National Endowment for the Humanities, William Bennett. Only four of the twenty-three Commission members were black. They released a report whose mixed review for the South was summarized by: "There was the promising beginning of growth in the 1960s and then a mighty surge in the 1970s. But the heritage of the South's impoverished past lingers." Two linked problems were the South's economy and its children.

### The Economy

The Commission noted that by being "more like the nation, the South is inevitably losing some of its advantages" in luring people and jobs. Higher wages, energy costs and taxes were among the costs of progress. A 1981 Bureau of Labor Statistics

---

electricity. Since the Indians are 90 percent dependent on federal aid, the Reagan cuts fell disproportionately on them. Those cuts also devastated Puerto Rico, which lost 25 percent of its food and nutrition funds. The island also lost all its 25,000 CETA jobs, which boosted unemployment to 24 percent.

survey found Houston with higher wages in thirteen of twenty occupations compared to New York. The same pattern was seen in a 1981 Urban Institute study of municipal wages: Houston was second for recent wage growth among police officers, New York eleventh. As well, the 1980 Commission on the Future of the South noted that the cost of living soared 66 percent in southern cities between 1972 and 1978, "more than in any other region."

Cheap energy had been a southern staple for years, but the deregulation of natural-gas prices after 1974 and oil prices after 1979 cut that regional edge. As energy prices down south rose to OPEC levels long suffered in the Snowbelt, the Commission noted how the South

> with its dependence on trucks and automobiles for moving goods and people, is at a disadvantage in comparison to the Northern industrial states with their highly-developed rail and rapid transit systems. Likewise, the South's energy-intensive industries, built during the halcyon days of low-energy costs, suffer in comparison with more energy-efficient ones in other regions.

There were also light tax loads, long a southern lure. The South had to upgrade urban services as populations grew, so taxes rose, since "sophisticated migrants to the region are joining native Southerners in demanding better public services. . . ."

The Commission on the Future of the South hoped that "more production in Southern staples like agriculture" might ease "the considerable poverty which exists in the rural South." The idea of farms as a major new employer was absurd since so many were already highly mechanized. A federal study showed that 926,000 black-run farms of 1920 were down to 57,000 by 1982. Rising land values, industrial growth and lack of wills from intestate black farmers cut black-owned acres nearly in half since 1969 alone. This is hardly a growth sector, and is, instead, one more reason for more black poverty down south.* Also unrealistic was

---

* As for farm labor, some of the worst examples of migrant exploitation are in the South, where Cesar Chavez has had little success. Many of 23 recent Justice Department convictions under antislavery laws were in the South, where literal peonage has been found among workers whose life expectancy of 49 compares with 73 years nationwide, whose living quarters are far below the worst city slum, and whose average income for a family of six of $3,390 in 1982 compares to a poverty-line standard of $9,287 and a national family median of $22,380.

the Commission's hope for more development of the South's coal, copper, iron, oil, phosphate and timber resources. Much of this is specialized work in an era of strip-mining and computer-aided oil drilling.

Fortunately, the Commission urged better schooling for the region since "low levels of educational achievement and low per capita education expenditures will remain a problem in the face of increasing demands for better schools and a better trained labor force." A rapid rise in labor skills was certainly needed to expand high-wage growth areas like electric equipment and machinery, the South's two biggest factory growers in the late 1970s.

### Children

Education was only part of the picture for a high-tech future down south. Meager welfare grants, low health standards and rising illiteracy were serious problems for southern children— the future work force. The Commission's chapter on children was the longest in the final report, the special focus at the urging of conservative Governor James B. Hunt of North Carolina. The summary of the severe problems from the Commission:

> More of the children of the South are growing up as part of a poor family than children in other regions of the country; their health is poorer; and they have less chance of graduating from high schools.
>
> All available measures indicate that the needs of children in the South are more acute than in other regions. Yet Southern children receive smaller public allocations than children in other states.

With higher birth rates than other regions, the South has a higher share of young citizens. In the post-baby boom of the 1970s, children under eighteen dropped by 11 percent nationally but declined only slightly down south. What is more, southern children under five actually grew in numbers during the 1970s. As other regions closed schools, the South was opening them, and a lower median age for parents and a higher birth rate insured more of this ahead.

The South with far more children has far lower welfare grants for a far lower share of its poor children:

- Outside the South, almost all poor children were on welfare. In the South, only about half were.
- Outside the South, children on welfare averaged $127 a month in the grant. Down south, they got only $58 a month.

Put another way, only half of poor children down south got welfare, and those who got it received only half of what children got elsewhere.

Every effort is made to keep mothers and children off welfare in the South. Fourteen southern states saw these shares of poor children kept off welfare:

| | | | | | |
|---|---|---|---|---|---|
| Georgia | 35% | Arkansas | 45% | North Carolina | 53% |
| Virginia | 36 | Mississippi | 45 | Florida | 62 |
| Tennessee | 39 | Oklahoma | 48 | Texas | 67 |
| Alabama | 41 | West Virginia | 52 | Kentucky | 69 |
| Louisiana | 43 | South Carolina | 53 | | |

The same grim data is seen for Medicaid. The South in 1976 had 40 percent of America's poor children, but only 22 percent of its child Medicaid recipients. As with welfare, for every child on southern Medicaid rolls, another was waiting for health coverage. Many of them came from "working poor" families.

Among the unusual southern crises for children seen in the Commission's thorough report:

- 72% of America's high infant mortality areas are in the South, which has only 30% of our people.*
- In education, per pupil outlays in the South were 25% less than the non-South. The South's drop-out rate was 51% higher.
- While 30% of our children live in the South—45% of the children in our poorest families were in the South.

* Pregnancy rates were also rising down south among girls under fifteen, the mothers most likely to have the low-weight babies prone to ill health. So mortality rates may get worse, without more federal aid through programs like the Women, Infants and Children (WIC) nutrition program, expanded by Richard Nixon, but threatened with cuts by Ronald Reagan.

The Commission urged higher welfare grants and broader eligibility standards, so children in two-parent families could get welfare and Medicaid. Until southern states take such steps, the region will remain a Third World enclave. It will also fail to sustain its transition from an industrial to postindustrial economy. Too many southern children are being crippled in the crucial one-to-three-year phase of child development, which determines cognitive skills.

Full employment, national health insurance, and adequate aid to mothers and children have long been familiar givens of all other advanced Western democracies. The South must join the Snowbelt in fighting for such routine amenities for America as well. Until it does, the South will remain "our No. 1 economic problem" and the "stepchild of the nation." Anything, in short, but the "New South" that is hyped today.

# CHAPTER 3

# SOUTHERN CITIES

## Florida

Florida has had an amazing census and job growth since 1970. A crowded peninsula of 6.7 million became one of 9.6 million, the 41 percent growth being the third highest in America. Half of the ten fastest-growing metro areas in America were in Florida, and Census Bureau projections through the year 2000 see our two biggest growers as Orlando at 44.7 percent and Fort Lauderdale-Hollywood at 58.2 percent. The fastest growing among 435 Congressional Districts was the 5th CD of Florida, which grew from 465,000 to 880,000 in the 1970s. There was one place in Florida that didn't grow in the 1970s. Instead, it lost 6 percent of its people. That was warning enough about Miami.

Jacksonville exemplifies Florida's economic growth. At 834 square miles, it is the world's largest city—almost as big as Rhode Island at 1,049 square miles. Jacksonville began the 1970s poorly, when Westinghouse convinced the Chamber of Commerce that floating nuclear plants were the new wave. Jacksonville proposed a bond of $2.2 billion—twice the size of any previous municipal bond in America—to buy two of the floating plants. Debate over the bond broke the nuclear fever, and Jacksonville thrives today. With thirty-four insurance firms, it's the state capital for the industry. Jacksonville also has the busiest port on earth for auto imports, with a huge Toyota plant for assembling parts. In 1975, it had the dubious honor of having the lightest tax load of our thirty biggest cities. A family earning $5,000 in New York City paid more taxes than one earning $40,000 in Jacksonville and got far better services.

In central Florida, a new high-tech strip grows on IS 4, the highway bisecting the state from Cape Canaveral on the Atlantic to Tampa on the Gulf. The Cape has been revived by the space shuttle after its nose dive in the wake of the finished Apollo project, when 25,500 space jobs in 1968 shrank to 9,000 by 1975. "The shuttle is to Apollo as a Mack truck is to a Ferrari," sighs a spacenik to *U.S. News & World Report*. "The Gold Coast isn't a 'Silicon Coast' yet" admits a state ad, but there is the IS 4 strip; Harris Corporation is the state's second biggest *Fortune* 500 giant, and Orlando has plans for new plants from Burroughs and Westinghouse plus a possible doubling of Martin Marietta's 7,000 jobs.

Jobs expanded 66 percent in Florida in the 1970s, while they grew 21 percent in America. In the 1940s, there was one job per 4.5 Floridians, by 1980 one for every 2.7 residents. The job boom was led by three Sunshine State staples: real estate, recreation and retirement.

For 1980, real estate earned $12 billion. But the sector has gone sour twice before, and the 1982 recession plus heavy condo speculation could mean further collapse. The first disaster occurred as 2.5 million people arrived in Florida in 1925, many to find that the deals they had made up north had bought swamps or tidal marshes. Then in 1926 northern banks got out of mortgage financing. The early 1970s saw a second spree, led by speculators, in an overbuilt market. The 1974 recession pulled the plug. There were over 1,000 foreclosed Florida projects by 1976, among them 32,000 unsold condo units in Dade and Broward counties. Broward's retirement market in Fort Lauderdale could absorb twenty units a day, but REIT fever was opening sixty apartments a day, which left many empty in 1976. "People got drunk on Florida," noted the former head of the Federal Home Loan Bank Board, adding that "people who didn't know Fort Lauderdale from Pumpkin Corners were building or financing projects there. They produced row on row of junk. Bulldozers should go in there and tear them down."

Five years later, the Florida market was again on fire. In 1925, 4.07 units were built per 100 existing units. In 1981 Fort Myers built 8 new units per 100 extant and Naples 23—and this was during a recession. One Miami broker bought a two-room condo for $153,000 and resold it in six months for $297,000. These rapid doublings in value made Florida condos an "informal futures" market. Wealthy Americans, Europeans and Latin Americans bought unseen units as they were built and sold them months later for huge gains. High interest rates and devalued Latin-American currencies upset the market in 1981. Speculators could no longer hold a dozen condo "futures" at once, and prices no longer doubled. Foreclosures piled up by late 1981, with 7,000 unsold condos in Miami alone.

For recreation, there were 36 million tourists in 1981. Orlando also has the world's top tourist site. Disney World greeted its 150 millionth visitor in 1983, only a dozen years after opening on 27,400 acres. In late 1982 the $1 billion Epcot Center opened—the Experimental Prototype Community of Tomorrow. This will be a permanent world's fair, with some 8 million annual visits on top of Mickey's 15 million next door. After all, as a Disney official observed, "There are still 20 million people who come to Florida and do not stop at Disney World." To make sure they do, Orlando opened a $300 million airport in the fall of 1982. This will break the Mickey-Miami syndrome: "When foreigners think Disney, they think Miami," noted an Orlando air official. In 1981, Miami International handled 8.5 million foreign arrivals, Orlando only 350,000.

For retirement Florida has no peers. The elderly grew 65 percent in the 1970s, Social Security payments and military pensions add more than $8 million to the state economy, and 83-year-old Representative Claude Pepper of Miami is the nation's leader against Social Security cuts. Economists have projected that each retiree generates a job in trade and services.

The only jobs shrinking in Florida are ones on farms. The citrus-and-cattle belt of central Florida yields to theme parks, high tech, retirement condos and the census bulge, which, a local economist suggests, makes the area "the southern California of the second half of this century." Growth is retiring farmland at a terrible rate. Cecil Andrus, the Secretary of the Interior to Jimmy Carter, summarized the problem for *The Wall Street Journal:* "What happens by 1990, when there is no more farming in Florida? They're chewing it up that fast and turning it into asphalt and concrete. What happens to the citrus industry in America?"

Citrus and central Florida are still symbiotic. The $4 billion crop is our largest. When three Medflies were found in traps in 1982, Tampa quickly sprayed Malathion over sixteen square miles. During the severe frost that destroyed 25 percent of the Florida crop in 1982, it turned out that—even in normal times— we imported more orange juice than we produced, with Brazil the main supplier, together with Canada, Germany, Israel and Sweden. In early 1982, *The New York Times* reported that Brazilians were "watching land development in Florida with an eye toward how it might benefit Brazil. Mr. Quintella said that in a 90-mile drive on a visit to Lakeland, Fla., he had counted 196 For Sale signs. The thinking here is that farmers in Florida may decide that it is more profitable to plant condominiums than oranges.''

The condos-over-citrus trend is part of a larger problem: Florida is running out of water. The state grew 143 percent in two decades, and managed to survive the 1971 drought. Then the state grew 41 percent more in the 1970s, mainly in central Florida. By 1979, salt water was intruding into the overworked wells of St. Petersburg. Then in 1981, the ground fell in.

It began in the central Florida town of Winter Park on the evening of May 8, when a sinkhole appeared, eventually becoming 1,000 feet wide and 170 feet deep and consuming a three-bedroom house, a camper, six Porsches and half of a municipal swimming pool. Before low water tables from an overworked aquifer imploded a limestone cavern, Winter Park was best known as home to U.S. Senator Paula Hawkins. Soon the town of 22,000 swarmed with tourists. If crowds got too big around the hole, needing 10,000 truckloads of dirt to fill, they could go and gape at two lesser sinkholes nearby, each about 200 feet wide. The state legislature, alarmed by eight sinkholes in parched Florida that year, began looking at sinkhole insurance. Since Florida is mainly at sea level, low wells plus spring tides threatened a lot of salt-water contamination.

In April, only 0.05 inches of rain had fallen at Miami International Airport. With more than a third of the state census, South Florida had to quickly cut water use 10 percent one week and 25 percent the next week. A 50 percent cut was washed out by late spring rains. Before then, Miami lawns could be sprinkled only on Mondays, Wednesdays or Fridays if you had an even address. By July, more than 500,000 acres of Florida forest had burned. The Everglades were so dry that alligators ran out of muddy burrowing ground and headed for open irrigation ditches. As water tables fell and sinkholes grew, surface water dwindled elsewhere. Our third biggest natural lake, Lake Okeechobee, is the water main for 80 percent of South Florida. By late July, the lake was down to 9.8 feet against a normal depth of 17.5 feet. Torrential rains from tropical storm Dennis in August caused major crop damage, but for the most part skirted the lake, and cloud seeding began the same month, with iodine crystals fired into cumulus clouds over the river feeding the giant lake. Four sugar counties flanking the 650-square-mile lake faced disaster unless the rains fell.*

As the ranking engineer of United States Sugar complained about the census bomb of South Florida:

> You have to funnel the water down there to keep the salt-water intrusion back. Now here we are with a lack of rainfall last year coupled with a lack this year and while the demand is greater and greater. . . . It was critical when the lake reached 12 feet. From then on, it's just been a higher degree of critical.

By late 1981, the "liquid heart" of South Florida was at its lowest level in forty years. The next harvest was threatened. Foliage must be burned off stalks before the cane is cut, and water must control these fires while it saturates the muck below. Farmers drew on 1982 water supplies to save the 1981 crop without burning out the muck and the industry itself.

In 1906 developers and engineers used a 1,400-mile network of canals and waterways to dry wetlands, thus launching the Florida building boom of the next two decades. That lost source of ground water and the census bomb after 1950 led to the drought crisis of 1981. A chief state environmental official has recalled how the wetlands were dredged into finger canals "to give everybody their childhood dream: a waterfront lot in Florida. . . . We're talking about thousands and thousands of homesites. We

---

* One of the sugar counties is Palm Beach County, which has 30,000 of our richest and 30,000 of our poorest citizens. The rich live in the famous enclave to the east. The poor live to the west, mainly in rural shacks near Lake Okeechobee, where Bahamians, Jamaicans, Haitians and Mexicans cut cane or harvest celery. This is the squalid town of Belle Glade, a major focus of Edward R. Murrow's *Harvest of Shame* film in 1960. A few years ago, a TV crew returned to find little change in the squalid town. Its wretched residents even lost marginal jobs after 1981, as some growers left, while more Haitians arrived.

found that basically the only water we have is the fresh water that falls on the state from rain. All we have is what we get every year." *

As growth soars in Florida, taxes and services stay low. For example, in welfare, Washington pays 79 percent of the bill against 50 percent in New York. Virtually all children in poverty get welfare in New York, but only 38 percent of poor children in Florida receive it. The light tax burden sustains this percentage.

A constitutional amendment approved by voters in 1980 let anyone with a home valued under $25,000 pay no property taxes. "We have a new tax phenomenon in the Panhandle: representation without taxation," said a lobbyist for strapped county commissioners. Business taxes were cut four years in a row. There is no state personal income tax and per capita taxes are the twelfth lowest in America (and the welfare grant is the tenth lowest).

Even the middle-class migrants of the last thirty years are affected. For example, there is Seminole County, near Orlando, which grew 114 percent in the 1970s. Many new arrivals were young singles in garden apartments, lured by the boom of Disney World, Epcot Center and the new airport. The county administrator told the *Washington Post* in 1981:

> There are some conflicts coming. Those people who left the industrial centers of the North are coming here fleeing high taxes and old, decaying facilities in the cities. They are anti-tax but high-service oriented. Now, when they complain about the level of services here, we ask them if they recall how much they paid in taxes where they came from. . . . It will take time for the public to understand that the cost of all this growth has not been paid for.

Florida pioneered in neonatal intensive care, yet hospitals were so overcrowded in 1981 that premature babies were turned away from ICUs in Broward County, Tampa and West Palm

---

* Another water pressure is from the big phosphate mining belt near Sarasota, most of it in Polk County. This area produces 80 percent of our needs and 33 percent of the world's. It also uses and pollutes water on a grand scale: 10,000 gallons to process each ton of phosphate, with 85 percent of the water recycled. The water is from the vast Floridian aquifer, further depleting ground supplies and leading to nearby sinkholes in drought years. The radiation that normally occurs in phosphate may also lead to higher cancer rates for those in the Polk County area.

Beach, and in each instance, the baby died. The University of Miami's teaching hospital has one of America's biggest neonatal ICUs, with fifty-nine beds, but it was so crowded that more than 300 referrals were turned away each year. A twenty-four-hour "Care Line" to find free neonatal ICU beds had helped Florida cut its infant mortality rate from 14.2 per 1,000 births to 10.8 in 1976, matching the national average, but the massive overcrowding and denials of care in 1981 could mean a reversal. The state is running out of geriatric care as well. In 1981, of 150 students at the University of Miami nursing school, not one trained to be a geriatric nurse.

With 17 percent of the state over sixty-five, this is our biggest retirement state. Yet a Chase econometrics study in 1981 placed Florida in ninth place among the states, down below even depressed regional neighbors like Alabama, South Carolina and Louisiana, as a place for the elderly. Seventeen percent of the Florida elderly are poor, often living in "gray ghettos" like South Miami Beach. That area has seen a battle between builders and landmark preservers over Art Deco hotels in a 125-block area, easily the biggest such "historic district" in urban America. These handsome, unique hotels contain many elderly residents on fixed incomes, who can't afford to live anywhere else.*

Dade County has an astonishing number of disabled, an estimated 262,000 of 1.6 million residents. The County cut special rides down to just 500 per day, 450 reserved for those with jobs or needing three or more medical trips a week. As *The New York Times* observed, that "left one of the largest concentrations of the nation's disabled with 50 rides, or 25 round trips, up for grabs each day."

The catalyst for the Dade cuts of 1981 was Reaganomics. Lost federal aid—$19.6 million—meant Dade was forced to propose closing the Legal Aid office for the 14,000 elderly poor of Miami Beach, lay off 1,700 county workers, and end most drug rehab programs in our drug capital. The housing authority faced bankruptcy, and a huge cut in CETA training funds—from $70 million to $19 million in one year—would lay off 17,000 workers in this

---

* A wave of condo conversions in 1981 forced a lot of Miami seniors into a 1 percent vacancy market. In four months, 2,800 units went condo in Dade County. A University of Miami study of two buildings with large shares of the elderly found those in the condo conversion suffered more dizziness and hypertension than those in a similar, protected rental.

county. The private sector, which Reagan urged to the rescue, had, by late 1981, hired only 100 of the first 2,650 CETA workers to be fired.

To cover the federal cuts, property taxes would have to be hiked 34 percent in Dade. Since Reagan had carried the normally liberal county by 50,000 votes in 1980, and since a property reassessment had just raised tax bills, the new hike was resisted.

## Miami

On the one hand, there is in Miami what a travel writer has termed "The Baghdad of Biscayne Bay": the serried ranks of Morris Lapidus palazzi along Collins Avenue, the foot-high cheesecake at Wolfie's, the airport where almost half of Florida's 12 million airborne tourists debouch each year. And there is the other Miami: the blacks of Liberty City, some 35,000 Haitian refugees in "Little Haiti," and 120,000 Cubans who arrived like a tidal wave in the spring of 1980.

Eighty-nine years ago, Miami was just three shacks on sandy ground when Mrs. Julia Tuttle sent some orange blossoms to H. M. Flagler, who had just opened his Breakers Hotel in Palm Beach. The blossoms proved that Miami had been spared a frost that had destroyed citrus in central Florida that year. Flagler made Miami the terminus for the Florida East Coast Railway in 1896, and opened one of his hotels.* By 1900, there were 2,000 Miamians, and tourism and business expanded rapidly over the next twenty-five years. Neal R. Peirce in *The Megastates of America* describes a scene where "hundreds of thousands of land speculators poured into the state—2.5 million people in the year 1925 alone—and prices zoomed to many times real value. But in the spring of 1926, the bubble broke; banks began to fail; paper millionaires became paupers overnight."

The biggest expansion occurred after 1950, as airplanes and air conditioners made Florida the tourist and retirement mecca of

---

* Flagler later went beyond Miami and into the water. Joel Garreau recalls in *The Nine Nations of North America* how seven hundred men died laying steel, island by island, until "Flagler's Folly" got to Key West in 1913. Flagler's next stop, literally, was Havana . . . a goal the state of Florida actually began to implement in 1934. This plan might have had an awesome effect on the region's twentieth-century history, had it not been for the hurricane of '35, which wiped out forty-one miles of railroad track and trestle and forced the abandonment of the Havana bridge.

the East. No state grew as fast; from 2.5 million residents in 1950 to 9.6 million today. Miami Beach alone has 400 hotels, 600 motels and 4,000 restaurants, as trade and services create half the jobs in Miami's metro area. Retiree pensions of $11 billion in annual deposits, an international trade role, and the drug smuggling trade helped push Florida, and especially Miami, bank accounts to several times the national average. An Atlanta banker analyst in 1981 called the Miami sector "probably the most attractive in the East, if not in the country."

Perhaps the most distinctive force in Miami has been the banking and trade boom since the late 1970s, which helped fuel a building binge downtown on Biscayne Bay. Miami hadn't built a major skyscraper since the early 1970s, but in 1982 five blocks had new projects: a thirty-five-story World Trade Center from I. M. Pei, a $180 million project for twin towers called Miami Center I and II from Pietro Belluschi, a fifty-five-story Southeast Financial Center, and one more pair of sixty-story towers for a future Miami Center III. The *Wall Street Journal* called these five blocks a "towering $750 million monolith set on the very edge of Biscayne Bay," similar in impact to the Renaissance Center opened on the Detroit River in 1977. An economist told the *Journal* that Miami had finally found "an identity other than pink pants and lawn chairs." The paper amplified that "what the movies have done for Hollywood, cars for Detroit, steel for Pittsburgh and oil for Houston, international trade and finance are doing for Miami."

The base for much of this was laid on January 1, 1959, when the rebel troops of Fidel Castro entered Havana, and the exodus of the Cuban middle class to Miami began. Over the next decade, commercial or special U.S.-paid flights ferried more than 230,000 Cubans to America, most of them settling ninety miles from home in what became the 600-block "Little Havana" section of Miami. Many were professionals, and within a decade, Miami had 6,000 Cuban businesses. A labor force of 65,000 revived a dying Miami downtown, with Neal R. Peirce observing in 1971 how these exiles were

> the cream of Cuban society. Of those who worked in Cuba before the revolution, the average annual income was four times the average on that island. . . . Among these educated Cubans, the period of manual labor in Miami—lawyers wash-

ing dishes, engineers tending gardens, physicians working as lowly helpers in hospitals—was short-lived indeed.*

In 1961 the Miami exiles reopened Fidel Castro's alma mater, using Al Capone's old liquor warehouse in "Little Havana." The Colegio de Belen (or Belen Prep), a Jesuit school, was padlocked by Castro when he banned the Catholic church in his new fiefdom. The school had been Cuba's version of the St. Grottlesex preps of New England, located on twenty acres in downtown Havana. Twenty years and 800 graduates later, Belen Prep opened a $3.5 million campus on ten acres. The school teaches its privileged students to care about social issues, its rector informing the *Post* that "we try to make students aware that life doesn't revolve around the Fontainebleau Hotel. We try to help them realize there are so many people in need who are friendly and full of joy. . . . "

During the 1960s, the exiles revived downtown. In the 1970s, they helped launch Miami as a banking and trade center. The *Wall Street Journal* has called the Miami Cubans the "Phoenicians of the Caribbean," the middlemen for North and Latin America. Foreign trade in Florida went from $600 million in 1962 to $18 billion for 1981, half of this flowing through Miami. A state ad in *Fortune* said that

> In the last 20 years Miami has become the communications and transportation capital of the Western Hemisphere. No other city funnels so many Latin links into North America. It is now easier to fly or telephone to any point in Latin America from Miami *than to make connections between many points on the southern continent.* . . . In the end it may be the Cubans in Miami, and not Havana, who will get credit for internationalizing the Americas. (emphasis added)

Forty-six percent of Dade County speaks Spanish, so Miami became what Ecuador's president-elect Jaime Roldos termed

---

* "Economically, the Cuban community is the best thing that ever happened to Miami," claimed Dade County's mayor to *Nation's Business* in 1972. The magazine noted some examples of the "Cuban renewal" downtown. A Havana banker was told he was "overqualified" for banking. He worked as a clerk at a shoe factory, became its comptroller, and within eight years was named president of the Fidelity Bank—on the day he became an American citizen. In 1963, some 45 percent of the Cubans got aid from the most extensive refugee aid program in American history. By 1972, only 10 percent were aided, of whom eight in ten were elderly.

"the capital of Latin America" in a speech at a Miami trade fair in 1979. Two years later, Prime Minister Edward Seaga's first trip here after his victory in Jamaica was to keynote the fourth annual Miami Conference on the Caribbean. More than 200 multinational corporations have Latin-American operations offices in the Miami area, with half of them in suburban Coral Gables. A recent tenant at The Gables is DuPont, with some $700 million in Central and South American sales in 1980. DuPont moved there after rejecting Bogotá, Buenos Aires, Caracas, Mexico City, Rio and São Paulo.

From 1977 to 1980, Florida's share of our exports to Latin America and the Caribbean (excluding Mexico) jumped from 20 percent to more than 32 percent. Export-import volume of $13.5 billion in 1979 rose to $18 billion in two years. Joel Garreau noted that in the past, most Miami capital came from northern pensioners and tourists, while now, "the economy and culture have turned completely around, and are now facing due south." This is true, but tourists and retirees are still driving forces in South Florida's service and real-estate sectors. As Garreau notes, however, Latins even influence tourism, since they spend billions each year in Miami for consumer goods. The cameras, clothes and watches are often 100 percent cheaper than in their homelands, so many Latins cover their Florida vacations with resales back home. Garreau adds that Latins also open "the hitherto-dead summer season to vibrant activity. J. C. Penney now even stocks fur coats in Miami in August to appeal to the tourists from south of the equator who arrive during their own winter." Latins were more than half of the 12.6 million visitors to Miami in 1980.

Related to trade in Miami is the new force of international banking. Florida banned foreign banks until 1977, but now Miami has forty, including Lloyd's, Crédit Suisse and the Bank of Tokyo. Forty American banks also have Miami offices to tap into the foreign trade generated by the Cuban "Phoenicians." Other forces join foreign trade in piling up the Miami deposits. Growing instability in Latin America encourages more of its rich to put funds in Miami banks. The growing share of the elderly in the 1970s added even more pension capital. Above all, there are billions in funds from drug smugglers. All these factors added up to a local Federal Reserve branch with a $5 billion surplus in 1981 —in contrast to shortages in other Reserve branches. The Southeast Banking Corporation of Miami is America's thirty-fourth largest bank. It leads a Miami hot market, even though some bankers think that Latin-American instability in politics and economics may stall much of the Miami boom.

Banking is a narrow career ladder for Liberty City blacks, or Haitians, or Cubans. Insurance is not much help either, although this sector and banking created 25 percent of all new Miami area jobs in 1980. As with Miami banks, a strong Latin focus would be inevitable for a newly planned insurance exchange. As oil fields expand and skyscrapers grow in Latin America, more high-risk coverage will be needed. Noting the region's instability, an organizer of the new Miami exchange observes that "Lloyd's has never been unwilling to write insurance even in areas undergoing guerrilla warfare. They just charge more." A Lloyd's officer would run the exchange, and the *Washington Post* noted in 1981 that organizers were already "concerned about possible attempts to launder drug money through the exchange. . . ."

Drug funds are part of a kaleidoscopic cancer in Miami today. Drug smuggling is estimated to be from $7 to $12 billion a year in South Florida, and Joel Garreau observes that it "is shredding the institutions theoretically committed to other economic and social goals and standards of morality. Professions founded on trust, such as banking, accounting, and the law, are thoroughly compromised." Many sectors are affected.

Drug money inflates the real-estate market. Realty analyst Charles Kimball estimates laundered cash alone hiked home prices $5,000 in 1980. Looking at all sales over $300,000 in the Dade and Broward county markets, Kimball found 42 percent were made to foreign firms or investors with half these sales to anonymous, offshore firms. An assistant U.S. attorney told the *Washington Post* that the building boom along Brickell Avenue downtown is part of the picture: "The avenue's not all built on dope money, but some of the foundations were certainly laid. . . ." A realtor notes the difficulty of telling clean from dirty money, but "if someone says, 'I want a house. I don't care what it looks like, as long as it has a dock,' we report it. That sounds pretty suspicious."

A $5 billion surplus at the Miami Federal Reserve branch was more than the combined surplus of the twelve Federal Reserve banks. *Time* claimed that some forty banks failed to report cash deposits over $10,000 in 1981, fouling federal probes like Operation Greenback, which traced $2 billion in suspect funds to fifty-one indicted suspects. Investigators suspected that four banks were run by drug rings. Joel Garreau observes that "outlaws used to rob banks. Now they buy them."

Successful investigations were made. The first payoff came in early 1981, when the Drug Enforcement Administration (DEA) drew the net on Operation Grouper, hauling in fourteen gangs that accounted for 25 percent of America's smuggled drugs. One billion dollars in marijuana was seized in that one raid. Another DEA raid seized $150 million in mob assets, including a night-club, airport and Miami hotel. But investigators were swamped. South Florida was where 70 percent of our cocaine and 80 percent of our pot was smuggled in. Some idea of the scale and frustrations of the fight were noted by a Customs man to *The New York Times* in mid-1981:

> Take marijuana. In 1970, it was a media event when we seized 850 pounds on a single-engine plane. Then they went to light twin-engines. Then medium twins to heavy twins. Now they've got DC 6s, DC 7s. We even seized a Constellation. But in this town, it may be the only one in the United States where, if you seize a few tons of marijuana and 100 pounds of cocaine, it's got to be a slow news day or it's hard to get the media out.

Ronald Reagan took action in early 1982 and formed a South Florida Task Force from the DEA, FBI, Coast Guard and Navy under the chairmanship of Vice President Bush. The Task Force was a spectacular success. Inside a few months, smugglers began using New England ports last used for contraband in the eighteenth century. In the first nine months of 1982, 100 tons of pot were seized in New England, against 9 tons of pot for that time in 1981. In New York City, 363 tons of pot were seized by October against 70 for all of 1981. Smugglers were even switching trade routes from the East Coast to the West Coast. But South Florida remains the main funnel. Task Force seizures in 1982 were ten times those elsewhere. The Reagan crusade is only a strong first step.

Drugs mean crime, death and chaos in slums across America. The drug trade corrupts cops and bankers in South Florida, while creating a broad spectrum of local smugglers.

Fishermen can make six months' pay in one night picking up a "square grouper," bales of pot dumped from a mother ship. CBS reported that in the bayous of Dixie and Taylor counties smuggling was replacing shrimp and mullet fishing. Perhaps half the local fleet was involved. The entire sheriff's office in Dixie County was under surveillance at one point. One 1983 bust in the small town of Everglades City seized $140 million in smuggled marijuana.*

Customs officials estimate eighty nightly flights for cocaine. Joel Garreau pointed out that Florida is on average, the flattest place in North America, perfect for illegal night landings. Plane crashes have increased in the area as more planes fly in under coastal radar, without lights, to improvised strips. "Smuggling dope into the region is about as difficult as buying a souvenir in Miami Beach," notes *Time,* quoting a policeman from Dade County patrolling 550 square miles of local waterways. "Hell, they even fly coke in from a ship in one of those remote-controlled toy planes and land it on a bayshore condo."

Colombians play a major role in the smuggling. *Time* says that it is a family affair, where "wives, brothers, sisters and children all help out." "Someone lays out $100,000 from a paper bag, it's no big deal," yawns a young shop manager. A Florida official said that Colombian smugglers have practically declared his part of the state "a free-trade zone."

FBI data show Miami as our most violent city for both 1980 and 1981. Murder escalated rapidly in Dade County: from 360 murders in 1979 to 567 in 1980, then 610 homicides in 1981. The Dade homicide chief had a framed bar graph of murders in his office. A *New York Times* reporter noted how the red column for murders "climbs right out of the graph, over the wooden frame and onto the wall." Twenty-three percent of all homicides that year were done with machine guns, a weapon whose use for anything gets life terms up north. To ease a crowded morgue, the Dade medical examiner rented a refrigerated truck from Ryder to hold thirty-five corpses.

Tourism was hit hard by rampant crime. Miami's tourist bureau began a "witness retention" program offering visitors free

---

* On August 4, 1981, Cubans were prominent among 60 smugglers arrested in Miami. The CIA had trained 2,000 Cubans for a possible invasion 90 miles to the south, so they knew the 300-mile coastline of South Florida and the Keys from endless practice landings. An ex-CIA man told CBS that his old comrades now "see the Coast Guard as enemy units."

return trips and rooms for testimony in court. All the tourist had to do was get mugged. TV monitors were installed on the main drags of Miami Beach. Some of the hooded boxes have cameras; some are dummies. Asked if the wiring of Collins Avenue wasn't a bit of Big Brother on Biscayne Bay, a police officer from Oceania-on-the-Ocean told *The New York Times* that "in *1984,* we are talking about an oppressive government watching everything. In this case, the public is demanding relief from the oppression of criminals." Tourism was off by $1 billion in 1981. Forty percent of Miami hotel rooms were vacant early in 1982, when a hotelier informed *The New York Times* that "it's the worst winter in 30 or 40 years up north, and they're staying put. Somebody has to get the message out that if you're not a narcotics dealer and if you're not standing in the middle of Liberty City at sundown, the chances of getting hurt here are no higher than they are in Peoria." (Well, not quite Peoria, which had 5,542 crimes per 100,000.) Miami was the most violent metro area, with 11,582 crimes. Florida had six of the top ten metro areas for crime rates in 1980:

| | | | |
|---|---|---|---|
| *Miami* | 11,582 | *Orlando* | 9,512 |
| Atlantic City | 11,481 | Sacramento | 9,373 |
| Las Vegas | 10,292 | *Fort Lauderdale* | 9,345 |
| *Gainesville* | 10,254 | Phoenix | 9,308 |
| *West Palm Beach* | 9,824 | *Daytona Beach* | 9,107 |

Gun licenses in Miami went from 24,000 in 1979 to 49,000 in 1980 and nearly doubled again in 1981. In five years 220,000 guns were sold in Dade County. Guns grew seven times faster than new households. A thief who found one handgun in every ten cars he rifled in 1980 found one gun in every four burgled in 1981. A legal researcher describes people "openly carrying guns, some in their hands, others in their holsters. You don't dare honk your horn at anybody; you could end up dead."

Yet as crime went wild in Miami, cops were cut 30 percent after 1977. This helped fuel crime, hurt the arrest rate, and made 911 response times average twenty-seven minutes in 1980, or twenty-three minutes more then the national average. Dade crime soared 31 percent in 1980 while arrests inched up only 2 percent. The huge gap between crime growth and arrest rates meant too few cops and deterrent force. In 1981 *The Miami Her-*

*ald* recalled how "in the years when . . . police forces were at their peak, county crime figures shrank. In 1976, Dade crime declined 9.6%, in 1977 by 4.3%. In 1978, crime increased only 3.5% countrywide."

After five years of cop cuts and crime waves, Dade County finally hired 1,000 new officers in late 1981. In per capita coverage, however, Dade still remained short.* Meanwhile, taxpayers protested that the police didn't sufficiently cut down on crime. A healthy contrast to this is rising demands across Florida for a 1-cent hike in the sales tax to hire more police. Lobbying for the tax in Tallahassee, the head of the Miami Chamber of Commerce urged, "Tax us, so that we can protect ourselves."

Finally, there is the uneasy mix of Cubans, blacks and whites in Miami. The Liberty City riot of 1980 and the mayoral election of 1981 showed the social divisions. The ethnic splits are unusual. Whites and blacks united behind a Puerto Rican mayor to keep Cubans out of City Hall in 1981. These strains, the severe problems of Miami blacks and the crime wave fueled by drugs have meant a city of dangerous extremes.

Despite the lively trade of Little Havana and the Cubans' role as Phoenicians of the Caribbean, problems are growing. Miami is our third main garment center, but so many sweatshops are manned by Latins that the city was one of four investigated by a federal Sweatshop Strike Force in 1981. Or there is the prominence of Latins in the drug trade. Anger about this helped repeal Dade's legal status as a "bilingual county" in a 1980 referendum backed by whites and blacks (in theory, the repeal could have ended letting Spanish operators handle 911 emergency calls).

The main catalyst for the Latin crisis was the freedom flotilla of 1980. Of some 120,000 emigrants from the port of Mariel, more than 80,000 "Marielitos" remained in Dade County. Low literacy in Castro's Cuba and few unskilled Miami jobs meant 25 percent unemployment for the group in 1981. Thirty-six of the first 113 people slain in Miami had come from Mariel in 1980.

Since 1976, Miami blacks had seen Washington try to deport

---

* Palm Beach is the world's richest island, the average home costing $1.5 million. Thirty of its ninety-five police have college degrees, a SWAT team is trained in hostage tactics, and the photos and prints of 200,000 servants are on file. With the highest ratio of cops to citizens in America, Palm Beach has one of our lowest crime rates. If all else fails, a "code red" signal raises three bridges to the mainland. The mainland city of West Palm Beach is staffed at low Miami levels of police and was our fifth most violent metro area in 1980.

some 16,000 Haitian refugees who had traveled 700—not 90—miles in search of a better life. Then in 1980, Jimmy Carter waved the Marielitos in. The light-skinned Cubans got $635 million in federal aid to smooth their path. Miami blacks had seen it before. They had seen Cuban refugees in the 1960s get relocation aid to better job markets while Cuban males in Miami got $100 a month in welfare, as jobless black males got nothing. Studying the riot of Miami blacks at the 1968 Republican national convention, a presidential commission found resentment of Cuban welfare one of the causes. In 1971, Governor John Gilligan of Ohio took note that Cubans had received $300 million in relocation aid after 1959 as southern blacks driven north to states like Ohio received no aid. Gilligan complained to Neal Peirce: "You say you're anti-Communist and you get the best of everything. The Negroes should be treated as political refugees."

Over the next decade, things got worse for blacks and better for Cubans in Miami. In a report for the Ford Foundation on the causes of the Liberty City riot of 1980, Professor Marvin Dunn of Florida International University and Bruce Porter of Brooklyn College focused on the black-Cuban problem. Among other things, they found that:

- Between 1968 and 1978, blacks went from owning 25 percent of all Miami gas stations to just 9 percent of them. Meanwhile, Hispanics rose from a 12 percent to an 18 percent share of these entry-level firms.
- Between 1968 and 1979, federal Small Business Administration loans in Dade County went as follows: Hispanics $47.3 million, whites $46.8 million, blacks $6.4 million. Blacks were half of the Cubans in numbers but got only 13 percent as much in SBA loans.
- 10 percent of black workers were machine operators in 1968, only 2 percent were by 1978. Meanwhile, the share of unskilled workers among blacks rose from 12 percent to 25 percent in Miami.

Some of this, however, has nothing to do with blacks and Hispanics. Fewer black machinists result from a shrinking factory base in Miami. And as Professor Lisandro Perez of Louisiana State University observed about the Ford Foundation report, blacks doing poorly on the job ladder are a result mainly of centuries of "racism in this country, and not in Miami's newly arrived Hispanic people, who are now being scapegoated . . . "

The final blow came on May 17, 1980, when four white cops were acquitted of the charge that they had beaten to death a black insurance salesman named Arthur McDuffie. Within a few hours, the first major American riot since 1968 broke out. The three-day tragedy was unusual in several ways. Eight whites had been beaten or stoned to death—the first time blacks had rioted against whites since the slave uprisings before the Civil War. And these were middle-class looters. Watts in 1965 and Newark in 1967 both saw 74 percent of arrested adults with police records. But only 32 percent of Miami's adult arrests had a yellow sheet. An area once called the "Black Gold Coast" had seen jobless-ness triple from 6 percent in 1970 to 18 percent by 1980. A census share of 28 percent who were poor in 1970 had zoomed to 52 percent by 1980. Many middle-class residents had been jolted suddenly from stable lives.

A week after the riot, Jimmy Carter was advised that a Miami trip would be unsafe. Carter pledged $83 million to rebuild Liberty City, and half of this arrived before Reagan froze the funds. Reagan's urban cuts hit Liberty City hard. The small area lost 1,000 CETA jobs. A 25 percent cut for Family Health Centers threatened a clinic that provided everything from drug counseling to advising diets for teen-age mothers hit elsewhere by proposed Reagan cuts in the Women, Infants and Children (WIC) program for maternal and infant nutrition.

Dade County lost 6,500 CETA jobs all told, the worst such cut in any major area.* William Kolberg, who administered CETA for Presidents Nixon and Ford, noted on *The MacNeil-Lehrer Report* in 1981 that Puerto Rico and Miami took the worst cuts, "and we know what happened in Miami-Dade last year."

Fifty-two businesses were burned out in the Liberty City riot. One owner relocated his jet engine repair factory to suburbia, explaining to the *Wall Street Journal* in 1981: "Am I supposed to look at those burned-out buildings and those empty lots for the next 10 years? Who's going to build in that area? Nobody. They can talk all the reconstruction they want to. There isn't anybody with any money and any brains that's going to build anything."

There was desperate talk of Liberty City seceding from Miami, as a new city of 103,000 people. That would hike taxes 37 percent

---

* A U.S. Conference of Mayors survey in 1981 showed that while Dade, with 1.8 million people, lost 6,500 CETA jobs, Los Angeles with 2.8 million lost 4,500. Outside mainland America, Puerto Rico took the worst losses, losing 21,000 CETA jobs out of the 301,000 cut nationwide.

for the empty symbolism of a new black mayor. Meanwhile, Latins took over some white stores abandoned after the riot. A former school official claimed in *Time* that "the only things blacks have in Miami are several hundred churches and funeral homes. After a generation of being Southern slaves, blacks now face a future as Latin slaves."

This was a bit much. After all, blacks would be crucial in re-electing Puerto Rican mayor Maurice Ferre over a Cuban challenger in 1981. But a city with secession fantasies was in bad shape, as exhibited by a former school principal taking a *New York Times* reporter down 27th Avenue in 1981: "These were all burned down in the disturbance. That used to be Noroton Tire Center. It burned. It employed 200 people. That's the post office. That they torched. That used to be a Firestone Tire & Rubber. That used to be a theater."

City Venture Corporation, begun in a dozen American cities by Control Data Corporation (detailed in Part II, pages 244–46), decided to create 4,000 new jobs in Liberty City. Also helpful was the Greater Miami Association, which raised $6.9 million to rebuild the area. These were notable acts of voluntarism, but by 1982, $100 million was still needed for the job.

Also inflammatory in 1981 were closed deportation hearings for Haitian refugees. After the freedom flotilla of 1980, the 35,000 Haitians in Miami were granted amnesty. But 6,700 arrivals since then were subject to deportation, unless political asylum could be claimed. On June 4, 1981, after unprecedented, closed-door hearings, eleven Haitians were deported by plane to Port-au-Prince. Seventy-six more were set for such peremptory deportation, but lawyers opened up the hearings, and a federal judge put the procedures on hold. Washington then agreed to review the refugees on a case-by-case basis.

Meanwhile Haitians kept arriving by boat in 1981, 600 landing in the first week of June. Some 2,000 Haitians were languishing at Krome detention center by late 1981. Cold weather and Coast Guard ships intercepting boats from Haiti put a general end to emigrations, but not before a tragedy in which thirty-three Haitians died as their flimsy boat broke apart in the Fort Lauderdale surf. In the summer of 1982 the Krome inmates were released to sponsors, pending a case-by-case review of their applications for asylum.

So Liberty City simmered in 1981. Twenty-five percent of its housing was substandard; 30 percent of its adults were jobless; 50 percent of its students were dropouts; 52 percent of its people were poor; 100 percent of its CETA jobs were gone. And its death rate was 117 percent higher than that of Dade County whites. A cop drove a *Los Angeles Times* reporter around, casually observing how, in the housing projects, "if they start throwing bottles and stuff at us, we just leave. If we stayed, it would just get worse. . . . To tell you the truth, there's just nowhere we could go in Liberty City and eat safely."

Until 1976, Cubans stayed out of local politics for a simple reason: they wanted to go home. Expecting Castro's fall, they avoided citizenship, and were characterized by Joel Garreau as "not refugees, but exiles." But in 1976 Cuban terrorist groups began to break up, and citizenship papers began piling up. Twelve hundred applications poured in every month, and Cuban leaders asked President Ford and Congress to shorten processing so they could vote. *U.S. News & World Report* observed that "for the first time, they sound like a minority . . . organizing to get things done." Cubans were 33 percent of Dade County but only 8 percent of its voters in 1976. This was a minority with potential clout.

Cubans had quadrupled their voters to 33 percent of Miami's electorate when they backed Reboso in 1981. The *Washington Post* observed how Reboso as mayor would be "the highest elected Cuban official in the free world—in effect, a president in exile. . . ." Just before the vote, Reboso, a close friend of the late Nicaraguan dictator Anastasio Somoza, flew to Washington for a photo session with Ronald Reagan. He later conceded he should have visited Liberty City instead, for Ferre won 95 percent of a huge black turnout, split the white votes, and pulled in 30 percent of the Latins to win easily by 56 percent. The blacks and whites of Miami had won a remarkable victory.

But for what prize? Our most violent city in 1980 and 1981. The capital of our drug trade. A city whose suburbs grew 28 percent in the 1970s—as the city shrank 5 percent. A city where 95 percent of canceled voter cards were from departing whites. A city where "Anglos" felt so alienated that only 38 percent of them bothered to vote in 1981, Ferre observing that "we've become a boiling pot, not a melting pot. The Anglos can't adapt.

They can't take it, so they're moving." For all the $2 billion in building on Brickell Avenue or the world's fifth biggest air-cargo volume or Miami as Hong Kong of the Americas—for all this, Miami was also a disaster. It was a place where impoverished pensioners scrambled for free transit rides. It was a place where 52 percent of Liberty City lived in poverty. It was a city where murder tripled after 1979, and where guns grew seven times faster than new households.

A city of extremes indeed.

## Atlanta

The King was gracious on the December evening in 1939. Forty thousand wanted to see him, but only 2,000 got in, as scalpers got $200 a ticket for the event. As the mob roared in the street, Clark Gable stepped up to the microphone to observe, "Tonight I am here just as a spectator. I want to see *Gone With the Wind* the same as you do. This is Margaret Mitchell's night and the people of Atlanta's night. . . ." So it was, for until the 1940s, Atlanta's fame was as home to our popular novelist and as inspiration to her work. But just two years after The King's modest words, World War II made Atlanta part of the "arsenal of democracy." A huge bomber plant in nearby Marietta, and other defense plants, brought in skilled workers to lay the base for Atlanta's postwar industries. Two decades later, it had become the "city too busy to hate," * a center of economic boom and racial harmony long before the New South was baptized by Jimmy Carter's inaugural speech of 1971, a speech made on the steps of a state capital where, in the 1930s, cows had grazed on the grounds.

Today, a first glance shows Atlanta to be a vital hub of the Southeast for construction, conventions and transportation. Yet as Andrew Young prepared to be Atlanta's fifty-fifth mayor in 1982, *The New York Times* summarized his agenda ahead: "The tax base is shrinking, population is declining, almost a quarter of his constituents exist under the poverty level, neighborhoods are

---

* The famous slogan was from Atlanta's mayor of twenty-four years, William B. Hartsfield. In 1961, the city had put nine black children in white schools and President Kennedy saluted this notable act at a press conference. Hartsfield replied with the famous phrase.

deteriorating, unemployment and crime rates are high and the city is polarized racially.''

Atlanta's problems began long before the 1980s. As Atlanta became a beacon of racial harmony for the South in the 1960s, its white citizens began to leave. The 1970 Census showed that this was the first big Sunbelt city with a black majority. In the 1970s, as big towers rose on Peachtree Street, many whites left the troubled city, which soon elected its first black mayor. The 42 percent exodus of local whites was second only to a 50 percent white flight from Detroit in the 1970s. Atlanta lost 14 percent of its residents, the worst such loss among big Sunbelt cities. Most of the emigrants moved to thirteen bedroom counties, and Atlanta's suburbs grew 28 percent in the decade. Today 1.6 million suburbanites circle the 420,000 left in Atlanta. Blacks went from being 50 percent of the city in 1970 to 67 percent of a smaller and poorer Atlanta.

In the 1960s, Mayor Ivan Allen joined with Martin Luther King to lobby on the civil rights front in Washington as an integrated team. Meanwhile, even as big buildings began rising on Peachtree Street, as metro area jobs doubled from 300,000 to 600,000, the central city was dying. The jobs grew mainly in the bedroom counties. During the 1950s, Atlanta grew by a striking 47 percent, but in the 1960s, it grew by a feeble 2 percent. As it became the first big Sunbelt city with a black majority, the media stage was held by the boom downtown.

The downtown noise centered about the colorful persona of architect John Calvin Portman, Jr. Portman's forte is, as described by *Time,* what are ''known in the trade as 'Jesus Christ' hotels: when visitors walk in for the first time, their eyes bulge and they gasp 'Jee-sus Chee-rist.' '' This blasphemous salute was mainly inspired by vast atrium lobbies, starting with the twenty-two-story interior of Atlanta's Hyatt Regency Hotel in 1967. Then there was the silvery silo of his Peachtree Center Plaza Hotel of 1976. At seventy floors it is the world's tallest inn, its seven-story lobby described by Horace Sutton in the *Saturday Review:*

> fountains, pools of water, twittering birds, ''floating'' cocktail pods, make the lobby seem a stage set for ''Star Wars.'' The hubbub of chatter and running water renders conversation as successful as a symposium held under Niagara Falls. For those who can get a reservation, two express elevators shoot sky-

ward through glass tubes, landing in eight seconds, on the seventieth floor.

All this was only part of a vast Peachtree Center below, a $200 million complex covering dozens of acres, including five office towers and the Merchandise Mart, one of the South's biggest buildings. This is called a "megastructure" in Atlanta, which has a second mega on Peachtree Street at the Omni International. The Omni is fourteen stories high and, in addition to a convention center, has two office buildings, six theaters, a 17,000-seat arena for the hockey Flames and basketball Hawks, a hotel, a skating rink, and the world's first indoor theme park.

Writing in *The Progressive,* Jonathan Schlefer noted in 1981 how the Omni and Peachtree Center kept out "undesirables." The Center had no bus stops, and used planters or spikes to keep out interlopers. The Omni required adult escorts for those under eighteen, which "should stop a few black teenagers," gibed Schlefer. He added that a third megastructure had been planned by the Chamber of Commerce for a run-down shopping area nearby the so-called Gulch, which was patronized mainly by blacks. But architect Richard Rothman found that the old Gulch had all of downtown's nineteenth- and early twentieth-century architecture and did more trade than the two Peachtree Street megas, while paying more sales taxes. The Gulch remains, though under the city's sweeter name of "Heart of Atlanta." Schlefer concluded that Atlantans with their passion for excess "have learned their lesson. The streets make the city." *

An important lesson is that downtown drama alone can't revive cities. The media today confuses new malls or office towers downtown with the "revival" of dying Snowbelt cities. In Atlanta's case, people gape at the Peachtree glitz and believe all must be well for the city. As Portman told *The Wall Street Journal* regarding inner city decay, "I know that I have the philosophical solution—there's absolutely no question about it."

Even the U.S. Chamber of Commerce grasped that reality in a profile of Atlanta in *Nation's Business* in 1976:

> Glitter and glamour are what impress the casual visitor . . . But behind this exterior . . . Atlanta has crime, racial friction, and

---

* A lesson in liveliness that John Portman understands. He acknowledges Tivoli Gardens and the southern front porch as influences since "it all comes back to one thing—people enjoy looking at other people."

unemployment. In some areas, real estate development has gone from boom to bust. Whites continue a flight to the suburbs, and the quality of public school education is in question.

Four years later, Atlanta was our ninth biggest builder of office space. But the new Census showed that of our ten big urban builders that year, only Houston's population had grown faster than America's. Seven of the ten big builders in 1980 had actually lost 5 percent to 15 percent of their residents in the 1970s. Atlanta's boom on Peachtree and depopulation offstage fit the national picture.

Of those left in Atlanta, few can land jobs on Peachtree Street. Their skills are for manufacturing, which provides only 15 percent of local jobs. Few skills and too much crime were cited by a 1981 Chamber of Commerce study, which found business relocators favoring Dallas, Denver and Orlando. The Chamber described clerical help as "increasingly hard to employ for center-city business" in Atlanta. This was one more reason for America's biggest glut of office space downtown: a 13 percent vacancy rate in 1981, and 20 percent in 1982. Meanwhile, some 2,900 CETA jobs lost under the Reagan cuts hit the unskilled local workers hard, with Atlanta's research director telling the *Los Angeles Times* that the few private jobs for the poor "are the lowest-paying, least autonomous and most dead-end imaginable."

Presiding over an emptying, poorer city was Maynard Holbrook Jackson, mayor from 1974 to 1982. His first year in office inspired a seven-part series in the Atlanta *Constitution* about "A City in Crisis." A *Time* story on Jackson's first fifteen months reflected a basic problem in its headline: "A Mayor Learning on the Job." The young black mayor was accused of polarizing the city and retaining dubious cronies. The *Constitution*'s associate editor told *U.S. News & World Report* in 1975 that "the mayor's mind often seems to be 'If you don't agree with my policies, it is racially motivated.' The mayor has stimulated white flight and white concern about racial matters in issues that a lot of other people don't see as black-white issues at all." Even John Portman, a big Jackson backer, told *Time* two weeks later that "he's perceived as taking every issue and turning it into a race issue. His biggest problem right now is raising white confidence. He has absolutely none."

Some of this criticism was self-serving. White power brokers were furious when Jackson reasonably asked for a 15 percent property tax hike to maintain city services. The City Council cut that in half, as Jackson assailed a "victory for the rich against the poor." But accurate class analysis was a far cry from yelling racism. Unfortunately, Jackson did that in defending his police commissioner, Reginald Eaves. Eaves had been a college friend of Jackson's, then an aide to Boston's Mayor Kevin White. Some cited his lack of legal background and charged Jackson with cronyism. To this sensible point, Jackson swung back wildly with "racism" charges. Later, Eaves's personal secretary turned out to have a police record, and Eaves's nephew was discovered to have gotten a public service job after "my uncle told me who to see at city hall." Mayor Jackson "was surprised, to say the least" and fired both employees. A year later, Eaves pointed to the fact that crime in Atlanta had risen only half as fast as in America but dragged in race again when he said that "what we've learned in Atlanta is that a black chief can make a difference in fighting crime. Other cities ought to try it."

Another problem for Jackson was Atlanta's shrinking tax base. The old Sunbelt standby of annexing rich suburbs for new revenues was considered. But while boomtowns like Houston could grab at will, fading ones like Atlanta, Miami or New Orleans lacked annex appeal in the 1970s. Also, annexing suburbs would dilute Jackson's black voting base. He told *Time* that he could only annex on "terms I can sell to the black community," keeping black votes above 45 percent of all registrants. Again, Jackson reduced big issues to petty racial lines. The fact was that without the white suburbs and their taxes, the black majority of Atlanta would inherit the wind. Jackson failed to lead Atlanta's blacks, the city declined, and suburban whites lost interest in annexation. Stanley Crouch observed in the *Village Voice* in 1981, "the plight of Atlanta's poor doesn't move those affluent whites who believe their home town is now perceived as a black city, and who lend their voices to periodic rumblings about incorporating greater Atlanta's other 13 counties to bring about a resurgence of white political control."

With no land to grab, a City Council resisting taxes, and a taxpayer exodus afoot, Maynard Jackson cut services. As revenues shrank, Atlanta budgets grew 20 percent less than inflation between 1974 and 1980. Eight hundred and thirty city workers were cut from a small work force, but Jackson bragged to the

*Los Angeles Times* in 1981 that "we've been successful in producing more with fewer people." Jackson similarly told *Nation's Business* that "we are ideologically liberal and fiscally conservative. That's a combination that can work, and we are proving it." Census results and crime data proved otherwise.

While part of a national trend, the Atlanta crime wave reflected a strapped city losing police at a phenomenal rate. Cops shrank from 1,700 in 1975 to 1,100 in 1979. Meanwhile, between 1977 and 1980 the crime rates soared: rape up 30 percent, robbery up 36 percent, murder up 51 percent. An affirmative action suit in 1975 froze new police hires. Finally in 1979, a new public safety commissioner broke the logjam. Lee P. Brown quickly hired 200 cops, and Atlanta's crime rate rose 1 percent in 1980 against 10 percent nationwide. That still left crime at very high levels. Atlanta in 1981 was #11 for robbery, #4 for murder and #2 for rape and robbery among the fifty big cities. Even the "fiscally conservative" Jackson dropped his pretense about "producing more with fewer people" in 1981 to urge the City Council to hire 400 more police.

The thin blue line, the 51 percent rise in murder since 1977 and Atlanta's growing poverty formed the background to the tragedy that ended the myth of a successful city. Twenty-three black children and five young black adults were murdered during twenty-two months from mid-1979 to mid-1981, almost all of these acts probably done by Wayne B. Williams.*

The Atlanta murders became national news in early 1981, after a sixty-seven-year-old Philadelphia grandmother put on a green ribbon to symbolize "life"—and launched a sea of green ribbons and concern across America. There was a torchlight parade of 20,000 in Harlem, a rally at the Lincoln Memorial, and a major effort by the FBI, with strong backing from President Reagan, to trap the shadowy "child snatcher." Hucksters also appeared. Having counseled the Reverend Jim Jones in Guyana, Mark Lane preyed on a bereaved Atlanta mother. CORE leader Roy Innis kept the three TV networks spellbound for forty-eight hours by claiming he would "arrest" the Atlanta killer. Even the usually stable Dick Gregory fantasized that the Atlanta-based Center for

---

* Williams, convicted of killing two of the five adult victims, was informally linked in court to thirteen of the twenty-three child murders as well. Since no known child murder victims by strangers occurred after Williams' arrest in 1981, he may well have killed all of the 28 victims.

Disease Control was spiriting away the black children for experiments.

The twenty-three child murders remained an open case for two years, reflecting murder by strangers preying on the poor. Until an educational campaign and a curfew got Atlanta's children off the streets, they were easy targets for the lunatic involved. One journalist found that for $10 most poor children in Atlanta would get into a car with a stranger. All the murdered children were poor. The media expressed surprise that "street wise" children could be abducted and killed.

The child murders divided Atlanta's black community along class lines. There had long been a strong black elite, Stanley Crouch recalled how "as early as 1873, 100 years before Maynard Jackson took office, a black church ran three health centers so successful that the death rate among those it served was one-third less than that of the white population."

In 1936, Atlanta was the site of a prophetic voting rights march led by the Reverend Martin Luther King, Sr. Recalling his Atlanta youth around that time, on *60 Minutes,* Vernon Jordan noted "great models in Atlanta, there were the black college presidents, the black lawyers. . . ." With five black colleges, the city was either campus or home for major leaders like Jordan, James Weldon Johnson and Martin Luther King, Jr., as well as for Andrew Young, John Lewis and Julian Bond.

Crouch notes the division between the middle-class, light-skinned Morehouse-Spelman college set and the rest of black Atlanta. When Maynard Jackson "does something the black community likes, the entire group takes credit for it; when mistakes or unpopular decisions come down, he is seen as a high yellow selling out blacks." This is schematic, but it took much agitation by the Atlanta victims' mothers before Jackson set up a task force on the murders in 1980. His delay is understandable, for when does one form such an expensive, police-consuming group? But only in the spring of 1981 did other light-skinned Atlantans like Coretta King and Andrew Young "speak out" on the murders. Their tardy reaction almost confirmed Thomas Sowell's view that many black leaders—especially, he argues, light-skinned ones—have lost touch with the black urban poor, as they pursue middle-class goals like open housing or affirmative action, while ignoring gut issues like jobs, health or welfare. Five years before the child murders divided Atlanta's blacks, local teacher Flora Stone told *U.S. News & World Report:*

A lot of Atlanta's problems are class problems, and Mayor Jackson represents the middle-class blacks. I don't think lower-class blacks can identify with him. I like him as a person but, looking at him as a politician, I don't think he is doing anything. The whites moved out with their money and when they leave us here in the inner city, nobody is going to be able to do anything.

Until the arrest of Wayne B. Williams on June 21, 1981, the tragedy of the Atlanta children hung over the election for mayor. Barred from a third term, Jackson endorsed his old friend Andrew Young. Young's belated press conference on the murders and black anger against Jackson for not arresting the strangler threatened to convert a mayoral blessing into a curse. Two months before Williams was arrested, NAACP lawyer Dwight Thomas told Art Harris of the *Washington Post:* "Just watch. In his final days, Jackson will be struggling harder than Jimmy Carter trying to get the hostages out of Iran. They've got to make some kind of arrest, otherwise heads are liable to roll."

Not since the 1979 blizzard in Chicago drove Michael Bilandic from City Hall and blew in Jane Byrne had one issue so dominated a mayoral campaign. Leading the Atlanta mothers had been Camille Bell, a college dropout and former SNCC worker who had fallen on hard times. She was living in a project with her four children when her son Yusef disappeared. Yusef had been a remarkable nine-year-old, helping adults balance their checkbooks at the local markets, one of them recalling for the *Washington Post* how "if you wanted to know how to spell something, you'd just ask him and he'd tell you. He knew math and history, what was what and how to do it. He was somebody like Abraham Lincoln." Six days after Yusef Bell was found, strangled and stuffed in the crawl space of a vacant school, his mother organized the Committee to Stop Children's Murders. A few months later, the Atlanta mothers got the task force from City Hall. At a Sammy Davis-Frank Sinatra benefit for the children in March 1981, Mrs. Bell was found by *Post* reporter Harris sulking on the sidelines amid "the swirl of well-heeled blacks." She observed sourly, "They aren't as far from the projects as they think. When Reagan cuts the social programs and their jobs, they'll be moving back to my neighborhood. It's going to be fun to see them on the way down."

One of the few bright notes during the tragedy was Public Safety Commissioner Lee P. Brown. He was America's first black Ph.D. in criminology, and had been with the San Jose police before he accepted the Atlanta post in 1978. Brown rapidly ended the five-year hiring freeze, and in 1980, despite the child murders, Atlanta homicides had dropped 13 percent.

During the complex hunt for the strangler, Brown was a model of discretion and calm. Brown showed good sense when the Guardian Angels of New York came to help Atlantans organize "self-protection patrols." He denounced them on arrival and they left. When local black vigilantes organized a "Henry Aaron Bat Patrol," Brown quickly arrested two leaders, who, it turned out, toted guns as well. As for reports on ABC about a "conspiracy" of stranglers in Atlanta, Brown coolly observed that "your network has made a religion out of trying to create the impression of a 'conspiracy.' "*

Ronald Reagan and Congress in 1981 made major cuts for programs vital to the welfare of slum kids: food stamps, school lunches, health centers, and the WIC maternal and infant nutrition program. But many liberal leaders let the huge federal cuts go by without objection, settling instead for rallies expressing "concern" over the young Atlanta victims. So much money flooded Atlanta for the families of the murdered children that local politicians insisted no more funds be sent the bereaved. As state representative Tyrone Brooks said, "Once we bury the children, take care of the funeral expense, I don't think we need to pay the families. We have children dying of leukemia in this city, for example, but nobody's rushing to say here's some money to tide you over."

With Wayne B. Williams arrested and indicted, a recovering city was polarized by racist mudslinging from its chief magistrate. As the mayoral primary between Andrew Young and white liberal Sidney Marcus headed for a photo finish, Jackson revived the racism that had divided Atlanta six years ago. At a black luncheon Jackson claimed white business leaders wanted a

---

* His aplomb and success in the Williams case impressed Mayor Kathryn Whitmire of Houston. So in fourteen years, Brown has now gone from San Jose to Atlanta to the fifth biggest American city, where police brutality and thin police ranks are notorious. If Brown can cut Houston's high crime rate while restoring confidence in police from the 46 percent minority share in the city, he could prove a formidable opponent for Whitmire later on.

"white mayor," and that black Marcus supporters were "Negroes" who were "shuffling and grinning around the campaign." One of Marcus's leading black supporters, state representative Douglas Dean, sneered that "I would rather have him call me a nigger." He added that Jackson's fusillades were "worse than slave plantation politics . . . an attempt to control black people's minds."

The national media usually tries to pretend that such black bigotry doesn't happen, but Jackson's blatant racism was too much. It got major coverage. Meanwhile, Andrew Young claimed that "race is clearly an issue; it always has been an issue in the campaign. But I've always agreed with whoever it was who said that racial need not be racist. If everybody's concerned about the racial factor, and I think they are, then I think it's important to discuss it openly." *

Young beat Marcus with 55 percent of the vote, which divided mainly along racial lines. During the campaign, Andrew Young had talked up his ties to the Third World. He recalled how in 1979 he took people from twenty-three American firms to Africa, and came back seventeen days later with $2 billion in contracts. He complained that only sixteen foreign banks had branches in Atlanta, as all those Eurodollars floated about "looking for a place to invest." Probably a few more banks will invest in Atlanta, but most will focus on Miami as the center of hemispheric trade and commerce. Regarding more foreign contracts for Atlanta firms, Young called this his "International Solution." At one point in the campaign, he was convinced that his contacts abroad would somehow cover any Reagan cutbacks at home.

Parts of his claim made sense. The Brandt Commission report of 1980, which inspired the Cancun economic summit in 1981, showed how economic interdependence of have and have-not nations is crucial for ending hunger and laying an industrial base in the South. This would open new markets for the stagflated nations of the North. There is merit in Young's view expressed to *The New York Times* on the eve of his 1982 inaugural that

> pragmatic businessmen would have realized the market potential around the world and would have begun to internationalize

---

* This disingenuous comment was hardly surprising for Young, who had negotiated with the PLO, branded the English and Swedes as "racists," and found "political prisoners" in America as well as the Soviet Union.

our economy to make it more competitive. . . . The new frontier is the developing world. What we're doing is trying to use Atlanta as a gateway to opening up a totally new market in Latin America, Africa and the Middle East.

The next day his inaugural address called for "a new consciousness of Atlanta as a regional center of international finance and export trade." The ceremony was attended by representatives from Liberia and Nigeria, a former foreign minister of Panama, and the Secretary-General of the Organization of African Unity.

Six weeks later, however, the *Times* business page noted questions from Peachtree Street about the "International Solution." Atlanta businessmen liked Young's pledge to get tough with crime. But a hub for Third World trade? One Peachtree power called the notion "pie in the sky," and added that Young should first improve services. Young's worthy but vague North-South idea seemed a strategic diversion from pressing tactical needs.*

Atlanta didn't explode during the long, frustrating crisis of the children's murders. For once, one agrees with Young's racial analysis that "the presence and involvement of a black power structure in the city is the reason why Atlanta responded to this, the murders and the trial, with confidence that justice will be done." But this hardly swept away class divisions obvious long before the recent tragedies. Until Young, downdown leaders and all parts of the black community agreed on a plan to restore services and stability to a dying city, businesses and taxpayers would keep moving to suburbia.

The day Young took office, so did a new councilman. John Lewis had led SNCC in its pre-black-power days. Then he ran the Voter Education Project in Atlanta, which is credited widely with the sharp rise in black voters and officials in the South. Always a realist, the new councilman bluntly described Atlanta in late 1981: "What you have is something like a festering sore,

---

* The main problem with the North-South strategy is the need for huge shifts in development, monetary and trade priorities from the North—outlined by the Brandt Commission. Jean-Jacques Servan-Schreiber suggests a second Marshall Plan to build up the Third World as producer and consumer, the way we revived Germany and Japan after 1945. Even before that, he adds, "the Third World needs . . . a complete network of infrastructures that will establish the foundations of development." It must be done. But it means many hurdles before Andrew Young plugs the Third World into Atlanta's potential ex-im outlets.

a white ring around a poor, black core with a few prosperous black and white neighborhoods . . . we've got to do something about it. If we don't, the sore is going to burst."

## Birmingham

Birmingham has been a bench mark of civil rights for two decades. The Freedom Rides were often focused here in 1961, and police chief "Bull" Connor unleashed his police dogs on children in this city in 1963. A decade after Dr. King and the children triumphed over the dogs, clubs and fire hoses, the media portrayed the old steel town as a symbol of regional rebirth. What had stood for the worst of the old regime now symbolized a New South.

Typical of this picture was a *Time* article on "A City Reborn," in its special "The South Today" issue of 1976, which said that "Alabama's largest city . . . has become a model of Southern race relations." It marveled that blacks could "dine freely downtown" as they had in much of the South for a decade. It made much of 34 black cops, out of 616 police, in a city that was half black. It praised school integration, although white flight meant city schools were 70 percent black. A shrinking U.S. Steel payroll meant fewer blue-collar jobs for unskilled blacks, while a growing University of Alabama meant more white-collar work for commuters. *Time* merely said that "White collars demand more culture than blue: a $60 million civic center nearing completion includes a 2,900-seat symphony hall and 1,000-seat theater, as well as a colosseum and exhibition hall." While white mayor David J. Vann admitted to *Time* that "we don't make any claim that we've licked racism, but we've learned to face the problem candidly and not play games," black city councilman Richard Arrington suggested that much of the racial improvement was "still very much tokenism."

Birmingham was dying. Census was shrinking, crime was rising and the key steel sector was cut in half. In late 1980, this was the only Sunbelt metro area with double-digit unemployment, its 10.2 percent rate nearly double America's 5.6 percent rate. Playing up civil rights gains, *Time* in 1976 confused the absence of racism with the presence of stability.

Councilman Arrington became Birmingham's first black mayor. On May 10, 1981, some of the old Freedom Riders, led by John Lewis, boarded a Greyhound to celebrate the twentieth anniversary of the Rides. The media trumpeted New South progress since 1961, but failed to note that the Greyhound with its celebrants was the *only* bus running in Birmingham that day. On March 1, a deficit at the Transit Authority took buses off Birmingham streets, leaving Mayor Arrington to say simply that "a story going out over the national wires and networks indicating a shutdown of buses in a city of over 700,000 cannot be viewed in any vein except a negative one." Only five years after being "A City Reborn," Birmingham was the only big Sunbelt city with 10 percent unemployment, and the only big American city with no mass transit.

Like those of its English namesake, Birmingham's coal and iron reserves made it a major steel town. Its first building was a blacksmith's shop in 1871, and there were twenty-five blast furnaces by 1890. By 1900, Birmingham exported 85 percent of our pig iron. The city's population went from 38,400 in 1900 to 132,700 in 1910. The panic of 1907, however, saw U.S. Steel buy out independent furnaces, with a U.S. Senate committee later charging that this had meant "the practical monopoly of the iron and steel trade of the South. . . ." Convict labor was leased, unions were broken and U.S. Steel had kept other industries out of Birmingham. The city's lack of economic diversity was matched by a sharp social division between the nonunion poor and the very rich. No middle class grew in Birmingham as a moderating force, since U.S. Steel managers lived "over the mountain" in the suburb of Mountain Brook.

At Birmingham's semicentennial in 1921, a segregated audience of 20,000 whites and 10,000 blacks heard America's first citizen make an eloquent plea for moderation. Warning that democracy was a "lie" unless blacks won equality, the orator put forth a bold dream: "I want to see the time coming when black men will regard themselves as full participants in the benefits and duties of American citizenship. We cannot go on as we have gone on for almost half a century." But the whites of Birmingham had ignored Warren G. Harding. The polarized city remained, and forty years after Harding's speech, Freedom Riders were beaten up on Mother's Day by white thugs. Two years later was "The Year of Birmingham," with the street protests and the killing of four black girls by a bomb explosion during a Sunday school class on "the love that forgives."

Birmingham's violence contrasted with the calm in Atlanta, where white mayors Hartsfield and Allen worked with Dr. King. *The Almanac of American Politics* observed that investors "don't like commotion of any kind. During the 1960s, metropolitan Atlanta grew 37 percent while metropolitan Birmingham grew 3 percent." Meanwhile, the central cities saw Atlanta grow only 2 percent as Birmingham lost 12 percent of its residents. Neal R. Peirce noted the saying that "When you're in Atlanta, you can forget you're in Georgia," then he added that "When you're in Birmingham or Montgomery, you *never* forget you're in Alabama."

Meanwhile, the steel that built Birmingham was cut in half by competition and automation. Using our technologies, Europe and Japan captured 25 percent of our market by 1980. U.S. Steel waited until the late 1970s to modernize three Birmingham furnaces, replacing open hearths. The upgradings cut the city's daily discharge of particulates sharply, from 38,000 pounds to only 19. Automation meant big factory losses in a city increasingly dominated by unskilled blacks. Production expanded in more modern productive mills, but U.S. Steel's payroll dropped from 25,000 to 12,000 by 1976. The University of Alabama, with 6,700 local jobs and 13,000 throughout Jefferson County, was threatening to become Birmingham's main employer in the skilled work that suburban whites tend to dominate.

Six years later came the worst blow of all. In May of 1982, U.S. Steel announced the closing of its huge Fairfield works, a loss of 7,5000 jobs. This trauma was noted lightly in the business section of *The New York Times* a month later, Lydia Chavez reporting how "the local chamber of commerce could proudly claim that it did not matter so much. The plant had already been usurped by the local telephone company and university as the city's largest employer."

Four months later, on October 8, CBS ran a special report the day America hit 10.1 percent unemployment. Steve Croft noted how "Birmingham used to forge steel . . . but most of the plants have been quiet for some time now." Fifty-five thousand were jobless in the metro area, a 14.4 percent unemployment rate. Referrals to the mental-health center had quadrupled in two years.

Even by 1980, only 15 percent of the Birmingham work force was in manufacturing against a 22 percent national rate and a 29 percent factory share in Huntsville.* Even then, Birmingham had 10 percent unemployment when deficits at the Transit Authority put the buses in the barn on February 27, 1981. Thirty thousand daily riders were affected, many of them low-income workers. Black churches, which had fought City Hall in 1963, now had to improvise a jitney system to help a black mayor. The missing buses hurt downtown. Trying to diversify, Birmingham had been redeveloping downtown as a shopping magnet for 700,000 residents of Jefferson County. Mayor Arrington told *The New York Times* that "what you're doing by letting a system shut down for any length of time is severely hampering economic growth, and you're losing ground you'll never regain."

Three months went by. The legislature in Montgomery sat on its hands. Service was finally restored by hiking the fare for the aging fleet from 60 to 80 cents and cutting rides almost in half. Arrington suggested that without further aid the system might close down for good. Twenty-five percent of the budget came from Washington, and Ronald Reagan's threat to end federal operating subsidies for mass transit by 1984 would end the Birmingham line.

Birmingham's crisis of 1981 was an extreme version of what happens in many cities today as the downward spiral of higher fares . . . fewer riders . . . even higher fares proceeds. This spiral got a big shove in 1980, when urban fare increases across America equaled all those of the previous six years. The press focuses on strapped systems in Snowbelt cities like Boston, Chicago, Philadelphia or New York, but Sunbelt cities also suffer. Beyond the Birmingham bus crisis in 1981, an official of the Washington-based American Public Transit Association warned that "Houston, Atlanta, Miami, Denver and Los Angeles all face terrible problems with their systems." †

---

* Huntsville's growth was based mainly on the Redstone Arsenal of Wernher von Braun: NASA and the Pentagon spend more than $500 million in the area each year. Fourteen thousand people in 1950 has become 140,000 today.
† Meanwhile, the media pretends that mass transit is a "failure," with lack of federal and state aid unrelated to the disease. Exemplifying this was an *NBC Overnight* lead in 1982: "In the United States, it is fair to say that mass transit is a mess . . . ," after which came a feature on San Diego's successful new trolley. Mass transit "works" if you have a prosperous city like San Diego and a limited jitney like its "Tijuana Trolley" for tourists. The press often reports on the "success" of subways in London, Montreal, Paris or Toronto, but all are backed very heavily by national subsidies from governments.

Birmingham is far from the polarized city of old. Operation New Birmingham, begun in 1963 by *News* editor Vincent Townsend, led to many racial advances. For example, there was attorney Arthur Shores, who was barred from an Alabama law school in the 1930s, but later was the lawyer who got Autherine Lucy into the University of Alabama in 1956. In 1967, Shores was elected to the City Council and in 1975, the seventy-one-year-old Shores got an honorary degree from the University of Alabama. Or there was a moving symbol of racial progress from the Jefferson County delegation to the state legislature. Fourteen white and seven black members elected as their chairman Representative Chris McNair, the father of one of the four little girls killed in the church bombing of 1963. Finally, there is Mayor Arrington, a Ph.D. in zoology, who told *Nation's Business* in 1975, "I'm not opposed to school busing, but I don't think it's good for Birmingham. I would give more priority to government structures. In other words, upgrade the schools and give more representation to the blacks, from superintendents and principals on down."

It took guts for a black leader to oppose busing in 1975. But Arrington reflects a sophisticated constituency. Despite Arrington's opposition, an odd coalition of conservative blacks and whites teamed up with liberal whites to elect a mainly white Council slate in 1981. In a sense the fact of blacks backing a white slate against a black mayor in Birmingham tells a dramatic story of progress.

This said, a troubled city remains: 14.4 percent unemployment in 1982, the central city shrinking 16 percent after 1960, 1,000 black-owned businesses in 1960 down to less than 500 by 1981. While murder rose only 5 percent after 1977, the rate was already so high that Birmingham had the eleventh highest murder rate among the fifty big cities in 1980 and the tenth highest in 1981. Despite the dramatic pollution gains noted earlier, a recent federal survey found Birmingham with the fifteenth worst urban air for 1980.

Nineteen eighty-three got off to a good start, with the opening of a new seamless-pipe factory and part of the old Fairfield mill. This $690 million investment from U.S. Steel should add 3,000 new factory jobs, and was a major shot in the arm. Otherwise, however, as Richard Nathan, director of Princeton's Urban and Regional Research Center, has observed, "Birmingham looks a lot like Cleveland, only it's smaller."

## New Orleans

New Orleans is the home of Mardi Gras, beignets, Antoine's and the cavernous Superdome, the largest finished building on earth. Nearly a third of all our farm exports passed through its ports in 1980, the docks a close second to New York for export-import volume that year. With more than 28,000 hotel rooms, this has long been a premier convention city.

For color and tourism, the Big Easy has no peers. A twelfth the size of New York, it had nearly half as many tourists in 1981. "Like Blanche DuBois, it is always depending on the kindness of strangers," noted Judd Rose on ABC, about the 6 million tourists who added $2 billion and 40,000 jobs to the New Orleans economy. Nineteenth-century neighborhoods like the Latin Quarter or the Garden District make this "the city that care forgot." Boston, New York and Philadelphia evoke the nineteenth century, but only New Orleans *lives* it in Victorian "guest houses." There are the nightly concerts at Preservation Hall, with Argentine poet Jorge Luis Borges a recent habitué. In his pinstripe suit, with cane, he sings "St. James Infirmary" with the other patrons, who have each paid $1 to sit on benches in the plain room to hear the most authentic jazz in America. Enchanted by "one of the most beautiful cities in the world," Borges at eighty-two considers relocation to a city praised in 1911 by the *Encyclopaedia Britannica* for "its cuisine, its speech, its 'continental' Latin Sundays, its opera, its carnival, its general fashion and manners, its intolerance of all sorts of rigours. . . ."

So it remains. There is Mardi Gras, now a year-round industry in a city with fifty-one parades a year. Walker Percy has called this an "organic, viable folk festival, perhaps the only one in the United States." And this remains the only city whose mayor once said of prostitution, "You can make it illegal, but you can't make it unpopular!" As New Orleans prepared to host the 1984 World's Fair, ten office towers and twelve hotels went up in the 1982 slump, with part of Jean Laffite's treasure dug up in the foundation of a Marriott hotel. The city hosts Super Bowl XX in 1986, only five years after XV earned some $100 million for New Orleans in a week-long corporate spree. The game is played in the Superdome, the biggest indoor stadium and structure on earth at 273 feet tall and 680 in diameter. Isamu Noguchi saw the Superdome soon after its opening in 1975. He gaped at its suavely curved exterior—which resembles a squashed nuclear cooling tower—and hailed "the greatest piece of sculpture I have ever seen. After this, we sculptors can quit."

But to live in—a disaster. New Orleans was rated the poorest of our fifty biggest cities in a University of New Orleans survey of 1977. It lost 11 percent of its people after 1960, going from a 37 percent black census back then to a 55 percent share today. It had the seventh highest murder rate in 1981. Extreme poverty, a narrow tax base, overcrowded housing and poor police relations further reflect one of America's worst cities.

Police brutality is a symbol of the growing distress. At least ten unarmed blacks have died during encounters with police since 1978. The most notorious incident occurred in the Algiers section in the fall of 1980. A policeman had been killed while apparently breaking up a drug deal. Five days later, officers with warrants swept through some frame houses near the huge Fisher Housing Project. Three blacks were killed during the search, all of them for allegedly having shot first. This episode and four more disputed killings of blacks by cops in 1980 upset the usual racial calm in "the queen of cities." Some officers were fired and others resigned, one of them the police chief brought in from Birmingham to clean up things. His successor observed that one might infer from news accounts "we are a uniformed mob of undisciplined thugs." Art Harris in the *Washington Post* suggests an odd explanation for some of the brutality: too much housing integration. As locals see it:

> Blacks and whites live close together in New Orleans, with stately Victorian mansions owned by white gentry often mere blocks away from blacks in rundown frame houses. Such proximity has kept many whites' racial fears simmering for generations, contributing to the apparent carte blanche enjoyed by the police.

The FBI got 105 brutality complaints from New Orleans residents in 1980 against 101 in four times larger Houston or 100 from even bigger Los Angeles.

Another symbol of racial tension in 1981 was a controversy over the city's Liberty obelisk. The monument marks the Battle of Liberty Place, an uprising in 1874 against one of our worst

Reconstruction regimes. In 1932 the inscription "White Supremacy" was chiseled into the monument, but a bronze plaque was later added to disclaim the phrase. Given the police incidents of 1980, Mayor Ernest (Dutch) Morial suggested it was "time to lay this monument to rest." His remark had been preceded by blind ads inviting bids to dismantle an unspecified monument. When the mayoral plan was revealed, a storm erupted. Perhaps the Solomonic solution of erasing the inscription and keeping the monument to liberty should be adopted.

One hundred years after the 1874 rebellion, an amendment to the Louisiana Constitution put New Orleans in fiscal chains. This was a tax cap to break all molds. The home of the Superdome has what amounts to a Superdeductible, for no one pays any property taxes on the first $50,000 of assessed value. This stupendous exemption meant 79 percent of New Orleans property owners paid no taxes in 1979. Another 10 percent paid less than $100 that year. When nine in ten property owners pay no taxes or less than $100 a year, the revenue base, and the services it supports, is going to be in ruins. As New Orleans' crime rates grew sharply between 1977 and 1981, so did cuts in cops. Murder rose 26 percent, robbery 44 percent and rape 68 percent while police forces shrank 10 percent. These officers were cut from a force already staffed a third lower than safer Snowbelt cities like New York, Chicago or Philadelphia.

"We don't have enough money even to put a coat of paint on our problems," sighed Mayor Moon Landrieu to Neal R. Peirce in 1972, adding that, "we tax everything that moves, and everything that stands still, and if it moves, we tax it again." The current mayor, Ernest Morial, is more of an optimist, brashly claiming to be "the best mayor in the country," in charge of America's "greatest city." His Kingfish swagger conceals a serious mayor who has focused on the growing problem of infant mortality in New Orleans—a teen-age pregnancy rate that is 40 percent higher than America's leads to low-weight babies at high risk, and the 20.8 deaths per 1,000 births is almost double the national rate. Despite the presence of major medical centers at Tulane and LSU, this data got worse in the 1970s. Designating 1983 as "the year of the healthy baby," Morial held a citywide forum of over 200 experts, cochaired by his wife, Sybil. This led to an action program which stressed more sex education in schools and use of prenatal care programs like the federal

Women, Infants and Children (WIC) program. Praising Morial's leadership, *The New York Times* editorialized that "the only thing wrong with what's going on in New Orleans . . . is that it isn't going on everywhere."

Most of the 3,200 preschool children of teen-age mothers in New Orleans live in some of our worst urban housing. Some inhabit rickety frame houses without basements, on spongy ground below sea level. Luckier ones live in some of America's worst public housing, like the shabby, wooden double-deckers of Fisher Houses, across the Mississippi in the forlorn Algiers section. This drab, muddy and obscure peninsula was the site of the notorious police raid of 1980. These hovels are in contrast to the rising new hotels and office towers of the carnival across the river. There is also a vast, unhealthy project named Desire. Back in 1972, Neal R. Peirce called it "a commentary on the city: it squats near the river, isolated by railroad tracks and canals, a home of sorts to more than 10,000 blacks, of whom 8,000 are under 21." These grim barracks compare poorly even with the infamous Cabrini-Green project in Chicago. Where the violent Chicago project crams 5.7 people in each apartment, Desire Houses in New Orleans stuffs 6.7 people. (By comparison, New York City's projects average 3.3 people.) Where 70 percent of Cabrini-Green residents were under the age of twenty, a striking 86 percent of Desire was in 1979. This may be the worst housing project in America—in a city so poor that 85 percent of its public school students qualify for the school-lunch program.

In addition to social turmoil and service crisis, the local economy faces trouble ahead. Even the three legs of port, oil and tourism are starting to bend. New Orleans had the second busiest port, employing almost 50,000, but with the opening of the Tennessee-Tombigbee Waterway, about 100 miles to the east, some of its vast inland trade will be taken away. The city is a major Sunbelt energy capital, but the exhaustion of domestic oil reserves in a few decades lies ahead. New Orleans receives 6 million tourists a year, which generates a lot of sales taxes and service jobs, but poor services make this a less pleasant and safe place to visit. Racial tension keeps the city close to a riot that could cut tourism badly.

Thus, the city that care forgot.

## CHAPTER 4

# TEXAS CITIES

### Houston

In 1836 on a humid, swampy site flanking the shallow, vegetation-choked Buffalo Bayou, fifty muggy miles inland from the Gulf of Mexico and the thriving port of Galveston, two realtors came from New York City. The Allen brothers bought it for a dollar an acre from the widow of pioneer Stephen Austin. They named the humid swamp after the man who had just driven the Mexicans from Texas at the Battle of San Jacinto, twenty-one miles away. Then the Allens got the Texas Congress to make Houston—on still vacant land—the capital of a new nation. For seven years, this was the capital of the Republic of Texas, one of our five cities to be a national seat (New York, Philadelphia, Washington, and York, Pennsylvania, the others).

Statehood in 1845 transferred the capital from the widow Austin's land to the city named for her husband. Houston lapsed into rich obscurity as the main rail hub for Texas. The real action was fifty miles downstream at Galveston, the only natural harbor on the Gulf Coast. Cotton, rice and sugar passed through Houston to America's second busiest port, with 10 percent of our exports in 1910. Only a decade earlier, however, two fateful events of nature had altered the two cities' destinies.

The first event was the worst natural disaster in American history. A hurricane hit Galveston on September 8, 1900, destroying 8,000 homes and killing more than 6,000 people in a city of 29,000. The second event came four months later, on January 9, 1901, when the Spindletop field blew out near Beaumont; more than 900,000 barrels of oil were lost before the first great East

Texas strike was capped. This made Houston a major oil exporter, while the Galveston tragedy led to Houston's later role as
the main regional port. Galveston recovered so rapidly that it
was our second busiest harbor by 1907. But the disaster gave
impetus to Houston's drive to be a major, inland port. The
clogged and narrow Buffalo Bayou was cleared, deepened,
straightened and widened for fifty miles to the sea. It still wasn't
deep enough, so a coalition of businessmen and politicians met
in Mayor H. B. Rice's office and from this came the then-biggest
federal grant in history, to dredge the Bayou. A "Deepwater
Campaign" overcame a brief tax revolt from the local middle
class. A bond was passed and a new Houston Ship Channel
opened in 1914.

By 1920, Houston had replaced Galveston as the biggest cotton
port on earth. It also shipped out rice, sugar and Great Plains
grain, and petrochemical firms opened on the Channel banks.
Early refineries had been near Spindletop, in Beaumont and Port
Arthur. But with Houston opened to the sea, refiners moved to
Channel frontage. World War II expanded petrochemicals as
Japan grabbed our Pacific rubber resources and America turned
to synthetic rubber. During the war, $325 million in new chemical
and rubber plants opened along the Channel. Three billion dollars
more was invested in them after 1945, as hundreds of chemical
plants lined a busy and polluted Channel. By 1947, Houston was
so diversified as our oil capital, the world's petrochemical capital, and our third busiest port that it let Galveston regain top rank
as our leading cotton exporter.

Yet by 1950, only 596,000 lived in this boomtown on the Buf-
falo Bayou, not much more than those in fading Buffalo, New
York. But another New York city, Syracuse, was perfecting the
Carrier air conditioner that helped Houston grow in the 1950s.
Air cooling was essential for this inland city on a swamp. Miami
and New Orleans had sea breezes to tame humidity; airless
Houston had humidity that was considered the worst in America.
People and industries in our most air-cooled city today pay $700
million for summer cooling, the bill higher than the GNP of thirty
nations. Before Carrier rode to the rescue in 1950, Houston was
so wretched that the British Foreign Service termed it a hardship
post, with three years on the Bayou counting as four toward
retirement.

Air cooling was the main force that tripled the Houston population between 1950 and 1980. As Joel Garreau observed, "Shell Oil didn't dream of leaving Manhattan for Houston until it became thinkable to air-condition an employee's entire life—home, office, automobile, parking garage, shopping center, redneck bar, bedomed baseball stadium."

Houston grew from 596,000 people to 938,000 in the 1950s—a 58 percent growth in one decade. Midway through this, in 1956, Houston annexed all 1,773 square miles of Harris County: "the blob that ate East Texas" went the local joke. If the City Council hadn't cut the annexation to 184 square miles, Houston would have been the world's largest city, almost twice the size of Rhode Island. Shortly before his death in 1956, Jesse Jones, head of the Reconstruction Finance Corporation under FDR and "Mr. Houston" for decades, summarized his hometown's growth over the years: "I always said that someday Houston would be the Chicago of the South, and it is. Railroads built this town, the port made it big, cotton and cattle kept it rich, oil boomed it, and now we're the chemical capital of the world. Growing, growing, growing, that's Houston."

Yet Houston in 1960 was still rural in ambiance, with rice fields, bring-your-own bars and just one big hotel downtown, the ten-story Shamrock of oilman Glen McCarthy. The next two decades saw Houston grow, grow, grow beyond Jesse Jones's wildest dreams. Building on its port, oil and petrochemical bases, it became office center to the West as well. On September 19, 1961, Vice President Lyndon B. Johnson hailed "the greatest thing for Texas and Houston since the Ship Channel," while Representative Albert Thomas predicted a "small revolution in Houston's business life." For once, Texas hyperbole fell short. As a study by William D. Angel shows, after the Manned Spacecraft Center of NASA opened, 150 corporations moved to Houston in six years, value added to manufacturing grew 118 percent in ten years and factories grew from 2,621 to 3,169 in just five years.

Angel sees the Spacecraft Center and the Ship Channel as products of the strong link between private and public sectors in Houston. The drawbacks to this nexus are the huge tax breaks for business and the resulting collapse of city services. The private-public link was forged early by Jesse Jones, who ruled Houston's business sector from Suite 8F of the Lamar Hotel. In 1947, John Gunther wrote in *Inside U. S. A.* that "the man who

'owns' Houston is of course Jesse Jones . . . to a considerable
degree responsible for Houston's giddy industrial growth, because—I mean no criticism—as head of the RFC during the war
he was in a position to locate new industry in the area." Gunther
noted that Jones's local holdings included the *Houston Chronicle*
and its radio station, the three leading hotels, chief stockholder
in the city's richest bank, and most of the property downtown.
"Oddly enough," Gunther concluded, "Jones, a builder, has
never paid much attention to oil."

The link of pols and plutocrats forged by Jones over four decades resulted in the Spacecraft Center of 1961. Lyndon Johnson
was chairman of the National Aeronautics and Space Council,
and Representative Albert Thomas of Houston ran the House
subcommittee approving NASA funds. Johnson asked his friend
George Brown, who was Houston's top contractor, to attend
Space Council meetings as a "responsible member of the public." Humble Oil gave a 1,000-acre tract to Rice University, then
Rice gave it to NASA for the Spacecraft Center. The chairman
of the Rice board of trustees was George Brown, whose firm got
a big Center contract later. Humble Oil also promoted a 15,000-
acre site for homes, industries and offices next to the NASA
complex on the Humble land at Clear Lake.

The Spacecraft Center meant 4,000 new jobs, and 10,000 more
in supporting industries. Neal R. Peirce noted in 1971 "the kind
of economic stimulus hundreds of American cities would have
loved—and which Houston, among them, probably needed the
least." He added that putting the Center at Houston, rather than
at Tampa, nearer Cape Canaveral, "added hundreds of millions
of unnecessary dollars to the nation's space budget—an egre-
gious example of Texas' private profit at the national taxpayers'
expense." *

Between 1960 and 1980, Houston grew 65 percent in both land
and population. Its downtown became the Sunbelt's front-office
capital. One *Fortune* 500 firm became a dozen, 10 million square

---

* One more reason for the Spacecraft Center's location was the narrow 23,000-
vote margin for JFK in the Texas vote of 1960. This close shave in an Electoral
College power was a warning for 1964. Houston had also been the setting for a
key turning point in the 1960 election: Kennedy's famous speech defusing the
"Catholic issue," given to Protestant ministers in the ballroom of the Rice Hotel.
JFK had observed how "side by side with Bowie and Crockett died McCafferty
and Bailey and Carey, but no one knew whether they were Catholics or not. For
there was no religious test at the Alamo."

feet of office space became 80 million. For census, jobs, geography and building, Houston had no urban peers for growth. Mayor Fred Hofheinz bragged in 1976, "We don't worry about so-called white flight to the suburbs, because we know we'll eventually annex them into the city."

Downtown grew like nowhere on earth after 1970. Sixteen million square feet of office space would become 108 million by 1984. An early catalyst was the $2 billion, 33-block Houston Center, an instant downtown on concrete stilts from Texas Eastern Transmission Corporation. Other megaprojects included the Galleria, a multistoried mall with ice-skating rink, a Sunbelt version of Rockefeller Center. In 1980 alone, 10 million square feet of office space opened in America's only city with no zoning laws. In just a few years, Houston built a "second skyline," dominated by instant landmarks like the twin black trapezoids of Philip Johnson's Pennzoil Place or the Texas Commerce Tower of I. M. Pei, the latter, at seventy-five stories, the tallest building in America outside Chicago and New York.*

One Canadian firm is now developing thirty square blocks downtown, which will add 3 million square feet of office space. Yet as other downtowns suffered an office glut in 1982, Houston had a low vacancy rate. The only cloud was noted by a Cushman & Wakefield official to *The Wall Street Journal* in early 1982: "Many Houston brokers look at what's under construction and with another 30 million square feet on the drawing boards and say 'Oh God, two years from now there's going to be a bloodbath.' " By the summer of 1983, a 3 percent vacancy rate had soared to over 10 percent, as a mix of recession and an overbuilt downtown took their toll. This office glut resembled that of New York after 1971 or of Atlanta after 1980, following their similar building sprees. Houston's 3 percent vacancy rate reflected demands from more than 200 American firms moving headquarters or divisions to Houston after 1970, or from foreign banks growing from six to sixty-five in eight years. Atlanta and Dallas had more convention trade and airport arrivals, but Houston's 1.1 million

---

* Up ahead is an eighty-two-story tower from Southwest Bancshares, modeled on New York's Chrysler Building. The textured obelisk with spire on top will be designed by Deco enthusiast Helmut Jahn. Bancshare's chairman suggests the tower will "enable people flying over the city to say 'That's Houston.' " Typical of the city's rapid growth is the fact that the building demolished for the tower was only eighteen years "old."

foreign arrivals in 1980 were third only to Miami and Los Angeles among Sunbelt cities.* Beyond air travel, outer-space business was reviving at what is now called the Johnson Space Center. The space shuttle dusted it off, Joel Garreau noting how "civic boosters like to recall that the first word spoken from the surface of the moon was not the business about the Eagle having landed. The very first word was 'Houston?' "

Even by 1971, Houston was still Texas' second biggest cattle county. The area also produced 30 percent of our rice, and half the tonnage in Houston's port was from farm products. Then there was oil, with thirty-four major firms based in Houston, along with equipment giants like Hughes Tool and Geosource, and all the petrochemical plants, with $5 billion in factories near the Ship Channel—although only 16 percent of local jobs were in manufacturing, against a 22 percent national average. "No Detroit for Houston" bragged a city ad in 1981, boosting the highly diversified economy in The City of the Future.

The sequence of food, oil, shipping, chemicals, banks, factories, space, and front offices over a century made Houston America's job mecca. Even in the slumping 1970s, its jobless rate was often a third below America's. As Houston's census grew by 30,000 a year, jobs grew faster—by 35,000 a year. When America had 7.6 percent unemployment in 1980, Houston had 3.5 percent, which compared well with Atlanta's 5.5 percent, Denver's and Miami's 6.2 percent, and Los Angeles' 7.3 percent. As recession hit the Snowbelt in 1981, Houston became the El Dorado for laid-off factory workers. Joel Garreau called it "the biggest draw for opportunity-seekers of all colors and classes this nation has seen since Los Angeles." In truth, the Dallas-Fort Worth area had 60,000 more jobs than Houston in 1981, but a Michigan book store sold twice as many copies of the *Houston Chronicle* as *the Dallas Morning News*. The *Chronicle* want ads ran up to 170 pages on Sunday, reflecting a job surplus that writer William Appleman Williams called "an infinity of second chances."

As in films, so in life, Houston is where the Urban Cowboy goes. The president of the University of Houston chaired the urban subcommittee of the Presidential Commission of 1980,

---

* Houston had 668 convention and trade shows in 1981, only half the volume in Atlanta and Dallas. With the opening of a $28 million terminal in 1981, Houston's airport nearly matched Dallas-Fort Worth's for size. It may exceed it after 1985, when a giant "Terminal D" opens for foreign traffic only.

with its theme of "Go Sunbelt, Young Person." About that report, the *Chronicle* breezily headlined: "Feds Accept Inevitable: Future in the Sun Belt." Super City was so blasé about the federal report that William K. Stevens of *The New York Times* found the story had "disappeared inside the paper the next day, to be all but buried and forgotten by the dominant story of last week: the ouster of Bum Phillips as the head coach of the Houston Oilers. . . ."

Also drawn to Houston were the Arabs, the Saudis replacing the Japanese as the city's main customers abroad. The Japanese go back to the early 1900s when they had helped cultivate the local rice fields. By 1971, the Japanese were doing $400 million in trade, but inside a decade, the Saudis were the top traders, with $2 billion in 1980. Some of this was imported oil, but much of it involved exports to the Middle East—drill bits, pipes, valves and other petrophernalia, shipped from Houston to Jidda by a growing Saudi census in the Sunbelt energy capital. There were seventy-five Houston-based firms in Saudi Arabia and twenty Saudi firms in Houston. As Dan Balz reported in the *Washington Post:* "The cultural bond between Saudi Arabia and Houston has less to do with the natural atraction of rich Arab sheiks to free-spending Texas oilmen than with conservative values, the traditions of home and family and a society that is male-dominated." Also, as one Houston banker bluntly said to Balz, the "political link to Israel is much less strong here than in the North. . . ."

In 1947, John Gunther described a city where few thought

> of anything but money, where the symphony orchestra is of the feeblest, and where the only tolerable bookshop was boycotted by many patrons because the proprietor announced in 1944 that he would vote for FDR. It is also the noisiest city I have ever visited, with a residential section mostly ugly and barren, a city without a single good restaurant, and of hotels with cockroaches.

Today, money talks louder than ever in this undertaxed, poorly serviced city. But a thin cultural veneer has since been applied. At the lowest level, there is the Urban Cowboy crowd, with "cowboy chic" Houston's main cultural export. Even New York was awash in C & W bars by 1982. On a higher level of lowbrow culture were the sports teams of the Astros, Oilers and Rockets, all major contenders in the 1980s.

At a higher level, the Alley Theater is one of our better regional theaters, and the Houston Ballet one of the best companies. The feeble symphony of 1947 has improved, though it remains well below the Big Ten rankings. In opera, however, the Houston Grand Opera is one of our Big Five. Indeed, HGO is cited as Houston's main cultural lure for *Fortune* 500 firms. One Houstonian noted to *The New York Times Magazine:* "The town fathers said that Houston had to get its cultural act together. You couldn't move here from New York or San Franciso and go to midget wrestling."

There are five things Houston promoters push in selling The City of the Future: no corporate taxes, no personal income taxes, low property taxes, no zoning, and annexation. As the chairman of the Texas Commerce Bank told *U.S. News & World Report* in 1976: "We still believe in the free-enterprise system. We think healthy, growing businesses are the source of it, not government. We try to keep budgets balanced, taxes low. . . ."

The very low taxes lead to things like the 2.2 cops per 1,000 residents. The spirit behind Houston's wrecking of service is noted in a 1981 ad in *Forbes,* which says that in Houston, "the cost of doing business would warm Scrooge's heart, and special interests are respected."

There is also the very low property tax rate. In 1980, most Houston property owners paid only $0.28 per $100 in assessed value. By comparison the tax rate in New York City that year was $8.95 per $100 in assessed value, or thirty-two times as great. The low Houston tax rate means that a $100,000 property in New York would yield $8,950 a year in taxes and $280 a year in Houston.

On top of the low tax rates were wildly deflated assessments for commercial property. In the summer of 1981, mayoral candidate Noble C. Ginther charged that Houston had forgone $10 billion in corporate assessed values in exchange for political favors. A few months later, Houston's tax department was being run by a court-appointed special master. It was discovered that the big construction firm of Brown & Root had been throwing hunting weekends for city assessors at its lakeside lodge. B & R paid for everything down to the shotgun shells, listing it all in an "Entertainment Facility Use Report," entering under "Business Purpose" a desire to "acquire better understanding of taxes."

These seminars bore fruit. An appraiser testified that one meeting between city officials and B & R execs was a lively colloquium on equipment at a company yard. Brown & Root declared $10 million in value; a city appraiser suggested $233 million. A "compromise" of $62 million in assessed value was suggested. B & R allegedly blew up and the compromiser backed off. Other allegations were that 134 Houston banks got $89 million in taxable assets reduced, and that Exxon property was struck from tax rolls for no reason. One Exxon chemical plant was paying no taxes at all.

The state judge untangling this mess added more than $3 billion in assessed values to the Houston tax rolls, or 10 percent of the city's taxable property. This would add more than $58 million a year in new revenues for the lightly taxed and underserviced city. Most of the new assessments belonged to Brown & Root, or $52.2 million a year in new taxes. Appointing a special master to reform the tax department, State Judge Arthur C. Lesher observed, "It's apparent from the court record that the city needs help."

No city of such wealth in America has things like the shantytowns a few blocks from Pennzoil Place and the downtown boom. As *The Almanac of American Politics* points out, "Like many rapidly growing cities in developing countries, Houston seems to have unusually great disparities of income and wealth." To see the extremes, look at two adjacent Congressional Districts, one the most Republican in America, the other the most Democratic. The 7th District is the rich one, its voters including George Bush and John Connally. In 1970, it had the third highest share of white-collar workers among America's 435 Districts. In 1976, it had the biggest vote for Jerry Ford. In 1980, this was the third fastest growing CD in the Census, expanding from 466,000 to 868,000 residents.

The 18th District next door in central Houston, mainly black, was Barbara Jordan's base. Among the growing Sunbelt Districts, this was the fourth biggest loser of population, with 99,500 of 466,000 residents leaving this dreadful slum in the 1970s. This and other black Houston areas have had the biggest Democratic margin in America, an incredible 98 percent. Given its placement next to our most Republican District, *The Almanac of American Politics* observed that often

the real question in Houston politics is, who will outvote whom? In 1976, there were enough votes cast in the 18th—

nearly half as many as in the 7th—to help carry Texas for Jimmy Carter. But in 1978 enthusiasm and elan belonged entirely to the Republicans. More than four times as many people voted in the 7th district as in the 18th. If the ratio of turnout had been the same as in 1976, the statewide results would have been different . . .

A 12,000 statewide margin for Senator John Tower and a 17,000 edge for Governor William Clements would have been wiped out by black votes in Houston's 18th CD.

Forty-six percent of Houston was minority in 1980, and more annexation can only postpone the "tipping point" a few years. As minorities become the majority in any American city, the downward spiral seems to gain new momentum. When this occurs in a city like Houston, with no corporate taxes, no personal income taxes, and light property taxes, the gap between service needs of the poor and services provided gets even wider.

Thin police ranks have inspired rich neighborhoods to hire private guards for "site-specific enforcement." But it is the 46 percent of Houston that is black or Hispanic that is most likely to be victimized. Houston is seventh for per capita homicides today, and from 1977 through 1980 rape was up 41 percent, murder up 60 percent and robbery up 66 percent.*

Only a few blocks from downtown are shotgun shacks on cement blocks and dowdy double-deckers, described by Joel Garreau as being "out of the heart of Mississippi. They are so antiquely southern, they're not even urban." *The Almanac of American Politics* refers to the "sharecropper thirties," noting frame houses with "cracks wide enough to let in Houston's humid, smoggy air."

The heat wave of 1980 saw water rationing in Houston, not due to lack of supply but because of a cheap, badly maintained water system. With too many leaky pipes, the system could pump only 400 million gallons a day. All of Houston had to cut water use, even though the city receives four times the Los Angeles rainfall. Houston simply won't pay for a normal water system. And the

---

* Also related to Houston's treatment of minorities is the low share of them on the police force: only 16 percent, though 46 percent of the city is black or Hispanic. One more striking negative statistic about Houston's public safety is that fatal police shootings between 1975 and 1979 were 5.8 per 1,000 officers, or twice the national rate.

sewage treatment is so bad that Houston in 1981 imposed a moratorium on building all but small homes and commercial buildings in 75 percent of the city.

Floods also inhibit Houston's growth. Much of its Southeast section was hastily built on rice fields in low-lying areas, with the spongy land further sinking as new homes draw on ground-water supplies.* Big rains in this humid city can mean flash floods, a Southeast section going under for the third time in two years in 1981. Hurricane Alicia plucked hundreds of windows from Houston's skyscrapers in 1983 but, as in 1900, the eye of the storm hit Galveston. While $676 million in insured losses were found in an early survey of the Houston-Galveston area, Houston has still escaped the worst hurricane scenario.

Nearly equidistant from New York and Los Angeles, Houston repeats their mistakes. The unplanned sprawl of L.A. and the service crisis of N.Y.C. are both at hand in The City of the Future. The floods, the sewage system, the leaky mains and soaring crime since 1977 are unpaid bills coming due. The physical resemblance is to Los Angeles. William K. Stevens compared the two Sunbelt capitals back in 1979 in *The New York Times:* "With their freeways, their dispersed development patterns, their open spaces, their outdoor styles of living, their gleaming buildings, their atmosphere of gung-ho vitality and their very newness, they are urban brothers. Probably no two major centers in the country look and feel more alike." Joel Garreau notes this comparison, and quotes a Houstonian marveling "who would have thought that, given the opportunity to do different, anybody would have built a second Los Angeles?" He adds that, while Los Angeles voted bonds and built freeways long ago, Houston avoided debt and never built the roads to match its 503-mile sprawl, so "the evening rush hour, now over 4 hours long, will continue to lengthen until new transportation facilities are built, or the population becomes so outraged at the inconvenience of getting around the place that people begin to leave."

The service crisis and an incompetent mayor were the two

---

* *Life* reported in 1981 that Houston's water table had dropped in some places by five feet. So "if it continues to sink at its current rate, in two centuries the top of the 45-story Exxon building will be below sea level."

issues in Houston's election of 1981. The mayor's nest was striking. The vagrant, possibly corrupt, ways of Jim McConn's tax
office have been seen as has its later supervision by a state court.
And there was a 1979 episode that found the mayor phoning from
Las Vegas to a city official in Houston seeking $6,000 to cover
gambling debts. The official was later convicted of extorting
$6,000 from a city contractor on the day of McConn's call from
Vegas. He may well have done this without the mayor's knowl-
edge, but the appearance was dreadful. Then in 1981, McConn
was found guilty in civil court of conspiring to violate antitrust
laws in a cable TV franchise award. McConn did so badly in the
fall primary that he missed the runoff, pitting former police chief
Jack Heard against City Comptroller Kathryn Whitmire. Houston blacks were the runoff's swing vote, and Congressman
Mickey Leland led them in backing Whitmire, who won with 62
percent of the vote.

The national press hailed Whitmire's victory. "A new generation of Democrats in Texas," wrote William K. Stevens in *The
New York Times,* who described a new breed having "a fusion of
fiscal conversatism with a traditional liberal stance on social issues. It rejects what its adherents see as the wastefully free-
spending Democratic ways of the 1960s and 1970s, but it also
holds to the Democratic liberals' long-standing concern for the
poor and minorities." But one can't aid the poor without the
"free-spending" ways. In truth Whitmire's win was far removed
from Texas liberals like Maury Maverick in the 1940s, Ralph
Yarborough in the 1950s and 1960s, or Lyndon Johnson as Ike's
liberal "prime minister" of the Senate after 1954. Whitmire was
also detached from vigorous Houston liberals like former Representatives Bob Eckhardt and Barbara Jordan or Representative
Mickey Leland.

Whitmire says she is liberal on social issues but conservative
on fiscal ones. She is a registered Democrat, but her idea of
municipal reform in 1981 was management reform. Citing her
"ten years of working with a variety of corporate clients," she
promised voters that "Houston can be run like a business." But
once past computerizing files or trimming management fat, this
strategy runs out of gas. Eventually, money for new hires is
needed to improve services. This holds especially for "hands
on" services like fire, health or police. No amount of "civilian-
izing" desk jobs in Houston precinct houses can free enough

cops for patrols. Houston's police chief noted in 1981 that only a doubling of forces could control a soaring crime rate.*

A month after Whitmire's election, the city's service crisis was detailed in a candid, thorough survey by the *Houston Chronicle*. Its Sunday magazine for December 6 issued a ten-article broadside on The City of the Future. The traffic jams, soaring crime, housing crunch and plight of the poor were detailed in Jesse Jones's old newspaper. Breaking with the Jones ode to growing, growing, growing, the *Chronicle* wrapped up the mess under the title: "GROWTH and Our Threatened Way of Life."

The survey was damning for two basic reasons: it was written by Houstonians, and it was about the middle class. The sources were objective; the subjects were the very class on which a city's stability depends. If the middle class had it this bad, imagine life in Houston for its 46 percent minority share.

Some details:

• *Traffic*. This issue was cited frequently in the *Chronicle* survey. According to the article "the worst feature of life in Houston . . . will likely roll out in one word—traffic. There is crime, but for most the No. 1 daily horror is traffic." A recent arrival from the freeway capital of Los Angeles observed that people from one part of Houston who "don't need to visit another section, never do . . . people who live in LA know all of LA. Here, the traffic rules people. It paralyzes them." This agoraphobia was also based on erratic, aggressive Houston drivers. The president of the Driving School Association of Texas criticized "a melting pot of driving styles. There's no rhyme or reason in it. It's the worst I've ever had to deal with. Compared to Kansas City, St. Louis or even Chicago, this is a nightmare." In normal traffic life, he added, drivers entering a freeway yield the right of way, but in Houston "you don't know if that driver's going to move over, speed up, slow down or hit you."

Beyond this demolition derby were the traffic jams and four-

---

* Houston's crime got even worse in 1982, when the first six months found crime rising 17 percent. This was the largest rise among all big cities, contrasting with *falling* crime in Cleveland, New York and San Francisco, and a 5 percent decrease nationwide. By late 1982, Whitmire pledged to double forces by 1985, and dispatched seven Houston cops to New York, where they set up a recruiting table at the John Jay College of Criminal Justice.

hour rush hours. A state traffic report observed that while most cities had up to 20 percent of trouble spots in roads, Houston had 80 percent. Thus, an interchange between a crammed West Loop and a stuffed Southwest Freeway became a "clogged funnel for almost half-a-million vehicles a day." There was talk of double-decking the freeways, "but there is no money in the 20-year plan to implement. . . ."

• *Housing.* The survey wasn't about the shacks of the Houston poor, but the soaring prices and rents for the middle class. There were simply too many people bidding up too few homes in a familiar upward price spiral. Homeowner costs grew 104 percent in America for the 1970s, but 152 percent in Houston. The head of a builders' group saw local demand at 50,000 new units a year against 33,000 opened in 1980. The head of a Houston tenant group noted a syndrome familiar in older Snowbelt cities: "It's going to be more difficult to move to Houston. We'll see higher rents and lower turnover. Young people will stay at home longer than they used to because they can't find an apartment at a reasonable rate. More people will double up. . . . If people can't find a place to live, growth is not going to happen."

• *Crime.* Robbery, rape and murder mainly hit the poor on streets, but the article focused instead on burglary, the bane of the middle class. It reported on a "very private war" where people "are spending their own private money for their own private protection." The ethos here was spelled out by Barry Kaplan, a transplanted New Yorker, teaching history and urban studies at Houston U: "You want better police protection? Go out and hire some private cops. You want better garbage pickup? Hire it. You want a good education? Pay for it. Supposedly that philosophy went out with the New Deal. It's coming back again, and Houston is going to be one of its leaders." * More serious was a police captain, telling the *Chronicle* that, with so few police, people in Houston were realizing that they "can't rely on us for their first line of defense."

---

* Elsewhere, in an article on "Quality of Life," assistant professor Kaplan recalls a smaller Houston in the 1950s, which "was essentially Protestant and kept blacks and browns tucked away in neat recesses of the mind and geography, so there was a greater sense of cohesion. What Houston lost in becoming a major metropolis is the sense of consensus, cohesiveness. . . ."

The Harris County DA suggested that one in three Houstonians had guns when traveling in cars. The *Chronicle* added that "Houston ranks last among the nation's largest six cities in money per resident spent on police protection. The other five spent almost twice as much. . . ." With only 3,100 police, Houston needed 2,300 more to simply match the national average.

Privatism was the law for order in Houston. The sheriff's office even hired out officers as "contract deputies" to neighborhoods able to pay extra fees. Forty-five affluent areas were policed this way in 1981, with residents paying $1.8 million.

• **The Poor.** Finally, the *Chronicle* looked briefly at the other Houston, the Fourth Ward, with tin-roof shacks in the shadow of Pennzoil Place. During the 1950s and 1960s, not one new unit of public housing was built. Or there is public school. Neal Peirce noted how the school board in 1969 approved a lavish marble headquarters with fountains and gardens, but ended kindergarten classes for 18,000 kids.

The *Chronicle* also looked at psychological collapse. One psychologist saw a city of agoraphobes afraid to run the freeway gauntlet for a night at the Grand Opera. A city that won't properly tax itself loses the will to survive. Unwilling to provide adequate police, education, public housing or water supply services, rootless Houston breeds an anarchy of guns in cars and offensive driving on freeways. Sociologist William Simon told the *Chronicle* of a city where "people buy their houses the way they used to buy cars, with one eye on resale value, and we play musical houses. It's what sociologists like to call the community of limited liability. . . . There's so much anger, so much frustration." The *Chronicle* found twenty-six executives of U.S. Steel in Pittsburgh who refused a Houston transfer because Super City lacked a sense of "community."

The rare Houston defenders in the *Chronicle* survey seemed to be defensive transplants like Barry Kaplan, who said

> We drive to work in a private machine, we party in our fenced-in back yard with a pool and a spa. If we interact, we do it in our homogenous class, as long as they're the same class. It's a private city, built on the idea of privatism.
>
> These really are American values, and I think this is truly an American city.

Even before the service crisis erupted in 1981, there were signs of slower growth in The City of the Future.

• Jobs in the six-county Houston area went from 107,700 new slots in 1978 to 98,300 in 1979, then took a plunge to 59,700 in 1980. Since there had been no rise in the unemployment rate, this suggested far fewer people coming to Houston.

• Utility hookups also showed a slower growth rate. Entex added 16,408 new natural-gas customers in 1977–78, then saw connections drop steadily to 10,649 by 1980–81. Houston Lighting & Power saw 81,689 new customers in 1978 dwindle to 66,732 new lines by 1980. New telephone connections dropped by 24 percent.

• Census figures confirm 1978 as the peak of Houston's growth. The 97,200 new arrivals that year in the metro area steadily declined to 89,000 by 1980, just before the recession. Demographers noted how the other Big Five cities of New York, Los Angeles, Chicago and Detroit had also gone through similar high growth periods of thirty to forty years before they had also leveled off.

The binge of the 1970s had been impressive: 670,000 jobs had been added as the economy diversified, adding more than one job for every two new residents; bank deposits had soared from $6 billion to $24 billion in the decade; and office space had tripled.

The growth had overwhelmed already poor services, and even a seven-page "City of the Future" booster ad in *Forbes* in 1981 had paused briefly to admit that "city services have been stretched and pressure is mounting for massive public works outlays." The ad suggested that it would be better to wait for the Reagan cuts in spending to reduce interest rates and "when that happens, the city's streets, the water and sanitary sewer systems, and solid waste management will rank a top priority. Also at the head of the list will be the police department, frustrated by rising operating costs and manpower shortages."

In the 1960s, Houston oil tycoon George Mitchell saw that "our cities were getting in deep trouble." He dreamed of a new town. For eleven years, he bought up more than 300 parcels of land in a lovely pine forest 26 miles north of Houston. In 1974, he broke ground on his 23,000 acres for The Woodlands, a planned community. The new town was backed by a $50 million HUD guarantee. Today it is one of four successful HUD new towns.* With twenty years to go on its plan, it had 13,000 residents in two planned communities and 5,000 daily workers. Mitchell has put $500 million into the project, even moving in his Mitchell Energy and Development Corporation, #395 on the *Fortune* 500 list in 1981. Ultimately, this "downtown in the forest" would have 20 million square feet of office space, a quarter of what Houston had by 1982.

The oil tycoon has invested a lot in his ideal of a racially integrated, aesthetically pleasing new town. In design, The Woodlands seems a modest update of Clarence Stein's garden apartments at Chatham Village in Pittsburgh, or Stein and Henry Wright's great Sunnyside Gardens in Queens. But where Stein's homes were for workers of modest means, the Texas enclave is strictly upscale. At bottom, The Woodlands is a giant version of those "planned unit developments" in Sunday real-estate pages —bucolic, tasteful, and eminently for the upper middle class of both races. Houston is endless growth over three rampant decades, the slowing of the growth after 1978, the service crisis eruption of 1981, the new mayor pledging management reform in 1982, but not higher taxes and new hires. Management reform is fine for a homogenous enclave like The Woodlands, but not in the real, gamy, complex world of cities such as Houston.

The City of the Future goes on living in the past today.

## Dallas

As 45 million television viewers have known since 1979, J. R. Ewing doesn't live here anymore. The Iago of South Fork has lots of company, for as Dallas grew only 7 percent in the 1970s, its white suburbs expanded 58 percent. With only 1.9 cops per 1,000 residents, this open city had even fewer police than Houston did in 1980. Indeed, with 11,778 crimes per 100,000 people in 1980, Dallas had the highest crime rate of America's ten biggest cities.

Even a diverse, strong economy has had recent problems. Too many northern workers flooded Dallas after 1980, and the jobless rate soared. The six-county area grew by 64,000 new jobs in one

* The other three federal successes are Irvine, California; Reston, Virginia; and the "new town in town" of Jonathan, a subdivision of St. Paul, Minnesota. Two other successful new towns done *without* HUD loan guarantees will be discussed later: Las Colinas, outside Dallas, and Columbia, Maryland, developed by famed mall builder James Rouse.

year, but by the summer of 1981 the Dallas unemployment rate was only a point under America's. Then the 1982 recession hit Dallas. Its biggest employer, Texas Instruments, laid off 16 percent of its workers. Other high-tech firms on the "Silicon Prairie" strip out to Fort Worth followed suit. Then on the morning of May 13, Braniff Airlines suddenly went under. It grounded its seventy-one multihued planes, fired 5,500 workers, and filed for bankruptcy. Overnight, one of Dallas' three major employers was no more.

Dallas will survive with its diverse mix of banking, high tech, insurance and aerospace. The Braniff failure still left Dallas with one of America's seven major airlines. American Airlines' move from New York had led to a fare discount war between the two Dallas giants, with one analyst recalling what "became a bleeding contest. And Braniff bled to death faster." American survived as the host airline at the giant Dallas-Fort Worth Airport.

While Dallas absorbed the loss of one of its three biggest employers, the rising jobless rate caused by too many northern workers was a cause for concern. Worst of all has been a growing collapse of services. The token census gains in the 1970s, the alarming crime rate, and a brief tax revolt in 1980 all reflected a familiar downward trend. Like Houston, Dallas has a record of rampant growth, absurdly low taxes and insufficient services. Unlike Houston, Dallas lacks experience in the self-government so essential to municipal reform.

Up until 1976, 200 businessmen had run our eighth biggest city. They were either corporation presidents or chief executive officers, the sole criterion for membership in the Dallas Citizens' Council. The DCC handpicked mayors and city councilmen in a city free of partisans or primaries. The DCC tone had been set long ago by Washington's famous Farewell Address. With Hamilton writing the text, our first President had assailed "all combinations and associations, under whatever possible character, with the real design to direct . . . the constituted authorities." A similar fear of politics gripped Dallas until a few years ago.

The DCC ran Dallas through several techniques. First, Dallas diluted minority blocs by annexing white suburbs. Then it dissipated the diluted minority votes by holding Council elections on a city-wide, or "at large," basis, rather than a district-specific basis favoring local blocs. All this meant Dallas had a long line of mayors chosen from and by the DCC and an all-white Council in a city that was 33 percent black and brown by 1970. Then in

1976, Representative Barbara Jordan got the Voting Rights Act applied to Texas, and a federal court ended at-large Council elections in Dallas, Houston and San Antonio. Three of the nineteen Council members are now black, though by 1980, 42 percent of Dallas was black or brown.

"The truth is, there really isn't any reason for Dallas. It sits in the middle of nowhere and nothing. The land around it is dry, black and unproductive . . . a monument to sheer determination. Dallas doesn't owe a thing to accident, nature or inevitability." So wrote Warren Leslie in *Dallas Public and Private,* published in 1964. The sight of Dallas rising dramatically from nowhere was well described by *Fortune* in 1949: "skyscrapers soaring abruptly up from the black land like Maxfield Parrish castles," a pop-up kingdom on the prairie. Describing our largest inland city in 1972, Neal R. Peirce observed that

> Dallas, I heard it said, was the city born with a wooden spoon in its mouth. Its location was remote, it had no port or access to the sea, the farmland about it was not particularly fertile, and anyway neighboring Fort Worth soon monopolized the western cattle trade. Nor have gas or oil ever been found beneath it.

This is one of the most man-made cities on earth.

Dallas began as an unlikely distribution hub. In 1870, a new railroad had no interest in isolated Dallas, until local citizens gave it $5,000, 115 acres and several miles of right-of-way. After which, Warren Leslie recalls, "the railroad did a little bending around and managed to hit Dallas on its way north." In 1872, the Texas & Pacific showed no interest in bribes so Dallas boosters got the state legislature to insure the line went through their city. Suddenly the unblessed site had major north–south and east–west rail routes and a new life. Even better, when the T & P reached Dallas in 1872, it stopped there for four years, before going on to Fort Worth. During those four years, John Gunther notes, "dozens of big eastern firms—mercantile establishments, distributors, and the like—got nicely settled in Dallas, and have stayed there ever since. Dallas was the end of the line." In time, it became our biggest internal market for cotton as a leading distribution point for the region.

The next break from the hand of man came in 1913, when U.S. Treasury Secretary William Gibbs McAdoo assigned the 11th Federal Reserve district to Dallas, not Fort Worth. Noting an example of the West biting useful federal hands, John Gunther observed about a Texas acquaintance: "My banker friend may deplore the working of the Federal Reserve system—though he could not operate a day without it—but the fact that the Federal Reserve came to Dallas instead of Fort Worth is one of the reasons why his own bank, his own city, are so rich."

Another reason is the great oil finds of the 1930s in East Texas. The new fields made Dallas the home of billionaires like the Hunts and the Murchisons, while fueling the city's banking sector. Starting in 1933, Dallas banks began lending on the collateral of the new oil reserves. As the fields grew, so did the banks. Neal R. Peirce recalls how

> hundreds of Dallasites became millionaires, and the huge capital reserves created were then available to finance more exploration for oil and also diversification into fields like insurance and electronics manufacture. Dallas also became a great gateway for the Southwestern trade, leading the region in banks, distribution, and even fashions.*

In 1975, *Nation's Business* picked Dallas to launch a fifteen-part "Bicentennial Salute to American Cities." The editor of the house organ of the U.S. Chamber of Commerce noted the city's selection as series leader as testament to a very pro-business city. Dallas had eight chambers of commerce, more than any other city. All told, there were thirty chambers in the six-county metro area. Beyond all this lay a rich, diverse economy. In addition to the role of banks and oil, some other Dallas bases of growth include:

• *Trade.* In 1872 Dallas became a rail distribution center, and was our third biggest convention city in 1981. A landmark was the

---

* Fashion is led by Neiman-Marcus, long run by one of Dallas' few liberal leaders, Stanley Marcus. N-M's chief Texas rival, Sakowitz of Houston, opened a big Dallas branch in 1981. Its president, Robert Sakowitz, noted that Dallas as a mercantile and distributive center was more of a taste-setter, while Houston, with its muscular economy based on the processing of natural resources, had customers focused on the goods themselves. In Dallas, he observed, you could sell the sizzle—in Houston you had to sell the steak.

1936 Texas Centennial Fair, landed by a major effort by corporate leaders—leading the next year to the founding of the powerful Dallas Citizens' Council. The leaders, organized by R. L. (Bob) Thornton, chairman of the Mercantile National Bank, raised $3.5 million and got the fair. Meanwhile, Fort Worth hired Broadway producer Billy Rose to throw a rival show, covering Dallas with signs stating "45 MINUTES FOR WHOOPEE! DALLAS FOR EDUCATION, FORT WORTH FOR ENTERTAINMENT!" But the Centennial Fair was a hit. It turned into the annual State Fair, luring 2.5 million visitors a year in the 1950s. This led to Six Flags Over Texas, the huge theme park outside of town, and the mammoth Dallas Market Center, the largest single-site merchandising complex on earth: 4.8 million square feet of exhibition space, or 100 city football gridirons. All of this made Dallas our third biggest host for conventions and trade shows in 1981. Its 1.6 million visitors were far short of New York's 4.2 million, but its 1,661 separate shows nearly doubled New York's events. Among Dallas' many events in 1984 will be the Republican National Convention.

• *Aerospace.* Airplane factories opened here during World War II. Dallas lured Vought from Connecticut in the 1950s, that firm later part of Ling-Temco-Vought (LTV), at its peak #14 on the *Fortune* 500 list. Airlines saw Braniff go from a regional to a national line in the 1960s, putting an "end to the plain plane" with its fleet of many colors, one plane painted handsomely by Alexander Calder. In 1979, American Airlines moved its front office here from New York. The world's largest commercial airport opened in 1973. The $700 million Dallas-Fort Worth Airport is even bigger than Manhattan Island, and is hailed as the inland metroplex's harbor on the "ocean of the air."

• *Electronics.* Texas Instruments got a start-up loan before World War II and went from $800 million in sales and 45,000 workers in 1975 to $4.2 billion and 84,000 workers before a 16 percent staff cut in the 1981–83 recession. And there was LTV, begun by ex-roustabout James Ling. The small electronics firm of 1958 has become a huge conglomerate today, #40 on the *Fortune* list in 1981 with $8.8 billion in sales and 53,000 employees. With Texas Instruments, Ling-Temco-Vought is one of Dallas' three biggest employers. Manufacturing of all kinds took off in Dallas during the 1960s, the city adding 7,000 new factory jobs a year. The same industrial growth continued through the early 1980s, with high tech playing a lead role. Other electronics firms in the area include Mostek in Carrollton and Tandy in Fort Worth, plus the main plant for Apple II computers in Carrollton. The Dallas-Fort Worth metroplex strip of high-tech factories is called "Silicon Prairie." After Silicon Valley and Route 128, this is America's third biggest high-tech concentration.

• *Office Space.* All of the above created a tremendous demand for offices. Back around 1950, the Dallas skyline had been dominated by Sir Alfred Bossom's Magnolia Building, with its famous Flying Red Horse at the top. Then Dallas went on a building binge in the 1950s, with only New York building more office space in the decade. By 1964, Warren Leslie was describing "a low-flying horse, dwarfed by the deathly competition between the banks and insurance companies," as Republic Bank, Fidelity Union Life and Mercantile Bank threw up new office towers.* By 1969, 38 of the top 100 Texas-based companies had Dallas headquarters against 31 in twice-larger Houston. By 1975, *Nation's Business* found Dallas third among the cities for headquarters with more than $1 million in assets. By 1981, the metroplex of Dallas-Fort Worth had 1,100 of these firms. Land in downtown Dallas was so hot that between 1977 and 1981 some parcels grew ten times in value.

Oil. Banking. Trade. Aerospace. Electronics. Insurance. Office Space. There is all this diversity in a city that began with no major river, no port, no farmland, no reason for being. The city grew from 294,000 people and thirty-first rank among cities in 1940 to 904,000 residents and seventh place by 1980. It has poor services and social crisis, as we shall see, but it is an economic triumph.

A man-made city inevitably leads to stern, go-it-alone, conservative ways. Another barren outpost, Salt Lake City, had required a harsh theocracy to grow. Dallas became a right-wing

---

* The Dallas insurance sector is sizable. By 1975, 198 insurance firms had Dallas headquarters, with $4.5 billion in combined assets. Only Hartford had more insurance front offices back then. Another 387 firms had Dallas branch offices as well.

center, where business and religion were often fused.* In the early 1960s, Dallas had the biggest Baptist and Methodist churches on earth, with one church for every 900 residents. The Social Darwinist gospel was heard in many a pew. In 1972 Neal Peirce found a city with Sunday services "where sermon titles like 'God's Business Is Big Business' are not considered offensive, and where the churches have steered deliberately clear of social action. In this milieu, bland Protestantism seems to give way to uninhibited superpatriotism."

Where the Elders of Zion ran Salt Lake City, Dallas was ruled by a secular conclave, the 200 members of the Dallas Citizens' Council. This group of corporate presidents and chief executive officers ran Dallas from 1937 through 1976. Its guiding light was R. L. (Bob) Thornton, a four-time Dallas mayor and, as Warren Leslie suggests, "Mr. Dallas" for the 1930s, 1940s and much of the 1950s. Thornton gave Conrad Hilton his first loan and was the first Dallas banker to invest in automobiles.

The DCC was a spin-off of a business proposal: Thornton's drive to land the Texas Centennial Fair in 1936. Raising the $3.5 million for the event meant endless meetings, and Thornton later recalled for Leslie how the tedious fund raisings of 1936 led to the DCC elite after 1937:

> There was no organization. We had to have men who could underwrite. . . . Sometimes you'd get a bunch together. They couldn't say yes or no. We didn't have time for no proxy people —what we needed was men who could give you the box score. Then I saw the idea. Why not organize the "yes" and "no" people?

At first, the Dallas Citizens' Council was limited to the 100 leading company presidents or CEOs, then it expanded to 200. Proxies could not attend, per Thornton's law: "If you don't

---

* God and Mammon in Dallas were recently seen in a *60 Minutes* profile of the head of the Mary Kay cosmetics empire. Mary Kay informed Morley Safer that "God is using our company to make women the success they are." Safer said about her entrance at the annual Dallas convention that "other corporate stars walk on stage. . . . Mary Kay *levitates*." In Michael M. Thomas's novel *Someone Else's Money,* a character much like her appears as "Grenada Masterman, a Texas-born cosmetics queen whose products include Born Again Balm, a dermatological cure-all with a cocaine base. . . . The unguent was marketed under the slogan 'For Skin as Pure as a Christian Heart.' "

come, you ain't there." Given the context of "one company, one vote," this made eminent sense. Later, an outlet for younger presidents was set up as a Dallas Assembly. By 1971, however, Neal Peirce observed how even "the Assembly was beginning to age, and an even younger group of aspiring Dallas businessmen formed a group"—a sub-sub-DCC.

In theory, the DCC was nonpolitical, merely there to advise public opinion or lobby for the city in Austin. But through one more branch, a Citizen Charter Association, the DCC hand-picked Council candidates and all the mayors—virtually all the latter being DCC members. Warren Leslie describes what happened when Mayor Earle Cabell retired in 1964:

> . . . it was announced that J. Erik Jonsson [founder and head of Texas Instruments] had accepted the job. There had been no prior announcement that Jonsson had been offered the job. Five councilmen simply went out to ask him. They came back and announced that he had accepted.
>
> At lunch the next day Larry Kelly, executive director of the Dallas Civic Opera, laughed about it. "I think we have the only city in the world where it could happen."

The DCC led public opinion and rushed through special projects. Leslie recalls how Vought Aircraft's president called the DCC head, insisting the Dallas runways be lengthened as a condition of Vought's relocation from Connecticut:

> Three hours and forty minutes later, Hulcy telephoned Beisel that the City Council had been persuaded to call an emergency meeting and the $256,000 had been voted for the runways. Work would begin Monday morning. Out of this phone call came an enterprise which now employs more than 20,000 people in Dallas.

Sometimes these proclamations were for causes like racial integration. A DCCer at the key meeting in 1962 told Leslie how the eighty-two-year-old Bob Thornton

> told us how much business had suffered in Birmingham, New Orleans and the rest. He told us how much it would cost Dallas if we couldn't solve the problem quickly and peaceably. There

was not a single piece of sentiment at the meeting. It was not an argument over whether Negroes should be integrated or not. It was simply a matter of dollars and cents. . . .

Integration ordered by the DCC was carried out with dispatch. Hotels, restaurants, schools and stores rapidly carried it out. But there was a basic cost to this rule by DCC decrees, Leslie observing that "what seems to me to have happened in Dallas is that the people have not been made angry, they have been made apathetic. They have the feeling that all will be well and that their leaders will take care of them. . . . In the end, government by private club is government by *junta*, whether benevolent or not."

Unable to participate in normal civics or politics, many Dallas residents turned to virulent extremists. There was General Edwin Walker and the Birchers. Or Representative Bruce Alger, leading the mob that shoved around LBJ and Lady Bird in 1960, Johnson later lamenting "a mob scene that looked like some other country." Or there was Adlai Stevenson confronted by a mob of pickets in the fall of 1963. He went over to comfort a screaming woman, who then hit him with a placard as a student spat on him. "For my part, I believe in the forgiveness of sin and the redemption of ignorance," said the saddened U.N. Ambassador. Stanley Marcus called a DCC meeting, where some had suggested that President Kennedy's visit in November be postponed. For sound reasons, the trip went on. The tragic results made Dallas a household word for extremism and violence throughout the world.

The next year, Warren Leslie wrote *Dallas Public and Private,* and described five distant "cities." There was middle-class Oak Cliff, the new apartment houses near Turtle Creek, the building binge downtown, and North Dallas for the DCC set, who also occupy two separately incorporated enclaves, Highland Park and University Park. These two "Park Cities" had 34,000 whites and 0 nonwhites.

Then there was the fifth city, the West Dallas slum. It hadn't even been part of Dallas until recently, since "the city fathers simply did not wish to face the huge problem of cleaning it up. . . . the shacks and privies of West Dallas are now as definitely a part of the city as the million-dollar buildings downtown." Leslie took the visiting J. B. Priestley on a drive through the better parts of Dallas. Priestley thanked him:

Very nice. Now I know how Nieman-Marcus customers live. Tell me, where do your elevator operators live?'' We drove to West Dallas, trying to stick to the ten miles of paved streets and away from the thirty-three miles of dirt and gravel roads. We watched the dirty, ragged children playing stickball, and we passed the building where Brother Bill Harrod annually collects his donations of shoes so that these children can wear something on their feet.

"I think," Priestley said, "that you have a puncture in your balloon.

Back when 3,000 families in Dallas had no piped water at all, Mayor Earle Cabell proposed building 3,000 public housing units since the private sector couldn't do the job. The head of the Dallas Real Estate Board said, "It's doubtful in my mind that private industry can do it—but let's start saying no to Washington." Dallas already had 6,400 units of public housing, but Cabell was denounced for "creeping socialism," and his housing proposal lost. He retired, later emerging in 1964 to oust Representative Alger in the LBJ landslide that year.

The DCC thunderclap choosing J. Erik Jonsson as mayor has been described. He turned out to be a superb choice. A boyhood in liberal Brooklyn may explain why the founder of Texas Instruments brought "citizen participation" to the pocket borough of the DCC. In 1965, Jonsson convened eighty-seven unionists, businessmen, blacks, Hispanics and students for three days of talk about Dallas issues. This marathon produced a 300-page book sent to 20,000 Dallas residents, its contents later debated at thirty-three town meetings, then refined at a second marathon meeting. At last, a blueprint for Dallas emerged, with 114 goals. "Goals for Dallas" was a decalogue with clout. It soon led to the first Dallas kindergarten, a pretrial release system in the courts, expanded family planning services, and a community relations commission. This being Dallas, one goal was a major business idea: the 1967 bond for the Dallas-Fort Worth Airport. Recalling this debut for Dallas democracy, Jonsson had told Neal R. Peirce with modesty that "I look back on some of my early years as years when I didn't do well for my society. I didn't do what I could do. I'm accelerating as my life goes on. I'm trying to make up for what I should have done. It's that simple."

Jonsson retired in 1971, and the era of citizen power briefly routed the DCC from City Hall, as a sportscaster named Wes

Wise was elected mayor on a shoestring budget and populist platform. But the interregnum was brief. The last two Dallas mayors have been DCC members with no previous background in politics. The real march to democracy in Dallas came in 1976, as Barbara Jordan got the Voting Rights Act extended to Texas.

Early in 1981, Peter Applebome of *The New York Times* began a feature on Dallas with the claim that "a combination of prosperity and good investment has made Dallas a city where the streets are clean, the budget is balanced, and the populace is generally pleased—in short, a city that works." Applebome conceded that rule by DCC "fiat" continued. Still later, he added some truths about the "city that works":

> Most low-income public housing is in a state of utter disarray; a recent consultant's report said more than $133 million was needed for repairs. . . . Dallas is not immune to the demographic trends that have been disastrous for the nation's older cities. While Dallas grew by 7% in the past decade, its affluent, overwhelmingly white suburbs grew by 58%. Most of the gain in Dallas came from minorities.

The 2.2 cops per 1,000 Dallas citizens is the second lowest ratio of coverage among big cities after Houston. And like Atlanta and Miami, Dallas cut cops although crime rates were soaring. Between 1977 and 1980, assaults went up 31 percent, murder 32 percent, robbery 45 percent and rape 71 percent—as police were cut 4 percent.

In 1981, Dallas was twelfth for assault, eleventh for murder and fifth for rape among the fifty big cities. With 11,877 crimes per 100,000 in 1980, Dallas had the highest crime rate among the ten biggest cities. Inevitably the 42 percent minority share of Dallas suffered most of the growing crime, but even the middle class lacked police protection. A new condo colony for 10,000 singles called The Village had a rape rate four times that of New York City, so private patrols on horses began in 1980 with riders decked out in Texas Ranger outfits.

Another dying service was mass transit. Normal city tax support in America means that fares cover only 40 percent of operating costs. But in Dallas tax support for buses was so low that the fare box paid 63 percent of the costs and low-income users paid high fares. Meanwhile, the hired help was treated like the riders. When Dallas bus drivers struck in 1980, their modest goal was a union, but the company city of the Dallas Citizens' Council is so anti-union that average metro wages in 1980 were $6.96 against $8.53 in more organized Houston. The bus drivers were fired, scabs were hired, and the strike was crushed in a month. When the 340 drivers returned, only 160 of their jobs were still open. Those lucky enough to get their jobs back lost their seniority.

Dallas finished last in a "quality of life" survey of thirty-five big cities in 1976. Like Houston, which was twenty-seventh in the survey, Dallas has no corporate, personal or state income taxes, and very low property taxes. Dallas is also uninterested in federal aid. A 1981 congressional study on the impact of Reagan urban aid cuts observed Dallas as "among the least federally-dependent large cities." The myopia pushing Dallas into the spiral of service crisis and taxpayer flight was seen when the survey noted how in Dallas:

> City officials express strong support for cutbacks in federal spending and, unlike their colleagues in many distressed cities, favor the shift from categorical to block grants [the "new federalism"].

A tax revolt began in early 1980, when Dallas mailed its first property tax revaluations since 1975. Values had soared during a five-year hiatus and the new taxes were a shock. A second jolt followed, as three Dallas tax districts sent new bills. There was a 49 percent hike for Dallas County, a 25 percent boost in school taxes, and a 23 percent rise in a hospital tax. By freezing assessments for five years and Balkanizing taxes into special districts, the DCC had laid the ground for tax revolt in 1980.

The tax mailings were the powder; the match was lit by city audits reported in the *Dallas Times Herald*. Homeowners reeling from new tax hikes now read that booming commercial land downtown was underassessed by $1.1 billion. DCC powers owning much of that land got tax breaks as homeowners got tax hikes, so a Tax Equality Association, or TEA Party, was born. The TEA Party demanded a 30 percent tax cut. The huge tax cut would have slashed 1,500 city workers from an already-thin payroll of 13,000 (compared in per capita terms to New York, Dallas should have 25,000 municipal workers for at least minimal services).

In his book on tax rebellions, *Revolt of the Haves,* Robert Kuttner observed how the middle class starts tax revolts, then loses twice. Most of the new tax cuts go to the rich, as the middle class and the poor see services cut by strapped cities. This syndrome would have occurred in Dallas. The 30 percent tax cut would devastate already poor services, and businesses would get two of every three dollars in the new tax relief. Dallas Power & Light and The Southwest Bank both would have saved $1 million in taxes and average homeowners would have gotten $66.

By early 1981, the tax breaks for the rich and the service cuts for the rest were well known. So the Dallas tax revolt rejected itself in a January 17 vote, 69,000 to 33,000. The nationwide tax revolt started by Proposition 13 in 1978 had been dealt a major blow. The Reagan tax cuts continued the binge on the federal level in the summer of 1981, but the Dallas vote had at least braked the local and state madness.*

To end the poor services and unfair tax loads favoring downtown powers, TEA Party activists must somehow coalesce with minority voters to dilute the DCC's power. Blacks play the lead political role among the 42 percent minority share of Dallas. They have all three minority seats, and wisely defused a busing issue in 1981. When the first of many busing orders was imposed back in 1968, most eligible white children were in the Dallas public schools. A dozen years later, only 50 percent of the eligible white kids were in the schools. Early in 1981, the black head of the Dallas School Board joined with local minority groups claiming to represent 100,000 people to oppose an NAACP busing plan. Like Birmingham's black mayor, Richard Arrington, Dallas blacks wanted good, quality schools, not symbolic, divisive exercises like busing.

The black legislative caucus in Austin also opposed a new black seat in Congress for Dallas. The new seat was a divide-and-conquer ploy from Governor William Clements, head of the Dallas-based SEDCO oil equipment company. The black seat would eliminate one white, relatively liberal Democratic congressman from Dallas. Jim Mattox would be moved into a new

---

* Meanwhile, assessments stayed low in downtown Dallas even though land prices soared. One area saw land values rise so fast that a proposed arts center from I. M. Pei was scaled back. Ironically, it was the proposal of the center in 1977 that launched the rising values. Land values tripled, making the concert-hall site so costly that the Symphony Association dropped it in 1981.

GOP District. The Republicans would pick up one seat and get credit for the new black seat. The black caucus in Austin attacked this proposal, its leader, Representative Craig Washington of Houston, observing that Clements "doesn't care anything about the black people of Dallas County and never has. There's nothing magic about having a black person represent a black district." Yet some Dallas blacks backed Clements in the deal that cost Dallas one of its two liberal congressmen.

Footnotes on two more problems: the flood of high-tech Okies in Dallas and the expansion of suburbs in the "Mid Cities" strip between Dallas and Forth Worth. The high-tech Okies arrived in Texas after 1980. At first, many of them found quality jobs. But unskilled Snowbelt workers were soon panning fool's gold in El Dorado. As they poured into Dallas in 1981, a jobless rate usually well below America's rose to just a point under the national rate. Few of the northern workers could fit into the banks, oil firms, insurance companies, or electronic plants. Thousands of them arrived each week in Texas, some via things like the CETA-funded "Job Shuttle" bus, which made monthly runs from Ohio after 1980. By 1981, the Texas Employment Commission was reporting that one in three new job applicants was from out of state. The lucky ones found work at $4 an hour. But many were soon in unemployment lines, and some began returning home.

A U-Haul manager in Detroit told *The Wall Street Journal* in late 1981 that "a year ago we were getting two or three inquiries a day about moving rates to the Sun Belt, especially to Texas; now these inquiries have dried up and we've started to see people moving back." Dean Reynolds, the manager of a temporary employment agency in Dallas, told *The New York Times* about those hanging on:

> It's like the 30s when the Okies and people all over the country made a mass exodus to California . . . a lot of them don't have anything more than what they bring in the car. Most of them spend some time living out of it. It's the old ethic of "God will take care of us." Perhaps He does, but some of these people go through an awful lot. . . . We call them Red River wetbacks. Yankees coming from across the Red River. It's not derogatory. I'm a Red River wetback myself, from Kansas City, Missouri.

Meanwhile, the Dallas suburbs grow. A big spur was the 1974 opening of the Dallas-Fort Worth Airport, which had inspired a North Texas Commission. This intercity chamber of commerce promoted a new metroplex of more than 3 million residents in Dallas, Fort Worth and the rapidly growing "Mid Cities" strip in between. By 1980, the metroplex had edged out Houston as our ninth biggest metro area.

Back in 1969, the Dallas Cowboys scrimmaged on a Spartan practice field in what would become the Mid Cities area. There were flimsy walls of corrugated tin around a field in the midst of a vast plain. At sunset, and far away across the flat plain, there was the black silhouette of Dallas office towers against an orange glow and that was all. There was no airport, no Six Flags Over Texas theme park, no Rangers baseball team in Arlington, just flat prairie. Today, this Mid Cities strip of thirty-four miles is where people and jobs go. It has the Texas Stadium for the Cowboys in Irving, Arlington Stadium for the Rangers, the Six Flags extravaganza and the world's largest airport. It gets many of the high-tech growth industries. The Silicon Prairie of the metroplex is still led by the two Dallas giants, Texas Instruments and LTV, but the Mid Cities get their share. National Semiconductor plans a new Arlington plant, while 75 percent of all Apple II and III computers are made in Carrollton.

A new town of Las Colinas on the Mid Cities strip avoids HUD loan guarantees used by The Woodlands of Houston. It also es-chews any charm: where The Woodlands has forests and low-scaled offices, Las Colinas has prairie and high-rises. This new town came about when Ben Carpenter decided to do something with his ranch. Assuming it must "be converted from ranchland to urban use" like the rest of Mid Cities strip, he decided to convert it himself, and "I wanted it to be the best, most attractive development possible—because I live in the middle of it." De-spite the dull prairie site, Las Colinas had soon attracted 9,000 residents and 11,000 daily workers, and was well on the way to a goal of 53,000 residents and 100,000 workers.

J. R. Ewing doesn't live in Dallas anymore—and soon the middle class won't either. In its superficial way, the TV series reflects the real city: the mania for wealth; the invisible minori-ties; the media illusion of Dallas as neat congeries of high-rises, condos and boutiques. But as the middle class leaves a dwindling Dallas, the popular series needs some new plot lines ahead.

## San Antonio

> San Antonio is, next to San Francisco, New Orleans, and pos-
> sibly Boston, the most colorful, the most "romantic" city in
> America. . . . Also San Antonio is a slum. The west side has a
> Mexican population of around sixty thousand, which—some
> Negro communities in the South aside—is the largest solid bloc
> of underpossessed in the United States.
> —John Gunther in *Inside U.S.A.*, 1947

These two cities remain.

San Antonio has gone from being our twenty-fourth biggest
city in 1947 to our tenth biggest today, yet it had our fourth lowest
hourly wages in 1980. It elected its first Hispanic mayor in 1981,
but 54 percent of the city is Hispanic, and most of them are very
poor. It ended its version of the Dallas Citizens' Council a decade
ago, but its West Side remains one of our worst slums. San Antonio still has its charming and meandering river, flanked by oaks
and cypresses, with *bateaux mouches* serving gourmet meals in
lazy midstream. But tourism and the huge military payroll in this
"Mother-in-law of the Army" reflect an undiversified economy,
lagging behind Dallas and Houston.

Founded by the Spanish in 1718, San Antonio was the capital
of the province of Texas, ruled first by Spain, then by Mexico.
Five missions remain from the 1730s, among them the famous
Alamo. Also on its eighteenth-century site is San Fernando Cathedral, the current building dating from the 1870s. The original
was built in 1734 at the dead center of town, the city charter
mandating that San Antonio be "six miles square, of which the
sides shall be equidistant from what is known as the cupola of
San Fernando. . . ." The medieval centrality of the Cathedral
translates today into a dominant political role. Archbishop Patrick Flores is one of the most powerful leaders for reform. The
church's dominant role may also explain one of the lowest crime
rates in urban America.

As in Dallas and Houston, rail lines in the 1870s helped expand
San Antonio. By 1890, this was Texas' biggest city, and it remained so until 1930. As the first of the western cow towns at the
end of the Civil War, it was the base for the Chisholm, Shawnee
and Western trails to northern points like Kansas City and
Omaha.

Neal R. Peirce evokes a

> veritable cattle capital, filled with picturesque saloons and gaming tables where men whose herds ranged over millions of acres played recklessly for high stakes. Eventually the cattle trade began to share the scene with pedestrian breweries, cement factories, milling, and oil. San Antonio became one of the great military cities of the United States.

The military role began with the Alamo siege in 1836, later expanding with Fort Sam Houston in 1865 and then a major army hospital in 1895. "Fort Sam" is our biggest military base, the army hospital one of the biggest on earth, and San Antonio is, with San Diego, one of America's two main military retirement colonies. Teddy Roosevelt organized the Rough Riders on the International Fair Grounds here in 1898 and, two decades later, a young officer at Fort Sam named Eisenhower met and won Mamie Geneva Doud, a Denver socialite wintering with her family in San Antonio.

San Antonio lost its rank as the biggest Texas city in 1930. The war years revived it rapidly, as even more military bases opened. A 1943 economic study found San Antonio was one of six American cities to benefit most from the war. To hold on to census and job growth generated at the time, San Antonio began to annex new suburbs. The cupola of San Fernando Cathedral soon lost its centrality. Mayor Gus B. Mauermann later recalled how "I kept on my toes and never let any suburbs grow. I took them before they had a chance to grow." The annexations saw San Antonio land grow by 68 percent in the 1940s.

Gunther in 1947 saw a romantic and very troubled city. On one hand, there was his charming picture of evenings on the San Antonio River, the "Seine" of Texas. But there was the other San Antonio with some 60,000 Mexicans on the West Side. Even today, the West Side has dirt roads out of a Third World slum. Jim Crow customs were gone by the 1960s and Hispanics won City Hall in 1981, but Gunther's analysis of 1947 still has some force today:

> The Mexicans are miserably underpaid; hence, they don't get enough to eat, their homes lack sanitation, and their health deteriorates. So the white entrepreneur, having shoved the Mexican into the gutter by paying what are probably the lowest wages in the United States, asserts that the Mexican is too poor

or too dirty to be reclaimed, and thus keeps him down in a permanently vicious circle.

There was a fateful land grab in 1952 when the Council proposed an annexation of 120 square miles in one move. Trying to avoid a suburban noose made sense, the city manager noting the need to stop "parasite cities which would have lived off San Antonio for perpetuity without contributing a thing to its growth." A campaign to recall the City Council began, and the annexation was cut by a third. All this led to the founding of a Good Government League, San Antonio's version of the Dallas Citizens' Council. The GGL was at least a more inclusive elite— 2,000 rather than 200 members pulled the wires at City Hall. But otherwise it was like Dallas. It handpicked Council candidates, and writer Arnold Fleischmann describes GGL goals in terms familiar from Dallas:

> The city's boosters have viewed their relationship to local government as one in which the city is expected to be run like a private firm . . . Consistent with this ideological base has been the commitment to "reform," which the boosters have characterized as a means of taking "politics" out of local government.

The Good Government League ruled San Antonio for two decades, pushing growth while neglecting services for slums. Then it forgot its origins in the 1952 backlash against annexation, and proposed a lunge for 63 square miles. This forged an odd coalition between suburban developers eager to stop city land grabs and slum dwellers protesting endless growth as services declined. The GGL lost control of the Council in 1973 and quickly expired. During the GGL's two decades, San Antonio had annexed 110 square miles. Fleischmann observes that had the city remained within its 1950 limits, it would have "lost 55,000 residents between 1960 and 1975. As a result of its ability to incorporate these outlying areas, the city's population, instead of declining, grew by 169,000 . . ." This fed the illusion of a thriving city, when, in fact, some 55,000 people had fled a city in decline. Annexation was covering the tracks of a growing service crisis.

Gunther noted the civil rights leadership of Archbishop Robert E. Lucey, denounced as a "red" in a city where "the Hearst paper is the most liberal in the town!'' In 1961, Hispanics sent Henry B. González to Congress, but in local politics, the Good Government League kept on the screws. Hispanics slowly built up the parallel structures of the poor. From civil rights struggles and Great Society programs, new leaders emerged led by Archbishop Patrick Flores and Ernesto Cortez with his Alinsky-style Communities Organized for Public Service (COPS). Hispanic voter-registration groups worked to scrap the at-large Council elections, while also raising the Hispanic vote from 40 percent of San Antonio in 1975 to over 60 percent by 1980.

The first grass-roots victory came in 1976, after the Council gave a shopping mall permission to build on the San Antonio aquifer. An Aquifer Protection Association got a special referendum. Outspent by pro-growth forces 8 to 1, the environmentalists won at the polls by 4 to 1. This win gave West Side community groups a lift, then Washington gave them the game. Barbara Jordan got the Voting Rights Act extended to Texas language minorities, and a federal court ordered Dallas, Houston and San Antonio to end the at-large Council elections diluting minority votes. With district elections, Hispanics won the Council majority in San Antonio in 1977.

As the 1970s began, Henry Cisneros was a young White House intern under Richard Nixon. He moved on from the Nixon White House to maintaining close ties with neoconservatives like Scoop Jackson, and then on to a Council seat in San Antonio prior to the Hispanic triumph of 1977. On April 4, 1981, the Hispanics elected Cisneros as mayor by a 65 percent margin. The young Ph.D. was the first Mexican-American mayor of a city that was 54 percent Hispanic, and the tenth biggest city in America.

The Cisneros victory launched a new media star. *Life* said he "looks as if he should be wearing a headdress of rare bird feathers, a brightly colored cape to complement that royal Aztec nose profiled in pre-Columbian sculpture found in Mexico's temples." Yet under those feathers was a vague pragmatist who breezily observed,

> I've studied government programs and New Deal-type programs and the trouble with all of them is their impermanence. They offer a leg up, but then there is no chance to hitch onto real growth. We have to bring in jobs, get the hot industries— computers, electronics, aerospace, health-related services, energy companies.

To start with, Cisneros can strike both energy and aerospace from his list. Energy will stay in Dallas and Houston, near the east and central Texas oil fields, the banks, the refineries and factories along the Houston Ship Channel. Perhaps Cisneros confuses four Air Force bases in San Antonio with industrial production. In any event, this is a dubious growth sector, given the problems of domestic airlines after 1980, the growing Airbus consortium of Europe, and the huge Sunbelt plants at hand. The latter include the Los Angeles–Anaheim strip, the "city of Boeing in Seattle," the NASA outposts in Alabama, Florida and Texas, and the big General Dynamics plants in Fort Worth.

With health-related services, Cisneros is on firmer ground. The huge army hospital and University of Texas Medical Center are impressive local resources. More health services are needed for the city's poor, but expanding the existing health facilities is difficult. Reagan cuts in community health programs and Medicaid spending alone may make this a job-losing industry in a poor city like this.

That leaves the two hot industries of computers and electronics on the Cisneros list. Here Cisneros points with pride to a new Control Data factory that he helped land for San Antonio in 1980. Control Data is one of the few *Fortune* 500 giants willing to open factories in slums. It does this through the City Venture Corporation (detailed in Part II, pages 244–46), whose plans for Miami's Liberty City have been noted earlier.

Cisneros would be jumping into a very crowded high-tech pool, and one that needs close academic backup, e.g., the link of Stanford and Silicon Valley or MIT and Route 128. In contrast, San Antonio is limited to the University of Texas Medical School, a fine backup for genetic engineering, digital radiography or ultrasound firms, but limited to biotechnology.

San Antonio is still a lovely tourist town, with no regional peers save smaller Santa Fe. A new River Walk has been added to the grassy banks of the San Antonio River. The famous tourist boat, called "A-Drunken-Old-Man-Going-Home-At-Night" by locals, runs by a new Museum of Art, the first major museum to be opened in America since 1970. The new museum has charm as the recycled Romanesque hulk of the old Lone Star Brewery, which explains the coy opening night theme in 1981 of "We're Brewing Art."

Another plus is a very low crime rate: 1981 found San Antonio eighteenth for murder, thirty-eighth for assault and forty-seventh for robbery among the fifty biggest cities. That year saw Newark with 2,362 robberies for every 235 in San Antonio. In 1980, San Antonio compared very favorably with Dallas and Houston for crimes per 100,000 residents:

|  | Murder | Rape | Robbery |
|---|---|---|---|
| Dallas | 35.4 | 124.6 | 553.7 |
| Houston | 40.7 | 92.6 | 698.7 |
| San Antonio | 21.0 | 46.6 | 223.3 |

This immunity could be a business lure for San Antonio, should the service crisis rage on in Dallas and Houston. Also striking is the low ratio of police to people in San Antonio. Only 1.5 cops per 1,000 residents is lower even than the poor coverage in Dallas and Washington. Why this fewer police, less crime anomaly?

South Texas is a repressive area where virtual peonage existed along the Rio Grande not long ago. As for Catholicism, it has dominated San Antonio since the central placement of San Fernando Cathedral in 1734. It is an orderly faith, and socially active leaders like Archbishops Lucey and Flores have inspired the local flock to constructive ways. Finally, there is the trend of unusually high crime rates among blacks. This trend seems part of the low crime picture in San Antonio, where Hispanics outnumber blacks more than 7 to 1, compared to more violent Dallas where blacks outnumber Hispanics 3 to 1.

If 1.5 police per 1,000 residents were raised to the 4.0 standard of Chicago, San Antonio, ideally, would be nearly crime free. The low ratio of cops reflects poor city services. No amount of wishful thinking about high-tech jobs by Mayor Cisneros can obscure such current problems. To his credit, Cisneros quickly proposed higher taxes to upgrade weak services.

But only massive federal aid can help a city with a 61 percent minority share, a proportion similar to dead Snowbelt cities like Cleveland, Detroit and Newark, or Sunbelt relics like Atlanta, Miami and New Orleans. Too many unskilled minorities and too few unions meant San Antonio's average hourly wage in 1980 was $5.39 against a national norm of $6.86. Our tenth biggest city was #205 among 209 metropolitan areas for average hourly wages. Along with El Paso, this is one of two Texas centers for cheap labor and sweatshops. If the Reagan program of "guest workers" unleashes a new flood of illegal Mexican migrants, these pestholes will rapidly grow in San Antonio.

As to regular factory work, only 13 percent of San Antonio works in manufacturing against 22 percent nationwide. Cisneros wants high tech to join military bases and tourism as a "third leg" of a diversified economy. But limits to high tech have been seen, and the factory picture is otherwise dim. While the old Lone Star plant may be "brewing art" as a recycled museum, it hasn't done anything lately for the beer industry, once vital in employing unskilled labor in this old German town.

Government remains the big employer in this "Mother-in-law of the Army." There are Brooks, Kelly, Lackland and Randolph Air Force bases, and "Fort Sam" for the Army, all these combining for 40,500 active-duty personnel earning $830 million in 1980. There are also more than 42,000 military retirees in the area with $298 million in retirement pay for 1980 alone. The dry, warm climate makes this the Army and Air Force version of San Diego's famous naval retirement mecca. Add civil service employees at the huge Audie Murphy Veterans Hospital and at the huge Wilford Hall Air Force hospital and the total Pentagon payroll for 1980 in San Antonio was $1.5 billion.

Even Henry Cisneros is an army brat, his father a retired colonel. Twenty-five percent of San Antonio works for government against an 18 percent national share. While the metro jobless rate in 1980 compared well with America's average of 7.6 percent, San Antonio's lack of diversity made for poor comparisons with its two sister cities:

|  | Factory Share of Jobs | Government Share of Jobs | Jobless Rate |
|---|---|---|---|
| Dallas | 21% | 12% | 3.8% |
| Houston | 17 | 12 | 3.5 |
| San Antonio | 13 | 25 | 5.3 |

Given aerospace, energy and high-tech competition in Texas and the Southwest, it's hard to see San Antonio expanding a narrow industrial base. Among our ten biggest cities, only the other military giant of San Diego had fewer *Fortune* 500 front offices in 1981.

Beyond the narrow economy of San Antonio lies the vast West Side slum. In 1971, Neal R. Peirce examined our fourteenth biggest city and found the West Side "one of the most striking slums of the continent. For block after block, tiny shacks and hovels stretch out, many with outdoor privies and lacking water, the conditions not much better than those suffered by the destitute . . . along the Mississippi Delta."

In 1980, Joel Garreau went on one more tour of the West Side of San Antonio, and wrote that "in Holy Family Parish, we found dirt streets, some steers, a goat, and chickens that looked suspiciously pugnacious. . . . Portions of the barrio could just as easily have been a thousand miles south. Dirt roads, fences made of sticks lashed together, unpainted wooden shacks, crooked doors."

### Rio Grande Cities

The big Rio Grande city is El Paso, with its sister city of Juárez across the river in Mexico. Both were once the single city of El Paso del Norte, founded in 1581, then partitioned in 1848 by the Treaty of Guadalupe Hidalgo. The two border cities celebrated their joint quadricentennial in 1981, with festival organizers promoting the dream of a united, international city like Hong Kong or Trieste. One and a half million people live in this isolated spot, the desert stretching for hundreds of miles to the east and west. Between the two cities runs only the thin trickle of the Rio Grande, a border which, John Crewdson observes in *The New York Times:*

> makes some important differences, dividing as it does the third world from the first world. Juárez is shorter of almost everything than El Paso: sewers, houses, automobiles, electric lights, money, calories per person, longevity. The only thing it has more of is people, nearly twice as many.

A common crisis for both cities was the double devaluation of the Mexican peso in 1982. This sent economic shock waves through these and other South Texas border towns like Brownsville and Laredo. El Paso stores catering to Mexicans lost up to

80 percent of their customers, while Juárez stores became flooded with Americans buying things like sugar at 9 cents a pound.

El Paso, our third fastest growing big city in the 1970s, depends on an aquifer with only a twenty-year water supply. Residents face disaster unless an aquifer in New Mexico can be tapped. The rapid growth of our seventeenth biggest city is based on unskilled minorities. Twenty-four percent of El Paso consists of registered aliens. These and resident Hispanics were the base for two economic worsts in 1980: the highest metro unemployment rate in Texas, at 8 percent; the lowest hourly wages of all 209 metro areas in America, at $4.98 an hour. Illegal Mexican arrivals keep pouring in at a tremendous rate across the Rio Grande, with a 20 percent upsurge in their numbers following the second peso devaluation in 1982.

McAllen is in the extreme southern heel of Texas. This city of 67,000 grew 78 percent in the 1970s, and made national news in 1981 when videotapes showed local cops beating up prisoners in the booking room. In the cleanup, two police chiefs were fired, forty cops left the force, and a human relations commission was formed for complaints. But the police issue polarized the 1981 mayoral election, which pitted Mayor Othal Brand, one of the world's biggest onion farmers, against Dr. Ramiro Casso, who ran a free clinic. Fighting Cesar Chavez's drive to organize his workers, Brand had once waved a pistol at demonstrators surrounding his car. On election day in 1981, he photographed voters to deter "fraud," he claimed. The Voting Rights Act reform of Barbara Jordan required bilingual voting materials to aid linguistic minorities. This and a voter registration drive meant a phenomenal rise in the McAllen electorate—14,000 new voters in a city of 67,000 for 1980 alone. Although 60 percent of the (mainly new) voters turned out in 1981, Mayor Brand won a close victory. In McAllen, half of it under the poverty line, Brand called his vanquished foe "a doctor that ought to be back giving shots," while Dr. Casso assailed the winner as "the scum of the earth." The Mexicans should win the next time, but meanwhile, the polarization at the polls had few equals in America.

South Texas politics in general has few equals in America. The Rio Grande Valley has long had pocket-borough counties, ruled by "patrons" who paid the poll tax, then told peons how to vote. The most famous examples were the Parrs of Duval County.* The "Dukes of Duval" managed the 4,622-to-40 county vote for Lyndon Johnson's first Senate race in 1948.

Flanking McAllen on the Rio Grande are the two poorest cities of the South. Brownsville was #360 for income among the 363 American cities with more than 40,000 residents in 1976; Laredo was last. The low wages and hovels are luxuries compared to life in Mexico, so the region still plays the role described by Neal R. Peirce more than a decade ago: ". . . There is one great central migrant system, and its massive roots blanket South Texas like those of a mighty tree. The great branches push up through the heart of the continent."

Until 1964, the branches were legalized by the *bracero* program of temporary workers begun in 1942, when wartime labor shortages required more workers for Southwest military plants. Over two decades, the program brought in 4 to 5 million Mexicans who tended—like Common Market "guest workers" today —to become permanent residents. The *bracero* program depressed wages, increased unemployment, encouraged illegal migrants and undermined union drives. In 1961, Henry B. González defied the Good Government League and was elected San Antonio's first Hispanic congressman. In 1964, he and Lyndon Johnson teamed up to end the *bracero* program but it has been revived again. Fifty thousand "guest" workers a year from Mexico was the quota offered by Reagan to President López Portillo in mid-1981. This should repeat the *bracero* history, touching off a greater tide of illegal migrants from Mexico.†

---

* The last of the Parrs got nine months in federal prison for tax evasion in the 1930s, and was later convicted of mail fraud. He was also later convicted of menacing a restaurant owner with a gun, and was fined $100. Found guilty of tax evasion again in 1974, he was sentenced to five years. Seen carrying a gun while on bond, he was called for bond revocation. He committed suicide or, as *Time* said, "George Parr, a persistent piece of Western folklore to the end, decided not to go to the hearing—and picked up his pistol instead."

† Some crossing the border are refugees from Central American violence who should get temporary asylum here. But people fleeing El Salvador and Guatemala are not granted temporary asylum in America unless they can prove they are bona fide political refugees. In recent years, the State Department has given blanket temporary asylum, or "extended voluntary departure" status, to all those fleeing violence in Ethiopia, Iran, Uganda and Nicaragua. Until human rights violations and violence are reduced, this status should be given all arrivals in America from Guatemala and El Salvador—per pending legislation from Representative Theodore Weiss and Senator Dennis DeConcini on Capitol Hill.

The idea of a new flood of illegal aliens in the wake of 50,000 new *braceros* is terrible. These Mexicans are economic refugees, and America cannot mop up the failure of its oil-rich neighbor. Mexico's census grows 3.2 percent a year, or triple America's rate of increase. Seventy-two million Mexicans today could well be 134 million by the year 2000. As TRB observes in the *New Republic:* "To act as a good neighbor, as Reagan suggests, the United States might have to absorb half of the Mexican growth, say 30 million in the next generation." Most would wind up in the Southwest, with its meager water supplies, poor city services, and limited openings for unskilled labor. TRB may understate the numbers ahead—a Reagan task force on immigration projected that up to 60 million Mexicans could be here by the year 2030. Why Reagan would encourage this flood with the *braceros* is anyone's guess, especially given the huge annual influx of legal immigrants and political refugees from the Caribbean, Europe, Latin America and Southeast Asia. Some suggested Reagan wanted to revive *braceros* to help out California and Texas farmers with more cheap labor. The new "guest workers" let Mexico off the hook. A nation producing $18 billion in oil for 1982 must set its own house in order. It must curb census growth, create more labor-intensive jobs and, above all, carry out the land reform promised by the revolution of 1917.

Mexico has one of the world's highest birth rates. Too many people on too little land means one of the world's widest gaps between the few and the many in a nation with 45 percent unemployment in 1982. Even a dozen years ago, 66 percent of Mexico had no form of drainage or sewage disposal. This has been lessened by new social programs funded by growing oil revenues, but staggering problems remain:

• In 1970, Mexico had 48 million people, 40 percent of them under the age of twelve. Today, it has 72 million, half under the age of fifteen. This young and Catholic population means that even higher birth rates may lie ahead, absent changes in family-planning policies.

• In 1975, Mexico City was the world's fourth largest city, with 11.9 million people. As birth rates soar and peasants flee the meager land, U.N. projections see 31 million in the world's biggest city by the year 2000. The current biggest metro area of New York City-Northern New Jersey will grow 13 percent more by then, as Mexico City grows by 160 percent.

• Peasants work on land so unproductive that, in 1981, 80 percent of the 23,000 communal farms had no surplus crops. As an economist said to the *New Republic* in 1970: "Mexico after 30 years or more of agrarian reform is a country of large landowners." All this encourages even more migration to Mexico City and the western states.

Mexico has failed to focus on simple, unglamorous and labor-intensive jobs, especially in agriculture. Only in 1980 did Mexico turn from the fancy, capital-intensive projects that got it into debt to modest strategies similar to those advocated by the late Barbara Ward for Third World nations—food self-sufficiency and rural stability prior to industrial advance.

López Portillo began a food self-sufficiency drive in 1980, with grain production up 33 percent in a year. The drive means more farming jobs, fewer peasants in cities and improved rural life. New rural surveys found that 90 percent of Mexico's 21 million peasants were malnourished to some degree, while 19 million Mexicans overall needed urgent nutritional aid, nearly half of them children under fourteen. Food stamp and other nutritional programs are being devised today, although the explosive birth rates may yet sweep everything away. Without family-planning policies, Mexico will become even more chaotic, as will our western states.

Back in Texas, a main *bracero* booster was Governor William Clements. To those who suggest that new "guest workers" would induce a flood of illegal Mexicans to threaten our poorer workers, Clements cited the Help Wanted ads. Waving the classifieds about, he claimed that "anyone who really wants to work, who *wants to work,* in the state of Texas . . . can find a job." Among many disputing Governor Clements and his classifieds was *Post* columnist William Raspberry. He noted how Ronald Reagan had informed Walter Cronkite that the new "guest workers" would be a "safety valve" for Mexico which had "an unemployment rate that is far beyond anything." "Well, not quite beyond anything," noted Raspberry. "Mexico's jobless rate is estimated at between 30 and 40 percent, which is to say that it is roughly comparable to the unemployment rate among young black Americans in our big cities."

Henry Cisneros observed that Clements "is making tremendous inroads in the Mexican-American community." Reagan got from 20 percent to 30 percent of the Hispanic vote in Texas.

Some suggest that if he legalizes all illegal aliens who arrived here before 1981, the GOP might justifiably lock up a big Hispanic bloc.

Another example of Texas reactionism is its prison system. Courts are so punitive that, with 6 percent of our people, Texas has 10 percent of our inmates, a high share even for such a violent state. In 1982, Texas with Florida and Georgia had more than half of all America's prisoners on death row, for 13 percent of its population.

The Texas inmates live in America's worst penal conditions. By 1981 there were 32,000 inmates and 11,000 cells. Some 4,000 inmates lived either in tents or slept on floors, and many others were triple-celled in rooms originally built for one man. Prisoners were also used as guards, porters and supers, the 1977 per-inmate expense of $2,241 being the lowest for all states. Federal judge William Wayne Justice ordered reforms, which the state instituted in 1982.

Texas is in many ways like poor Mexico. Both are rich in oil, and in extremely poor peasants. Both have wretched prisons, and both until lately had one-party systems. One of them, however, is part of an advanced democracy, while the other is part of the Third World, and that distinction can be made.

# CHAPTER 5

# ROCKY MOUNTAIN CITIES

### Denver

Horace Greeley dropped by in the year of the city's founding in 1859. A hundred huts flanked the Cherry Creek in this mining town, and there was one hotel, with a canvas roof, no floor and two rooms—one of them a large bar. Recovering from injuries suffered when his stagecoach was hit by a buffalo stampede, Greeley got little rest in Denver. He wrote home about "black-legs" who rented "opposite corners of the public room and were steadily swindling greenhorns at three-card monte; one stage driver, who was paid off with $207 at noon, having lost the last cent of it to one of these harpies by 2 P.M. . . . I soon tired of hotel life in Denver." * In 1947, John Gunther found "quite possibly the best hotel in the United States" to be the Brown Palace, an atrium-lobby hotel built in 1892. Between Greeley and Gunther, Denver had grown indeed.

---

* Also in Denver was Henry Villard, then a stringer for the Cincinnati *Commercial,* later publisher of *The Nation,* owner of the New York *Evening Post,* president of the Northern Pacific railway, and occupant of the great Madison Avenue mansion bearing his name today. Villard noted how Greeley had limped to the bar, asking for quiet. "He spoke for nearly an hour, and was listened to with rapt interest and the most perfect respect. He succeeded, too . . . The gambling stopped, and the bar was closed at eleven o'clock as long as he remained."

The first rail line went through in 1867, and there were nine by 1910. The "Queen City of the Plains" grew from 4,500 in 1870 to 133,000 by 1900–then to 213,000 in 1910, as a major farm hub of the West. In 1908, the Democrats held their first western convention here, nominating Bryan for his final campaign. Only San Francisco was bigger out west in those days. But when Gunther arrived four decades later, the mines were long since exhausted, and Denver was in a rut.

> The city is one of the half-dozen richest in the nation; most of its money—as in Boston—is tied up in trust funds, and a great deal is held by women, daughters and granddaughters of the gold and silver kings. Denver has the largest number of bond houses per capita of any American city; its major banks put most of their money into bonds and are extremely chary of loans—which is one reason the city doesn't grow; the attitude is to hold tight, stand pat, discourage new industry (that might compete), and keep expensive labor out.

Gunther also had found "religious crackpotism on a lively scale" and called the *Denver Post* "for many years the most lunatic paper in the United States . . . Its front page looked like a confused and bloody railway accident . . ."

Over the next two decades, there was large-scale development downtown, Denver's airport was expanded and high tech grew in 1956 when Martin Marietta arrived to build the Titan ICBM. The company was soon Colorado's biggest employer, and today there are extensive plants from IBM, Hewlett-Packard, Eastman Kodak and AMAX. The Front Range area around Denver is one of our major centers for high tech.

But the big draw was the mineral wealth of the Rocky Mountain states, bringing cardsharps and Horace Greeley here in 1859. The silver and gold mines had given out long ago, their history now the stuff of musicals and operas. But just two months after Greeley's visit, oil found in Pennsylvania hinted at a second energy boom for Denver, 100 years in the future. By 1980, more than 2,000 energy firms were in the Front Range to develop oil, gas, coal and shale reserves. Majors like Gulf, Standard Oil of California, and Texaco set up Denver bases to exploit the oil and gas in the Overthrust Belt of Utah and Wyoming, or coal from the Four Corners section of New Mexico. Eight thousand energy jobs in Denver in 1977 became 21,000 in 1982, generating 20,000 more jobs in support services like banking, engineering and law. Denver has long been a center for militant farmers, from the National Farmers Union of the 1940s to the American Agriculture Movement, which blocked Capitol Hill with 3,000 tractors in 1978. The spirit of Horace Greeley and free soil lives on.

Denver has many roles today. It is the capital of Rocky Mountain energy as a "Houston West." It has been the capital of Colorado since the Centennial State's founding in 1876. It is a major regional center for federal offices and the jobs they generate. It is both a major farm hub from the nineteenth century and high-tech center for the twenty-first century. As a longtime rail town, it has the two *Fortune* 50 majors of Frontier Airlines and Rio Grande Industries, and its airport is the fourth busiest in the world. It remains an attractive tourist stop just fifteen miles from the Front Range of the Rockies. All these roles combined into a huge boom after 1970:

• During the decade, Denver's jobs grew 5.5 percent a year. As the seven-county metro area grew 31 percent, jobs grew 61 percent. Denver had the third highest growth rate in America for both personal and per capita income in the 1970s. The 1981–83 recession fell lightly here as job growth dropped to "only" 3 percent a year, with unemployment of 4.7 percent in late 1981 comparing to 8.4 percent nationwide.

• The Denver economy went from the coupon clippers found by Gunther in 1947 to risk takers seen by Neal R. Peirce in 1972 to the growing capital markets of today. *Congressional Quarterly* observed in 1980 how the growth of Denver and Phoenix as regional finance centers gave the "Rocky Mountain states a chance to break out of the colonial economic status that has limited its past development . . . [They had] looked east to Minneapolis and Chicago or West to Seattle for venture capital for resource development." Now they looked to Seventeenth Street in Denver, reducing the influence of regional finance rivals like Dallas and Houston, Los Angeles and San Francisco. Noting the former boom-bust cycles of the old mining towns, the head of the Four Corners Regional Commission observed, "The biggest change in the West is that it's developing its own capital centers. It's now developed the beginnings of home-grown capitalism."

• All the jobs and money fueled a phenomenal boom in office space downtown. Even during the 1982 recession, Denver together with Houston and New York had a low 3 percent vacancy rate—and a building boom to meet the huge demand. Houston had 28 million and New York 21 million square feet under construction; Denver had 15 million. Since the other two cities were three and fourteen times bigger than Denver, this was a sensational boom in what Joel Garreau calls "the nesting place of the forty-story crane." Three new towers would each be bigger by half than Denver's largest office building. Commercial space grew 76 percent between 1977 and 1982 and would grow 46 percent more by 1984. Vacancy rates were so low that in 1981 rents jumped from $19.50 to $28 a foot downtown. "Last year, I felt like a commodities broker in a pit," noted a realtor in 1982. "I had people literally screaming in my ear on the phone bidding for space."

Despite the 1981–83 recession, Denver kept building and growing, cashing in on the energy boom, expanding in new-wave industries. Among the latter was Storage Technology, founded in the Denver-area city of Louisville in 1969. It grew from 3,000 workers in 1978 to 8,000 by 1982 as #325 on the *Fortune* 500 list. Denver also has Joseph Coors. His grandfather built the brewing barony, then went broke during Prohibition. His father saved the firm by producing malted milk until Repeal, and today Coors heads our fifth biggest brewery.

Coors is a prime mover in the sagebrush rebellion. He has been founder and chairman of the Mountain States Legal Foundation, which fought grazing quotas, strip-mining reforms and even a utility break for the elderly (unfair to other consumers, went the line). In 1977, Coors picked a young federal bureaucrat named James Watt to run the Denver-based foundation. As Interior Secretary, Watt later hired Coors's friend Robert Burford to head the Bureau of Land Management, which runs the vast federal lands out west. Through mining leases on government lands in Colorado, Montana, Utah and Wyoming, Coors's two Interior protégés can make Denver even more of an energy center. A third Coors disciple is Anne Gorsuch, current wife of Burford and former head of the Environmental Protection Agency, and a former Colorado state representative.

In terms of recent Denver problems, there was the drop of oil prices after 1981. Oilmen could grouse over their turkey wings in red wine at the Brown Palace, but oil prices will rise again. More serious was the glut of office space after the building binge. By the middle of 1982, three downtown projects were on hold, and a new tower of fifty-seven stories was cut by several floors. By the summer of 1983, the office vacancy rate was a staggering 19.3 percent. Finally, there was the flood of high-tech Okies in 1981 and 1982. The last year saw the number of transients grow 40 percent at the Denver Rescue Mission. Often whole families were involved, and few jobs were available. Even roustabouts on oil rigs need special skills, and those jobs shrank as the oil glut deepened after 1981.

The long-term problems for Denver begin with the issue of growth. A 1971 state commission saw a four-county Denver metro area of 1.2 million, and urged a census limit of 1.5 million. The no-growth cause was taken up that year by a young member of the state legislature named Richard Lamm. In an article for the *New Republic*—titled "Is Bigger Also Better?"—Lamm noted recent studies on the link between growth and urban costs as of 1971:

• Once cities got too big, economies of scale no longer applied, but service demands grew. A California study found that where cities under 300,000 spent $14.60 per capita on police, those from 500,000 to 1 million spent $21.88.

• There was the old link of more commuters and more city roads. A city could grow 100 percent, but commuters drawn to it could mean roads growing by 1,200 percent.

• As cities grew, so did their crime rates per 100,000 residents:

| City Population | Assaults | Robberies |
|---|---|---|
| Under 10,000 | 28.9 | 12.8 |
| 100,000–200,000 | 83.3 | 56.5 |
| Over 250,000 | 154.1 | 117.6 |

In 1972, Lamm led a campaign to revoke Denver's selection as the site for the 1976 Winter Olympics. This dubious bit of no-growthism led to a stunning victory. The invitation to host the Games was withdrawn. Lamm was elected governor in 1974.

But no growth was soon overgrown. Denver's metro area of 1.6 million in 1980 breached the outer limit of 1.5 million urged by the state commission of 1971. Apart from the foolish barring of transient athletes and spectators from the XXI Olympiad, Lamm and the no-growthers had failed to stop an influx of permanent hordes, part of a huge regional tide. Among the eight Rocky Mountain states, only Montana failed to double America's growth rate in the 1970s. A Harvard-MIT study suggested that 75 percent of the region's growth was from migration, and the big growth cohorts in Colorado had been under the age of forty. Projections for 1990 suggest more of this, with Colorado expected to double America's growth once more in this decade.*

In 1947, John Gunther saw the state reacting to postwar arrivals, in a split "between old-timers born locally and those who moved in from outside; I felt this more strongly in Colorado than anywhere else in the country, except possibly New England." The xenophobia grew in the 1970s again. Colorado expanded 30 percent as eastern lawyers and bankers, western oilmen, Canadian developers and young job seekers piled in. By 1982, both U.S. senators and four of six U.S. representatives had been born outside Colorado, as had been Governor Lamm. In 1980, he sighed to *Congressional Quarterly:* "I see nothing short of an energy depression that will alleviate our growth rate. Colorado is just a boom state, growing three times the national average. That's highly likely to continue." Most of the growth was suburban; most of the problems were in the shrinking central city of Denver:

• As Denver grew only 2 percent in the 1960s, bedroom counties grew several times over. Jefferson County to the west grew 318 percent, Arapahoe to the south grew 211 percent, Adams to the north expanded 361 percent. By 1970, these three bedroom counties had 580,000 residents—already 70,000 more than the city in the center of the suburban noose. In the 1970s Denver was one of the West's few major cities to lose census. Although the Rocky Mountain states were growing two and even three times faster than America, Denver lost 5 percent of its people. Meanwhile, its four-county metro area expanded 25 percent.

• The only groups growing in Denver were minorities, who went from a 23 percent census share in 1970 to 31 percent by 1980. Nineteen percent of Denver is Hispanic today. In the 1940s, Gunther found more black homeowners in Denver than in any American city. This stability was noted twenty-five years later by Neal R. Peirce, who recalled how Pullman porters and teach-

---

* One minor result was a bumper-sticker war. Old Coloradans had "Native" stickers, later arrivals had "Semi-Native," newcomers sported "Aliens."

ers, waiters and government workers had come to Denver hoping for "a less abrasive environment than the South. Essentially [they are] middle class in their views . . ." He noted how in 1956 the first black elected to any state senate west of the Mississippi had drawn more than 109,000 votes from Denver, which had only 2,500 registered black voters.

This racial harmony was upset by a violent busing battle in 1970. Dynamite destroyed twenty-three school buses, and homes of people on both sides were bombed. This dispute may finally be resolved by a "magnet school" plan.

• Prominent in this crisis was crime. Denver is in the middle ranks for violent crimes like assault, murder and robbery among the big cities, but its overall crime rate is extremely high. With 12,020 crimes per 100,000 residents in 1980, it was within range of Miami, Newark and St. Louis, Since Denver has a far lower share of minorities and poor people, the high rate is striking and ominous.

• There are growing air and water problems in Denver. The thin air of the Mile-High City is very susceptible to auto-exhaust pollution. As more commuters drove into a booming downtown, a federal survey in 1981 found the second worst urban air in America. Data from the Sunbelt's three most polluted cities showed two improving, as Denver declined, in annual number of unhealthy days:

|  | 1975 | 1978 | Change |
|---|---|---|---|
| Los Angeles | 264 | 206 | − 22% |
| Riverside, Cal. | 193 | 146 | − 24% |
| Denver | 157 | 172 | + 10% |

A 25 percent metro growth since 1970 put big strains on water supplies. At the recent rate of water and sewer hookups, the Denver area could open 8,000 new connections a year until roughly 1987. After that, new ways to draw from the Rockies runoff must be found. And there's the dormant synfuel industry with the vast shale reserves of the Piceance Basin nearby. If synfuel is revived by a third OPEC price shock, its huge demands could further crimp Denver's ability to sprawl more, while also impacting on the rich farms of Greeley and Weld County to the north.

Perhaps the 1982 oil glut and recession will slow Colorado growth. But Colorado was still three points under our jobless rate in 1982, and late that fall a *U.S. News & World Report* cover story on the nation's mood observed "only in the Rocky Mountain area did the survey find many voters saying they were living better." The Denver area sprawl and air and water problems should get worse. Without more cops and better services, the 488,000 Denver residents should be quickly reduced.

Denver remains a regional center for agriculture, with farms still a vital part of the Rocky Mountain states. But here as elsewhere in America, a mix of shoddy farming and rampant development is retiring land on a grand scale.

In national terms, America has been losing an average of 3 million acres of cropland a year—roughly the size of Connecticut. In addition, there have been ominous losses of topsoil to erosion. One federal estimate saw America losing 5 billion tons of topsoil a year to water and wind erosion—compared to peeling an inch off the state of Missouri. That state once had from twelve to sixteen inches of topsoil, but was down to five inches by 1981 and losing topsoil at the rate of two and a half inches every ten years. That could mean no topsoil left in Missouri by the year 2000. Land speculators have ignored routine conservation methods like crop rotation, cover crops or windbreaks. Marginal, erosion-prone land is pressed into service: "It's a case of plant now, pay later," notes Tom Wicker in *The New York Times*.

Ronald Reagan cut soil conservation funds 22 percent in 1981, as his agriculture secretary warned of a looming erosion crisis. Reagan proposed useful federal bonuses for states with strong conservation laws, but without strong federal funds, things run down. Experts estimate that $3 billion must be spent each year in public and private funds on soil conservation, but only $1 billion is spent today.

Greeley, Colorado, began as a Fourierite commune on 12,000 acres in 1870. Its namesake and founder found a "bare, bleak prairie," whose soil "could not be cultivated to any purpose without irrigation." But Horace Greeley also saw about 2,000 people and

an irrigating canal which takes water from the Cache . . . and distributes it over one thousand acres, as it will do over several thousands more . . . We are soon to have a newspaper (we already have a bank) and we calculate that our colony will give at least five hundred majority for a Republican President in 1872 . . .*

By 1899, Greeley was the hub of the state's biggest irrigation project. Its irrigation system was copied so widely that Colorado was sued by Kansas in 1902 for drawing too much water from the Arkansas River. This was one of the first state wrangles over western water, just as Greeley's irrigation project was one of the last built without federal aid (and built by socialists). By 1947, John Gunther was observing a major farm state with a major water problem: "Touch water, and you touch everything; without water the state is as sensitive as a carbuncle. . . . Water is blood in Colorado; only California among American states has a greater irrigated area. And I know no state with quite so many water issues . . ."

Thirty-five years later, Colorado, and Greeley, were running out of water and land. As Denver became the energy El Dorado of the Rockies, Colorado projected another million people moving into the East Slope, where 2.6 million live today.

By 1980 Weld County, of which Greeley was the seat, was second only to Fresno County in California for farm wealth. The old socialist colony was also home to one of Colorado's few *Fortune* 500 firms, Montfort of Colorado, a food giant with sales of $816 million in 1981. But the 1970s had cut deeply into Greeley's farm base. The city grew from 39,000 to 53,000 in the decade, as housing tracts, shopping centers and low-slung factories ate up the land. Weld County lost 189,000 acres of cropland in just ten years, almost as many as the 226,000 acres *developed* as farmland between Greeley's founding in 1870 and 1900. These losses occurred despite a plan issued by Weld County in 1973 to regulate growth and protect farmland. Even after this useful edict, Weld lost an average of 18,000 acres of cropland each year through 1978.

*The New York Times* in 1981 saw Greeley annexing a "560-acre site on prime farmland . . . where the Hewlett-Packard Company plans to build an electronic plant." The local ecology was endorsed by the prairie sphinx moth, a rare local species that

---

* The opponent turned out to be Horace Greeley. This amazing switch occurred when Democrats adopted a platform of GOP reformers led by Greeley: equal rights for blacks, civil service reform, an end to Reconstruction.

had disappeared in 1934, and had become a "holy grail" for lepidopterists ever since. Suddenly, the "lost colony" of prairie sphinxes was found in 1981, the reappearance a tribute to Greeley's environmental stability. But the moths and water surplus notwithstanding, the 189,000 acres of cropland lost in Weld County since 1969 was warning enough for our second richest farm county. As a realist from the Soil Conservation Service at the Department of Agriculture told the *Times:* "When you get that much influx, agricultural water is going to be the first to go. It's really kind of frustrating when you look right here in Weld County—some of the best agricultural land in the world they're building houses on and someday there's going to be a food shortage in the world."

## Phoenix

In 1960, Alfred Hitchcock's *Psycho* opened on a flat, sprawling city dominated by one TV tower. That was Phoenix, and when Janet Leigh sighed with ennui in the first reel, a boozy rancher leered, "What you need is a weekend in Las Vegas. . . ." In 1975, the heroine of *Alice Doesn't Live Here Anymore* fled a piano bar and a brutal boy friend in Phoenix for Tucson and a new life. The city had grown by more than 200,000 since Janet Leigh drove off in dismay. Even by 1968, John Barbour of the Associated Press was reporting how

> Phoenix is wrenched with change. In less than 10 years, 500 industrial plants move into town. Manufacturing now outsells the tourist trade 4–1. Now people come to Phoenix for jobs more than for the sun. They have built a city on wheels, built around more than 100 bustling, extravagant shopping centers, a city of near strangers where six out of 10 families moved into new homes in just six years.

The growth was sensational. Thanks to the mass production of air conditioners after 1950, Phoenix exploded from 107,000 residents in 1950 to 781,000 in 1980. This was a 630 percent gain, as our ninety-seventh biggest city became our eleventh in only three decades. A city of 10 square miles in 1940 has become one of 350 square miles today. "If Phoenix has any sacred value, it is growth," wrote Neal R. Peirce in 1972, noting how it "brings to mind the culture and attitudes of a Dallas—economically dynamic, fast-building, dedicated to wealth and free enterprise and right-to-work laws, sometimes tolerant of John Birchism . . .''

Barry Goldwater was on a reform slate for the City Council in 1949 when conservatives drove corruption from City Hall. Goldwater went on to bigger things, but the Charter reformers continued to rule Phoenix, businessmen running the city like their peers in Dallas and San Antonio. The growing and diverse economy evolved in four overlapping stages: copper, cotton, coolers, computers.

• *Copper.* Early settlers looked for gold and silver in Arizona, only to find 95 percent of America's copper reserves. By 1976, Arizona supplied 55 percent of our copper needs and 13 percent of the world's. *Nation's Business* observed how "Arizona, not Canada or Zaire . . . is the world's copper king." But cheap labor and foreign subsidies abroad reduced that share, and the 1982 collapse of world copper prices, the worst slump since the 1940s, forced Phelps Dodge to halt production. Mines were closed for the first time in eighty years, though huge reserves remain.

• *Cotton.* The catalyst here was the first federal water project, dedicated by Theodore Roosevelt in 1911. This irrigates the rich soil of the Salt River Valley: 13,000 square miles of watershed for 250,000 acres of crops in 1976. Cotton was lured from the South to Arizona and California during World War II by richer soil and a three-crop year. Soil often thirty feet deep and more than 4,000 hours of sunshine a year were producing an average of 1,188 pounds of cotton an acre, against a national average of 443 pounds. As early as 1944, Arizona's cotton, cattle, citrus and the like earned $124 million, overtaking mineral production of $112 million.

• *Coolers.* Mass production of air conditioners by Carrier after 1950 was a main spur to Sunbelt growth, like the Gold Rush of 1849, Homestead Act of 1862 or federal water projects after 1911. Cooling was crucial for Phoenix, whose annual precipitation of 7.05 inches makes it our driest big city. As copper capital, cow town and part-time spa, Phoenix had only 40,000 residents in the 1930s. Lawyer Frank L. Snell recalled for *Nation's Business* how "you had to wrap yourself in a wet sheet to get any sleep." Snell got the first custom-built, air-cooled home here in the 1930s. Two decades later, Willis Haviland Carrier's factory in Syracuse, New York, made the first mass-produced air conditioners.

### POPULATION

| | 1950 | Rank | 1980 | Rank | 1950–1980 |
|---|---|---|---|---|---|
| Houston | 596,000 | 14 | 1,554,000 | 5 | 161% |
| Dallas | 434,000 | 21 | 901,000 | 7 | 108 |
| San Diego | 334,000 | 28 | 870,000 | 8 | 161 |
| San Antonio | 408,000 | 24 | 783,000 | 10 | 92 |
| Phoenix | 107,000 | 97 | 781,000 | 11 | 630 |
| San Jose | 95,000 | 109 | 625,000 | 17 | 557 |

Also fueling Phoenix's growth in the 1950s were new industries noted below, and the city's role as a major training center for American and British airmen in World War II. Many British fliers returned to live here. One told *Nation's Business* how fellow cadets killed in training accidents were buried in Phoenix, and how on Decoration Day "the post puts two little flags—one the Stars and Stripes, the other the Union Jack—on every grave." Tourism also grew and by 1976, this was Phoenix's third main earner, with more than 100,000 part-time residents attracted by the dry, hot climate.

• *Computers*. The computer industry began in Chicago in 1946 when the developer of the walkie-talkie told Motorola's founder: "I'd like to build a solid-state research laboratory down in the Southwest." Dr. Dan E. Noble was dispatched to open the one-room shop in Phoenix that grew into two of Motorola's four major divisions, semiconductors and government electronics. With 22,000 jobs at peak production in 1976, this was Phoenix's biggest single employer. Computers led an industrial boom. In the late 1930s, only 2,000 Phoenicians were in factories, producing $8.4 million in annual value added to raw materials. By 1976, some 72,000 in factories produced a valued added of $1.8 billion. Governor Bruce Babbitt's election in 1978 gave an added push to high tech. A moderate who hasn't forgotten his days as a ranking VISTA official in Washington, Babbitt has also helped business, encouraging high tech with state grants and training programs at the University of Arizona. Arizona is now third among the states for high-tech jobs. If new-wave firms need venture capital, Phoenix has the Valley National Bank of Arizona, the largest western bank outside the four Sunbelt finance centers of Dallas, Houston, Los Angeles and San Francisco.

Fund raising led to the Dallas Citizens' Council in 1937, backlash against annexation had launched the Good Government League of San Antonio in 1953, and a drive to end things like gambling, prostitution and graft led to a Charter Government Committee for Phoenix in 1949. The Charterites swept the Council elections, cleaned up City Hall, and began the huge annexations. City borders grew more than 1,400 percent in two decades. By expanding its tax base through mindless sprawl, Phoenix avoided raising property taxes for several decades. Predictably, this lengthy vacation from higher taxes led to hysteria later on over *any* tax hikes in Phoenix.

In 1972, Neal Peirce observed that some academics had found "one of the best examples of nonpartisan and business-dominated government in America." But he added, "The danger of such a government, of course, is that it may be insensitive to needs of the poor and minorities. Milton H. Graham, the mayor for several years during the 1960s, was a definite exception to this rule . . ." Peirce recalled how Graham

> quickly threw aside Phoenix's old bugaboo about accepting federal money and tried to get all the help he could from Washington. Some called him the most liberal mayor in the southern half of the country; this was probably an overstatement, but in 1969 the Phoenix establishment, including Barry Goldwater and the Pulliam papers, decreed Graham's defeat. He barely lost to the new Charter-backed candidate.

The Charterites went back to running Phoenix into the ground. By 1976, they had a hefty electoral batting average of .976 off ninety-three Charter candidates, with ninety-one council or mayoral wins. The current mayor, Margaret T. Hance, was a Charter pick for the Council in 1974. As a former businesswoman, she fit the group's picture. Appearing on *The MacNeil/Lehrer Report* in 1981, Hance defended Reagan urban aid cuts, while insisting that the state legislature in Phoenix was the main enemy of its host city. The reason for this animus, she contended, was a rurally dominated legislature. Twice in the program, a fellow guest, Governor Babbitt, reminded Hance that "one-man, one-vote" long ago gave Phoenix and Tucson, with 80 percent of Arizona's people, 80 percent of the seats in that "rural" legislature. Babbitt also noted that the Reagan cuts in urban aid for 1981 meant cities "*are* going to suffer . . . [as] the federal government abdicates its responsibility."

Hance reflects the rigid conservatism of a rootless city that grew too fast.* This remains Goldwater country, with moderates like former Congressman and House Minority Leader John Rhodes rare in the Valentine State. In commenting on Supreme Court-designate Sandra O'Connor Representative Morris Udall recalled in *The Washington Post* how a Republican friend from Tucson told him that the state party was in two camps: "conservative and very conservative. . . . The very conservative believe nothing should be done for the first time, and the conservatives believe that a few things should be done for the first time, but not now."

Phoenix sneers at federal aid, but without water from the Central Arizona Project, it will soon shrivel up. And as Phoenix grows, so has Washington's share of the city budget, with a 9 percent federal share in 1972 becoming a 25 percent one by 1978. A Princeton study of 1980 suggested that if Washington cut all aid overnight, Phoenix would have to suddenly raise local taxes 66 percent.

As Reagan cuts federal aid, Phoenix is unlikely to cover the losses. In 1977, the City Council tried to raise the sales tax 1 percent, but voters quickly repealed the minor burden. This hurt already meager city services for the middle class and the poor. While Phoenix ranks in the bottom third of the fifty big cities for violent crimes, it's among the highest for overall crime rate: 11,322 crimes per 100,000 residents in 1980, the rate up 20 percent in three years.

The poor of Phoenix live in a "poverty pocket" of forty square miles, cut off from public view by an interstate highway. Andrew

---

* Another conservative force may be the elderly, who grew by 24 percent in America while growing 61 percent in Arizona. A mild offset within the age cohort may be a sharp rise among traditionally liberal Jews. "Never in my wildest dreams did I imagine Phoenix would ever become a major Jewish community," marveled a local rabbi, as 3,500 Jews of 1955 became 35,000 by 1980.

Kopkind described the slum for the *New Republic* in 1965 as "a cross between a Mississippi Black Belt Negro ghetto and a Mexican border town." Seven years later, Neal Peirce found "many unpaved streets, unconnected sewers, and houses with outdoor toilets—conditions which many leading Phoenicians seem to ignore completely and which, of course, might be substantially corrected by passage of a building code." Phoenix voters had rejected a code, so nearly "alone among major U.S. cities, Phoenix has no housing code and as a result is ineligible for federal urban renewal aid." This amazing neglect of simple housing standards was matched by the fact that, until Governor Babbitt led the way in 1982, Arizona was the only state not in the Medicaid program.*

In 1981, John Herbers of *The New York Times* visited the South Phoenix slum to find "old farm shacks, junkyards, sagebrush, vacant lots and some recently built low-income housing, all within sight of the city's gleaming downtown skyscrapers." One hundred twenty-five thousand lived there, or one in six Phoenicians. Adding more land meant spreading city services even more thinly. Although the city was 19 percent minority, Herbers recalled how Mayor Hance told *Fortune* that "the poor are a Federal, not a local, responsibility. If Washington cannot afford these programs, we certainly can't. Local people do not feel that welfare programs should be financed by local taxes."

Another problem of Phoenix annexations involves more commuters, drivers and exhaust fumes. Fumes wed to desert dust particles meant our tenth worst air between 1976 and 1978—in a once famous health spa.† Phoenix had early warnings about pollution. Neal Peirce recalls how, for eleven windless days in 1969,

---

* Even states like Alabama, Mississippi and Texas have had Medicaid coverage for years. Arizona's late entry was under a unique three-year "Arizona Experiment," loaded with cost controls and big gaps in coverage, such as long-term nursing care in a major retirement state. At least this restricted version of the real Medicaid program cuts indigent care costs for Arizona localities from $145 million a year to $75 million, as Washington ($50 million) and the state ($20 million) pick up the rest.

† Federal highway safety data in 1980 found Arizona's cities the deadliest places to drive in America. More than 40 percent of Arizona traffic deaths were on metro streets with California second at 37 percent. Phoenix voters long feared that safer freeways would turn the city into another Los Angeles, but endless annexation did that anyway. Finally, after two decades of debate, a federally funded Papago Freeway will be completed around 1990.

Phoenix's "famous mountain skyline disappeared behind a thick brown pall . . . filling the city and the mountain canyons with smog and even forcing Williams Air Force Base to close its runways." Phoenix kept annexing land. More drivers drove longer distances, stirring up more desert dust wed to more fumes. By 1981, this produced what Robert Lindsey described in *The New York Times* as "a cloud of pollution that smears the crisp, desert sky above Phoenix with a puffy, opaque crown of dirty air reminiscent of a giant chef's cap. On many days, it can be seen more than 40 miles from the city."

As the air thickens and services decline, a taxpayer exodus is on. Exodus from a city that grew 33 percent in the 1970s? Phoenix suburbs grew 48 percent in the decade, which was the fastest suburban growth in America. Since Arizona lacks the liberal annexation laws of Texas, Phoenix may be approaching the end of its amoebic expansions. A symbol of this suburban trend is reflected by 15,000 people of Casa Grande who want an NFL franchise for their desert town, between Phoenix and Tucson. Phoenix may well win the vote of Governor Babbitt's search committee for a possible NFL site. But that tiny, ex-ex-urban Casa Grande is even in the picture is a warning for the poorly serviced capital city. *The New York Times* notes that NFL fever has Casa Grandees "yearning for a pro football stadium the same way other small towns a century ago looked to the coming of the railroad. It would not only bring trade and commerce and tourists: it would also put Casa Grande on the map." Railroad terminals made Atlanta, Dallas and Miami. A domed arena may expand Casa Grande and start up a new Mid Cities strip for the 119 miles between Phoenix and Tucson.*

Even if Phoenix gets the NFL site, the rise of that Mid Cities strip may occur. What characterizes Phoenix are poor services,

---

* A new urban strip would also mean more "light pollution" in once pristine night skies. Tucson astronomers complained in 1982 about a 15 percent rise in "sky glow" and warned that their observatory may become obsolete. Lowell Observatory in Flagstaff, which discovered Pluto in 1930, seems safe in the less-settled north. In California, Palomar has lost 33 percent of its power due to sky glow from the suburbs of Los Angeles and San Diego, and Mount Wilson's view is also in danger. One solution would be to switch from gleaming mercury lamps to softer sodium lights. This is also cheaper for cities. Meanwile, an astronomer told Harold Dall of CBS that "the fight against light pollution is a fight for precious ground. There are only so many sites . . . we can't afford to lose any of them."

growing crime and pollution—a city that grew too fast too soon with too few taxes.

This Phoenix is sinking into the ashes today.

A note on water and growth in Arizona begins in 1912 with a thirty-four-year-old congressman from a brand-new state. Fifty-six years later, Carl Hayden would crown the longest term on Capitol Hill with the biggest victory in his career: the $1.8 billion Central Arizona Project.

When Hayden went to Washington in 1912, Arizona was mainly a mining state, and both Phoenix and Tucson had under 7,000 residents. Pleasant resorts for the elderly and infirm, the two spas were also in verdant areas with rich alluvial soil and lots of sun. But the word "Arizona" means "few springs" in Indian. The state comprises 113,090 square miles, only 329 of them liquid. For crops and cities to grow in this very arid state, imported water was essential. From the 1860s on, early settlers had used a 600-year-old canal built by the Hohokam Indians, Then in 1911, Theodore Roosevelt dedicated the first federal reclamation project at Salt River, whose dams and aqueducts would store and ship water to Phoenix and the rich croplands nearby. In 1947, John Gunther described how this

> project, on which Phoenix rises from the desert that would otherwise be its ashes, is the most spectacular thing of its kind I have ever seen. Pass over in an airplane; the burgeoning green of the irrigated valley overlays the desert as if painted there with shiny lacquer.

Meanwhile, the potential water solution for Arizona was flowing nearby. This was the Colorado River, which defines the border of Arizona and California; its annual flow of 15 million acre-feet make it "the Nile of the West." When the historic river compact of 1922 portioned out the annual Colorado flow among states, several Indian tribes and Mexico, only Arizona refused to sign the compact. Citing a federal "prior appropriation" law on homestead water rights, Arizona demanded full use of all Colorado waters flowing along the border of the dry "land where time stands still." In the 1930s, Arizona actually dispatched its national guard in an attempt to stop the Hoover Dam, fearing that the dam would deflect the Colorado River to California and other alien parts. The foray failed, and the dam opened. Arizona's governor signed the compact in 1944, citing the need for teamwork in a time of war. Arizona got more Colorado River flow, including 18 percent of the Hoover's hydropower. Gunther noted in 1947 that "give Arizona another million acres of irrigated land plus cheap power, and the state can go anywhere."

So it did. With new water supplies, cheap hydropower and air conditioning, Tucson grew five times over between 1950 and 1965, and Phoenix tripled its ranks. This rapid growth put tremendous strains on local water supplies. As Tucson grew more than 500 percent in fifteen years, its well dropped seventy feet. As Phoenix grew more than 300 percent, wells providing a third of its water fell 210 feet. The two cities, and the rich farmland between them, were quickly draining two aquifers dry.

New surface water supplies were required. So the reluctant joiner of 1944 sued for a better share of the Colorado River in 1952. Eleven years later, the Supreme Court ruled in Arizona's favor. A new portioning of the river among three downstream states saw California get 4.4 million acre-feet a year, with far smaller Arizona getting 2.8 million acre-feet. The Court edict encouraged eighty-six-year-old Carl Hayden to revive the Central Arizona Project in the Senate. Five years later, at the age of ninety-one, he saw the $1.8 billion water project approved.* This 400-mile system of dams and aqueducts would ship an annual 1.2 million acre-feet of the Colorado from Lake Havasu, sending it to Phoenix, Tucson and nearby farmlands.

In 1972, Neal Peirce found Arizona aquifers dropping by ten feet a year for an aquifer "overdraft" of 3.5 million acre-feet a year. Peirce noted that this nearly equaled the water used for irrigating "feed grains and animal forage, both crops of low cash value that are easily grown in more moist eastern sections of the U.S." Arizona's water wasting on these crops was summarized by one fact: 90 percent of state water went to farms that were 10 percent of the economy.

This may explain a drastic Arizona law of 1980, hailed by Washington as the toughest aquifer protection law in America. The new law gave first call on water to people and industries, and

---

* Carl Hayden's other notable achievements on Capitol Hill include sponsoring the 19th Amendment guaranteeing women the right to vote, authoring the bill for Grand Canyon National Park, and coauthoring the law leading to the interstate highway system.

least priority to farms, a "condos over cows" ranking. A western state had finally passed a law setting policy for water use, but the law was too harsh on farms. There would be no new irrigation in major areas of census growth. When lands ceased to be irrigated, they ceased forever as farms. New pumping of aquifers was a felony unless it fit state plans. Water duties were imposed on each farm, the money to be used later to buy and retire croplands elsewhere. The water fees were overdue in a region spoiled by cheap federal supplies. Also useful was a ban on development unless durable water sources were at hand. But the sweeping attack on farms was senseless and an ominous signal from the West. The idea of retiring the very rich soil of central Arizona so people could move into Phoenix and Tucson was absurd.

The main way to cut water wasting by farms is through irrigation reform. Lubbock, Texas, with 25 percent of our cotton, saw wells go dry in the 1977 drought and was forced to cut production by 20 percent that year. Lubbock has since led the way in cutting irrigation waste. It helps farmers install dikes and dams to catch irrigation runoff and return it to the soil; it cuts water pressure on sprinklers; it has better irrigation scheduling, through electric sensors buried in fields to measure soil moisture. Lubbock has cut water pumpage by 33 percent since 1975. This buys it twenty or thirty more years of mining water from its local aquifer. Arizona could similarly subsidize farmers to install devices to cut irrigation waste.

The mining of Arizona's aquifers by an overgrown state was so intense in the 1970s that *Life* observed in 1981 that "as strict as Arizona's new law is, even if it is honored up to the letter, the state's underground reservoirs will not be replenished until the year 2225." For now, some Arizonans see shortages before the new aquifer law takes hold around 1985. And even the Central Arizona Project coming on line that year will cover less than half Arizona's annual "overdraft" of aquifer supplies. Tucson's aquifer is nearly twice the size of Lake Mead, but the city's census growth in the 1970s meant the water level in 250 wells dropped two feet a year. John Opie observed in *The Progressive* in 1981 that, even after the CAP water arrives, "the demand on the Colorado will have already exceeded the flow available. Energy costs to pump water from Tucson's deepening wells will become prohibitive. Tucson will run out of water."

This is apocalyptic: at worst, crops will be retired so Tucson can live. But that's the "condos over cows" priority of the 1980 aquifer law, in a rich farm state basic to our own and the Third World's food supply. George Will decries the 1980 aquifer law as a "plan that viewed against the backdrop of American history, is historic and a bit sad." Recalling America's first political argument, pitting Hamilton for industry against Jefferson for farms, Will accurately concludes that "Arizona's answer to the hard questions posed by water is redundant evidence that, although we worship Jefferson, we live like Hamilton."

## Las Vegas

The games that drive Las Vegas are in trouble today. The spread of legal gambling to forty-six states and competition from Atlantic City have hobbled the Vegas action. Thirty percent of Nevada's recent census gains are attributed to what is called "gaming" here, so the economic crisis for Vegas goes beyond the recent recession. Since 1980, its jobless rate has often matched or exceeded America's in what was the second highest metro area for crime in 1980. By late 1982, "recession-proof" Las Vegas had 12.4 percent unemployment. Some big casinos were closed, gaming revenue growth of 20 percent a year was down to 7 percent, and many felt Atlantic City could replace Vegas as our biggest casino city by 1985. State revenues were so depressed that Nevada was last for per capita spending in education. Jobs were so scarce that 16,000 applied for 1,400 positions at the new El Rancho Hotel. The boom-bust cycles of mining in the old Silver State were revisiting its mildly refined descendant.

Nevada and gambling go back to mining-camp days, and the twenty-four hour play with the stress and violence it creates live on in Vegas today. In the past, however, Neal Peirce recalled how "casino gambling has been in and out of the door several times in Nevada. It sprouted naturally in the first mining camps, was illegal from 1864 to 1869, then legalized for 41 years, outlawed in 1910, then made legal again in 1931 . . ." Mormons from neighboring Utah were the main force against gambling. But their numbers were diluted by 1931 and, as John Gunther later wrote, "to clean up gambling in any mining area is like trying to mop up the Mississippi with a dishrag." People were also fed up with the corruption and payoffs that kept the "illegal" sport alive during the long prohibition of 1910–31.

After the final legalization of 1931, gambling went untaxed for fourteen years in a state with no corporation, inheritance, personal income or sales taxes. Nevada bragged about this, but Gunther noted "the inadequacy of the schools and hospitals makes this boast a mockery." Since Washington owned 87 percent of the state's land, property taxes were a weak revenue base for anemic services. The state was barely able to pay its teachers; the secretary of state back then drew the fattest government salary—$3,600 a year. Above all, Gunther recalled how "day by day, armored cars rolled and rollicked out of Las Vegas for Los Angeles, carrying cash away." At last, this colony of southern California rebelled and a 10 percent tax on the gambling gross was proposed in 1944. Later, this was cut to 1 percent on the premise that people didn't want gambling to run Nevada. The vestigial bow to Mormonism made, the tax was imposed.

In the 1930s, the action was in Reno. Back then, Vegas, with 5,000 residents, was a short stop on the Union Pacific. The Reno clubs were like those in mining camps, dark, hot and small. Then came Harolds Club, well lit and ventilated. Peirce charmingly recalls Harolds as exuding the air of a kind uncle, far removed from the grim gaiety of Vegas today, a place to

> encourage gambling by the common man and, even more assiduously, the common woman; warn customers not to gamble more than they can afford to lose; be kind to losers (Harolds Club traditionally lets no one go home broke); foster a family spirit (even with baby-sitting); and advertise, advertise, advertise.

The link of gambling and crime in Las Vegas was forged early on. From the opening of the Flamingo in 1947 by Bugsy Siegel to the purchase of the Stardust in 1960 by Moe Dalitz, the mob and The Strip were often synonymous. Although Frank Sinatra lost his state gambling license in 1963 for having entertained Sam Giancana at the Cal-Neva Lodge, Giancana and Tony Accardo would be identified as among the owners of Caesar's Palace in 1966. Late that year, however, the Mormons made a remarkable re-entry into the Nevada gambling scene.

The agent of change was Howard Hughes. During his reclusive four years at the top of the Desert Inn, he bought nearly $250 million in Nevada properties, starting with the D.I., going on to the Landmark, Sands, Frontier, Castaways and Silver Slipper casinos. By 1970, Peirce recalls, "the Hughes operations in Nevada had some 7,000 employees, with an annual payroll estimated at $50 million. Through his extensive holdings, and the fantastic wealth held in reserve, there was no question that Hughes was the most powerful man in Nevada." Anaconda and Montana, Phelps Dodge and Arizona, the Mormons and Utah, Hughes and Nevada—the West had its fourth company state, with then-Governor Paul Laxalt saying that Hughes "is the greatest thing that has happened to Nevada since the Comstock Lode."

Hughes quickly bought the mob off The Strip. His Mormon advisers cleaned up what their forefathers couldn't close down. The purge of the hoods was welcome, although Peirce recalls the ironic drawback of the Mormons trying to sell Vegas as a "family resort." After Hughes slipped away to the Bahamas in 1970, casino owners "got together and agreed to go back to a hard-sell portrayal of Vegas as an uninhibited action town." Hughes was soon replaced as the main property owner by the Teamsters. In 1981, Teamster president Roy Williams was indicted for allegedly trying to bribe U.S. Senator Howard Cannon with an option on union land in Vegas. Two weeks later, Williams got his salary raised from $156,250 to $225,000, then informed the annual union convention in Vegas that "a strong labor movement is the only way to fairly distribute wealth." (Williams was convicted of attempted bribery in 1983, and stripped of his office.)

Gambling is doing a slow fade in Vegas today. The reasons run from the recent hotel fires to high fuel costs inhibiting West Coast players. But the main cause is the Vegasization of America. In broad cultural terms, Vegas is no longer the unique Sodom. Ten years ago, this city had no peer for gambling, nude shows, prostitution at the Mink Ranch. Times Square and Club Med have since cut into Vegas for middle-class fantasy life today.

In economic terms, Vegasization is the rapid growth of state-run gambling elsewhere. Bingo, dogs, horses, jai alai, lotteries, numbers, even legal football betting in Delaware, Montana, Nevada and Washington have become prevalent in America. Thirty-two states with legal betting in 1976 became forty-six by 1983, the holdouts being Hawaii, Indiana, Mississippi and Utah. As legalized gambling grew in more populous states like Michigan and New York, Nevada fell to fifth place among states paying gaming taxes to the IRS.

Many criticized the new state games for raising little revenue, while diverting people from the need for equitable tax reforms and better revenues. Defenders could point to Thomas Jefferson, endorsing lotteries for the thirteen original states as a "salutary instrument wherein the tax is laid on the willing only." But this voluntary taxation is a costly way to raise revenues. States were spending 60 cents in prizes and overhead to collect one lottery dollar and only 5 cents to collect each tax dollar, yet lottery revenues grew twice as fast as Vegas revenues in 1982.

Atlantic City had lost half its hotel rooms and a third of its residents since its glory days as "The Garden City" of the 1920s. In 1976, Atlantic City gave a desperate throw of the dice and voted for casinos. The result was a quick rise in land values, the eviction of a lot of elderly and poor people, and the third highest metro crime rate in 1980.

Within five hours' drive of 25 percent of America's population, Atlantic City is a major drain on East Coast junkets to Nevada. There are nine casinos on the boardwalk, and 1981 saw a binge of promotions to lure some 250,000 high rollers from the Vegas credit list.*

Other cities have examined casino gambling as well. We shall later see how Detroit made a fleeting pass in 1981, and Florida only rejected a 1978 referendum when Governor Reubin Askew led the attack on a new source of violence for Miami. New York City also survived a casino threat in 1980, after some cautious promoting by Mayor Koch and financier Felix Rohatyn. Even usually sober Massachusetts got the bet bug. Having wrecked revenues with the 2.5 percent tax cap of 1980, the Commonwealth had to cover $250 million in lost property taxes. So casino gambling raised its ugly head, promising $50 million a year in new state revenues. Owners of the MGM Grand Hotel in Las Vegas, where eighty-four died in a 1980 fire, negotiated to build a casino near Boston in 1981. There was also talk of a gaming house in Adams, a dying mill town in the Berkshires.

The fire at the MGM Grand Hotel had killed 84 and injured 700

---

* The Sands instituted Monday-Night Football parties. The Tropicana flew in Hong Kong topliner Roman Tam to headline a party for 7,200 Chinese plungers. The Sands threw a "World Championship of Casino Games" where entrants bought $2,000 in chips to play for a $90,000 purse. The Hi-Ho had the wildest casino promotion of all, "Whirlwind of Money," as described by The Wall Street Journal: "The winner of this drawing will be locked in a glass cage with $2,500 to $5,000 stashed in the bottom. Suddenly a fan will start blowing and he will have one minute to catch as many of the bucks flying about as possible."

more. Eight months later, the hotel reopened as "one of the safest buildings in the world," with a new stage show that included simulated aerial dogfights and the voyage of the *Titanic*. *The New York Times* noted that by usual Vegas standards this was "subdued." Another hotel fire killed eight people. Weak fire codes and missing sprinkler systems were cited. Today, Nevada has one of America's toughest fire codes. But the two fire tragedies and a fire code decades behind those in most big cities pointed to a city living too fast and too cheap. For stress, Nevada had both the highest alcoholism and suicide rates in America for the mid-1970s. Infant mortality, child abuse and life expectancy also fared poorly here. Among cities of more than 150,000, Las Vegas in 1981 was #9 for assault, #6 for robbery, #3 for murder and #2 for rape, and had the second highest crime rate for all metro areas in 1980.

The only superlative is that Nevada is #2 for millionaires among the states. With 76.1 millionaires per million people, the old duchy of Howard Hughes is second only to the pocket borough of the Du Ponts in Delaware with its rate of 94.0.* The other end of the Vegas income spectrum sees a 15 percent black share of census, many of them in a west-side slum. Even in the better times of 1972, Neal Peirce found 20 percent unemployment among black males, a high rate even today. The west side had also been the scene of three days of burning and looting in 1969, which left two killed and a badly damaged community.

This company town may have to hold a "World Series of Card Counters" in its fight to survive.

---

* Third place went to Washington, D.C., with 65.4 millionaires per million. Another Nevada-D.C. link is a high share of people in service jobs: Nevada with 42 percent of all jobs, D.C. in second place with 29 percent. A third link is a very high infant mortality rate. Washington's is so high that it is double the national rate—higher even than Third World nations like Costa Rica, Cuba and Jamaica. The nation's capital has too many out-of-wedlock babies from too many teen-age mothers, leading inevitably to too many low-weight babies and the extremely high mortality rate.

CHAPTER 6 |

# CALIFORNIA CITIES

## Crime and Taxes

> When I am in California, I am not in the West, I am west of the
> West.
> —Theodore Roosevelt

• *Crime*. This has been a staple in California since the mining
camps of the forty-niners, and it is growing sharply in big cities
today.

By the 1940s, various California cults had produced what John
Gunther termed a "theology *in extremis*." In Southern California
they are the "ultimate segregation of the unfit," as Bertrand
Russell said. These cults tended to get buried like time capsules
as the postwar industrial boom of California produced the good
life. At the same time, however, huge migrations after 1940—
California grew from 6.9 million to 23.5 million in four decades
—heightened rootlessness in a state prone to mobility, mass
media and mass politics. All that was needed was one long economic slump to revive the old cults and their "leaders."

At first, the madness was limited to drug covens like the Manson "family" or to lone psychotics like Juan V. Corona, the
Hillside Strangler or the Zodiac Killer. As the California economy went into a slow nose dive after 1978, however, violence
grew in cities among the hopeless and jobless poor. Its most
extreme and tragic expression was with the mass suicide of more

than 900 California cultists, victims of the People's Temple in the jungle of Guyana. It's an ongoing symbol for the virulent culture of survivalism.

The rationale for survivalism is a complex brew, concocted of every fear from earthquakes to OPEC boycotts, volcanoes to rioting blacks, Weimar-scale inflation to The Bomb. At a benign level, survivalism in 1981 meant one million tear-gas grenade carriers in California, as the fear curve rose sharply in what one entrepreneur called "a growth industry that you can't comprehend." Los Angeles firms paid tuition for tear-gas classes as fringe benefits, *The New York Times* observing how it was common for "church and social clubs to plan meetings around a program of tear-gas instruction."

A 1980 *Times* survey of California groups found a "Christian preparedness" group called the Legion of Zion Army; a sect of Sikhs known as the Healthy Happy Holy Organization, teaching armed self-defense; a monastic band of organic gardeners called The Brotherhood of the Sun whose arsenal featured semiautomatic weapons; and some Hare Krishna acolytes with a submachine gun for "protection of the deity," despite Lord Krishna's strictures on violence.

The secular side of this madness includes things like Survival Inc., a Southern California mail-order house hawking storage food, survival books, and sundry gear from radiation suits to an $8,000 pair of night-vision glasses. A magazine titled *Soldier of Fortune* from Colorado is read by 210,000 each month, and it gives advice on such things as blowing up a railroad or a recipe for prussic acid. A survey of the magazine's readers found 33 percent had managerial, professional or technical positions, 63 percent had handguns, and 87 percent kept back issues, "much like the *National Geographic*," suggested the managing editor to *The Wall Street Journal*. There is also a magazine titled *Victoriana* for female survivalists.

Or there's that Sunbelt sine qua non, a survivalist condo. One 240-unit job, built underground in the desert outside La Verkin, Utah, was romantically titled Terrene Ark I. At its start, the threat of MX missile bases in Utah made this a timely buy, its developer telling *The New York Times* of a long waiting list in 1981: "Almost all are professional people or own their own business. Half believe there will be a nuclear war and half believe there will be economic collapse followed by complete chaos, riots, that kind of thing." For $39,000, a buyer at Terrene Ark I gets a twelve-by-thirty-foot cell with blastproof doors, eight inches of reinforced concrete overhead, and four years of food in the walls. The developer suggested that people might dynamite mountain passes or interstates, since "the authorities will try to take our weapons away. We won't let them." An Oregon firm is building twenty hideaways across America, selling at $100,000 to $800,000 per lair.

The toll on families is sad. Unlike the mass doomsday movements of the past, survivalists are often isolated family units. Peter Arnett of the Associated Press wrote about the Richard Johnson family in Oregon, and their "Camp One," a mountain fortress reached by a three-hour climb over ridges and streams. "Nobody could find this place, not tracking dogs, not the National Guard, not fighter-bombers," observed Mr. Johnson. Camp One had 1,000 pounds of canned food and C rations, the Johnsons backpacking all of it to their retreat. In winter, they squirreled away a weapons cache. Along with several other families, they also stored explosives for tunneling into the mountain. To while away idle hours before It or They or Whatever drove them to the hills, Johnson told Arnett the families liked to "practice tactics, laying booby traps and ambushing each other along the trails. We'd put the M-80 machine guns over there. As far as our family is concerned, we've invested more in Camp One than in our regular home, and we figure it's worth it." *

However, there are some very useful anticrime groups in California. The most famous is Mothers Against Drunk Drivers, started by housewife Candy Lightner in 1979, after her daughter was killed by an intoxicated driver. Within two years, MADD inspired a state law with teeth, including license suspensions and mandatory sentences. California traffic deaths over the Christmas holidays fell from 64 in 1980 to 31 in 1981. Within a year of MADD's law in California, a dozen states had passed similar laws, and later on, President Reagan appointed a Commission on Drunk Driving headed by former Transportation Secretary John Volpe. Since drunk driving leads to about half of 50,000 annual auto deaths, the laws and educational campaigns may greatly

---

* The survivalist's mountain or desert lair recalls the question raised by French ambassador André François-Poncet, following a trip to the Eagle's Nest at Berchtesgaden in 1938: "Was this edifice the work of a normal mind or of one tormented by megalomania and haunted by visions of domination and solitude?"

reduce the casualties. Mrs. Lightner and her MADD women had launched a useful national movement in only three years.

Another useful California anticrime group faces a long struggle in a state where 325,041 new handguns were registered in 1980 alone. Led by Victor Palmieri, former ambassador for refugee affairs for Jimmy Carter, this group would (a) register all 4 million handguns in California, then (b) freeze the purchase of unregistered handguns six months later. The first idea is sound, the second so extreme that even America's leading gun-control activist, Pete Shields, flew out from Washington to urge only the first, milder course. The moderate proposal for gun registration went on the 1982 ballot as Proposition 15, but despite heavy editorial backing, 15 was defeated 63-37 on November 8.

Rather than fund police or right the social causes of crime in slums, many Californians rely on private arsenals of guns, teargas grenades or attack dogs—or on harsh new laws. One example is Proposition 8, put on the ballot in 1982 by Paul Gann of Proposition 13 fame. Proposition 8 proposed to end most felony plea bargaining, back preventive detention by judges, and allow the use of illegally gathered evidence. The ACLU attacked it as "garbage," as did the Bar Associations of Los Angeles and San Francisco. The voters passed it in June, though it may be repealed later in court.

Seventy-one-year-old retired Army colonel Earl Huntting is the leader of one of California's most vocal anticrime groups, the 6,500-member Citizens for Law and Order of Oakland. Huntting formed the group after hearing a speech by then-DA Lowell Jensen, now the assistant attorney general at the criminal division of the Department of Justice. Another Huntting adviser has been Herbert Ellingwood, now deputy counsel to Ronald Reagan.

Despite his clout, Earl Huntting seems not to support his local police. As we shall see, he led Oakland voters against a 1981 tax hike that would have put more cops in a city that was #4 for rape, #5 for robbery and #9 for murder in 1980 among cities of more than 300,000.

In fairness, Earl Huntting led one useful crime crusade in 1981. Having undermined law and order by killing the Oakland police tax, he went north to Sacramento to lobby against Jerry Brown's plan for a $5 billion anticrime program, much of it focused on prison construction. As Tom Wicker has observed, opening new jails today virtually invites new ways to fill them. Harsher laws, less parole and fewer work-release programs are encouraged by opening new cells that are "unproductive" unless filled. Over-building urban freeways after 1945 led to more traffic and pollution and less mass transit; new jails should lead to even more inmates than the record 412,000 in cells in 1983.*

• *Taxes.* The tax revolt since 1978 has led to growing, and predictable, fiscal chaos. First, the Proposition 13 vote of 1978 cut 60 percent of all local property taxes, then Jerry Brown and the legislature added to the fiscal fire by cutting 14 percent of the state revenue base in 1979 through things like the indexing of income taxes. Then the deep recession of 1981–83 cut even more revenues.

Brown and the legislature made huge cuts in 1981 to cover a $1.6 billion budget gap. But later that year, recession plus the weak tax base produced a new deficit of $460 million—and a new 2 percent state service cut by Brown. Six months later, in early 1982, people saw a $1.4 billion shortfall for the coming fiscal year, and again recession and the ravaged tax base had created the huge new gap. One month later, the gap had expanded to $3 billion.

A Field Poll in late 1980 found 78 percent of those polled still felt taxes were too high—which was more than the 70 percent who thought so before the tax cuts. The poll also showed taxpayers inclined to spare education any cuts, but to swing the ax against services like fire and police. Welfare cuts in the poll were predictably the most popular. By the spring of 1982, everyone knew of the huge budget gaps produced by the tax cuts and the recession, yet the June ballot saw one more tax-cap referendum, which would repeal all inheritance taxes. Although California was facing a $3 billion budget gap for fiscal 1982–83, the estate tax was repealed, adding a new annual revenue loss of $600 million. This led to wholesale cuts by the state and the localities that deepened the downward spiral in the older cities.

In the three years before Proposition 13, the California economy had grown spectacularly. In those days, this was a "full-service state," with services helped by a tax rate 27 percent

---

* California is considering a plan for prefab jails. The first modular example could be a nine-story county jail for San Jose, put up in less than a month. This could launch a new era of prefab prisons.

higher than America's. Then came the supply-side cuts of 1978 and 1979. As writer Harold Mayerson has noted, the state tax rate was now only 1 percent above America's, services were cut to cover the revenue losses, and jobs declined sharply:

| Fiscal Year | New Private-Sector Jobs |
|---|---|
| 1977–78 | 587,000 |
| 1978–79 | 490,100 (83% of 1977–78 jobs) |
| 1979–80 | 202,100 (34% of 1977–78 jobs) |
| 1980–81 | 204,500 (35% of 1977–78 jobs) |

All the tax cuts meant more social and economic instability. They damaged the state education aid needed to produce or retrain a skilled work force for a high-tech era. California had been the fifth highest per capita state spender for education in 1978. After the tax cuts, California plunged to forty-fourth place. This threatened the high-tech sector that California has projected for 42 percent of its new jobs in the 1980s.

An example of this threat was seen at San Jose State's School of Engineering, a major technical backup, along with Stanford, for nearby Silicon Valley. Due to state education cuts the San Jose State faculty was being paid $5,000 to $7,000 less in 1982 than counterparts in other states. The dean of engineering told *The Wall Street Journal* how "one third of our 100 engineering faculty positions go unfilled, and we're forced to turn away half the qualified students applying for admission." Firms in the Valley were short of engineers, which was one reason why the area's biggest employer, Lockheed Missiles & Space Company, with 6,000 potential jobs, moved a military communications complex to Austin, Texas.

The roots of the tax revolt lay in the rootlessness of California itself. Midwest migrants in the 1920s and Okies in the Depression helped fuel "crackpot cults" on the social side and "funny money" crusades on the economic front. The latter began with Upton Sinclair's variation on Henry George in the EPIC campaign of 1934, *Time* noting that "no politician since William Jennings Bryan has so horrified and outraged the Vested Interests." Then came the Townsend plan of $200 a month for jobless senior citizens, to be funded by a national sales tax (which was similar to the value-added tax used in Europe today, and briefly examined by President Nixon in 1971).

The Townsend plan was followed by the Ham & Eggs movement, which proposed $30 every Thursday for the jobless elderly —on a ballot initiative that nearly passed with 1.1 million votes in 1938. This close vote led in 1939 to the wildest California ballot initiative ever, a 12,000-word constitutional amendment that, Gunther recalled, would have "transformed California into a Ham & Eggs dictatorship." Gunther quotes Walter Lippmann, warning that the issue "was not whether retired citizens over fifty should be given $30 of doubtful money every Thursday; it was whether the people could be bamboozled into surrendering sovereignty of the state."

After the Depression came the "Second New Deal" and the later prosperity of war. California's arsenal of democracy saw Lockheed produce 20,000 planes and Henry Kaiser train 300,000 welders to build 20 percent of our merchant fleet in his Richmond shipyards. After the war, aerospace drove a booming state. It grew 228 percent as California's economy grew 81 percent. Huge federal contracts poured into the state. At one point, 24 percent of all prime defense contracts and 40 percent of all R&D contracts went to California. Add to aerospace the farm, entertainment and oil legs of the state economy, and California in the 1960s had a net gain of 2.1 million migrants, or 69 percent of all net migration in America.

Then aerospace experienced a slump as 616,000 jobs in 1967 shrank to 450,000 by 1972. The Apollo moon program was winding down, the arms race was declining, and Lockheed begged Congress for a $250 million loan guarantee to finish TriStar in 1971. Thirty percent of all California jobs were related to military or space programs. In 1971, California with 7.2 percent unemployment compared with 5.5 percent nationwide. The state slump wore on through 1975, the deep recession then seeing America at 8.3 percent joblessness—California now up to 10 percent. The state that had grown by 26 percent in the 1960s had grown only 6 percent by 1975.

Even in the trough of 1974, California generated $125 billion in personal income, 11 percent of America's wealth. *U.S. News & World Report* observed that if California "were a nation, its gross national product would rank among the world's top 10." Then California had a new and unprecedented job boom. From August of 1976 through August of 1979, California added 1,484,200 new jobs, an amazing growth of 18.2 percent for a state adding 8 percent more people. By 1981, California's output of wealth was higher than the continent of Africa.

Yet 65 percent of the state wanted relief from taxation as they voted for Proposition 13 on June 6, 1978. The symbiosis of a booming economy and a tax revolt was odd, even for California. Among the causes was an early dose of Ronald Reagan, an odd pinch of Jerry Brown, too many ballot initiatives and too few settled people. The infusion of wild property tax hikes brought the mess to a boil in 1978.

An early example of what lay ahead was Governor Reagan's cap on Medicaid spending in 1971. This threw the working poor off health insurance and onto the mercies of strapped localities. The fiscal shock wave was later described in *The New York Times* by California health analysts Philip R. Lee and Barry Ensminger:

> Suddenly, counties were faced with many sick patients ineligible for state payments. State costs were reduced but local health expenditures soared. Counties began painful retrenchment: more than 20 public hospitals closed, basic clinical services were curtailed. . . . A 1978 state health department report concluded: "Medicaid recipients, medical indigents, and the working poor have often been left with no place at all to go for medical or hospital care."

Four months after Jerry Brown took office, *Time* quoted a former Reagan state Cabinet officer, claiming his old boss "thinks Jerry Brown has gone too far to the right *[sic]*." Indeed, Brown's budget raised spending only 4.6 percent, against a 12.2 percent average in the Reagan years. Robert Kuttner observed in *Revolt of the Haves* how candidate Brown in 1974 had pledged to end a business tax if elected, even though "Reagan, as a conservative, had traded business inventory relief for other taxes. Brown, the Democrat, was prepared to give away $450 million in business tax relief and get nothing in return, at a time when homeowners were crying for property tax relief."

Homeowners were suffering huge tax hikes raised by a state tax escalator tied to rising property values in a hot housing market. Between 1974 and 1978, Los Angeles homes went from an average value of $37,800 to one of $84,200—a 120 percent growth in value against 48 percent nationwide. Orange County prices soared to an average of $107,000 by 1977, with lotteries often held in new subdivisions to award the "privilege" of buying in. California housing values doubled, even tripled, in just four years, pushing up the automatic tax escalator.

The result was a dramatic tax shift. Kuttner recalls that California homeowners had paid a steady 32 percent of all state property taxes for years, then the hot housing market yoked to the tax escalator saw them pay 45 percent of all taxes by 1978, the year of Proposition 13. Months before the 13 vote, Brown and the legislature could have modified the fateful tax escalator and put out the fire.

The 13 vote was a famous initiative in California. In 1971, Neal Peirce noted how voter initiatives, instead of aiding the grass roots, "may now be a device for special interests, interests wealthy enough first to buy their way into an election and then to seduce voters with come-on advertising." This was very much the case with Proposition 13. Kuttner points out that landlords and corporate property owners got most of the tax relief, and the homeowners who made the crusade got only minor cuts. Big winners included Pacific Telephone and Telegraph, saving $130 million a year; Pacific Gas & Electric, saving $91 million; and Southern California Edison, saving $54 million. Edison vice president Howard Allen organized a coalition against Proposition 13 in early 1978. Allen felt the huge tax cut would be "fiscally irresponsible and potentially catastrophic for the state's economy." He met in Los Angeles with business leaders like A. W. Clausen, head of the Bank of America and later head of the World Bank. Then Allen held a press conference to warn voters that "although business stands to receive at least $4 billion of the anticipated $6 billion in property tax relief, we felt it was time for the private sector, among others, to stand up for principle and fight this measure as unsound."

This dramatic and wise move by the chief beneficiaries of the tax "revolt" might have killed 13. As Kuttner concluded: "It is no small irony that the initiative, brought to California by the great trust-busting Gov. Hiram Johnson, became the indispensable tool of a campaign to produce a massive tax windfall for business."

Proposition 13 cut $7 billion in annual property taxes for cities and counties. About 66 percent of the relief went to corporate property owners, or landlords represented by that famed "populist" leader of the 13 revolt, Howard Jarvis. California helped the localities by covering some of the local tax losses from a huge state revenue surplus in 1979 and 1980. But localities already began cutting services as the legislature and Jerry Brown went off on a new tax-cut spree, indexing state income taxes after 1979. This fought off "bracket creep" two years before Ronald Reagan discovered the disease in 1981. It also cut $2.5 billion in annual state revenues. This and other tax cuts saw $4.3 billion carved from 1982 revenues, or 14 percent of state collections.

Something had to give. Someone had to pay. January 9, 1981, found Brown telling the legislature that "the moment of truth is upon us." Rather than pass new taxes to cover the deficit they had created, Brown and the legislators proposed service cuts. Some even suggested freezing grants for welfare clients, the blind and handicapped. The poor were spared, though the legislature had to double Brown's niggardly raise of 4.8 percent in a welfare grant normally indexed to inflation.

At the same time, however, Brown also proposed a sales tax to raise $5 billion over ten years to fight crime. But rather than use the funds for preventive weapons like cops, judges and job programs, he aimed the tax mainly at building more state prisons and county jails. Meanwhile, the legislature was rejecting a sales tax aimed at helping cities hire more police and firemen. Arguing for his bill, Senator Daniel Boatwright noted that since 1975, state census grew 9 percent as crimes against people zoomed 38 percent and police forces inched up 2 percent.

In the end, huge and unprecedented cuts were proposed. The Assembly proposed to cut 18-, 19- and 20-year-olds off welfare, slash state aid to localities by $250 million, and restrict eligibility for in-home services for the aged, blind and disabled. The Senate proposed to cut $350 million from the localities, while shifting new alcoholism, drug and mental health costs on them as well. Twenty health-care clinics faced closing in Los Angeles. Although illegal aliens from Latin America and Asia had boosted TB by 30 percent in Los Angeles County in only one year, money needed to buy drugs for that very contagious disease was cut from Watts and East Los Angeles. Child immunization funds were cut by 33 percent statewide.

San Francisco had offset early Proposition 13 losses by doubling its bus fare, landing $2 million in corporate gifts to save its cable cars, and starting an "adopt an animal" fund for its zoo. But the 1981 state cuts meant losing 1,000 of 24,000 city workers, and Reagan CETA cuts would lay off another 1,400 public and private workers. Los Angeles faced losing $50 million in state aid and up to 5,000 CETA jobs. There were relatively harmless cuts like a few less library hours and streets that went unswept. But Mayor Bradley also threatened to cut half the city's recreation programs and close twenty-four recreation centers. Almost 200 murders in 1980 were related to teen-age gangs in L.A., so these cuts were virtual recruiting posters for some 350 gangs. On top of this, the County Board of Supervisors proposed to close the twenty health clinics in Los Angeles.

In the fall of 1981 California landed in the fiscal soup again. Recession combined with a weak revenue base for new budget gaps. California borrowed $1 billion to maintain cash flow, and Jerry Brown made a quick slash of $460 million, cutting all state services across the board by 2 percent. Up ahead, the state treasury would be losing $230 million more under Reagan cuts in federal aid that Brown had done nothing to avert.

Six months later, the California fiscal crisis erupted again. A $1.4 billion deficit was forecast for the new fiscal year of 1982–83. *The New York Times* reported that "public officials say that California has not faced such financial problems since the 1930s. . . . According to some estimates, state and local government *might have had more than $14 million more* [emphasis added] to spend if the tax cuts had not been passed." A month later, the budget gap doubled again. A $3 billion deficit was forecast for the next fiscal year, as recession depressed tax collections. California's fiscal fiasco was exceeded only by federal follies as Reaganomic tax cuts in 1981 induced the huge Washington deficits that intensified the recession in 1982.

Two and a half billion dollars in new cuts were made for fiscal 1983. Some of this was through painless but nonrecurrent taxes and wage-hike deferrals for state workers. But $1.2 billion in new service cuts occurred, with state spending down from the previous year, for the first time since wartime austerity in 1943. By the fall of 1982, a new round of deficits was projected. California was now spending $2.5 million a day more than its starved tax base took in, and some saw from $600 million to $1.2 billion in new shortfalls by July 1, 1983. A few months later, in early 1983, Standard & Poor lowered the state's bond rating from AAA to AA.

The lesson of this interminable, self-inflicted fiscal crisis is simple: taxes can only be cut in moderation, not by 14 percent in one year. Anything other than that wrecks services in the short term, while plunging states into needless fiscal chaos and more service cuts once a recession occurs. None of this benefits the poor, elderly, or middle class, nor does it create jobs.

Jobs grew by 587,000 the year before Proposition 13, then dropped to an average of 299,000 for the three years after the 13 vote. In 1981, Jerry Brown's director of economic policy told *The Wall Street Journal* that a sharp drop in state education funds since 1978 meant "education has become our most serious long-term economic development problem. Without educated workers, we won't be able to attract high-technology business." Early in 1982, Jerry Brown warned that Silicon Valley could be the depressed "Detroit of the next generation." In 1982, California electronics firms employed 25 percent of all factory workers and the state had 40 percent of America's electrical engineers and computer professionals. But the education cuts threatened the future work force, and Arizona, Idaho, Oregon and Texas had lured away California high-tech firms.

As new-wave companies left California, aging state factories from the 1940s were closing elsewhere. From 1980 through mid-1982, 979 California factories closed permanently, for a loss of 105,000 jobs. While the UAW worked with Ford and GM in a new program to retrain 11,000 workers from three plants closed in 1982, a state official noted that "this kind of problem happens in Detroit or Pittsburgh, not California; we open plants, not close them, and we now have to deal with the reality that things have changed." The old plants included a Firestone factory with 1,700 workers in John Steinbeck's Salinas, an old Kaiser steel mill, and a Mack truck plant with 3,000 workers. Suddenly, California had 7.2 percent unemployment against 6.8 percent in New York and 6.6 percent in New Jersey.

Where 48 percent of state factory workers were unionized in 1956, only 23 percent were by 1981. This would soon be an either/or industrial state: either high-tech firms with a work force crippled by state education cuts, or sweatshops for unskilled labor. The stable middle ground of union shops and heavy industry was eroding fast. A Bank of America projection saw 330,000 new state jobs in 1982, but only 50,000 would be in manufacturing, mainly in high tech.*

One footnote involves the growing role of Japan in the California economy, the two giants being linked in a growing Pacific Basin market. The Japanese cars that cause 14 percent unemployment in Michigan create thousands of jobs on busy California docks, then thousands more in final assembly and detail work nearby. After seeing twice as many Japanese cars on the Coast than he did in the East, Joel Garreau concluded that "one of the reasons North American auto-makers were slow in meeting the Japanese challenge is that they didn't live on the West Coast . . . You look out your Detroit window, and you still see people driving Chevys. Here, you don't."

Japanese electronic giants are buying into Silicon Valley. Fujitsu has a disk memory plant in Santa Clara, and owns a third of Amdahl computers. Toshiba bought up Maruman Semiconductors in 1979, and Toyo helped found Exam Systems in Sunnyvale back in 1971. But the leader here, as in Japan, is Nippon Electric Company. NEC is building a $100 million highly automated chip factory in the Sacramento suburb of Roseville. By 1985, this may be one of the biggest such plants on earth, producing perhaps $200 million in chips a year.†

The big minus from Japan is a huge imbalance of trade. Garreau notes Pacific Basin states had a $3.6 billion deficit with Japan in 1978—twice their 1976 trade deficit. While 835 Japanese firms had opened American headquarters in California by 1981, most of the Basin trade went Japan's way. Coastal resources like fish, food and timber were often processed in Japan, making our states a "colony" of sorts. Garreau quotes a Japanese banker in

---

* Even worse was a study from Security Pacific National Bank. This saw only 518,000 jobs added to the California economy for five years through 1983. Jobs would grow only 4.9 percent, as the work force grew 9.3 percent. This meant just one job for every two new workers. This reversed the earlier boom between 1976 and 1979, where the state census grew 8 percent, as jobs grew 18.2 percent, which meant two jobs for every new resident.

† Other high-tech plants opening in the Roseville area, 150 miles north of San Jose, come from firms squeezed for space in Silicon Valley. This cheaper, inland area may become Silicon Valley II. San Jose's alarming sprawl should be warning enough: it went from 95,000 people in 1950 to 626,000 today. "You'd think we could learn from San Jose," noted a Hewlett-Packard official, as his firm planned a new Roseville site.

San Francisco: "We see California already as part of Japan. Oh, yes. California Prefecture." *

## San Francisco

At first glance, San Francisco is a paragon. "Everybody's favorite city" employs some 90,000 in its main industry of tourism. Hills, bridges, fogs and vistas. Ethnic diversity, tolerant ambiance, and a human scale, despite the "Manhattanized" skyline downtown. These make San Francisco second only to New York for tourist visits. There are few factory jobs on the confined and hilly peninsula, but many service openings for unskilled minorities who comprise 47 percent of the city. The city seems nearly recession-proof: 5.4 percent unemployment in 1980 compared well with 8.3 percent in New York and 7.3 percent in Los Angeles.

But like N.Y.C. and L.A., even "The Paris of America" is slowly turning into the polarized residence of the very rich and very poor. Most of San Francisco is black, Hispanic or Oriental, and housing is scarce as single-person households grow. The poor can't leave, but the middle class can: 470,000 whites in 1970 shrank to some 360,000 by 1980. While Los Angeles, San Diego and San Jose grew in the 1970s, San Francisco lost 6 percent of its people. Even its suburbs grew sluggishly. The 8 percent expansion was second only to Los Angeles' 6 percent as the worst growth among big Sunbelt cities in the 1970s.

In 1980 the city lost 8 percent of its tourist trade. Some cited a stronger dollar scaring off foreign visitors, but the same year New York gained 17 percent more tourists. San Francisco took even more tourism losses in the 1981 recession. The only good news was a slight rise in police hires and slower growth in crime than most cities, although crime remained at a very high level.

Violence is an old story here. As 1,000 residents of 1847 became 30,000 by 1849 in the rush for Sutter's gold, this was Amer-

---

* Japan may soon be selling us a "bullet train," which will whiz at 160 mph beween Los Angeles and San Diego, connecting the antipodes of Southern California in just fifty-nine minutes. Our labor would build the roadbeds and lay the tracks, but Japan would fund 25 percent of the $2 billion project, and the trains would be Japanese. There has also been talk of a Los Angeles–Vegas bullet train. France, not Japan, may get this one. Since the 1970s' slump, California's aerospace firms have had ample time to follow Grumman in the East and diversify to mass-transit production, but they stay tethered to the Pentagon and NASA.

ica's most open city. The city was full of gangs, kangaroo courts, lynchings and vigilantes, and more than 1,000 murders occurred between 1849 and 1856, when the mines gave out, miners left, and the rule of law began. The Comstock Lode revived the anarchy after 1859, but in time a real city emerged, as a port, mining base and financial center for a new West.

This was the biggest Sunbelt city when a tremendous earthquake hit at 5:12 on the morning of April 18, 1906. Twenty-eight thousand buildings, a total of $500 million in property, were destroyed, and more than 500 were killed. The rebuilding renewed civic pride, and a campaign began to make this "The Paris of America." The notorious Barbary Coast section of the city was finally closed down in one day in 1917. Eighty-three brothels were closed, and 1,073 women were driven out with their goods. Two days later, forty saloons closed.

A new era began. By 1950, this was America's eleventh biggest city, and by 1970, a major financial, shipping and headquarters city for the West. Los Angeles had picked up many front offices since 1950, but San Francisco built twenty-one office towers in the 1960s, then twenty-three more from 1970 to 1975—when an overdue zoning code stopped the destruction of a once-charming skyline. The city also remained a major financial center in 1981 with America's second biggest bank, BankAmerica, and other major banks like Wells Fargo and Crocker National, as well as the eleventh biggest diversified financial corporation, Transamerica.

As a place to live, however, San Francisco was becoming a smaller city of income extremes. Even by 1971, Neal Peirce found "the highest crime rate of any city—bar none—in the USA," inducing the usual taxpayer flight. The 1970s intensified this trend. The metro crime rate soared from 5,411 crimes to 8,540 per 100,000 residents, and the housing market shrank from sight. Housing was so tight that by 1981 San Francisco had the highest median cost of all cities: $129,000 per home, against $118,000 in Los Angeles and $90,000 in New York. San Francisco was losing people but gaining households from a lot of singles, among them its sizable gay community. All of this put even more demand pressure on rental and sales markets. As average households shrank from 2.7 people in 1970 to only 2.1 by 1981, more people were bidding up even fewer housing units.

The big losers in this housing squeeze are the majority of San

Francisco that is not white or English-speaking. Blacks actually declined by almost 10,000 in the 1970s, but many remained in subcode shelter like the "temporary" World War II housing at Hunters Point. There were the Hispanics of the Mission District, their numbers up 30 percent in the 1970s. An overcrowded Chinatown was swamped even more in the 1970s by new arrivals from mainland China, Hong Kong, Korea, the Phillippines and Vietnam.* Orientals went from 13 percent of the city to 22 percent in the 1970s. Peirce called Chinatown "perhaps the most or only glamorous slum in America, but still a slum." In 1972, Peirce found that a third of the Orientals were poor, half lived in substandard housing, 60 percent either lacked or shared a bathroom, there was a "suicide rate [that] is far above" already high San Francisco rates, and the TB rate was three times that of whites citywide. Then 50,000 more Orientals arrived in the 1970s.

Public health declines as Proposition 13 and Reagan federal cuts grow. Too few nurses at San Francisco General meant the city's only public hospital lost accreditation in 1981. Two-thirds of General's patients were indigents covered by Medicaid. Reagan cuts threw 23 percent of working poor families off coverage, which meant even more debts and service cuts at General. The city health department also took cuts in preventive programs like family planning, health education and rat control. A health official noted that San Francisco had the highest alcoholism and suicide rates, and the highest single-parent ratio in America, adding that "if the funding for these programs disappears, those figures will go through the roof."

Suicide brings us to the main problem for the growing poverty census and the crucial tourist industry: crime. In the past decade, this city has witnessed the Zodiac Killer, the Patricia Hearst kidnapping, the near assassination of President Ford, the People's Temple massacre in Guyana, and the assassinations of Supervisor Harvey Milk and Mayor George Moscone. This is also a city where crowded neighborhoods and a high share of elderly and single-person households mean a suicide rate of 27.5 per

---

* Orientals grew by more than 100 percent in California during the 1970s, and migrants from abroad are now more than a third of annual census gains. A RAND demographer claims that "California has become the Ellis Island of the 1980s," a new melting pot for Hispanic and Oriental arrivals. Former Lieutenant Governor Mervyn Dymally, a black, claimed that by 1990 California would be "the country's first Third World state" as minorities became the majority there.

100,000—higher even than the 19.0 murder rate in 1981. The Coroner's Office projected that 10 percent of all murders in 1980 were caused by sadomasochistic acts, and the Coroner now gives "preventive counseling" to cut the death rate.

Mayor Dianne Feinstein might be called one of those "liberal on social issues, conservative on fiscal affairs" types. She hired more cops in 1980. That still left San Francisco with a low ratio of cops to people, but it slowed the increase in crime, compared to other cities. The murder rate actually dropped 5 percent after 1977, but assaults rose 20 percent, rape 26 percent and robbery 39 percent, and San Francisco ranks high among the fifty big cities for crime rates in 1981: eleventh for robberies, twelfth for rape, sixteenth for assaults.

Crime also seems a key reason for a 14 percent drop in tourism after 1979. The Convention and Visitors Bureau issued new city maps in 1981, printing warnings about crime areas in even quaint Victorian enclaves. The police failed to get hotels to carry pamphlets about these areas, the head of the policemen's union saying it was "an economic thing. They don't want to scare the hell out of people." When a British tourist was mugged and shot in the Western Addition area, Mayor Feinstein invited her to recuperate at her home. She added fifty police in the area, and robberies fell 25 percent in one month. This "tactical police force" gambit has been used in New York City for several decades. It works for a while, but muggers catch on and move to areas stripped of cops covering the target area. Only higher levels of citywide police can have the thorough, suppressive force to cut crime in all the high-risk areas of San Francisco.*

In the fall of 1982, the cable car system was closed for a twenty-month overhaul costing $60 million. Barry Peterson of *CBS Evening News* noted this latest tourism setback in a city "already reeling from one of the worst slumps in history." The 3.5 million tourists of 1979 were down to 3 million in 1982, and "without the cable cars, some feel . . . as much as 40 percent" in tourism would be lost. This was hyperbolic, but the twenty-month retirement of the cable cars was one more blow. "It's like

---

* In 1983, Feinstein examined Japan's *koban* system, in which one-room police offices cover every 10,000 residents in a model of community crime control. But like "quality circles" in factories, this Japanese device needs a lot of money and manpower. Tokyo has 5.2 cops for every 2.6 in San Francisco, and Japan has an absolute ban on guns.

trying to sell Disneyland without Mickey Mouse," groused a retailer.

In late 1981, there was the dedication of the $126 million George Moscone Convention Center. There were plans to open up 5,000 new hotel rooms nearby in three years, and by late 1982, 263 major events were already booked into the long-awaited convention center, which will host the Democratic National Convention in 1984. While #2 for tourists, San Francisco was only #8 for convention and trade shows in 1981 and the Moscone Center should improve that rank. But this dramatic symbol of downtown renewal cannot reverse the tourism slump.

Crime is also a force in business relocation, and since 1978 San Francisco has lost more than 10,000 jobs to other Bay Area cities. Contra Costa County received most of this movement. Standard Oil, San Francisco's leading headquarters and #5 on the *Fortune* 500 list, doubled its Contra Costa work force to 3,000 and some project 10,000 there by 1985. BankAmerica plans a $200 million office-computer complex for 4,000 workers in Contra Costa by 1985. The county will also get 500 workers from another San Francisco giant, the Bechtel Group.

San Francisco's violent sister city of Oakland has no peer for crime in California. The old stage for Black Panthers and lunatic offshoots like Symbionese terrorists, Oakland goes beyond New Left posturing to the real violence of a very poor city. With less than half of San Francisco's census, Oakland had more murders in 1980.

With only 1.9 police officers per 1,000 citizens, Oakland had the lowest ratio of cops outside Dallas and San Antonio. Due to Proposition 13 tax losses, Oakland cut its officers another 8 percent in 1981 and turned off another 1,000 streetlights. Although a third of its crimes were committed by teen-agers, it ended afterschool recreation programs.*

A 1981 referendum proposed to raise local taxes for more cops. Proposition 13 mandates a 60 percent vote in order to hike local property taxes, this barrier defeating forty of fifty-four local votes in two years (forty-one of the fifty-four votes would have been

---

* A noncrime service affected in Oakland by all the cuts since Proposition 13 is street maintenance. "We're on a 200-year maintenance schedule now," observed the city finance director to *The Wall Street Journal* in 1982, "so if your street was paved during the Revolutionary War, you're up for repaving this year."

won under a simple majority). But even a majority was beyond reach in Oakland. Led by crime "fighter" Earl Huntting, voters rejected the minor tax hike 55–45 percent. Rich precincts in Oakland Hills supported the tax, but an odd coalition of poor blacks and the Huntting set prevailed. Oakland's black mayor cited "mistrust of the police" among the poor.

Gertrude Stein, who spent her childhood in Oakland, once observed: "The trouble with Oakland is that there's no *there* there." There is, however, enormous crime.*

## Los Angeles

In 1980, Los Angeles-Long Beach replaced Chicago-Gary as the biggest factory town on earth. There were 911,000 manufacturing jobs here, against 895,000 for Chicago-Gary, 604,000 for New York-New Jersey and 486,000 for Detroit. As the old Snowbelt cities lose industrial jobs to foreign competition, Los Angeles should widen its lead. It has few peers in areas like aerospace or high tech. As the Reagan defense spending binge grows 50 percent in constant dollars by 1986, the gap between Los Angeles and the rest of our cities should widen some more off the large defense sector in the Los Angeles-Long Beach area.

Los Angeles even raids New York's longtime industrial leader, the garment trades. As fashion trends go from the West to the East Coast, jobs are going the other way. Seventh Avenue lost 50,000 jobs between 1970 and 1978 while L.A. gained 30,000. As New York lost 23 percent of its publishing jobs and 8 percent of its finance jobs, Los Angeles gained 32 percent and 23 percent more of such jobs. All of the above added up to immense wealth. Joel Kotkin observed in *the Washington Post* in 1980 how "the economy of the '60-mile circle' around downtown Los Angeles exceeds $110 billion: if taken as a country, it would rank 12th in terms of gross national product and its per capita income would put it fourth, behind oil-rich Kuwait, Qatar and Saudi Arabia."

---

* A rare cloud passed over Neal Peirce's crystal ball in 1972 when he predicted that the new BART subway might encourage San Francisco firms to put "runover office space, computer installations, and the like" in Oakland—now only nine minutes from Montgomery Street via BART. But as seen above, BankAmerica put these "back office" functions in Contra Costa County instead. The one plus, noted by Joel Garreau, is a new Oakland container port, which draws cargo from San Francisco docks. Otherwise, as Peirce noted a local saying in 1971 about BART: "Why should anyone get off in Oakland if Rome is only nine minutes away?"

The Mexicans who founded Pueblo de Nuestra Señora la Reina de los Angeles in 1781 may threaten its future as well. Two centuries later, L.A. has more Mexicans than any city save Mexico City, and what Mexicans wrought, they may yet take away. As the boomtown passed its bicentennial, there were too many Mexicans, and their impoverished numbers grow at too rapid a rate. The Hispanic median age in Los Angeles is nineteen; these are Catholics, and peasant backgrounds mean big families. A 28 percent Hispanic share of Los Angeles could approach 50 percent by 1990. Add a 21 percent black census share in 1980 and a quickly growing Oriental share of 7 percent, and this could be *the* minority city of America by 1990.

It couldn't happen at a worse time. Pentagon funds will soon mean more jobs for the aerospace sector driving Ronald Reagan's adopted town. But Reagan urban aid cuts, Proposition 13 revenue losses, state aid cuts and rapid minority growth mean disaster. Compounding the problem would be the flood of illegal Mexicans unleashed by the revived *bracero* program and the peso devaluations of 1982. Even now, state officials estimate that perhaps 70 percent of California's unskilled jobs are filled by illegal entries in a sweatshop industry that made Los Angeles one of four targets in a federal probe of 1981. Beyond these pestholes, where do growing and youthful minorities go in Los Angeles after CETA jobs cuts? Some will go to crime.

This is the West's crime capital, with murders up 27 percent and other crime up 30 percent in 1980 alone. Only Miami had a faster rise in violence among big cities that year. Crime has dominated L.A. in a way few cities understand. Many of the 2 million California gas grenadiers are here. There are more than 350 teen-age gangs with perhaps 35,000 members, police crediting their activities with nearly 200 of a record 1,010 murders in 1980.

Long before the 1980 crime wave, however, taxpayers were already decamping the scene. Los Angeles grew only 5 percent in the 1970s, less than half the national rate. That sluggish growth was based entirely on young minorities, as some 300,000 whites left a city that soon may be split between the polar extremes of Bel-Air and Watts.

One hundred years ago, Los Angeles was a small town of 11,000 and New York a metropolis of 1,911,000. Then the Santa

Fe Railroad reached L.A. in 1885 as a link to the East. The Santa Fe competed with the Southern Pacific for the right to open up Southern California. John Gregory Dunne recalls in *New West* a rate war that

> defied common sense. From the jumping-off point in the Missouri Valley, passage to Southern California dropped from $123 to $100, and then, in a maniacal frenzy of price-cutting, to $12, $8, $6, and $4. Finally on March 4, 1887, the rate went to one dollar. . . . Bargain basement pioneers . . . flooded into Southern California, 120,000 of them trucked into Los Angeles by the Southern Pacific alone in 1887, the Santa Fe keeping pace with three and four carloads a day.

The next spur to growth was the Second Street Park oil field, discovered by Edward Doheny in 1892. By 1895, a contemporary described oil wells "as thick as the holes in a pepper box." A Salt Lake Field of 1902 was the biggest in California. Then the immense plays of the 1920s in Huntington, Long Beach and Whittier made Los Angeles the world capital of oil. The lowly by-product of gasoline was found useful for cars. *Congressional Quarterly* recalls how "as early as 1925, Los Angeles was heralded as the unabashed leader of the car culture, with one automobile for every three residents."

A second leg for the L.A. economy was added in 1915 as "No Dogs or Actors Allowed" signs were taken down, and the movies arrived. After D. W. Griffith finished shooting *The Birth of a Nation* in Brooklyn and Fort Lee, New Jersey, he and the films had moved west. Hollywood had only 4,000 residents in "the most beautiful suburb in America" in 1910. It had 36,000 in 1920 as silents took off, then 250,000 by 1930 as talkies caught on. By 1938, films ranked fourteenth among all American business for gross value, eleventh for total assets. By 1979, the entertainment sector in Los Angeles was annually grossing $13 billion off films, TV and records.

As oil and films boomed and Los Angeles grew in the 1920s, an inevitable third leg of real estate was added to the prosperous economy. Los Angeles had still been America's richest farm county until 1920, but oil and film wealth, plus the new mobility of cars, meant the paving of the L.A. Basin. At one time Los Angeles had a vast mass-transit system. By 1930, the Pacific

Electric rail system had 1,200 miles of rails for the biggest mass-transit system in America.

Back then, there were only three miles of freeways. At 451 square miles, Los Angeles was the largest city on earth in 1947, when Gunther characterized it as "nineteen suburbs in search of a metropolis." Mass transit still played a vital role and all it needed was maintenance and political support. Alas, the freeways expanded in crisscrosses, cloverleaves and curlicues. The three miles of 1930 centupled to 325 miles by 1970, when Neal Peirce updated the phrase to "40 suburbs in search of a city."

By 1980, there were some 1,500 miles of freeways—the 1,200 miles of trolley rails long since torn up. For the past two decades, this has been one of the few major cities on earth without a viable mass-transit system, where once had been the biggest such system in America. The freeways, the city and the county grew. L.A. County nearly tripled in those four decades, growing from 2.8 million to 7.4 million. Combined with the Long Beach area, this was the fourth biggest metro area on earth in 1980. A 1980 survey by *Congressional Quarterly* now raised the Gunther-Peirce appraisals, finding "100 suburbs in search of a metropolis."

The oil, the films, the real-estate boom pushed Los Angeles from a city of 100,000 in 1900 to a metropolis of 1.9 million by 1940, then World War II made it an industrial power. Los Angeles landed $10 billion in war contracts as industrial jobs soared 75 percent. Journalist Carey McWilliams later wrote that Southern California "unlike other areas . . . did *not* convert to war production, for there was nothing there to convert; what happened was that *new* industries and *new* plants were built overnight."

The main force was aerospace. Giants like Douglas, Hughes, Lockheed and Northrup made the Los Angeles area America's main aviation arsenal, with Lockheed producing 20,000 fighters and bombers during the war years. The draft depleted the work force and defense plants faced labor shortages in Southern California, so the *bracero* program was begun in 1942 to bring in needed Mexican labor. Between 1941 and 1956, Los Angeles County grew from 3 million to 5.5 million, an 83 percent growth in fifteen years. Only New York City's 65 percent growth during the peak years of European immigration from 1900 to 1920 compares to this.

As industry expanded, the economy diversified. Workers who arrived to man the war factories needed shelter and services. There was a binge of small business, as Los Angeles replaced imports with homemade goods. In *The Economy of Cities*, Jane Jacobs observed that one-eighth of all new American businesses began in the L.A. area in the late 1940s. All this, plus oil, films, realty and aerospace meant huge income growth over three decades: $3 billion in personal income for 1940 skyrocketed to $48 billion by 1970, a 1,500 percent income gain, although the county census grew only 150 percent. By 1981, Los Angeles had the ninth and eleventh biggest banks in America, and also the sixth, eighth and ninth biggest diversified financial corporations on the *Fortune* 500 list. Trade was also a major growth industry. By 1970, this was the center for both western and Pacific Basin trade as one in four Angelenos worked in jobs related to foreign trade.

Above all, there was aerospace. Peirce noted its lead role in expanding the city's export base, starting with its revival during the Korean War and continued growth in the Cold War years as the most dynamic element in Southern California's

> postwar economy. Through aerospace, California became the leading defense contracting state. . . . By the 1960s, people were talking of Los Angeles as a "federal city" because of the close relationship between its economy and that of Washington. Some 40 percent of the area's manufacturing employment was tied directly or indirectly to defense and space spending.

By 1970, California was getting 19 percent of all military contracts, with twice the dollars going to New York and Texas. A slowed-down space and arms race saw California lose 25 percent of its aerospace jobs between 1967 and 1971. Peirce suggested a way out: "How can aerospace avoid the disarmament blues and survive? Its brightest future would logically lie in fields like mass transit design, environmental control or information systems— those areas which require systems analysis and a high technological component."

A decade later, high tech was indeed in vogue, but aerospace had failed to diversify. By 1981, Joel Kotkin was observing how aerospace remains the largest cog in the Los Angeles area industrial machine, providing some 200,000 jobs. While the civilian end of the aerospace industry—communications, satellites, solar cells, corporate jets, gas lasers—has expanded, federal dollars still play a key role. In 1978 California received more than $10 billion in defense contracts, the most of any state, while capturing more than 40% of prime NASA contracts.

Kotkin added that between 1945 and 1975, Southern California's professional, scientific and technical workers grew more than 200 percent, four times the Snowbelt rate. Yet by 1980, even more skilled workers were needed: "At a time when some 200,000 auto workers are out of jobs, companies like Hughes Aircraft, Lockheed and Douglas Aircraft have been sending recruiting teams to depressed regions to find workers."

In 1982 one Wall Street aerospace expert said, however, that "research and development programs will not be completed until 1984, with the bulk of the profitable production not due to take place until the period of 1958–88. That's moons away. A lot can happen in between." Anything from SALT pacts to policy changes in Washington can reduce the binge ahead for L.A. firms: Rockwell with two MX contracts and the B-1; Northrup with the gyro system for the MX and the Stealth bomber; Lockheed, the likely contractor off its past record for Trident 2 advanced missiles.*

Furthermore, the nearby desert town of Palmdale may be landing many of the future big defense contracts. Located an hour from Los Angeles and near to Edwards Air Force Base, this town of 14,000 is where Rockwell builds its huge assembly plant for the B-1, creating 4,300 permanent jobs, and thousands more for subcontractors. Lockheed also has its TriStar factory here, and there may soon be a new international airport—with 30,000 more jobs for the town of 14,000. This may be California's version of Huntsville, Alabama, with the Pentagon building up one small town with billions of public funds as a big city dies nearby. It happened to Birmingham in the 1950s; now Los Angeles will lose

* A battle among California aerospace giants could occur over the $20 billion Stealth contract for the 1990s. This bomber would use a mix of materials, coatings and surface shapes to absorb or deflect—rather than reflect—radar beams. Northrup has the current Stealth development contract, but Rockwell and Lockheed may make a Stealth version of the B-1, then bid for the 100-plane contract whose first product is set for 1991.

aerospace jobs to another federally sponsored "speck on the map."

The outstanding problems in L.A. involve water, air, earth, and a service crisis linked with crime and tax revolt.

Water problems reduce to: how does Southern California cover water losses after Arizona gets the Colorado River bookings in 1985? The obvious solution is a long overdue end to water wasting by Imperial Valley irrigators and conservation by 12 million residents of Southern California. Slower regional growth is also essential and seems well under way: A peak gain of 3.2 million new residents in the 1950s declined to one of 2.7 million in the 1960s and then to 1.9 million in the 1970s. If growth keeps slowing, the region can probably handle the Colorado River losses. If not, the first drought after 1985 could mean major crop losses.

As to air, this city virtually named smog. The growth of freeways and decline of mass transit combined with local topography to create and trap what Peirce called "a veritable chemical factory in the sky." The saucer-shaped basin and surrounding hills of Los Angeles trap cool Pacific air in thermal inversions, with auto fumes producing 90 percent of the resultant smog. Fortunately, auto-emission controls cut unhealthy days 23 percent between 1976 and 1978 alone. But 206 days a year are rated "unhealthy," nearly three times the average of 23 major cities.*

What about mass transit to cut the smog? A 1968 proposal for a $2.5 billion system to replace the old Pacific Electric system was voted down. Mass-transit talk since then has focused mainly on helping businesses downtown. In the 1970s some useful rooming houses for the elderly were replaced by high-rise apartments in a new "Bunker Hill" neighborhood. To make life even easier for these affluent residents of urban renewal land, a $167 million Downtown People Mover was proposed to shuttle workers from

---

* L.A. recently issued a plan for clean air by the year 2000, but the details are fantastic. Homes and offices would be concentrated into a network of mini-cities. Gas would be replaced by methanol or electricity. Commuters would do more walking or bicycling. Home computers would see more people in cottage industry. The only exception to the smog syndrome lately is noted by Joel Garreau. Los Angeles imports much of its power from Arizona and Utah, exporting "its pollution to these distant outposts . . ."

the new high-rise homes to work in the office towers downtown. This mass transit for the elite would have done the work of 50 buses for the cost of 2,000 buses. In 1980 Angelenos finally voted to raise a sales tax for mass transit. Long-suffering riders of the slowest buses on earth would see fares cut from 85 to 50 cents. A rail system may be built.

The problems of earth in Los Angeles are the most fateful of all. Along with San Francisco, L.A. should be one of the two main victims of a probable Great Quake within the next forty years. The California coast is part of the "ring of fire," a circum-Pacific earthquake chain shaped like a huge horseshoe that starts in New Zealand and goes up to Indonesia, to Japan, then across to Alaska and down to the California coast, Mexico, Latin America, and finally to Peru and Chile. This horseshoe produces 80 percent of all earthquakes, its California section experiencing some 500 tremors a year. Mount St. Helens in 1980 and the even bigger eruption in 1982 of El Chichon in Mexico were also part of the same chain.

The main problem for California was described by Neal Peirce, who noted how the two abutting edges of the San Andreas fault were frozen together for now, although "the longest and most exposed fracture anywhere in the world's crust . . . has been in motion 65 million years, with slippage between the two sides of 300 miles." Southern California south of Bakersfield has experienced nine Great Quakes on a cycle of 120 to 160 years. The last one to hit Los Angeles was in 1857, so the city is now within the forty-year time frame of greatest danger. Los Angeles got a frightening prelude of what lies ahead in late 1971. A 6.5 Richter quake hit the San Fernando Valley and a crack appeared in the Van Norman Dam, which looms over 150,000 homes. Had the quake lasted a few seconds more, the dam might well have broken above 350,000 residents below. The earthquake killed sixty-five people, forty of them trapped in a collapsed Veterans Administration hospital.

A National Security Council study group examined the California earthquake problem for Jimmy Carter in the wake of the Mount St. Helens eruption. The NSC group predicted Great Quakes for both Los Angeles and San Francisco, the latter due for a repeat of the 1906 tragedy by the year 2006, based on a 60-to-100-year cycle in the area. The group told Carter that the next Great Quake in California would be the worst natural disaster in

American history and warned that both Los Angeles and San Francisco were unprepared.*

The group added that Los Angeles had a 50 percent chance of being hit in the next thirty years. The worst scenario they created would be a 7.75 Richter quake along the Newport-Inglewood fault at rush hour killing 23,000, injuring 100,000 and leaving 250,000 homeless. The chief surgeon at San Francisco General Hospital suggested that an 8.3 quake similar to the one in 1906 could leave 10,000 dead and 40,000 injured. He also projected 7,000 hospital beds destroyed, leaving no first aid for the 40,000 injured, and difficult evacuation for them from a city bound on three sides by water, its two great bridges badly damaged.†

Most seismologists and geologists in California agree with the National Security Council group that there will be a Great Quake within thirty years. The only defense is preparation, and L.A. and San Francisco held alerts after the NSC report was issued. A Red Cross spokesman said in 1981:

> The first thing we're trying to tell them is that they must get ready for an 8.3 earthquake—it is going to occur. Second, they will be on their own for up to 72 hours. They won't be able to depend on the Red Cross. We'll need 1,000 shelters alone, and we don't even have 1,000 shelter directors.

California first budgeted $4.3 million for earthquake studies in 1981, then dropped this to $2.4 million, then to $319,000. "This is a tight fiscal year," noted the state's Director of Emergency Services in what may prove a tragic understatement. Three months later, as Los Angeles celebrated its bicentennial birthday

---

* Also unprepared is American public opinion. In 1975 a Berkeley earthquake specialist, Karl V. Steinbrugge, identified by *Time* as "perhaps the country's leading expert on designing quake-resistent buildings," projected the probable impact: "Thousands of lives snuffed out in 30 seconds is going to blow the roof off this country. And it's going to happen."

† Earthquakes have been predicted in China, Greece, Mexico and Russia, but the science is inexact. There was the animal activity seen at the Tientsin zoo just before a 1969 quake where swans suddenly left the water, a tiger stopped pacing, a panda began to moan with its head in its paws. More precise was Dr. James Whitcomb, a Caltech geophysicist, who in 1973 examined the speed of sound waves sent through the earth's crust and correctly predicted a shock near Riverside within three months. In 1976, he used the same "P-wave" velocities to project a Great Quake for Southern California within twelve months; the quake did not occur.

on September 4, there was a brief tremor.* Mayor Bradley vowed L.A. would stand "for many years to come."

But bravado doesn't stop Great Quakes. Los Angeles and San Francisco must prepare, or an unprecedented tragedy will occur. Tokyo lost 143,000 people in the Kanto earthquake and firestorm of 1923, and is on a quake cycle of about 69 years. Japan has spent $6 billion on quake preparations, including a six-week store of provisions for a projected 4 million people.

Crime, however, has been the main issue in Los Angeles in the 1980s. As a city of cars, L.A. lags behind New York in the street crime of robbery. But in murder and rape it trounces its East Coast rival in both the rate per 100,000 citizens and the rate increase since 1972:

| | Los Angeles | | | New York City | | |
| | 1972 | 1980 | Change | 1972 | 1980 | Change |
|---|---|---|---|---|---|---|
| Rape | 76.2 | 96.2 | 26% | 41.2 | 52.9 | 21% |
| Robbery | 491.9 | 870.7 | 77% | 991.2 | 1,433.2 | 31% |
| Murder | 17.3 | 34.6 | 100% | 21.4 | 25.8 | 17% |

In per capita terms, Los Angeles in 1980 had 35 percent more murders than New York and 40 percent fewer cops. Put another way, 6,600 Los Angeles police in 1980 fought a severe crime wave that 9,500 would have battled in New York. Most of the violence inevitably occurred in slums like Watts and East Los Angeles. Gangs and their violence have escalated rapidly in Los Angeles. Some gangs were black ones from Watts, but many were groups of Mexicans from East Los Angeles. Since the 1930s, this area of wooden bungalows near the Civic Center downtown has been what writer Tracey Johnston described in 1979 as the site of

> a violent and unique subculture based on continuing gang warfare. . . . In their own fantasies the *vatos locos* [crazy guys]

---

* A note on the Diablo Canyon nuclear reactor. Begun in 1968, it was designed to survive a 6.75 Richter quake. Then in 1971, offshore oil explorers for Shell found a new fault nearby on the ocean floor. This Hosgri fault, two and a half miles west of the reactor, may have been responsible for a 7.25 Richter quake back in 1927.

are Homeric heroes; soldiers of an ancient battle, whose origin is unknown. . . . The sociological reality is that these are ghetto boys who live in the worst pocket of poverty, unemployment, drug abuse and family disintegration in the West.*

The police handle the gangs in several ways; the main thrust is a CRASH program (Community Resources Against Street Hoodlums). This focuses on "war zones," including Hollywood Boulevard in 1981. During the first half of 1981, there were fifty murders on Hollywood Boulevard, five of them involving gangs. Another gang-control program fields a dozen unarmed community workers, using a successful model from Philadelphia— where there were no gang murders in 1980. After pushing it in the media, Mayor Bradley failed to set aside $800,000 for the new program in 1981, so funds were taken from a tight police budget. This threatened to take forty or even fifty cops off the streets during a massive crime wave.

Late in 1980, Police Chief Daryl Gates proposed a special tax to raise forces from 6,600 cops to 8,500—the 8500 Plan. Despite crime rising 30 percent in 1980 alone, Bradley at first opposed the new tax. Only after several violent incidents in late 1980 did he follow his police chief's lead and back the 8500 Plan. Also following Gates were the *Los Angeles Times,* the Chamber of Commerce, and the local Urban League—the last gamely backing the plan although polls showed Los Angeles blacks opposed more police. The 8500 Plan would have meant a 19 percent boost in patrol forces to fight a 30 percent rise in crime, an inadequate proposal but a first step toward crime control. On June 2, 1981, however, it was rejected by voters 58–42 percent.

There was a blind belief in "management reform" to fight crime. One report claimed extra forces could be raised at no cost by just filling vacant police slots, civilizing desk jobs, and cutting police brass. With good reason Chief Gates literally attacked the report—he hurled it to the floor and stomped on it at a press conference. The LAPD had already civilianized many jobs, the brass was not top-heavy, and filling vacancies would obviously leave police short of the 1,354 hired for the 8500 Plan.

---

* Within the slum is Los Angeles' oldest structure, an 1818 adobe home in a landmark district of brick and tile called El Pueblo de Los Angeles. The Latin custom of *Las Posadas* (The Inns) occurs here on the eight days before Christmas, Mary and Joseph seeking shelter each night without success until December 24. Then a *piñata* of gifts is broken.

Also, there was the voters' inability to see past some minor inequities in the 8500 Plan's form of taxation. Proposition 13 limits property taxes to 1 percent of assessed value, so Chief Gates was forced to suggest flat surcharges on cottage and castle alike. A small home in Watts and a Hollywood mansion would both pay the same $12.30 a year in extra taxes. With commercial property, the sole criterion was lot size. If they had equal ground area, an office building and a parking lot paid the same flat fee. "ARCO, with ARCO Plaza, may be paying as much as a service station," carped one critic. Alexander Pope, the L.A. County assessor, called the 8500 Plan and its trivial inequities "a work plan for attorneys."

The day after the 8500 Plan defeat, the City Council began talking of new police cuts. Marvin Braude, chairman of the Finance Committee, said that if it came to "cutting the Police Department a very little bit against closing down parks and libraries, I think the people of this city may decide that parks and libraries should not be closed." Since Sacramento was cutting $50 million in local aid to Los Angeles, more cops might be cut indeed. Chief Gates sent a videotape to precinct roll calls the day after the June 2 vote. In it, he wrote an epitaph for America's tax revolt in general, when he pithily observed how Los Angeles voters "want more police officers, they just don't want to have to pay for them."

Presiding over the mess was Mayor Tom Bradley. When this ex-cop took office in 1973, there were 490 murders that year—against 1,010 in 1980. While decent to the poor, Bradley is slow to lead on services. With strong business ties, he played fiscal conservative in 1981, hinting at $80 million in service cuts. The legislature cut local aid by "only" $50 million, and Bradley's cut to match the loss would mainly affect recreation programs.

Bradley did face, however, huge pension giveaways to firemen and police. Approved by voters in pre-tax-revolt days, the pensions rose an incredible 300 percent since 1970, and by 1981 they ate up 18 percent of the city's operating budget. In 1979 a Los Angeles citizens' committee demanded "drastic changes" in the pensions to avoid "eventual financial disaster similar to that of New York." Of an $80 million deficit faced by Bradley in 1981, $50 million was from pension costs.

For fiscal 1981–82, Bradley proposed cutting 6,000 of 26,000 municipal jobs. But nearly 4,000 of these were CETA employees cut by Reagan in Washington. Also hard hit by Reagan cuts was the L.A. public hospital system, which had already been swamped by uninsured indigents kicked off Medicaid by Governor Reagan's cuts after 1971. As President in 1981, Reagan also cut federal community health funds by 25 percent. His cuts in food stamps, school lunches, home health care for the elderly, and the WIC maternal and infant nutrition program would also affect the health of the poor, working poor and elderly in Los Angeles.

In 1982, Bill Moyers examined the impact of federal and state cuts on L.A. public health for *CBS Evening News*. Noting an overall cut of $65 million, Moyers found that "the deficits land in the County's lap." The conservative County Supervisors had put the screws on tight. Public hospitals no longer advised working poor patients of their right to free public care. Apart from emergencies, patients had to pay clinic costs up front. That ended a lot of preventive care for the uninsured working poor, Moyers noting the impact on premature births. Indigent mothers could no longer get free prenatal exams, so the risks of premature birth had grown—those babies increasing 7.5 percent in 1981. Apart from the health risks involved for mothers and babies, Moyers also noted the fiscal costs. The County "saved" $600 in free prenatal care per indigent patient, then lost an average of $80,000 in caring for every premature indigent baby in neonatal intensive care.

Another example of the Reagan cuts was in Legal Aid, a program Reagan wanted to end by 1984. The Los Angeles branch in 1981 had to close half its offices and cut its case load by 66 percent. This helped to double illegal evictions in 1981.

Noting all the Reagan, state and local cuts in 1981, *Los Angeles Times* city bureau chief Bill Boyarsky suggested a "war room," complete with aerial maps, population bar graphs, charts on housing shortages, areas of potential unrest, to manage the growing chaos. But this couldn't replace the thin ranks of cops, the closed health clinics, the shut gyms, the cut of 6,000 city workers out of 26,000 in one year. There is no substitute for things like the huge federal cuts by Reagan. And a city whose voters won't raise taxes for more cops has lost the will to survive.

The main agents of crisis in Los Angeles are in Sacramento and Washington. Those broader taxing jurisdictions have the fiscal power to resolve the urban crisis. All they lack is the will to do the job. Los Angeles with its immense wealth can play a stronger role in defending its services. Unless its voters regain the instinct for survival, however, the city is lost. Until they elect a mayor pledged to raise taxes and improve services, the growing census of jobless and hopeless minorities will produce more crime . . . more taxpayers will leave a chaotic city . . . and "demography as destiny" will claim one more rich Sunbelt city unwilling to save itself.

# PART II
# THE SNOWBELT

# CHAPTER 7

# THE THREE MYTHS

DESPITE SNOWBELT DECLINE over two decades, the media has lately portrayed urban revival in the aging region. Young couples revive townhouses in the Queen Village section of Philadelphia as urban pioneers. New York City expands its office space more than 25 percent since 1980, with 46 million square feet opening by 1986. Handsome malls bristling with bistros and boutiques dust off dead ports: Quincy Market in Boston and Harborplace in Baltimore. New sports stadiums and convention centers open up; two even open in dying Detroit, one the setting for the Republican National Convention of 1980, the other host to Super Bowl XVI in 1982.

But beyond these Potemkin villages are the old Snowbelt scenes, as aging cities continue to lose people, jobs, taxes and stability. With a few exceptions noted in Chapter 8, most Snowbelt cities are deep in the downward spiral of service cuts and taxpayer flight. Urban-revival images are flimsy façades to general ruin.

*Philadelphia* has major town-house revival areas and the big Gallery shopping mall from the developer of Quincy Market and Harborplace. But it also lost 43 percent of its factory jobs after 1970. It recently lost its rank as the region's #1 port area to Hampton Roads. And it has the second worst black and teen-age unemployment rates in America. The fairy-tale film *Rocky II* is a sadly realistic picture of Philadelphia's growing mismatch of unskilled youths and a service economy. Too ignorant for office work, unable to find work on the dying docks and laid off from a meat-packing plant, Rocky settles for being heavyweight champion.

*New York City* had 35 million square feet of office space planned through 1985, plus a $250 million South Street Seaport mall opened in 1983, a $292 million hotel from John Portman to open in 1984 and a $500 million Convention Center from I. M. Pei also set for 1986. But while the city had gained 108,000 jobs after 1978, its residents had lost 16,000 jobs. This isn't a puzzling exercise in New Math, it's simply that almost all the new jobs were in specialized service areas like banking, insurance and real estate, while 48,000 factory jobs were lost at the same time. Commuters landed virtually all the new jobs. As well, a growing service crisis is driving the middle class from New York. Eleven percent of the city left in the 1970s—the first major census loss since the first census of 1790.

*Baltimore* has the colorful Harborplace arcade for shoppers and a new National Aquarium for tourists, both reviving the waterfront with more annual visitors than Disney World in Orlando. But the big Florida park brings in far more tax income to an area which often has 3 percent unemployment. And beyond the publicized waterfront, Baltimore is a city with the second highest unemployment after Detroit, and 60,000 substandard housing units.

*Detroit* hosted the first Super Bowl in the Snowbelt since the 1960s and the first Republican Convention in its history. But this is a huge company town, with one in every three workers in auto-related jobs, and the auto slump since 1979 is dragging down Motor City. Detroit in 1981 led all big cities in the three main categories for unemployment: blacks, teen-agers and all workers. At one point, 60 percent of Detroit was getting some form of public social aid.

I will discuss these and other Snowbelt cities in Chapters 8 through 10. Chapter 8 will look at four regional paragons: Minneapolis, Milwaukee, Kansas City and Wichita all have low jobless and crime rates. Each has a diversified economy able to ride out the boom-bust recession cycles that have ravaged Snowbelt cities since 1970. The four cities built their economic immunity over many years. They teach few lessons to other, failing cities of the region.

Chapter 9 will examine five disaster areas. Philadelphia and Baltimore may be salvageable, but a growing mismatch between residents and jobs sees commuters land most of the new office work downtown. Both have notable downtown revivals—but also severe census and job losses since 1970. St. Louis, Detroit and Newark are cities past the point of no return. St. Louis is the Carthage of the Midwest, with a 630-foot Gateway Arch looming over 5,000 vacant lots in the city. Detroit has had the auto slump since 1979—and faces a strategic crisis in that industry as domestic demand declines, more work is exported, and robots expand. Back in 1950, Newark had more residents than Dallas, Denver, Phoenix, San Antonio, San Diego or San Jose, to name six of the ten biggest Sunbelt cities today. But Newark today is the worst big city in America with dramatic losses in property values since 1968 and a 93 percent rise in violent crime after 1977.

Chapter 10 details the service crisis of New York City: crime, housing, health, subways and jobs. The city slowly splits into the gentrified island of Manhattan and four dying Outer Boroughs. The middle class leaves en masse. New York is rich in untapped revenue sources like the booming office towers of Manhattan. But Mayor Edward Koch refuses to tax developers adequately, thus keeping the service crisis alive. Claiming to "save" New York by balancing its budget, the mayor destroys its economic and social stability with relentless service cuts.

Before looking at the Snowbelt cities in Chapters 8 through 10, let's examine three key problems for all of them: money, crime and jobs. These problems are reflected in what I shall call the Myth of Limited Resources, the Myth of Uncontrollable Crime and the Myth of Reindustralization.

## 1. The Myth of Limited Resources

This is a favorite rationale for endless service cuts by mayors and governors in Snowbelt states. First, they cut taxes in a vain effort to lure business or as a reaction to tax revolts. Then they bemoan the "limited resources" that result from their own tax cuts. This forces them inevitably to "do what they have to do": make relentless service cuts to balance budgets. The cuts hurt the poor and the elderly, drive taxpayers from cities, frighten away business, and deepen the downward spiral. Recent tax-cut sprees have seen even liberal states like Minnesota, Michigan and New York swing the ax. Massachusetts joined the party in 1980, its Proposition 2½ tax-cap vote perverting Sam Adams' famous cry to read "No Taxation with Representation!"

The tax cuts ravaged the revenue bases, then recessions caved them in. Snowbelt states in the 1980s faced a self-imposed Hobson's choice between tax hikes or service cuts to fend off fiscal crisis. The choice was predictable: taxpayers went on getting tax breaks; the poor got more service cuts. Reagan's cut of $29 billion in social programs for fiscal 1982 was a big fat pitch to hit out of the park.* But the Snowbelt mayors and governors kept the bats on their shoulders. Only after Reaganomics collapsed in late 1981 did Mayor Ed Koch attack the new federalism as a "sham and a shame," or Governor Richard Snelling of Vermont denounce it as an "economic Bay of Pigs."

As we've seen in California, tax cuts do little for business. A National Governors' Association report in 1981 was the latest survey to make this familiar point. Tax cuts are always far down the list of business lures—well below labor costs, local labor skills or, interestingly, the quality of public services. In his *Revolt of the Haves,* Robert Kuttner notes that "ironically, the erosion of the tax base to attract industries often depletes the money to pay for good schools, parks, police protection, and other things that make cities attractive to corporate executives contemplating where to locate."

How do these tax cuts affect Snowbelt states and cities? For an example, look at New York. After 1978, Governor Hugh Carey and the legislature cut $2.3 billion in recurrent taxes, or 12 percent of the state revenue base. Full-page ads trumpeted New York as "The Best Place in the World to Do Business," the copy gushing like Molly Bloom: "Yes! A sweeping deregulation of the overly regulated banking industry. Yes! 33% off the top tax rate on earned income. Yes! Next year we bid farewell to the unincorporated business tax and sales tax for manufacturing supplies." But no! It does nothing much for jobs, far less for social stability.

Supporting the huge tax cut, *The Wall Street Journal* saluted

---

* The Reagan cut meant that cities of more than 250,000 lost 13.3 percent of their federal aid in one year. An Urban Institute study suggests that if the "new federalism" is fully realized, Washington's share of state and local budgets could plunge from 25 percent today to 4 percent by 1991.

Carey the Democrat while assailing the Republican former governor, Nelson Rockefeller, for trying "to soak the upper middle class" with a higher top rate on income taxes. The *Journal* claimed success for the Carey tax cuts: New York had lost 367,000 jobs between 1970 and 1976—but lost no jobs during the 1980 slump. But the 1970 to 1976 period had featured two virulent and lengthy recessions—quite different from the 1980 dip. The 367,000 jobs lost back then had mainly been in factory cities like Buffalo and New York City, the latter losing 270,000 manufacturing jobs during those six years. With factory jobs combed out, the state was more "recession-proof" against boom-bust cycles of heavy-industry states around the Great Lakes. The Carey tax cuts did little for business.

Meanwhile, what had $2.3 billion in annual tax cuts done for people depending on Albany for welfare, mental health and health—three services traditionally supplied for local government by stronger taxing powers at the state level.

• Welfare saw an unprecedented seven-year freeze on the state grant. Even Nelson Rockefeller and his more conservative successor Malcolm Wilson had raised the grant twice in two years to offset two cuts. But Hugh Carey let a family of four feed and clothe itself on a montly grant of $258 for seven years. Meanwhile, OPEC inflation between 1974 and 1981 reduced the grant's purchasing power by 55 percent.*

• Mental health cuts meant patients dumped from state hospitals. Some 36,000 homeless vagrants roamed the streets of New York City: bums and bag ladies, subway sleepers or people living in steam tunnels beneath Grand Central Station. Instead of paying the full bill for their care in hospitals, the state abandons them and pays 25 percent for whatever outpatient care they receive.

• Health care has been plunged into fiscal chaos under the harshest Medicaid cost controls in America. As Medicaid costs rose 48 percent across America, they inched up only 13 percent in New York State. Public and private hospitals had to care for millions of uninsured indigents sliced from Medicaid by Albany. The sixteen public hospitals of New York City give about $250

---

* New York was also the only state requiring localities to pay a 25 percent share of welfare and Medicaid costs. Indeed, forty-four of the fifty states demanded no local payments at all. So as New York State passed out tax cuts like a drunken sailor, New York City paid $832 million for welfare and Medicaid in 1981, while cities like Chicago and Philadelphia paid nothing.

million a year in free indigent care. Twenty-six private hospitals have closed in the city since 1976. Two hundred and twenty-two hospitals in the state had to cannibalize $494 million in assets over four years trying to stay open. Albany could have deferred 12 percent of its tax cut. Two hundred and seventy-five million dollars of the $2.3 billion cut would have raised the welfare grant 10 percent, kept more patients in mental hospitals for treatment, and covered most indigent costs at hospitals.*

Minnesota is another example of how tax cuts destroy social stability. The state of liberals like Humphrey, McCarthy and Mondale was also the pioneer for the indexing of income taxes. Minnesota did this in 1979, well before Ronald Reagan decried "bracket creep" in 1981. Indexing did for Minnesota then what it does for America now. After thirty-five years of unbroken prosperity and state budget surpluses, "recession-proof" Minnesota became an overnight, self-made pauper. Indexing converted a $292 million state surplus in 1979 to a $195 million deficit in 1980. High taxes, fine services and low unemployment had been Minnesota traditions. But the huge tax cuts plunged the state and its Twin Cities into a self-induced downward spiral of fiscal crisis and service cuts. At last look, Minnesota was facing a $768 million deficit for the biennium ending in July of 1983.

In between cutting state taxes and services, there is the fantasy of "taxurbs," whereby the old Snowbelt cities would annex rich suburbs and expand their tax base. This nostrum was suggested by investment banker Felix Rohatyn, hailed by the media as the "wizard" of Lazard Frères, who had helped to "save" both New York State and City from default in 1975. Rohatyn had demanded service cuts and tax cuts to balance those budgets. His advice to cut, cut, and cut again since 1975 had helped induce service crisis in Lazard Frères clients such as Cleveland, Detroit, New York City, and Washington, D.C. By 1981, rising crime, slipping services and disappearing taxpayers in those four cities were hard to ignore. So Rohatyn turned around 180 degrees, urging his client cities to raise taxes to end those service crises. The media hailed him for saving his clients from his own previous advice.

---

* Few in New York link the service crises in welfare, mental health and health to all the tax cuts since 1978. Future governor Mario Cuomo in an interview in 1981 praised the tax cuts as good for business, deplored the service crisis partly caused by the cuts, and urged more tax cuts—once that mysterious service crisis was under control.

Why would Snowbelt suburbs want to be annexed by the very cities from which their residents flee? The last big annexations by these currently troubled cities were in the nineteenth century. Historian Richard Wade recalls how in 1886 "Chicago acquired more than 125 square miles in one quick seizure. And, of course, in 1898 New York added the outlying boroughs to Manhattan. In this fashion successive rings of early suburbs were incorporated into municipalities."

Wade points out that the wholesale opening of the suburbs by the automobile ended annexation after 1920 for all but a handful of very stable Snowbelt cities. Since 1950, only rare cities like Columbus, Indianapolis, Kansas City and Milwaukee were able to annex suburban tax bases. Only Sunbelt cities are attractive or strong enough to annex at will, with Houston and Phoenix adding inner- or outer-ring suburbs year after year.

There is also the panacea of management reform. Having cut taxes with one hand and services with the other, the mayors and governors roll out management reform with the slogan of "more services for less money." Computers, work-rule reforms, shuffling boxes on flow charts will exorcise the specters of Waste, Fraud and Mismanagement. Money will be saved, services improved, and tax cuts elsewhere can be ignored.

Young technocrats like David Stockman began to "manage down spending." As an Arthur D. Little executive told *Business Week* in 1980: "Large corporations have been virtually overrun by a proliferation of profit-zealous MBAs who are turning every nut another half-turn to get a payoff." Incessant service cuts were made to build character among "profligate" cities. In reality, however, management reform was a limited way to overcome limited resources.

• A key goal of management reform is getting municipal union costs under control. Ford can frighten the UAW into wage concessions with the threat of plant closings. But no mayor can scare his troops by threatening to move the city. The only credible threat for city workers is bankruptcy. This wipes out labor contracts, including the lavish pension plans that got New York and Los Angeles in fiscal trouble. But mayors let this weapon rust in the sheath. Instead, they talk about trivial "givebacks" in work rules. The unions lose more jobs, and the service crisis spiral deepens. This happened in Detroit until 1981, when Coleman Young used a mix of bankruptcy and layoff threats to force unions into a long overdue wage freeze. Had Mayor Abe Beame called the unions' bluff early in 1975, New York could have avoided much of the later needless fiscal crisis. But Beame didn't impose a wage freeze, the crisis got out of control, and the work force was cut 20 percent in the first of many drastic slashes.

• The big tickets of management reform—wage freezes and work-rule changes—are useful but limited techniques. One can computerize clerks and improve services: 1,300 New York City welfare clerks were replaced by a data system keyed to thirty-two welfare centers, with more than 240,000 cases easily accessible by punching keys. One can put civilians in a few precinct jobs, freeing police for street patrols. One can trim some middle-management fat through span-of-control studies. One can monitor service productivity through management-by-objective indices: the number of potholes filled, good arrests made, code violations cleared, schoolchildren immunized, or catch basins cleared.

One can contract out services. Many cite San Francisco's use of private carters for sanitation. Others note the Mafia dominance of carters in eastern cities. There's also the dubious bet of casino gambling with its ties to organized crime, its twenty-four-hour cities where crime breeds.* A more useful management reform is purchasing in bulk, such as fuel-oil purchases. Or one can increase parking-fine revenues with more meter maids or tire "boots": New York made $92 million from such fines in 1981 alone. Finally, one can hire more auditors and assessors for better returns on business, income and sales taxes—and more timely assessments on rising values from commercial property downtown.

• The bottom rung of management reform is voluntarism such as the teen-age Guardian Angels patrolling the subways of New York. These young citizens divert us from the real issue of why there aren't more real cops guarding the subways. Voluntarism is an American tradition. Thirty-five of the fifty-five signers of the Declaration of Independence were volunteer firemen, and De

---

* A better gambling idea: legalize numbers. This gets minorities into legitimate, taxpaying jobs in a major slum industry. Or there is the more controversial idea of legalizing prostitution, putting it and smut films into defined red-light areas as in Western Europe. This would also raise new tax revenues, reduce street crime, help get prostitutes off drugs and out of their trade, and improve public health through regular doctor checkups of the women to control and reduce VD. Unlike drugs, prostitution is endemic to society—even Warsaw Pact nations wink at the trade.

Tocqueville found many mutual-help societies 150 years ago. But voluntarism's corporate revival by Ronald Reagan has limited use for cities today. Corporations can help with job-training programs, but otherwise they tend to boost things like culture, parks or public schools. More controversial help like legal or health services for the poor tends to find fewer pro bono servitors.

A voluntarist variation comes from Professors Raymond Horton and Charles Brecher in their fine analysis of New York City's budget, *Setting Municipal Priorities, 1982.* They would modify citizen behavior to improve services. For example, they note that only 25 percent of 7 million annual calls on the 911 system are real emergencies. They suggest that if only 10 percent of the frivolous calls were not made, 500 cops would be freed from needless radio calls. Or why not cut the false alarms that tie up firemen? And why can't the poor stop using hospital emergency rooms for common colds?

In a perfect world, why not indeed. But until the poor have regular doctors and continuity of care, they will rush to hospital ERs if their child has a fever of 99 degrees. And until slum kids have jobs in summer, there will be false alarms—a famous index of slum anger, as Moynihan noted in his "benign neglect" memo to Nixon.*

In truth, only minor changes in citizen behavior can be made. A law against dog excrement means fairly clean New York streets; a ban on smoking in elevators works.† But the only major change in citizen behavior comes during water-saving campaigns in droughts—a common crisis. Mutual aid is otherwise remote from an era of tax revolt and human-potential movements. A law against loud radios has quieted the New York subways, but meanwhile graffiti go on visually raping trains, and kids kick out car windows in a perverse "game." Given the service neglect, joblessness and growing despair of the urban poor, these things happen when politicians limit resources.

---

* I rode in a South Bronx fire engine one evening. What a lot of excited kids were rushing about as this awesome monster arrived with its bells, lights and sirens on those dull, dimly lit summer streets.

† New York's many antilitter drives have mainly been failures. "Don't Be a Litterbug," "Pick It Up, Pal" and "Don't Dump on New York" are past slogans recycling a necessary and endless plea. Too few garbage collectors is one problem, with the other stated candidly by former sanitation commissioner Anthony Vacarello in 1977: "New Yorkers are slobs."

## 2. The Myth of Uncontrollable Crime

The Gallup Poll finds crime the main force driving people from cities. The notion is that we just don't know how to stop all that crime since 1977. It's an unfathomable scourge, a medieval plague. This myth is a fine rationale for cutting police to balance budgets. Even sophisticated analyst Nathan Glazer shrugs that while cities can fix potholes, repair bridges or pick up trash, "there are other things we don't seem to be able to do: educate those who will not be educated, teach to work those who don't know how and don't want to learn, reduce crime, prevent those who destroy themselves with drugs or drink from doing so."

Ronald Reagan informed a police convention in 1981 that controlling crime "isn't simply a question of more money, more police, more courts, more prosecutors. It is ultimately a moral dilemma, one that calls for a moral or, if you will, a spiritual solution."

Things like pornography, TV violence and broken families certainly undermine stability today. But Mr. Reagan's spiritual strategy is only a small part of a much bigger picture. Also small in the picture is the recent outcry for harsher laws and sentences. This means a huge leap in prison populations, with 292,000 inmates of 1977 up to 412,000 by early 1983 (off recent growth trends, some see 500,000 convicts by next year). As mandatory or sterner sentences and less use of parole fill the cells, the *Washington Post* ran an editorial saying how "fewer and fewer of us talk much about the 'root causes of crime' any more." By the middle of 1983, there were 1,202 prisoners on death row, the highest number ever. Twenty states were under court orders to relieve things like overcrowding, as two inmates arrived for every new bed added in 1981. Only Russia and South Africa had more prisoners per capita.

• *Jobs.* Jobs are inevitably the main problem. As the federal definition of "full employment" rose from 4 percent joblessness in 1971 to 6 percent today, the violent crime rate also rose by half. Another coincidence: 69 percent of New York State welfare clients in 1980 were from New York City and 69 percent of state prison inmates were also from that city. The crime-poverty link is long established.

As work and hope receded from slums in the 1970s, crime rates replaced riots as a fever chart of unrest among the poor—the implosive rage of crime replacing the explosive chaos of riot. The media saw slums cooled off. The Miami riot of 1980 was the only major outbreak since the hot summer of 1967 and the disturbances after the assassination of Dr. Martin Luther King in 1968. But as former New York City mayor John V. Lindsay has observed, the crime wave after 1977 has been "the slow-motion riot" of dying cities. Thus for every person killed in the Detroit and Newark riots of 1967, forty-five people were murdered in New York City in 1981. Riots make great copy, but they pale next to the murder wave that since 1977 has killed more Americans than all the soldiers we lost in the Korean and Vietnam wars. New York City set world murder records for 1979, then 1980, and then 1981, the last year with 1,834 homicides.

Robots in factories and automation in offices threaten even more unemployment. The federal definition of "full employment" could rise to 8 percent or even 10 percent joblessness by 1990. A massive federal effort to train, retrain and employ a lot of displaced blue- and white-collar workers is needed, otherwise the Luddite protests of 1810 will be revived by a broad range of the dispossessed. No such employment policy is in view. President Reagan cut CETA and similar job programs in half in 1981, and only a revived Congress prevented him from phasing out the remains in 1982. Black teen-age joblessness in the past dozen years has risen from 29 percent in 1970 to 40 percent by the late 1970s, then a phenomenal 51 percent in 1981. Since the sixteen-to-twenty-four-age cohort is traditionally the leader in crime data, the rise of teen-age joblessness is ominous.*

• *Kids.* The baby boom is over. The point was made by former Attorney General Griffin Bell and Governor James Thompson of Illinois in a report on violent crime to Ronald Reagan in 1981.†

---

* A controversial 1976 study by sociologist M. Harvey Brenner of Johns Hopkins University contended that a 1 percent rise in unemployment was accompanied by murder rising 5.7 percent and state prison populations growing 4 percent, with suicide up 4.1 percent as well. Brenner saw the worst stress among unemployed males from fifteen to twenty-four. He noted that murder and imprisonment rates in the Depression were only matched in recent years, the years when the definition of "full employment" went from 4 percent in 1971 to 6 percent today.

† The Bell-Thompson report put a strong focus on preventive detention, stronger sentences and more prison construction. But better halfway-house use could cut today's terrible prison overcrowding.

In past terms, they had a point. In his book on the baby boom, *Great Expectations,* Landon Y. Jones notes that the sixteen-to-twenty-four-year-old group hit its peak in 1976, the year that our crime rate dropped after five years of growth. Even violent crime dropped 4 percent in 1976, the first drop since 1960. Then came 1977. Crime rose again and kept rising through 1980. It rose again even though President Carter expanded CETA and public works employment programs and cut joblessness by several points. More people had jobs, there were fewer kids and there was more crime. Why?

One reason then and now is that the poor in cities haven't heard about the end of the baby boom. Many of them are first- or second-generation migrants from farms in the South, Puerto Rico, Latin America, Southeast Asia and, most ominously, Mexico with its explosive birth rate. They are peasants from cultures that encourage big families to overcome high infant-mortality rates even though little farmland remains. This cultural heritage is hard to overcome, and many of these recent arrivals are Catholic, another strong factor for high birth rates among the urban poor.

The flood of Mexicans out west results in things like 350 teenage gangs in Los Angeles, credited with up to 192 of the 1,020 murders in 1980. Or there is the steady rise of illegitimate children in our cities: 36 percent of all Boston and New York births, 44 percent in Chicago and 55 percent in Washington. With more than half of Washington's babies illegitimate, the infant mortality was almost double the national rate. More unhealthy illegitimate and battered kids from slums means more teen-age violence ahead. Consider two facts from 1981: 55 percent of all black births in America were illegitimate and 51 percent of all black teen-agers were unemployed.*

• *Guns.* A 1980 Treasury Department estimate counted 143 million guns in private hands. As America grew 11 percent in the 1970s, guns escalated by 36 percent. Only the civil war of North-

---

* When crime dropped 5 percent in the first half of 1982, some hailed the fading of the baby boom and the start of a new, downward trend. But a small drop after four years of escalation hardly qualified as a trend, and while all crime dropped 2 percent, *violent* crime rose 1 percent. Hailing this "apparent reversal" of crime after two record years, even Attorney General Smith was careful to note how "the fact that the all-time high was reached and maintained for a two-year period should be a major concern for the nation."

ern Ireland has inspired a higher murder rate among industrial democracies. In 1979, America had 10,728 gun murders. England had 8. Japan, with more than half our population, had 171 gun crimes. We had more than 337,000. A similar ratio was found for our other main trade rival: only 1 West German was killed or robbed in a gun crime for every 1,300 Americans victimized by guns.

Federal gun controls? Even the bipartisan proposal of the Bell-Thompson panel to ban imported handgun parts was rejected by Ronald Reagan. His counterproposal was mandatory sentences for federal gun crimes. This is fine after the fact, but it is no deterrent. A similar bill from then-Governor Reagan of California in 1969 added five to fifteen years for California gun crimes, but Los Angeles had a murder rate three times that of America in 1980. Stronger gun controls are needed, like a 1975 Massachusetts ban on the carrying of handguns. The law was effective: where Boston had 134 murders in 1974, it had 80 by 1979. As writer Michael McManus points out, quarrels among family or friends lead to most murders and "other weapons—such as barstools—just aren't as lethal as guns." Yet a Massachusetts ban on gun *possession* was defeated by more than 2 to 1 in a 1976 vote. Only the small town of Morton Grove, Illinois, has imposed such a ban. Beyond its 23,000 residents are 230 million Americans with 143 million guns. The one bright note on gun control was that California's moderate Proposition 15 of 1982 did somewhat better than the Massachusetts ban. In time, its proposal to let people keep registered guns may be passed.

Or there are the Reagan cuts in the Bureau of Alcohol, Tobacco, and Firearms of the Treasury Department. Half of all gun dealers were inspected a dozen years ago. But as their numbers doubled, the BATF inspections declined:

| Year | Gun Dealers | Inspections | Inspections per Number of Dealers |
|------|-------------|-------------|-----------------------------------|
| 1969 | 87,000 | 47,000 | 54% |
| 1980 | 185,000 | 12,000 | 7% |

The thin ranks are obscured by high-tech efficiency: BATF computers took only sixteen minutes to trace the gun fired at President Reagan by John W. Hinckley, Jr. Recovered from this assault, Mr. Reagan proposed to further decimate BATF inspectors: four of five to be cut, leaving twenty-eight inspectors to keep an eye on 185,000 gun dealers. The dealers could stop keeping accurate records, or worrying about background checks for criminal acts or drug use. *The Washington Post* recalled how a Tennessee investigation was scrapped after Bureau agents "for lack of money backed out of an undercover deal to buy some dynamite and a number of machine guns, and in Florida, BATF cancelled a deal for a car full of plastic explosives."

• *Drugs.* The FBI projected drug sales in 1981 were at $79 billion, almost equaling the earnings of the *entire Fortune* 500 list of $81 billion. When drug use reaches such levels, social stability declines, and crime is fueled. At the center of the mess is cocaine, its projected sales of $32 billion in 1981 representing twice the combined earnings of Exxon, Mobil, Socal, Gulf, Amoco, Arco and Shell. Hollywood cocaine use is familiar, but it is also popular among less glamorous professionals. *U.S. News & World Report* quotes an accountant who praises the drug in hair-raising terms: "I can grind out accounting studies all coked up. Do a little line at 9 P.M., and work far into the night, awake, alert and happy."

The growth in cocaine use has been spectacular. Once the drug of the poor, cocaine became the "drug of choice" for upscale addicts, its traffic up 50 percent between 1980 and 1981. Investigators estimate more than 10 million users, of whom half deal in it as well. The product has been grown for $4 (sic) a pound in Peru or Bolivia, processed at $6,000 in Colombia, then sold at well over $100,000 on the streets of New York. The indictment of John DeLorean was only one of hundreds of such white-collar arrests, his alleged cache of $6.5 million in cocaine only enough to meet California's needs for a day. Federal officials seized 3,748 pounds of cocaine in Florida, and asserted that businessmen, doctors, lawyers and bank officers were among the ringleaders involved.

The other main drug is marijuana, with $24 billion in estimated sales for 1981. This is also a major American crop; some estimates assert $10 billion grown annually, which would make it our third biggest crop. It may be the second crop in Florida after oranges, and at $1.5 billion may earn as much as California's grapes and raisins combined. Its use has been declining in high schools. A Michigan study found a sharp drop in pot use among students, and student arrests for possession in Los Angeles dropped 40 percent between 1976 and 1982. But while 74 percent of America opposes legalization, the market is still so great that many failing family farms turn to it in desperation, the way that impoverished farmers in Peru and Bolivia turn to coca as their cash crop.

Perhaps only a spiritual solution can overcome such madness. Drugs are hardly "recreational." Cocaine overuse often leads to psychosis. Quaalude abuse in Florida led to an escalation in traffic arrests in 1981. Marijuana may impair lungs, reduce immunity, decrease sperm counts and affect unborn children. A recent Temple University study found that 237 heroin addicts in Baltimore committed more than 500,000 crimes during eleven years. The Reagan war on drugs was at first a sluggish crusade. Late in 1981 Marvin Stone, editor of *U.S. News & World Report*, wrote an editorial titled "What War on Crime?" He noted the cuts in BATF gun inspectors, the loss of 1,000 FBI employees, and some proposed Reagan slashes on the drug control front.* A main target for the proposed cuts had been the Drug Enforcement Administration. Reagan planned to cut DEA funds by 12 percent for 1982, and Marvin Stone observed how "investigations shatter because there is no money to pay informants. A major suspect has to be released because the DEA could not afford an agent's fare to go and identify him." Attorney General William French Smith intervened, and the Reagan cut of 12 percent for the DEA became a 6 percent increase instead.

Federal troops were also diverted by the drug war. As the South Florida Task Force doubled its ranks in 1982, some 300 agents and prosecutors were pulled from other regions. With smugglers now working beyond the Florida net and federal offices stripped to strengthen that net, the Justice Department needed a new, national strategy. On October 14, President Reagan announced plans for a new web of twelve regional Task Forces in Atlanta, Baltimore, Boston, Chicago, Denver, Detroit, Houston, Los Angeles, New York, San Diego, San Francisco and St. Louis.

Beyond the Task Force war on the home front is the main war on drugs at points of origin abroad in Southeast Asia, the Middle

---

* Beyond the FBI loss of 1,000 employees, Stone noted cuts in the Bureau's arson and fingerprint services, both crucial to local law enforcement. A *Washington Post* summary of proposed Reagan crime cuts for fiscal 1983 quoted an OMB analysis on the FBI which predicted "probably no new undercover operations will be authorized" against organized or white-collar crime.

East, Sicily and South America. The DEA exposure of the Bolivian government's drug ring helped oust the military regime running a $1.5 billion business. President Nixon retired Turkish heroin by spending $35 million in helping poppy farmers convert to regular crops. President Ford later destroyed most of Mexico's marijuana crops. With a mix of subsidies, responsible pesticides (i.e., no Paraquat) and pressure, more can be done today.

The main heroin suppliers are the Golden Triangle of Burma, Laos and Thailand and the Golden Crescent of Afghanistan, Pakistan and Iran, with Sicily the final processor. Some areas are beyond our control: Afghanistan and Communist areas in Burma, and the hashish crop in Lebanon.* Although heroin use grew in America after 1977, both Jimmy Carter and Ronald Reagan had cut funds for drug wars abroad. When the Golden Triangle tripled heroin output in 1981, the DEA office in Bangkok was threatened with cuts, although a dozen refineries operated openly, most of them run by a drug lord with a private army of several thousand.

It is imperative to destroy the heroin crops of Southeast Asia, the coca crops of Bolivia and Peru, and the marijuana and coca crops of Colombia that hook our children and ruin their lives.

• *Cops.* As we saw in Part I, thin blue lines in many Sunbelt cities fed the crime wave after 1977. Cities like Houston, Dallas and Phoenix had, in per capita terms, half the cops of Chicago and twice its crime. This seemed to confirm Chief Justice Warren Burger's remark to the American Bar Association in 1981 that deterrence is undercut since "many large cities have either reduced their police forces or failed to keep them in balance with double-digit crime inflation." The same goes for Snowbelt cities. Newark, for example, cut its police force by 33 percent between 1977 and 1980 and its violent crime rate soared 93 percent. Philadelphia cut its cops by 10 percent in that time, as its violent crime rate shot up 47 percent.

By 1981, police were in such short supply across America that for every cop on the beat there were two private security guards

---

* Despite Communism's professed scorn for opiates, Cuba, Bulgaria and China peddle drugs. Four Cuban officials have been indicted by a Miami grand jury for smuggling, two of them being members of the Communist Party Central Committee and Castro intimates. Bulgarians sometimes help ship Middle East heroin to Sicilian processors. Red China is the main source of illegal methaqualone in America, with up to 200 million Quaalude tablets attributed to its supplies.

elsewhere. Indeed there were more private guards in the sixteen municipal hospitals of New York City than real police in either Minneapolis or Memphis that year.

New York City illustrates the Snowbelt tale. It had 31,104 cops in 1974 and 22,165 by 1981, a 29 percent cut although the population shrank 7 percent. In late 1980, the city's Police Commissioner told *The New York Times* that "this city, in effect, is conducting a vast social experiment. The experiment is 'How far can you cut back your police forces before crime runs rampant?' " Six months later, a study showed crime complaints up 16 percent and arrests down 5 percent. This time, Commissioner Robert McGuire didn't ask questions about "social experiments." Instead, he told the *Times* that the rising complaints and falling arrests meant "our manpower losses finally caught up with us." Police were so thin in 1980 that it took 6.9 minutes to respond to a 911 emergency call against 2 minutes in 1977.

The more cops = less crime formula is seen in New York subways. After two months of subway crime stories in 1979, Mayor Koch put on overtime patrols and crime fell nearly 40 percent. A year later, Koch cut back the patrols and crime shot back up 70 percent. Only after more pressure from the City Council did Koch start hiring more subway police. Meanwhile, his uneven war on subway crime inspired the famed Guardian Angels. These teens in red berets were great copy. When Lieutenant Governor Mario Cuomo threw a wine-and-cheese party for them in 1981 he referred to "the most extraordinary social phenomenon of the last few decades. It is outstanding that out of the wreckage which we, the politicians, have created [comes a group] that helps people instead of mugging them."

But is it outstanding or depressing? The kids are dedicated and decent, but what are we to make of a society that won't tax itself to hire adults to patrol subways? The Guardian Angels reflect a growing and desperate belief that we can magically cope without cops. In suburbs, citizen CB patrols can supplement cops, alerting them to strange vans or people. But citizen vigilance in cities is limited. Too often it's an excuse to avoid paying for protection, as people play cops on the cheap. The idea of citizen "eyes and ears" on city streets was popularized by Jane Jacobs in *The Death and Life of Great American Cities*. It works in Mrs. Jacobs' former neighborhood of Greenwich Village, with its middle-to-upper-class milieu. But not in slums, save in controlled areas like housing projects. This distinction is lost in the press. Narrating an otherwise useful television program on crime in 1982, even *New York Times* columnist Tom Wicker fell into the trap.

Wicker reported on a large area of the South Bronx which had one of the lowest crime rates in New York City: the Belmont section up near Fordham University, which had 16 percent of the people in the 48th Precinct but only 5 percent of its crime. It also had a lot of middle-class Italians. Italians are noted for family stability, and are famously xenophobic about strangers, the *forestieri*. Italians are known for lively street life in cafés, markets and restaurants. Belmont is such a lively enclave that it was used for street scenes in *The Godfather*. Similar Italian pockets of stability are found in the west end of the Coney Island slum in Brooklyn or the tiny Pleasant Avenue strip in East Harlem. Belmont is not the South Bronx; it's middle class. And middle class means very little street crime.

Articles about effective citizen patrols tend to be set in suburbia where the patrols work. The Neighborhood Watch program claims more than 5,000 groups across America, and the National Sheriff's Association projects 25,000 community crime groups. TV spots urge viewers to form such groups to "take a bite out of crime," and FBI data for 1981 showed only a mild rise of 7 percent in suburban crime since 1975. Even *U.S. News & World Report* confuses the stable suburbs with a nationwide "People's War Against Crime." A 1981 survey led off with the notion that "fed up with being victimized by crime, harried Americans are doubling up their fists and fighting back."

But most of the story was set in suburbia with CB patrols. There was a new "buddy system" in Ronald Reagan's former residence, Pacific Palisades. There was Harlingen, Texas, where "volunteers patrolling in golf carts" cut burglary to nearly zero. There were enclaves like Sugar Creek in Houston with perimeter walls, guarded gates and private security patrols. The one urban example in the *U.S. News* survey showed how misleading "people's war on crime" stories can be. The story was about 13,000 public housing tenants who patrol in 764 groups in the projects of New York City. The tenant patrols in blue Windbreakers are familiar and welcome sights.

A final example of our feeble war on crime concerns arson. The FBI made arson a major crime in its Uniform Crime Reports.

Magazines and television report on crime that kills thousands of people a year and costs perhaps half of $6 billion in annual fire losses. But where is the political will to fight it? Arson cannot be stopped without more social stability. Failing business firms will have insurance fires, and slum pathology will feed arson from spurned lovers, addicts, derelicts, or disturbed kids with matches.

But one major source can be controlled—landlords torching for insurance. Some cities settle for computer "models" to predict likely arson targets. But these merely complement the main weapons. More fire marshals are needed to deter arson through patrols as are tougher laws requiring landlords to use insurance payouts for repairs only.*

## 3. The Myth of Reindustrialization

The cry for reindustrialization went up after 1980, but the groundwork for crisis was laid in the 1950s. Countries like France, Germany and Japan began opening new plants with new production modes, many of the latter American discoveries. They opened the oxygen-process steel plants that we invented as we stuck to the old open hearths that lose price wars. They drove about in small, fuel-efficient cars as we laughed at George Romney and his Rambler, and his attacks on "gas guzzlers" in the 1950s. In 1959, Joseph Engelberger developed a pioneering industrial robot in New York. Ignored at home, he was invited to Japan in the early 1960s, where "at the first meeting, there were 600 people . . ." †

The Sputnik launching in 1957 briefly woke up America to foreign advances. In 1961, John F. Kennedy got into the Sputnik

---

* Arson in Boston was rampant until a ring of thirty-one torchers was broken up in the late 1970s. Then arson shot up to old levels in 1982, as part of a 23 percent rise across America. Meanwhile, Boston firemen had been cut 20 percent under the Proposition 2½ tax cap that "limited resources" after 1980, with money also running out for an effective arson warning system. As the firemen dropped from 2,000 to 1,500, their average age rose to forty-nine.

† As foreigners applied our technology in the 1950s, a popular film warned of America's failure to reindustrialize. Robert Wise's *Executive Suite* (1954) concerned a factory that was being milked for profits. A battle for the presidency pitted comptroller Fredric March against designer William Holden. March claimed the aging factory was only a "financial institution yielding the highest return on investments." Holden argued for reindustrialization, noting that "sometimes you have to use the profits for the growth of the company." Holden got the job in the film, but America failed to get his message.

spirit by pledging to put a man on the moon. We won that walk-over in 1969, but as Armstrong and Aldrin walked on the moon, an industrial moonscape was emerging in Akron, Youngstown and Detroit. A dozen years later, four Snowbelt heavy industries had collapsed:

- Some 30 percent of our auto workers lost their jobs after 1978. Imports led by Japan, Germany and France went from a 10 percent to a 32 percent market share in a dozen years.
- In 1947, we produced more than half of the world's steel. But 57 percent of our steelworkers lost their jobs after 1957. Meanwhile, imports led by Japan, Canada, Germany and France rose to a 22 percent market share.
- The last tire produced in Akron rolled off the General's line in 1982, in what John Gunther once called "the rubber center of the universe." France and Japan alone have a 10 percent market share here.
- Machine-tool imports were 10 percent of our market in 1977, but an incredible 41 percent in 1982. Ironically that share may rise as America reindustrializes to compete with Europe and Japan, since their machine-tool firms are more flexible in handling the rapid-change orders involved.

America's science teaching is in crisis, as Japan widens its awesome lead in numbers of engineers. The number of science teachers shrank by 64 percent in the 1970s. In 1981, half of our new math and science teachers in high schools were not even certified to teach their subjects. Noting how the Pentagon got $30 billion more in fiscal 1983 as education got only $70 million extra, astronomer Carl Sagan said that "the United States is behaving as if it thinks it doesn't have a future." *

As science declines in schools, an engineering gap grows. Where 6 percent of our college graduates had engineering degrees, 21 percent did in Japan and 37 percent did in Germany.

* Six months after Dr. Sagan's remark, the National Commission on Excellence in Education issued its report on our education crisis, "A Nation At Risk," and the debate was on. Beyond this issue lies a larger, current crisis: 26 million Americans are functionally illiterate, with 46 million more operating at a "marginal" level. The Labor Department has recently projected that 75 percent of our unemployed lack reading or communications skills for work in this high-tech era. Our school crisis, then, is only the main part of a huge, transgenerational crisis.

We now have 20 lawyers for every attorney in Japan, while they have six engineers for every one of ours. With 60 percent of the world's lawyers for 5 percent of its people, America has a litigation binge that featured 12 million civil suits in 1977. The American Electronics Association estimates that we need 200,000 more engineers by 1985, while our universities can graduate only 70,000 by then. (A Japanese maxim says that "Engineers make the pie grow larger; lawyers only decide how to carve it up.")

Since 1971, Japan's R&D has soared 500 percent as ours grew 150 percent. Combined with Japan's larger output of engineers, this strengthens its high-tech challenge to America in the 1980s. The Pentagon and NASA actually outspent our private sector for R&D. This unproductive lead should lengthen with the Reagan defense binge, which could raise the Pentagon share of the federal budget from 24 percent in 1981 to as much as 37 percent by 1985. Apart from its inflationary role and the accompanying cut in social-program dollars, defense crimps high tech in some odd ways noted by Robert B. Reich of Harvard. Reich observes that the Pentagon spends as much in high-tech development as Japan's MITI, in areas like computers, lasers, robots and semiconductors. But while Japan puts subsidized companies into a competitive arena, the Pentagon tolerates cost overruns. MITI also helps companies through the long time needed to develop, test and market. Pentagon contractors are inevitably "subject to relatively sudden changes in national-security needs and prevailing politics." And where Japan encourages new factories to locate in areas with strong infrastructure and labor skills, Pentagon contractors tend to go to Sunbelt states, "where infrastructure has not yet caught up with economic development, and semiskilled labor is in short supply, while the industrial Midwest suffers unemployment and an underused, crumbling infrastructure."

More defense spending does mainly one thing for the Snowbelt. It hires its urban poor for a mercenary army. Reagan defense spending has led Republican Representative James Leach of Iowa to observe that enlistment may soon be one of only a few federal career paths. The "volunteer army" created by the unholy coalition of Richard Nixon and the New Left of 1973 may well prove a symbol of our social and economic decline. As Snowbelt factories close and CETA jobs are cut, chronic recession among the urban poor is a fine recruiting poster. Indeed the old patriotic appeal of "Uncle Sam Wants *You*" has been chanted to the career-pitch jingle of "Be All That You Can *Be*." *

Too few engineers and too much research money put into defense are threatening our high-tech lead. The collapse of our heavy industries is crisis enough. The main problem is meager capital spending after the 1974–75 recession. Just as six years of cutbacks after fiscal crisis in 1975 led to New York subway breakdowns in 1981, so with the old Snowbelt plants. Seven years of milking old factories meant higher wages for workers, more dividends for investors, and even older factories.†

American companies forgot the management principles they had taught the world: investment, testing, marketing and quality control. Quality was crucial; a Ford survey in 1981 found that 85 percent of Americans put quality above price in buying cars. As Robert B. Reich has observed, it is better quality that often loses market shares to Europe and Japan; our share of these markets has gone down by an average of 50 percent between 1970 and 1980:

| | |
|---|---|
| athletic equipment | hand tools |
| automobiles | industrial robots |
| cameras | machine tools |
| color television | medical equipment |
| computer chips | microwave ovens |
| electric motors | optical equipment |
| electron microscopes | radial tires |
| food processors | |

Then came the 1981–83 recession. Capital spending, already slowed from an annual average of 5.5 percent in the 1960s to 3.9

---

* The case against the volunteer army is easily summarized: it is too expensive, it leaves America without a trained reserve for a ground war in Europe, and it is undemocratic for reasons well stated by Joseph Califano, one of its few Democratic critics in 1973: "It is truly Kafkaesque thinking for public officials who call themselves liberals to support this six billion investment of scarce public resources so the lower classes can fight our wars."

† Capital itself went abroad. In *The Deindustrialization of America*, Barry J. Bluestone and Bennett Harrison note that where 10 percent of American-owned manufacturing was done overseas in 1970, about 25 percent was by 1980. Our investment abroad grew sixteen times between 1950 and 1980, from $12 billion to $190 billion. Some industrial giants added more foreign than domestic jobs, with GE adding 30,000 jobs abroad while losing 25,000 jobs here, and RCA adding 19,000 jobs overseas as it lost 14,000 jobs in America.

percent in the 1970s, declined 4.8 percent in 1982. The Commerce Department projected more decline in 1983, for what could be the first two-year drop since World War II. High interest rates, idle plant capacity and low profits held down new investment, as did the huge federal deficits fueled by massive Reagan tax cuts. Instead of launching an era of plant expansion, Reaganomics had intensified the capital crunch, and America's deindustrialization.

• America invented the basic oxygen process and continuous casting of steel more than thirty years ago, but Germany and Japan led other nations in opening plants with these new modes after 1950. By 1982, only 26 percent of our steel was made by continuous casters, where 75 percent of Japan's steel was.

• America did not invent the small, fuel-efficient car, but George Romney had introduced his Rambler in the 1950's. Two decades later, OPEC oil prices caught Detroit off guard: fuel-efficient imports went from 10 percent of our market in 1971 to 32 percent by 1982. Only in the late 1970s did our Big Three scramble to retool for small-car production. Although GM stuck with its $40 billion investment plan until late 1981, its former chairman Thomas A. Murphy conceded to *The New York Times Magazine* that the 1970s had been "all but a disaster. We seem to have spent most of our time not making decisions."

• American management expert Quentin Deming suggested worker "quality circles" to improve productivity back in the 1950s. The *Fortune* 500 ignored him. Japan Inc. was at his feet. Japan "discovered" quality circles, and West Germany evolved its similar "codetermination" policy for workers. Only in the 1980s did America rediscover its own idea, with Deming hired by Detroit. The guaranteed lifetime employment used by a third of all Japanese firms is now being discussed by the UAW and the Big Three. That is also an American invention. As Akio Morita, the head and cofounder of Sony, has pointed out, this Japanese "tradition" began in the late 1940s when General Douglas MacArthur ordered such guarantees as a way of stabilizing new Japanese firms during the American occupation.

• There is that typical Japanese invention, the industrial robot, invented in America in 1959. Japan now has 60 percent of all advanced robots. Robots and better factory organization meant Japan doubled car production in a decade, using the same number of workers. Japan also has a factory where robots make robots, just like England around 1850, when machines began to make machine tools.

• Three of our oil firms have dominated solar energy research, holding 80 percent of the world market for photovoltaic cells (PVCs) in 1980. But this dropped to a 55 percent share in two years, as Japan, Europe and some Third World nations entered the field. And as Ronald Reagan was cutting federal PVC grants by 66 percent from $150 million to $50 million, Japan's PVC outlays were rising 140 percent, to $30 million in 1982.

• Bell Labs invented the transistor in 1947, but Sony mass-produced transistor radios after 1955, and Japan has dominated consumer electronics for years. A new wave of electronic cameras and digital audio disks suggests more of the same ahead. And while America long dominated the semiconductor field, each new generation of microchips saw Japan make dramatic new gains. In 1970, Japan had no market share for the 1,000-function, or 1K, chip. Then it got a 12 percent share of the 4,000-function, 4K, chip market in 1975. Today's 64K-chip market sees Japan projected for a staggering 70 percent world share by 1986. When the 256K chip arrives, some think firms like Fujitsu, Hitachi and Nippon Electric will so dominate the market that only a few American giants like Motorola and Texas Instruments will remain. One reason for Japan's rapid dominance has been fewer defective chips. A Hewlett-Packard analysis of chip quality found that Japan's worst was often better than our best. Texas Instruments even makes most of its chips in Japan.*

• We made the first computer in 1946. It weighed thirty tons, was thirty by fifty feet, had 18,000 vacuum tubes—and today's pocket calculators can do as much. America still dominates computer markets, and new personal computers from Japan did poorly here in 1982. But some see Japan biding its time, studying our market for an onslaught around 1985. Meanwhile, she is beating us to Third World markets, with the Fujitsu Computer School training

---

* IBM produces more chips for its own use than all of America's and Japan's chips combined. Describing the fast strides from 1K to 64K chips, Stephen Lohr writes in *The New York Times Magazine* that had aircrafts progressed at such speed, "the Concorde would now hold 10,000 passengers, travel at 60,000 miles an hour and a ticket would cost 1 cent." *The Wall Street Journal* similarly notes the new "monomode" optical fiber at Bell Labs. Gutenberg took five years to set his Bible in print, while the new fiber may transmit sixteen Bibles in one second.

other Pacific nationals. Japan will invest $70 billion in computers in a decade, with nearly half that for computer teaching and training, spreading Japan Inc. products abroad. This is the "technology transfer" that the Third World asks of America at the U.N., and Japan is doing it today, opening new markets abroad later on.

• We also dominate supercomputers through Control Data and Cray, but Japan has two challenges under way. For beyond these machines capable of 100 million calculations per second is a future computer for 10 billion a second (or 1 quadrillion a day). Japan invests up to $200 million a year here, and also has two teams competing to invent a fifth-generation computer, or "superbrain," capable of understanding speech and possibly able to program itself.

• While America holds the overall computer lead, Japan makes far better industrial use of each new generation. Using a central computer from Digital Equipment in Massachusetts, a Japanese firm put more than 100,000 hours of programming into a new industrial art where computers direct robots, or "mechatronics." In the Yamazaki factory at Nagoya, our computer directs their robots in making machine tools. On the night shift, the only human is a watchman making rounds. All told, 12 men do the work of 220 in this pioneering mechatronic plant.*

America remains more productive than Japan, but the latter is fast closing ground. As Dwight Macdonald pointed out, America today resembles England around 1900: losing a longtime lead, as markets erode both at home and abroad. Let us examine this problem as seen in three industries crucial to the Snowbelt states.

• *Autos.* In 1979, the industry planned an $80 billion overhaul through 1985. But recession and interest rates cut sales and cash for reinvestment. The auto slump saw Detroit lose $4.2 billion in 1980, then $1.3 billion more in 1981. Working capital for reindustrialization dropped sharply: from $13 billion on hand in 1978 to only $300 million by late 1981. Even GM put its five-year over-

---

* Among the Japanese users of personal computers is Bendo Kagawa, an ad man turned Zen priest. With his Apple II, he designed a program for contemplation, where Sanskrit characters and images of Buddhist gods slowly change colors on the display screen as Indian music plays. "Now you don't need to spend long hours sitting in a temple to meditate," he tells *Newsweek.*

haul on hold. As well, the end of the baby boom meant fewer first-time drivers after 1980. Noting a "saturated" American market for cars, one survey projected that the 3 percent annual growth of the 1970s would slow to 2 percent a year in the 1980s, then down to just over 1 percent in the 1990s.

To revive sales in 1982, the Big Three quickly cut costs. A UAW-Ford agreement began to close a wage gap that saw $20 an hour in America against $12 in Japan. Another factor adding up to $1,500 per car was productivity. Through better-run factories, quality circles and robots, Japan went from 450,000 workers producing 5.2 million cars in 1971 to the same 450,000 workers producing 11 million cars in 1980.

Then there is quality. By 1982, our cars compared favorably with imports for miles per gallon, and an insurance survey found that small American cars were safer than small Japanese ones. Thirteen of the seventeen cars with the worst claims records over two years were Japanese, while American cars of comparable size had the best records. But as a Commerce Department study noted in 1981, "a poor quality image is difficult to turn around and the shift unfortunately requires an extended period of time." Even if costs are cut and consumers appreciate quality, domestic demand is declining, and three obstacles to revival remain:

• The immediate problem is that of auto parts manufactured abroad. A million engines bought abroad in 1979 rose to 3 million by 1981.

• The intermediate problem may be the diesel car. By 1985 Volkswagen may have finished developing a diesel car that will sweep the market.

• The strategic problem is robotization. With robots, GM cut 337 welders to 35 at a Pontiac plant, retraining the workers for other tasks. GM plans on using 14,000 robots by 1990, and this could replace 40,000 workers. A Wayne State University economist projects that by then robots could replace up to 200,000 auto and auto-supply workers.

• *Steel.* A long-term collapse became a severe depression in 1982. Since 1957, steel jobs had gone from 719,000 to 306,000—a loss of 57 percent. Then came the 1982 collapse in the Ohio Valley. By year's end, the mills were down to 28 percent capacity. Steel firms lost more than $3 billion that year. Yet twice in 1982 the steelworkers' union rejected a three-year wage freeze, although

27 percent of the workers were laid off and although their wages and benefits had zoomed 195 percent since 1973. (The average hourly worker costs were $19.42, or $9 an hour more than Japan, for the highest industrial wage on earth.)

As for management's bigger role in this decline, the buzzword among steel barons is diversification, not reindustrialization. Even before buying Marathon Oil in 1982, U.S. Steel had increased nonsteel assets to $4.7 billion, against $5.9 billion in steel holdings. While letting its profitable but aging Weirton, West Virginia, mill run down, National Steel was buying two large savings and loans. Armco purchased an insurance company, and dropped the five-letter S——l from a sanitized corporate name.

Meanwhile, an aging industry saw rail mills at a U.S. Steel plant in Alabama being powered in 1980 by the steam-engine process of 1785. The cost of a thorough steel overhaul was put at $30 billion. Updating plants on a twenty-five-year cycle meant $4.4 billion annually—but only $3 billion was invested in 1981. Then the bottom fell out in 1982, and even the tepid retoolings came to a halt. To gain time for reviving capacity and capital for renovation, the steel companies filed for federal relief from imports. But could that save an industry of overpaid workers, with managers diversifying portfolios?

• *Machine Tools.* Imports skyrocketed from a 10 percent market share in 1977 to a 41 percent share by late 1982. Ironically, American reindustrialization was a partial spur. As our industries retooled, America's less flexible tool firms saw Europe and Japan get the rush orders:
• When Detroit finally decided to make small cars to fend off imports, it put out rush orders for new tools in 1978. But as *Business Week* reports, our suppliers "were caught short. Lead times now stretch as much as two years for some tools." So, in order to compete with Germany and Japan in cars, Detroit bought their machine tools.
• When our steel firms finally installed the continuous-slab casting we had invented in the 1950s, twelve orders for the casting process went out, only one to an American firm.
• When our textile industry retooled for $12.5 billion in the 1970s, this was "accomplished largely by using foreign equipment," wrote *Business Week*. Our producers of textile machinery had

gone from a 93 percent market share in 1962 to only 54 percent by 1979.*

At a lower level of the tool art, the Commerce Department notes that eight of every ten nuts used in the U.S. are imports, while half of our carbon-steel valves come from abroad. Higher quality and lower costs are the reason; our valves cost $9,000 while theirs go for $5,000. A businessman told *The Wall Street Journal* that "when our client sees the difference in price, they say a valve is a valve." So many American foundries have closed that when Westinghouse needed castings for huge steam turbines, it went abroad. When General Dynamics sought large steel castings for the Trident sub, domestic suppliers were again hard to find.

The rise in imported tools is seen in one striking fact: in 1965, we exported five times the tools we imported; by 1981, we were importing twice the tools we exported. Recession cycles since 1970 have inhibited our toolmakers from updating production modes. *Business Week* observes that the tool industry's cyclical nature also probably "discourages the in-house training of workers, since it makes it less likely that individual companies will earn an adequate return on their 'human-capital' investments." The magazine suggested public grants to train machinists in a nation whose National Association of Manufacturers projects a shortage of 300,000 machinists by 1985. As they remain scarce and our industries retool, the 41 percent import share of tools could grow in a nation where two-thirds of its tools are more than ten years old, a third are more than twenty years old, and only 5 percent are numerically or computer controlled. An official at Japan's Makino company told *The Wall Street Journal* that our aging tool plants lack "the flexibility to change manufacturing schedules" for rush orders. New and better-organized Japanese firms can handle such demands. Since the Japanese are usually modest, the Makino officer's blunt view of our tool sector is devastating: "It's much easier competing against U.S. firms. In

---

* The textile retooling was one of our few timely ones. This plus the denim craze in Europe led to big U.S. exports after 1978. A flood of American and Far East textiles meant 150,000 lost textile jobs in Europe, as we captured market shares like 35 percent of all British bedsheets. Our textile overhaul was partly to comply with OSHA regulations to cut cotton dust and "brown lung disease" in aging southern mills. This meant more productive machines and mills, and the big export drive.

fact, I don't even think Japanese companies view American companies as competition."

The 1982 recession brought a nose dive in orders. As autos, aerospace and steel cut production, tool orders fell nearly 60 percent from 1981. Also shrinking our tool sector was the dollar's strength against English, German and Japanese currencies. As the dollar rose 25 percent against the yen, 19 percent against the pound and 14 percent against the mark, imports from those nations became even more popular here. A third of the exhibits at a huge Chicago tool fair in late 1982 were from abroad. By then, imports had temporarily risen to an alarming 49 percent market share here.*

As America starts to retool, the growing shortage of machinists will be felt. Over the long run, however, the main threat will be from robots or numerically controlled drills, lathes and milling machines. When one computer, a few robots and 12 men can do what 220 men usually do in the mechatronic plant of Nagoya, even machine-tool meccas like Milwaukee may be living on borrowed time.

In fairness, America's decline is not unique. England's long-term slump confirms Hannah Arendt's insight that one cannot base an economy on a tea break. Its steel slump and annual subsidy of $1 billion for British Leyland are old problems, accompanied by harsh Thatcher social cuts. France spends $20 billion on electronics through 1987, but a third of its steel jobs are gone and imports took 30 percent of its auto market, as Renault and Peugeot-Citroën took losses in 1981 and 1982. Even stable Switzerland has a run-down watch industry. Where Swiss watch exports tripled those from Japan and Hong Kong in 1974, the latter two exported more watches in 1981.

Even Japan has problems. It now faces the four "new Japans" of Hong Kong, Singapore, South Korea and Taiwan. Hong Kong and Singapore are mainly trading colonies, while Korean and Taiwanese dictators must trade more freedom for industrial progress in a climate of higher wages and more consumer goods. But all four will compete with Japan to some extent in the Pacific

---

* By the summer of 1983, the dollar's value had reached record heights against the franc, and an eight-year high against the mark. Machine tool exports had fallen by a third, and some 6.2 million export-related jobs in America were down to 4.9 million by the end of 1982, for a 40 percent share of all lost industrial jobs here during the last two years.

basin, even if Japan maintains a long regional lead in autos, ships, steel, machine tools or high tech.

More serious for Japan are internal problems. For all its R&D funds or its new "technopolis" of Tsukuba near Tokyo, this is still a consensus culture. "The 'eureka' phenomenon just isn't part of our culture," laments a Japanese businessman to *The Wall Street Journal*. This is also an aging nation. Japan's economic miracles mean that a life expectancy of fifty-five in 1949 soared to a world-leading seventy-six years today. By the year 2000, Japan will have the world's oldest population. By then, the current ratio of 7.5 workers per retiree will drop down to 3 to 1. Long overdue pressures for decent pensions will rise. Today, the Japanese face mandated retirement at fifty-five, with meager pensions starting at sixty. The result is the world's highest proportion of "retired" people at work, with an amazing 45.4 percent of those over sixty-five working in 1980. "This is the reality of lifetime employment, Japanese-style," notes Mitsuo Tajima in *The Wall Street Journal*. As the elderly grow and pensions finally become adequate, this will slow Japan's ability to invest and compete. Meanwhile, however, Japan had 2.7 percent unemployment—a record high—in 1983.

Three more factors may undermine Snowbelt economies as well: a brain drain of skilled workers to Sunbelt states; the growth of robots and factory automation; and a new drive for productivity in services.

*The Brain Drain.* Brain drains began around 300 B.C., when Greek scholars moved to Alexandria. During the 1960s over 400,000 doctors, surgeons, engineers and scientists left undeveloped nations like India, Pakistan, the Philippines and Sri Lanka for Canada, England and the United States. America has had an internal brain drain since around 1950, when Snowbelt accountants, lawyers, managers and other professionals began moving to the new boomtowns of the South or West. Then the 1980s saw a new drain with ominous signs for the Snowbelt's industrial future, as a growing share of technical graduates in areas like computing or engineering were recruited off northern campuses by Sunbelt aerospace, energy or high-tech firms. Some think this technician drain could undermine the reindustrialization of the Great Lake states. While 54 percent of Michigan State University engineering graduates took jobs within the state in 1973, only 19 percent did in 1981. Where only 3 percent of the M.S.U. graduates took Texas jobs in 1973, some 17 percent did in 1981, with the University of Michigan, Ohio State and Purdue reporting similar increases in engineering graduates headed for Sunbelt states.

Ironically, many of these young technicians were reversing their parents' career paths after World War II. Their unskilled parents had come from the South to man the postwar factory boom around the Great Lakes and, as Iver Peterson reported in *The New York Times,* "their children, first-generation college graduates, are departing. . . . 'The South gave us their poor,' said an official of the United Automobile Workers, 'and we gave them work and educated their kids. . . . And now those kids are taking their skills back down South with them.' "

The drain means skilled labor shortages in the Midwest and Northeast. A 1981 industrial survey of Ohio found that 39 of the state's 88 counties were short of engineers, 34 needed computer technicians and 18 even lacked accountants. By 1982, *U.S. News & World Report* noted how computer programmers and electrical engineers were "at a premium, with little relief in sight" in New York, with nearly a third of the engineer openings due to out-of-state moves. The head of the Indiana Society of Professional Engineers was warning that the brain drain could have "long term impact if the level of business comes back to where it was before" Indiana's industrial slump after 1981.

A popular notion is that Snowbelt industries "flee" to Sunbelt states. Recent studies by Sunbelt academics from Clemson and Duke, however, suggest that Snowbelt firms tend to close rather than move. But if the region's jobs don't move, its young engineers or scientists do. Describing "The Myth of Industrial Flight" for *Milwaukee* magazine in 1982, Gary Hoffman noted how brain drains harm the "synergy" needed for Midwest high tech.

• *Robots.* A Carnegie-Mellon University study suggests that today's robots may replace 1.2 million workers by 1990, in sectors like autos, electrical equipment and metalwork. The next robot generation may go beyond manual dexterity to crude vision and tactile sense, possibly affecting 3.8 million of *those* workers. Finally, the survey suggests that robots may do almost all factory work by the year 2025.

This is a sea change like the one that led to Luddism after 1811, as frightened English workers wrecked stocking and lace frame machines. A young member of the House of Lords made a notable maiden speech in 1812, attacking laws that would make machine wrecking a capital crime. Will there be Lord Byrons in our Congress to speak for the millions of American factory workers needing new jobs and training as robots mow down their ranks in the 1980s?

Robots are the third technology from the Snowbelt to undermine the Snowbelt in four decades. The three disruptions have followed Alvin Toffler's script in *The Third Wave*—through the agricultural past, the industrial present and the postindustrial future:

• Improved farm machines from Snowbelt firms like Deere and International Harvester were a major force driving southern blacks out of the fields and into Snowbelt factory towns after 1945.

• Cheaper air conditioners from the Snowbelt firm of Carrier sent white middle-class workers to the Sunbelt, as humid cities like Houston, Phoenix and San Jose expanded in an air-cooled era after 1945.

• And now the robots, also a Snowbelt invention. Unless Snowbelt industrial states get federal aid to retrain and relocate displaced factory hands, America's definition of "full employment" could go from 6 percent joblessness today to even 10 percent by 1990. With a new robot generation threatening up to 40 percent of factory workers, the crisis is now.

Japan's robot revolution gives some idea of what lies ahead. Japan has more than 14,000 advanced robots, compared with 3,300 here and 900 in Germany. The robots can work three shifts a day, and cost half a worker's wages to run and maintain. Since Japan is short 800,000 skilled workers today, robots are often needed simply to get work done. But more importantly, these "steel collar" workers mean huge productivity gains. Robots mean that Toyota can run factories at 70 percent capacity and still make money. Or that Fujitsu Fanuc, the world's leading robot firm, can break even at 30 percent capacity. Noting these remarkable advances in *The Wall Street Journal,* Kenichi Ohmae, manager of McKinsey & Company in Tokyo, writes that "these plants are extremely resilient in downturns. While competitors suffer from operating losses and sleepless nights worrying about layoffs and union resistance, robot-run plants can simply switch to one-shift operation."

Ohmae adds that the versatile robots can also help small firms overcome shortages of skilled workers in precision fields, improve flexibility in meeting new specifications and rapid change-over time, or do unpleasant tasks involving heat or fumes. All this applies strongly to machine-tool work, and three of the first mechatronic factories, where computers guide robots and numer-ically controlled machines, are the Yamazaki machine plant of Nagoya, a Fujitsu Fanuc factory near Mount Fuji, and a Sumi-moto Electric plant for machines in Hokkaido. There is even a robot sushi chef, which produces 1,200 neatly shaped cakes of vinegared rice an hour. Suzumo Machinery sold more than 500 of these for $7,000 per chef in 1982. For the future, a Japanese Industrial Robot Association survey of 1981 foresees "nurse ro-bots to take care of physically handicapped people and aged pa-tients in bed, to sweep the streets, to guide the blind and to serve on fishing vessels . . . spraying insecticides on farms, spreading fertilizer, inspecting eggs and packing them, milking cows, cut-ting lumber . . ." *

GM and GE are among America's leading robot users. GM uses low-tech robots today for spot welding and spray painting, and may use more advanced robots to fit bulbs in dashboards. GM has also joined with Fujitsu Fanuc to open a robot-making division. GE spent $500 million after 1980 in buying factory au-tomation firms, and $1 billion more to automate its own plants. It is promoting a "factory of the future" package, featuring robots, numerically controlled machines, computer-aided design and au-tomated warehouses. GE sees a $30 billion domestic market here by 1990, but Japan's lead in factory automation, union resistance, and our weak capital spending since 1975 suggest a far smaller sector.

Some see America's 6,000 factory robots turning into an army of 150,000 by 1990. Joseph Engelberger said in 1982 that "if we have our way, automation will do for factory workers what it did for farms." Farmers went from being 25 percent of our workers in 1950 to just 3 percent today. Since factory hands are 22 percent of our labor force today, they could be nearly extinct in a few decades at that rate.

With its policy of lifetime jobs until fifty-five and its consensus

---

* Just as recent textile automation increases productivity while reducing cotton-dust disease, the Japanese report sees worker health advances in robotization. Thus the "tree-cutting robot is expected to eliminate Reynaud's disease . . . caused by vibration affecting chain-saw operators." Divers would be aided by "submarine robots, which can construct fish farms and build marine structures in deep water."

form of labor relations, Japan views robots as friends of workers, the latter retrained for work elsewhere. But a 1982 poll in Japan showed that 97 percent of union workers and 79 percent of managers saw robots as an employment threat. Meanwhile in America, it's every man or machine for him/itself. Absent a major change in federal job policies and programs, robots may be a tidal wave for the Great Lakes industrial states.*

• *The White-Collar Noose.* As robots take over factory work, silicon chips move in on service jobs. Within a few decades, *Business Week* projects that up to 38 million of our white-collar jobs may be affected by automation. Snowbelt states and cities reeling from factory losses in the 1970s are also facing a white-collar noose.

Factories had employed displaced farmers after 1945, and services later employed some of the factory workers displaced by automation after 1970. But the drive to automate white-collar jobs in the 1980s will throw people—where? One can open just so many hands-on services like hospitals, hotels, restaurants or shops. Looking at the service automations ahead, an MIT analyst said to *The New York Times:* "I don't know where we can run to this time."

• Computers are a big growth sector. Some analysts project *quadrupled* earnings by 1986. An ominous exception could be keypunch operators. They may lose 15 percent of their jobs by 1990 —the first of many computer workers to be replaced by computers.†

• Automatic money machines are already replacing bank tellers. A French study projects that automation could replace 30 percent of all its banking personnel.

---

* Robots can't write, but Unix of AT&T tries. Used internally at Bell as a "Writer's Workbench," this computer program is described by *The Wall Street Journal:* "If a wordy writer types 'at this point in time,' a computer program will suggest a substitute: 'now.' It also will detect split infinitives and sexist phrases, tally the number of sentences written in the passive voice and, if need be, flash a warning on a screen that 'passive sentences are harder to understand than active sentences.' "

† Key-punch jobs can even be exported. National Demographics in Denver collects 5 million warranty cards with data on who buys what products. The cards are shipped by plane to Barbados where, for $1.50 an hour, they are key-punched into computers. An American union official comments that "we've exported a lot of manufacturing jobs . . . where do you go when they export service jobs?" Irving R. Levine of *NBC Nightly News* asks, "How do you impose a tariff on word processing, done abroad, then sent back by satellite?"

• Computer graphics speed up things like car design, and could replace 25 percent of our tool designers by 1990. Automated typesetting reduces printers; the Japanese newspaper *Asahi Shimbun* is fully automated.

• Baptizing New York City as "Info City" in 1981, writer Desmond Smith observed how in 1980 local clearing houses handled 38.2 trillion checks; Bell Telephone processed 200 billion phone calls; and the Stock Exchanges traded nearly 93 million shares on one of Joe Granville's "sell" days (this volume became routine after the summer rally of 1982). Smith also noted that "an information-based economy is labor-releasing, not labor intensive." Electronic switching systems, bubble memories or microprocessors enabled the city's biggest private employer, the New York Telephone Company, "to service 30 percent more callers than in 1969, with 15,000 fewer employees. . . . New York, after a hundred or so years as the melting pot, has entered the age of the Uncommon Man. The common man has virtually no future in the brave new city."

• The U.S. Postal Service has long been a classic entry-point for unskilled service workers. But an automation drive in the 1970s meant that by 1981, roughly 30 percent more mail was being handled by 71,000 fewer workers. Since costs of 670,000 remaining postal workers were 84 percent of operating expenses that year—and since Washington would phase out the federal subsidy by 1984—the drive to automate was crucial to keep postal charges under control. Even the rapidly growing "express mail" services seem unlikely to cover such job losses.

• The biggest example of the white-collar noose ahead is the "paperless office." Offices have recently spent more than $70 billion on automation. The paperless office will mow down secretaries, clerks and even managers with word processors, printers and computerized files.*

Automation affects 38 million of our white-collar workers. Robots will have replaced more than 3 million factory workers by

* The paperless office may bring health problems. One federal agency rates secretarial work as the second highest job for stress-related disease. Staring all day at video display screens in isolated "data centers" compounds this stress and, without proper lighting, can badly strain the eyes. Women have 90 percent of all clerical, secretarial or keypunch jobs, so the group Working Women claims that "the office of the future is . . . the factory of the past." In England, bank workers have been monitoring the health impact of new lasers and video screens.

the year 2000, and almost all of them by 2025. There is the brain drain from Snowbelt campuses to Silicon Valleys. If we add these trends to the decline in heavy industries like autos, steel and machine tools, we see a Snowbelt economic crisis on many fronts. As we shift from a goods to a service economy, the paperless office and automated banks are among the reasons why services can't pick up the slack. The only good news is the end of the baby boom. This could mean labor shortages in some areas by 1990. But the bad news is overwhelming: an increasingly unskilled, illiterate work force that must somehow be trained for new, more technical tasks ahead.

America's lack of a coherent industrial strategy was a major subject for Democrats in 1984 and has been fully examined in Ira C. Magaziner and Robert B. Reich's *Minding America's Business* and Barry J. Bluestone and Bennett Harrison's *The Deindustrialization of America*. Let us limit our look, then, to the failure of Reaganomics, the limits of high tech as savior for our economy, and the need for a thorough public works program to keep people employed.

The essence of Reaganomics was this projection from economist A. Gary Schilling in 1982: those who earned less than $11,500 would lose $24.8 billion in federal benefits; those who earned over $47,800 would gain $139.8 billion in tax breaks. In early 1983, there was 10.8 percent unemployment and a projected deficit of $189 billion for fiscal 1984. By the year's end, joblessness was "down" to 9.8 percent, although the deficits ahead were still unprecedented, due to the huge tax cuts of the "Reagan revolution" and the giant defense outlays.

Jimmy Carter had used EDA and UDAG capital grants to help revive aging factories, but Reagan proposed to end both programs. Congress resisted him here, but even in late 1982, Reagan was still trying to cut the UDAG grants. Reagan's idea for helping old cities economically is the "urban enterprise zone" of conservative Representative Jack Kemp and liberal Representative Robert Garcia. But without strong EDA, UDAG, CETA and public works programs, the new zones would be fifth wheels added to vehicles with four broken wheels. Leaving that larger reality aside, the zones still make no sense in terms of scale, design and impact on existing laws.

The scale drawback is simple: only $1 billion in tax incentives are involved—in a federal budget with more than $100 billion in such breaks for businesses, investors and owners. As to design, the zones are supposed to help the small firms that created two of every three new net jobs between 1969 and 1976. But tax breaks mainly help existing, well-capitalized firms, not small businesses starting out. Small firms need venture capital such as UDAG and EDA grants. Finally, the impact of the zones on local labor laws could be disastrous. Professor William W. Goldsmith of Cornell has observed that eleven urban enterprise zones from the Thatcher regime in England "had Draconian elements" that could see our fifty states wage "wholesale war on labor's 20th-century gains." Goldsmith noted an Illinois enterprise zone passed by the state legislature—before a wise veto by Republican Governor James R. Thompson. This bill would have "eliminated building codes, minimum wages, property taxes, and general state aid; would have weakened laws protecting health, safety and the environment; and would have enforced right-to-work laws in specific urban zones."

A better idea is Felix Rohatyn's proposal to revive the Reconstruction Finance Corporation. Before its demise in 1953, the RFC spent more than $40 billion in an orderly version of the recent bailouts for Lockheed and Chrysler. A new RFC could help Snowbelt industries quickly retool for competition with the Common Market and Japan. Even Charls Walker, the main lobbyist for the tax-break spree of 1981, is for Rohatyn's RFC revival. Left-wing economists attack it as a giveaway to bankers, while centrist Democrats like Charles Schultze point out that "the Government may have to bail somebody else out, but given the reality of our system, which rewards the wheel that squeaks the loudest, we may handle it a lot better if we do it ad hoc." Economist Lester Thurow suggests an industrial policy that promotes "sunrise" sectors like high tech, while shunning "sunset" ones like steel. This is fine in the abstract, for the future. It would be a disaster for Snowbelt industries today.

A new RFC is needed to revive viable heavy industries in a postindustrial era. In the meantime, however, more modest federal grant programs like EDA and UDAG must be revived, along with a full-fueled CETA panoply, public works and counter-cyclical job programs during recessions.

There are also what are referred to as the "Atari Democrats" in Congress. They would raise the share of GNP for research and development, rebuild our infrastructure, insure computer literacy in schools, make America a net energy exporter by 1990 and retrain workers for the high-tech era. Other Democrats would revive protectionism. They back the UAW's "local content" law, which requires high-volume auto imports to use more American-made parts. Reagan trade ambassador William Brock recalls the trade wars that followed Smoot-Hawley in 1931. His predecessor under Jimmy Carter, former Florida governor Reubin Askew, bravely launched his presidential campaign by attacking the "quicksands of protectionism." While Japan's informal barriers to our goods must be lowered, similar walls here won't fend off imports; only competitive products can do that job.*

Then there is the economic chimera of high tech. RAND Corporation economist Aaron S. Gurwitz claims high tech is to the 1980s as the "service sector strategy" was to the 1970s, or downtown malls were to the 1960s—one more buzz word, with limited impact. The main reason has been seen: a high-tech region needs a critical mass of skilled workers, fine universities and venture capitalists.

Not only does high tech require high-powered universities like MIT or Cal Tech, it also doesn't add many jobs. As Atari sends factory jobs to Hong Kong and Taiwan in recessions and Texas Instruments buys microchips in Japan, the sector creates few jobs at home. The personal computer problems of 1983 at Apple, Atari and TI, and the bankruptcy filing of Osborne, took even more spin off the high-tech ball. Columnist Joseph Kraft modified a glowing dispatch from Silicon Valley in 1982 with the fact that microprocessors added only 400,000 jobs to a nation where 11 million were out of work. In this context, he added, high tech as an economic savior for America "is about as effective as a cough drop for a case of pneumonia."

One way to quickly put millions of Americans back to work is to repair or replace nearly $2.5 trillion in bridges, dams, roads and sewers across America. A survey of our crumbling infra-

---

* Walter Mondale tempers his protectionism by noting the key role of exports, whose share of GNP has doubled since 1970. He suggests that 20 percent of our industrial output goes abroad, that 33 percent of all corporate profits are from foreign trade or investment, and that 40 percent of our farmland produces for export. Yet he supports what economics writer Hobart Rowen calls "a blunderbuss form of protectionism, certain to reduce imports, raise price, lower quality and invite retaliation."

structure by *U.S. News & World Report* in 1982 suggested that 20 percent of our interstates needed resurfacing, 22 percent of our dams needed safety improvements, and 45 percent of America's bridges were officially deemed "either structurally deficient or obsolete." John E. Jacob of the Urban League has proposed a $100 billion federal public works program to start the task, and Felix Rohatyn's idea for a new RFC includes loans to cities to rebuild infrastructure. *U.S. News* concluded that sewage, transportation and water systems

> cannot be cut back easily in a vigorous nation dedicated to long-term growth. America's competitiveness and economic well-being depend on an effective infrastructure. . . . After a decade and a half of neglect of public works, the U.S. thus appears to have no other course but a new and immensely expensive commitment over many years . . .

But does America have the will to meet the challenge of this business-oriented magazine? *U.S. News* reported that 80 percent of bond issues were approved by voters in the 1950s, but barely 50 percent are today. This is also a nation where employee theft amounts to $76 billion a year, where some $79 billion is spent on narcotics, and where the IRS projects $87 billion lost to tax shirking. Infrastructure rot seems likely to join overworked factories and underserviced cities in the downward spiral of a society unwilling to pay heed to Justice Holmes's dictum on taxes as the price of civilization.

Indeed the 1983 public works bill meant only 470,000 new jobs, barely enough to cover the 340,000 CETA jobs *cut* by Ronald Reagan in 1982. In contrast, the Urban League's $100 billion proposal would employ up to 3 million people on public works. That would approach the New Deal peak in 1936, when CCC, PWA and WPA programs employed 3.7 million, from a work force one-third that of today.* The Urban League program could

---

* Ronald Reagan's father ran a WPA program in Dixon, Illinois, which turned a swamp into a public park. Another New Deal beneficiary was Richard Nixon, who got 50 cents an hour as a National Youth Administration aide while studying law at Duke. Nixon later revived such programs by starting the CETA program in 1973, expanding it later to soften the 1973–74 recession induced by his economic policies. So Nixon the anti-New Dealer invented CETA and expanded food stamps, school lunches and the Women, Infants and Children's (WIC) nutrition program, while Reagan, the old New Dealer and Democrat, has cut them back.

cost Washington far less than $100 billion, since it would cut unemployment nearly 3 percent, and every 1 percent cut means $23 billion saved through fewer federal funds spent on unemployment, welfare, food stamps, health benefits.

America's crazy quilt of job training is led by corporations with $30 billion in annual programs, trailed by localities and states with $5 billion, and Washington's $3.5 billion for the CETA ruins. Corporations mainly upgrade internal skills. Labor analyst Sar A. Levitan observed how "business is in business to make a profit—not to train the unskilled." Three of the biggest in-house trainers are AT&T, IBM and Xerox. Our three somewhat "Japanese" giants stress things like "shared values," virtual lifetime employment, or, in IBM's case, company songs about founder Thomas Watson. Before its breakup settlement in 1982, AT&T spent $1 billion a year to train 20,000 to 30,000 people a day. As switches went from mechanical to electronic or telephone lines went from coaxial cables to fiber optics, the training needs grew at Bell.

Beyond this in-house upgrading from corporations, CETA was launched by Nixon and expanded strongly by Jimmy Carter. By 1979, it had helped some 4.3 million Americans. Beyond gutting CETA, Ronald Reagan would merely focus on the Private Industry Councils (PICs), which grew from CETA revisions in 1978. These 450 local bodies of business and government leaders give employers a big voice and, unlike CETA, give no training stipend or wage subsidy for workers. The PICs have been small beer to date. While New York City's PIC recruited 2,000 firms to take on trainees, it placed only 12,000 workers in private jobs from 1978 through 1981. That was 3,000 jobs a year, or only 0.1 percent of the city's work force of 3.2 million people.

Great Society programs had cut poverty's share of America from 22 percent to only 11 percent in 1978. Even before Reaganomics, the mismatch of unskilled workers and high-tech jobs was slowly expanding the poor's share to 13 percent by 1981. They were 14 percent of America in 1982, with the growth of the "new poor" so obvious that Reagan backed $250 million in rush aid for the homeless people showing up in all big cities.

The new poor grew with particular speed in our most depressed state, Michigan. Three hundred and fifty-five thousand families lost their health coverage in three years, with 16 percent unemployment added to stress and health problems. A national study from Johns Hopkins suggests that every 1 percent rise in unemployment means 1.9 percent more deaths, 4.1 percent more suicides and 5.7 percent more murders. A 1982 Michigan survey found rises in everything from hypertension to heart failure. Detroit opened an emergency program, where doctors and hospitals treated people who had lost health coverage on an ability-to-pay basis. Four states had similar programs, but only New York City has the universal coverage familiar in Europe, the city paying more than $250 million in annual free care. In the 1981–83 recession, 11 million Americans lost their health insurance in an economy that at full strength produces 10 percent of the world's food and 21 percent of its goods with only 5 percent of its people.*

One way to train the growing ranks of our structurally unemployed is an apprenticeship program like West Germany's, where half of their youth leave school by the age of sixteen for a three-year schooling in a chosen trade. In mid-1981, Germany's teenage jobless rate of 5.1 percent was *lower* than its adult rate, while in America the youth rate normally triples the adult rate. And where 5.1 percent of Germany's youths had no job in 1981, 51 percent of our black youths had no jobs. Germany's program sustains a first-rate work force. As teenagers get a solid dose of working life at an early age, employers gain confidence in their stability and ability to adapt to new technologies. This contrasts with America, where job training slows down, and Lester Thurow warns that "it is not only technical skills that atrophy, it is also work behavior." For all workers, Germany also guarantees job retraining with a family stipend. Just as the Japanese adapted General MacArthur's edict on lifetime employment, Germany used our G.I. Bill as the model for a 1969 law extending training and stipends to all. Germany and France both train 2 percent of their work force a year, as we train from 0.1 percent to 0.5 percent. As labor analyst Herbert Striner observes, we are the only industrial nation with no compulsory job reporting services. Without such a job bank, worker relocation to suitable job markets is haphazard. We also end unemployment benefits if

---

* One more grim fact from 1982: Where 66 percent of our jobless got unemployment checks in the 1974–75 recession, only 41 percent did in 1982. By the fall of 1982, only twenty-four of our hardest-hit states would pay extended benefits for an extra thirteen weeks of unemployment, and ten states would lose that ability by October. Finally, in 1983, Reagan backed a $2.9 billion bailout to extend benefits nationwide.

sign up for school. Jobless benefits of $16 billion over four years included only $53 million for training and relocation programs.*

Leaning on the three myths while pointing to new skylines in Baltimore, Boston, Detroit and New York, some think Potemkin village is real. The shopping malls of James Rouse or atrium hotels from John Portman are hailed as symbols of citywide revival. But as symbols of thriving cities, they are about as relevant as the *Ville Radieuse* abstractions of Le Corbusier in the 1920s. The Snowbelt culture centers, hotels, malls or office towers have little to do with cities where people live daily lives. They mainly service or shelter a transient census of commuters and conventioneers, tourists and traders. Beyond downtown or waterfront revivals, Snowbelt cities are dying as places to live and to work.

We will look at ten Snowbelt cities that illustrate the growing disaster. Chapter 9 will show that Baltimore and Philadelphia are at the brink, while Detroit, Newark and St. Louis are past the point of no return. Chapter 10 will look at New York—a city needlessly plagued by fiscal and service crises. In the next chapter, however, we will examine four Snowbelt cities that mainly succeed.

---

* By 1983, Ronald Reagan backed a law allowing states to use 2 percent of their unemployment funds for training or relocation, some $450 million a year. One more German idea is work sharing, and three western states use it today. Arizona, California and Oregon let companies with brief production cutbacks cut hours for workers—who then draw jobless benefits for the days "unemployed." The firms don't have to lay off skilled workers, and the latter lose only a small part of their income, while retaining company health insurance and similar fringe benefits.

CHAPTER **8** |

# THE FOUR PARAGONS

ODDLY, OUR FOUR paragons are in the Midwest, where heavy-industry states are America's leading victims of recession cycles. Minneapolis, Milwaukee, Kansas City and Wichita illustrate an old law: diversified economics succeed. Their jobless rates tend to be two or even three points below the national average, with Wichita at times five points below. Their stable economies mean steady revenues, generally adequate services and low crime rates.

Before looking at our four cities, a note on how misery loves company towns. In the Sunbelt, we saw how Birmingham and steel took a mutual dive after 1970. Several smaller southern cities yoked to a few aging factories also had growing economic problems. Out west, the reaction against nuclear power after Three Mile Island ruined uranium towns in New Mexico and Wyoming, while the housing slump after 1979 dragged down lumber centers like Boise, Portland and Seattle, the last also hit by Boeing's troubles.

But undiversified Midwest cities were the worst hit of all. Eleven of the fifteen highest metro unemployment rates in early 1982 were from just four Great Lakes industrial states:

| | | | |
|---|---|---|---|
| *Anderson, Ind.* | 17.7% | *Detroit, Mich.* | 15.0% |
| Modesto, Calif. | 16.9 | Johnstown, Pa. | 14.7 |
| *Muncie, Ind.* | 16.6 | *Gary-Hammond-* | |
| *Flint. Mich.* | 16.5 | *E. Chicago, Ind.* | 14.6 |
| *Janesville-Beloit, Wis.* | 16.1 | *Muskegon, Mich.* | 14.6 |
| Stockton, Calif. | 16.0 | *Jackson, Mich.* | 14.5 |
| *Saginaw, Mich* | 16.0 | Vineland-Millville- | |
| *Youngstown-Warren,* | | Bridgeton, N.J. | 14.5 |
| *Ohio* | 15.9 | *Bay City, Mich.* | 13.9 |

Ohio has some famous single-industry towns. The closing of the Campbell steelworks at Youngstown Sheet & Tube in 1977 was the single biggest overnight layoff in our industrial history. Almost 5,000 workers and some 6,000 people servicing them were hit in one blow. Just as the steel town of Birmingham lost its buses in 1981, Youngstown faced a similar loss at one point in 1982. We shall later see other troubled steel towns in the Ohio Valley like Steubenville and Weirton, or Lackawanna on Lake Erie, where the closing of one giant mill in 1984 could cut city tax collections by 70 percent. Other troubled steel cities are Lackawanna's neighbor Buffalo, and Gary. Buffalo was once envisioned by King Camp Gillette as the residence of 60 million people living in 24,000 glass-domed apartment buildings, with eternal energy from Niagara Falls. Gillette dropped his ''Metropolis'' vision to invent the safety razor, and Buffalo has lost half its people since 1950. Gary has been a famous company town since 1906, and its activist mayor, Richard Hatcher, landed over $300 million in federal grants after 1965, twice the aid for comparably sized cities. But the long-term steel slump meant Gary's median income fell by 25 percent in the 1970s.

Some Snowbelt company towns must square off to survive. As International Harvester faced bankruptcy in 1982, it decided to close a Midwest plant in one of two cities 150 miles apart: either at Fort Wayne, Indiana or Springfield, Ohio. Whoever made Harvester the best offer would save its factory. Springfield, at 13 percent unemployment, faced ruin if the Harvester plant, with nearly half the city's factory workers, closed. Fort Wayne, with 10,500 Harvester workers at peak production, felt that closing its plant would see 12 percent joblessness soar to 21 percent. *The MacNeil/Lehrer Report* examined this struggle, comparing it to a war between two medieval city-states. Neal Peirce suggested that Harvester raise funds from private capital markets, rather than "hornswoggle" the taxpayers of the winning city. Fort Wayne won the bidding battle with a $50 million package, but Springfield won the war. Its Harvester plant was only 15 years old, and that plus $30 million won the day.

Fort Wayne and Gary are two of many industrial cities in Indiana, where in early 1982 12.4 percent unemployment was second only to Michigan. Indiana's flat farmland has many troubled company towns. The auto slump since 1979 hit the Chrysler-dominated city of Anderson, whose 17.7 percent jobless rate was America's highest in early 1982. Even by 1980, Edward Kennedy was evoking "the closed factories and the stalled assembly lines of Anderson, Indiana" in his rousing speech to the Democratic convention. Another Hoosier company town was Kokomo, whose small-town stability was celebrated in a hit tune of 1947. In 1978, Kokomo was a booming auto town, where GM and Chrysler had a third of all jobs. That year found Kokomo 15th among our cities for average retail sales per family. Then the long auto slump began, and Kokomo plunged from 15th to 176th place. At one point in 1982, it had 23 percent unemployment.*

The Midwest's most troubled company town is often Flint, Michigan, where a third of the work force—some 80,000—is employed at 11 GM plants. During the 1975 recession, when Detroit had 15 percent joblessness, Flint had 18 percent. Early in 1983, Flint led America with 23.9 percent, which has twenty points more than the lowest rate of 3.9 percent in Stamford, Connecticut.† Flint's powerful Mott Foundation has proposed an industrial Disneyland, to be called "Autoworld." This would feature a three-story replica of an auto engine and a moving-

---

* Indiana is an innovative auto state, where over 370 makes were produced, starting with the horseless carriages of the 1890s. The more famous makes included the Dusenberg and Maxwell, the Studebaker and the Stutz. Hoosier Booth Tarkington's *The Magnificent Ambersons* described those early Indiana auto days.

† Stamford can be called a "company's company town." With only 102,000 residents, it has twelve headquarters from the *Fortune* 500 list. In per capita terms, that would be like New York City having 840 members of the *Fortune* 500. Most of Stamford's front offices came from New York after Stamford cleared 118 acres downtown in 1968, just before the big corporate relocations of the 1970s. Stamford's census shrank by 3 percent in the 1970s, but jobs grew by 20 percent, since almost all the new workers were commuters.

sidewalk history of the assembly line. "Is this what we mean when we talk of reindustrializing America?" asked writer Alex Kolowitz in *The New York Times*. There is irony here. Back in the 1930s, Henry Ford's premier theme park at Greenfield Village had celebrated our past with the log cabin where McGuffey of the Reader was born, and the buildings where Lincoln had practiced law. John Gunther had observed Ford as resurrecting "the America he knew as a boy . . . which, as much as any man, he helped to obliterate."

Another factory theme park is in Lowell, Massachusetts. It preserves the famous cotton mills which made Lowell the "Manchester of America" by the 1850s. A century later the mills were closed, and Lowell had 13.8 percent unemployment in 1975. Yet the deeper recession of 1982 saw only 6.8 joblessness, with many studying "the lessons of Lowell." A mixture of luck and geography were the saving graces here. One break was that Governor Michael Dukakis and Senator Paul Tsongas were both Lowell natives, but the main boost came when Dr. An Wang located his electronics firm there in 1975. Wang Electronics has since grown by about 40 percent a year, adding thousands of jobs a year, with suppliers flocking in as well. In one period of eighteen months, there were thirty industrial expansions in this city of only 92,000—and one high-tech dynamo.

As for geography, Lowell is 25 miles north of Route 128. Indeed An Wang graduated from Harvard, part of that critical mass of universities, cultural amenities and brainpower in the Northeast which is to high tech what coal fields or iron seams were to earlier auto or steel towns in the Midwest. Eleven northeastern states form a "Golden Corridor" from Maine to Maryland, which has 24 percent of our people, 29 percent of our college students, 37 percent of our bank assets and 50 percent of our venture capital for 1981. In Massachusetts alone, the 1981 recession saw a record year for factory expansions. The deeper slump of 1982 saw 185 more expansions in the first six months.

"Similar transformations are likely to occur in the Midwest," claims a *Wall Street Journal* editorial, but the Midwest brain drain is a problem, and the Northeast already has a huge lead. In 1900, Fall River and New Bedford were, respectively, the biggest and the second biggest cotton towns in America. Then textiles went south, and the sight of empty mills was familiar to anyone driving the Shore Route to Cape Cod. These two big cities today are best known for Lizzie Borden and Moby Dick, not An Wang or high tech. The recent opening of a major factory from Morelli Shoes of Italy may herald new times for New Bedford. Otherwise, America's two greatest cotton towns of 1900 were Massachusetts' two most jobless cities in 1980.*

Steel, autos, farm equipment, textiles and other heavy industries like rubber and machine tools which built Snowbelt company towns are now bringing them down. As we enter the postindustrial era, the Snowbelt company town without the luck of Lowell may well be doomed. There are, however, some diversified exceptions to the growing regional crisis. Cincinnati, Omaha and Rochester are cited by many, and so are Columbus, Indianapolis and Lincoln, the latter three doubly protected against bad times by huge state universities and state capitals. Then there are our four Midwest paragons, four cities which diversified long ago to build stable economies and societies.

## Minneapolis

This was rated America's best city in a quality-of-life survey by the Urban Institute. Minneapolis has a low crime rate, and an unemployment rate of 4 percent is rare. It has two major art museums, a Top Ten symphony orchestra and the Tyrone Guthrie Theater. Minneapolis also has an acre of park for every eight residents, a fine university, and a tradition of high taxes and high services. All of this so impressed Irving Wallace and his children that their *Book of Predictions* insists that America's capital will move here by 1999.

Yet this paragon lost 19 percent of its residents in the 1970s, and a winter average of forty-two inches of snow and 4 degrees may explain why. As jobs grow in warm Sunbelt states, Minneapolis must somehow hold on to the 364,000 people who remain. One means is to rapidly expand its glass-enclosed "skyways" downtown. Sixty-four blocks are linked by these heated bridges,

---

* New Bedford's decline is poignant. Not only does it have charming nineteenth-century neighborhoods and industrious workers, but it's an early example of timely "reindustrialization" in the 1840s. Back then, this was the whaling capital of the world and America's fourth busiest port, but it had the foresight to diversify with its first cotton mill in 1848. Eleven years later, the first Pennsylvania oil strike knocked out whale oil overnight. Four decades later, New Bedford was America's second biggest cotton town.

making most of downtown climate-controlled. Minneapolis resembles Toronto, where a honeycomb of corridors and tunnels lets people walk up to two miles underground, with Toronto's planning director warning of "a city of moles." *

In any event, the German and Scandinavian stock of Minneapolis thrives on harsh weather. Since both North European nations are ones where social welfare is a way of life, the high taxes and services of Minneapolis are inevitable. The services, a homogeneous population, low unemployment and cold weather help cut the crime rate. In 1981, there were only 621 violent crimes per 100,000 residents. Only Milwaukee among the major cities had a lower rate.

Minneapolis has a diversified stable economy. Ever since the Taylor and St. Anthony falls made this a hydropower center in the 1840s, the city has milled Great Plains grain. By 1900, it was the biggest primary wheat market on earth. Food giants like General Mills, Land O'Lakes, Pillsbury and International Multifoods are among the eight *Fortune* 500 companies that make Minneapolis the seventh biggest front-office city in America. With the addition of Investors Diversified Services, Dayton-Hudson, and such high-tech giants as Control Data and 3M, Minneapolis is truly recession-proof. Among Snowbelt cities, only smaller Midwest centers like Sioux Falls, Lincoln, Topeka and Wichita do consistently better for jobless rates. In 1979, the Minneapolis-St. Paul nexus had 2.9 percent unemployment against 5.6 percent nationwide. In 1980, the recession pushed it up to 4.6 percent.

Minneapolis was the third biggest loser of branch factories among Snowbelt cities between 1967 and 1976, as twenty of its plants relocated from the big headquarters city. Despite such losses, it finished a strong eighth among fifty-two big American cities for growth in manufacturing value added in a Princeton survey of 1980. With twelve *Fortune* 500 giants in the Twin Cities, Wold-Chamberlain Airport is the third busiest in America. Like other services in the area, the airport is well staffed and

---

* The director notes empty streets downtown, with only "a few brave souls dashing between buildings from urban fort to urban fort under the eye of skyscraper security guards." Apart from the impact on business, this also mocks the "eyes on the street" formula for security espoused by Jane Jacobs, now a Toronto resident. To break its growing suburban syndrome, Toronto now requires ground-floor stores to encourage sidewalk use. It may also start opening some landscaped shafts down below.

maintained, and its administrator observed on *The MacNeil-Lehrer Report* in 1981 that despite all the snow "we aren't experienced in closing the runways. The last time was 20 years ago for 30 minutes."

The European ethos and all those front offices have combined in a unique coalition of City Hall and corporations called the "Minnesota model." Forty-five Minneapolis firms tithe 5 percent of their pretax income for civic improvements as members of a 5 Percent Club. Mayor Donald Fraser, long a liberal leader in Congress and former ADA chairman, observes that "the most important things in this city have happened at the initiative of the business community, not because of government." This is the only city where Reaganite "voluntarism" is on the grand scale—in a state where liberal Republicans like Harold Stassen and ultraliberal Democrats like Hubert Humphrey, Eugene McCarthy and Walter Mondale have been the rule. It seems that voluntarism flourishes best in a city with fine services and liberal traditions.*

Leading the 5 Percenters in Minneapolis is the Dayton-Hudson Corporation, with nearly 1,000 stores nationally, including the B. Dalton chain. Dayton-Hudson gave $9.6 million for 1981 alone, and has given 5 percent of pretax profits since 1945. Unfortunately, it is only one of two corporations listed on the New York Stock Exchange to kick in 5 percent—the other Big Board benefactor being Cummins Engine of Columbus, Indiana, famous for its many brilliant commissions of modern architecture in that small town. If their 5 percent example was applied to the current 1 percent corporate average across America, some $10 billion more a year could close a third of the vast gap left by Reagan social cuts in 1981.

But this won't happen. Even Minneapolis finds its 5 Percenters aiding safe causes like Culture. General Mills invested $8 million in Stevens Court, a gentrified town-house area. Dayton-Hudson was a major donor for the new Orchestra Hall, the Hennepin Center for the Arts and a mall for shopping—the last hardly a daring move for a department-store chain. This voluntarism often "doesn't go far enough," observes William C. Norris, head of

---

* A prominent Eisenhower Republican in Minnesota today is Ike's former HEW secretary Arthur Flemming, who was, at seventy-six, a vigorous chairman of the U.S. Civil Rights Commission. Appointed chairman by Gerald Ford and retained by Jimmy Carter, Flemming was fired by Ronald Reagan.

Control Data Corporation. He adds that a lot of the Twin Cities tithing is a "cop-out that makes the giver feel good."

Norris is a striking figure in both business and philanthropy. The seventy-three-year-old founder of Control Data built it to 141st rank on the *Fortune* 500 list, 6th in rank among computer firms. He has led joint ventures with other office-equipment giants in developing computer disks and tapes, and *Business Week* saluted him in 1980 as a leader of farsighted reindustrialization:

> Under Norris, CDC has invested $150 million in Plato, a computer-based education system, and has still not broken even, yet he insists on continuing full funding . . . . Norris' attitudes —his willingness to back money-losing projects because he believes in them, his fearlessness of Wall Street, his willingness to cooperate with other companies and other researchers—are exactly what are needed in the next generation of managers.

Norris also leads the way for a kind of corporate giving quite distinct from "feel good" grants. Instead of lavishing gifts on malls, skyways and culture centers, Control Data capitalized a $3 million consortium of fourteen business and religious organizations as a City Venture Corporation. Within three years, Control Data factories under the CVC aegis were being planned for six of the worst slums in America.

CVC's goal is to help small businesses, always the best job creators in slums. Among its tools are sizable Business and Technology Centers for the areas involved. These BTCs have factory, lab and office space for small firms, as well as shared accounting, computer and legal services. City Venture also helps set up worker services like day-care centers, employee counseling and computer-based training to help unskilled residents get and then hold on to jobs.

The model for all this was a Control Data factory that was opened in the black Northside community of Minneapolis in 1968, after two summers of riots. A decade later, William C. Norris recalled some lessons from the pilot Northside plant. To cut absenteeism there among working mothers, one of America's earliest factory day-care centers was opened. To help workers with frequent credit problems, a pioneering credit subsidiary was opened. Some workers had legal problems with landlords or stores, and Norris later recalled how "Monday morning's production would suffer because part of the work force had landed in jail over the weekend." So a company lawyer visited the jail on Monday morning with a book of bail bonds. Finally, there was the usual employment form to fill out. Most workers could put little work experience on the form, and some had had experience with the law. Control Data simply ignored most background criteria, since, "in essence, we were saying we are more interested in your future than in your past."

All this tinkering paid off. A reliable work force trained at low cost emerged from the Northside slum. The average tenure at the factory would be five years, and the average trainee cost of $2,500 compared with $3,000 in federal programs. In 1970, Control Data opened a second factory nearby, in the Selby slum of St. Paul. This plant was manned only by part-time workers, like welfare mothers or high-school and college students. To fit their schedules, the early shift went to the mothers, while the late hours went to the students. The Selby plant was so successful that an even bigger factory was opened in 1974. It was the first new industrial building on an aging commercial strip since 1889.

From these Twin City pilots, the City Venture Corporation projects evolved in the late 1970s. Like Mallory on Everest, Norris took a "because they are there" approach in planning CVC projects for the worst slums. The first six projects were set for Baltimore, Miami, Philadelphia, San Antonio, Toledo, and Charleston, South Carolina. The Baltimore site would be in the Park Heights section, where 40 percent of the residents were unemployed in 1979. A Business and Technology Center would anchor an industrial park of forty acres with at least 350 jobs, a bindery from Commercial Credit Company would add 200 more jobs, and 1,750 new jobs was the ultimate goal. The Philadelphia project would be in West Parkside, which had 28 percent of its residents on some form of public aid in the nonrecession year of 1979. The Miami site seems a typical Norris gamble. It would be smack in the middle of the tragic, burned-out Liberty City slum. Norris later hopes to open an industrial park for the South Bronx as "the highest mountain" left. Oddly, the one setback was in Control Data's backyard. A Minneapolis project aimed at 3,000 new jobs blew apart when community residents claimed it was, to quote City Venture's own account, " a plan advocating relocation and displacement.'' But while the larger project failed, Control Data still put up a $12 million BTC, with 164 jobs for Minneapolis' poor.

Job creators. Five Percenters. Little crime. Low unemployment. A European ambiance. Since 77 percent of Minnesota's high-school graduates go on to college, and since this is a European enclave, culture comes naturally here. There are thirty-seven art galleries in the Twin Cities, among them the famous Walker Art Center and Minneapolis Institute of Fine Arts. There are thirty-nine theaters, including the famous Guthrie. There is the Minnesota Symphony, one of our Top Ten orchestras. All told, more concert and theater tickets are sold in the Twin Cities than any American city save New York.

With its culture, fine services, low crime and unemployment rates, and its tithing firms, Minneapolis sets many examples for the rest of America: decency, democracy, real interest in culture, stability, voluntarism and job creation for the very worst slums. It also shows concern for those abroad who depend on the vast grain trade here. Food for Peace may have been the greatest among Hubert Humphrey's many inspirations, while Walter Mondale was an early advocate of food stamps in the late 1960s, and of food relief for Southeast Asia during the region's refugee crisis in the late 1970s.

But even in this wintry Arcadia, there is the curse of the tax revolt. With the usually dominant Democrats crippled by internal party fights, Republican Albert Quie was elected governor in 1978 on a rash pledge to cut taxes 10 percent and to index personal income taxes. Quie ran against the highest state corporate and personal income tax rates in America, but high taxes bought full services and stability. State aid to localities was generous, the state had equalized the fiscal gaps between rich and poor school districts, and Minnesota had been ranked high among the states for its health, mental health and welfare programs.

A notable example of these fine services had been education. Back in 1973, while Minnesota was only our nineteenth biggest state, it had America's fourth biggest university system. Minnesota also had the lowest school dropout rate in America, with nearly eight in ten of its high-school graduates going on to college. Some of the economic results of all this were noted by Neal Peirce in the early 1970s: University of Minnesota researchers had found ways to convert taconite into high-grade ore, helping save the Iron Range near Duluth; the high-tech boom around the Twin Cities had drawn on a skilled work force trained at the University; and farmers were aided by the development of rust-resistant wheat and northern-growing fruits. The late 1970s would see America's pioneer in computer-based education, the Plato System of Control Data, emerge from this education-blessed state.

The high-tax, high-service state stabilized a prosperous economy. The state jobless rate was often two or even three points under America's. Tax cuts would be a fifth-wheel stimulus to the Minnesota economy, while threatening the usual revenue and service havoc that tax revolts produce. But 1978 was the year of Proposition 13. So Quie proposed his sweeping tax cuts and was elected. *The Almanac of American Politics* suggests that voters backed Quie thinking that "his reputation as a political moderate apparently reassured them that spending would not be cut to the bone."

This was not to be. In a classic example of the Myth of Limited Resources, the tax cuts did nothing for business, while causing endless fiscal and service crisis for a previously stable state. Supply side did for Minnesota what it did for California under Proposition 13 and the nation under Reaganomics. In Minnesota, the Quie tax cuts and indexings passed by a Democratic legislature in 1979 led to the prosperous state going broke in 1980, 1981, and 1982.

After thirty-five years of constant growth, Minnesota had a state surplus of $292 million at hand in 1979. Then Quie and the legislature swung the tax ax, and the $292 million surplus of 1979 was converted into a deficit of $195 million for 1980. Having created a huge deficit in a booming state, Quie wound up making predictable and unprecedented cuts in school and local aid. The resources got more limited as tax indexes worked away.

In 1981, Minnesota was $150 million in deficit. Quie abandoned his policy, recovered his common sense, and proposed surcharges on taxes. He issued his call on April 15, of all unfortunate days. His retreat angered Republicans since, once out of the bottle, tax revolts are hard to recant. Quie quickly backed down.

Then the Democrats got even by passing Quie's surcharge bill, forcing him to veto his own idea. This travesty of responsible government left Quie with an old conservative standby: a hike in the regressive sales tax. The Democrats reluctantly agreed and the story ended for the summer of 1981.

In the fall of 1981, the indexed revenue base acted up again, producing new deficits. That happens after tax revolts, especially when there is a recession. Hard times and a revenue base eroded by indexing had now produced a new deficit of $768 million for the biennium ending June 30, 1983. Since Quie had hiked sales taxes earlier, the fall saw him cutting state aid to localities. His two main victims, Mayors Fraser of Minneapolis and Latimer of St. Paul, warned that "our cities have already cut back for 1982 fire protection, parks, libraries, and street services. There is no way that 15 to 23 percent of the remaining expenditures can be cut without causing major hardships for people in our state." Quie's budget director blandly replied that cities could meet new state aid cuts with one of three "options": raise property taxes, make more service cuts, or draw on local budget surpluses. Once again, the stronger tax jurisdiction was sticking the weaker one with the bill, a travesty of civics seen nationally in the "new federalism."

The good news from the Minnesota mess was the rapid revival of the Democratic Farmer-Labor Party. Faction fights had cost the DFL its usual lock on both Senate seats and the statehouse. But the revenue debacle was soon the main course at the "bean feed" banquets of the DFL. With each new deficit projection from St. Paul, more groups rushed back into an expanding party tent. As Mayor Fraser told *The Washington Post,* "I think anybody would forgive him the first time, but the third or fourth?"

Although Minnesota continued to have lower unemployment than most states, residents who had seen their property taxes cut sharply after 1970 had to face up to higher taxes to retain the quality of life with which they led the nation.

## Milwaukee

Milwaukee is a bit like Minneapolis. Both have very diverse economies, are dominated by Northern Europeans, have few slums, and low crime rates—often the lowest among American big cities.

But only Milwaukee has had Socialist mayors for nearly half this century. Peirce and Keefe write in *The Great Lakes States* that Milwaukee's socialism was not the left-of-liberal brand usually associated with such ideologies. Instead it was a frugal, almost penny-pinching brand of municipal management, stressing practical, basic, and efficient services . . . often referred to as "sewer socialism."

"Sewer socialism" was founded by Socialists of the early 1900s. The national party's founder was Victor Berger, a three-term congressman from Milwaukee. His legacy is detected in the broad social programs of Milwaukee, his spirit in such ultraliberal leaders as Representative Henry Reuss from the German South Side, or the man who beat Reuss for mayor in 1960, Henry Maier. Reuss went on to become chairman of the House Banking Committee, the most respected economist on Capitol Hill. Maier was one of America's most outspoken urban leaders in the 1970s, as president of both the U.S. Conference of Mayors and the National League of Cities. After twenty-four years as Milwaukee's mayor he's still quite wild.

On January 19, 1981, the eve of Ronald Reagan's inauguration, Henry Maier was in vintage form. At a U.S. Conference of Mayors' meeting at the L'Enfant Plaza Hotel in Washington, most of the big-city mayors were biting nails over the budget and tax fights. There was one exception. As *The Washington Post* reported, "shouts and some screaming came from one of the U.S. Conference of Mayors' old tigers . . ." Maier charged over the top, yelling:

> I say to you that if you say [the cities] can live without federal help, God bless you. Some of us are on the brink of catastrophe. You don't believe me, go look at those bond ratings . . . We have city after city on the verge of collapse. Now we're being told as we are about to be booted down the hill further that we ought to allow them to boot us—take it in good grace —and I have only one thing to say to you. To hell with that!

The reporters asked the mayors what federal grants might not be missed under the Reagan regime. Militant Richard Hatcher, of Gary, Indiana, clammed up, and Mayor Dianne Feinstein of

San Francisco suggested that a look at Social Security might be useful. Henry Maier said, "I really think the most ignorant damn people in America are the media; I do because you're all middle class . . . you don't really get the smell of those central cities. . . ." Two weeks later a dozen mayors met with President Reagan. With Ed Koch of New York leading, they went into the Cabinet Room, and emerged radiant. Ironically, Koch and Tom Bradley of Los Angeles were especially elated even though they had united to ask the President to try out the subminimum wage in their cities.

Reagan got the picture. Apart from Henry Maier and Richard Hatcher—the latter blackballed from White House briefings by Reagan—the big-city mayors were his. Their mute protests during the budget and tax fights ahead were predictable. The media would later salute Reagan as a "brilliant" leader in the 1981 victories on Capitol Hill, but he had merely pushed through an open mayoral door. Only after the Reagan house of cards collapsed in the fall of 1981, with record deficits, recession and panic on Wall Street, did the mayors revive. As a $109 billion deficit and 8.5 percent unemployment hit the water, even Ed Koch became an overnight shark, tearing away at the "sham and a shame" that he had been zealously promoting for the past six months.

On February 14, 1981, Henry Maier warned that the Reagan promise of "milk and honey . . . may turn out to be a desert of rocks and dust for the older central cities . . ." No other mayor or governor save Richard Hatcher had even laced up the gloves. What may seem commonplace today were fresh and lonely fighting words from Maier back then:

> My concern is for the local costs of some of the cuts—more crime and possible urban unrest. What have we gained if we trade Federal red ink for blood in the streets?
>
> And, of course, my concern is also for the fiscal effect—bucking the bill from more-elastic Federal revenues to a local property tax that was never intended to pay the costs of social overhead.
>
> The forces at work are not turning back the clock, returning only a few hours in history. They are, in fact, turning back the calendar, reverting through decades to an earlier era when state and Federal Governments entirely disregarded the problems of our cities.

In early 1981, and through the awful budget and tax cuts that spring and summer, these words were ignored by mayors and governors. To them, Henry Maier was a cranky Cato, croaking *"urbs defendum est"* at the end of each tirade.

In his leader's role, Maier in 1981 recalled the earlier, militant days of Milwaukee Socialism, when Emil Seidel was the party's first mayor of a major city, and Victor Berger its first congressman on Capitol Hill. Berger had founded the Socialist Party with Debs in 1901 at a Masonic Hall in Indianapolis, the delegates rising there to sing the *"Marseillaise."* Back then, some thought the Socialists might be like the infant Labour Party in England, though a lack of overt class politics in America soon proved otherwise. Still, Debs got almost 6 percent of the presidential vote in 1912, and more than 1,000 Socialists held public office, including fifty-six city halls. Perhaps the biggest prize was Seidel's election as Milwaukee's mayor in 1910, the first of forty Socialist years in what was then our tenth biggest city. Abraham Cahan, editor of the *Daily Forward,* attended Seidel's inauguration and later described it: "A thrill passed through the socialists present. It was one of those moments which are a landmark in one's life. There were tears in some eyes, tears of the highest hope known to man . . . It almost seemed too good to be true. As Comrade Simons subsequently put it, 'Is this the United States?' "

Milwaukee also elected Victor Berger to Congress that year, where he was later followed by Socialist Meyer London, elected by the *Forward* readers of New York's Lower East Side. By 1917, there was even a Socialist mayor in the insurance mecca of Hartford, and that year the party received sizable urban vote shares: Cleveland, 20 percent; Buffalo, 25 percent; Chicago, 33 percent; Toledo, 33 percent; and Dayton, 50 percent. These 1917 results suggested that the Socialists might realign our party system, but then America entered the war and the Espionage Act was passed. Berger was indicted and given twenty years by Judge Kenesaw Mountain Landis, later appointed baseball commissioner after the Black Sox scandal of 1919. Landis remarked that he would have preferred "to have Berger lined up against a wall and shot." Congress expelled Berger in 1919. He was re-elected from his jail cell, then expelled again. Finally, he was vindicated by the Supreme Court and returned to Capitol Hill for three more terms. Around this time, a young Socialist public school teacher named Goldie Meyerson left Milwaukee for the Middle East and a new identity as Golda Meir.*

An influx of conservative Polish Catholics in Milwaukee soon diluted Socialism to "sewer socialism." But this was still a very different kind of government. Recalling a youth under Socialist rule in the 1920s, the Republican president of the state Association of Commerce and Manufacturers, Paul Hassett, told Neal R. Peirce and John Keefe:

> I was nobody in Milwaukee, nobody. In fact, my parents were unemployed. But I learned to swim indoors in Milwaukee over 50 years ago . . . people who grew up in Milwaukee became used to a high service . . . and while a few people complain about high taxes, I think generally speaking most people accept the cost of the high service they want.

The Germans who built Milwaukee socialism had also brought with them a strong sense of thrift. Sometimes this took reactionary forms; Milwaukee County was one of the first places in America to start a "workfare" program, before it became fashionable in parts of California. A Pay for Work program had welfare clients pick up garbage, shovel snow or serve food. However, the benefits of workfare are dubious in creating good work habits or finding real jobs for clients.

Otherwise, the thrift of Milwaukee Germans is a paragon for our economy. Few companies remained in family hands like those of the Uihleins at Schlitz, but many companies ran tight fiscal ships with little debt service and held on to skilled workers even in bad times. Thus while Milwaukee was the Snowbelt's second biggest loser of branch factories after 1967, more than 29 percent of its workers were still in manufacturing by 1981. The factory jobs were spread among many industrial sectors. This diversity avoided simultaneous slumps among a few big employers in a recession. Milwaukee usually compares well with America in recessions: it had 6.7 percent unemployment against the nation's 9.0 percent in 1975. In the good year of 1978, *U.S. News*

---

* Socialism yielded to Communism in a 1946 Republican primary for the Senate, when liberal incumbent Robert M. La Follette was beaten by a young circuit judge. La Follette had attacked Franco Spain, so Catholics backed his Catholic opponent. But, noted John Gunther, "more importantly, the strong Communist-inspired fringe of the Milwaukee CIO went all out to beat him, because he had often attacked Stalinist Russia." So the Communists backed Joseph R. McCarthy instead.

& *World Report,* noting 6.1 percent unemployment in America, reported that "the outlook is brighter in Milwaukee, which last year was the scene of about 500 separate industrial projects— both new plants and expansion. The city's unemployment, even during the bitter December to March period, dropped from 4.2 to 3.7 percent." Not everyone had jobs. In the fall of 1980, an ad for 150 jobs as busboys and maids at a new Milwaukee hotel drew more than 13,000 applicants on one cold morning.

On the whole, however, Milwaukee is a stable and diversified factory town. While machine tools are to Milwaukee what autos are to Detroit, they employ fewer than 10 percent of all workers (against the auto share of 33 percent in Motor City). Milwaukee's biggest employer, Briggs & Stratton, employs fewer than 2 percent of all city workers to make gas engines and car frames. While machine-tool giants like A. O. Smith, Bucyrus-Erie and Allis-Chalmers have headquarters in the area, other *Fortune* 500 members include Johnson Controls in electronics and Clark Oil. This beer-and-shot town even has some white-collar majors: Northeast Mutual, the ninth biggest insurer in America, and MGIC, the biggest mortgage insurer.

When *The Wall Street Journal* needed a broad array of factory workers for a feature on wage givebacks in 1982, it went to Milwaukee. The twenty-eight workers interviewed for the piece "brew beer, build motorcycles and automobile frames, make parts for jet engines and earth-moving equipment, and assemble electronic controls for cars . . . in a strong union town. . . ." Their worries seemed as diverse as their jobs. Since Milwaukee was the Snowbelt's second biggest loser of relocated factories, Richard A. Blavat, a worker for twenty-seven years at Ladish— a high-tech forging and fitting firm—worried that wage concession demands might find executives thinking: "Let's rattle their cage, let's take them by the throat and shake them and see how far we can get. If we can back them up against the wall and save enough money, we stay here. If they say 'No,' we can't bend'm, the hell with them, we go down there [South]." *

---

* Milwaukee was second only to Chicago for relocation of factories tied to headquarters in big cities. Curiously, sixty-five of the eighty-nine factories leaving Chicago, Milwaukee and Minneapolis went not to the Sunbelt but to nonurban areas in Wisconsin, part of the "rural revival" in the 1970s, where cities broke even in factory jobs as rural areas gained 878,000 manufacturing jobs. Snowbelt factories rarely moved to the Sunbelt. Either they closed or relocated to rural or small-town areas in the same or a neighboring state.

James Hoeppner, one of 4,800 union members at A. O. Smith, recalled how 90 percent of the workers voted for wage concessions to help land a contract for GM car frames. He had fourteen years' seniority, but without the GM deal, "I'd probably be working, but two years from now, I probably wouldn't be." Less realistic union leaders at Allis-Chalmers rejected a wage freeze in 1981, so machine worker James A. Kloss was laid off. He recalled for the *Journal* the UAW position on givebacks: "All they said was, 'No.' . . . They never asked us, we never had a chance to vote on it. It's *my* livelihood, it's all of our livelihoods."

Looking at two industries crucial to Milwaukee, start with the one that made it famous.* The couplet from Cole Porter's *Kiss Me, Kate* is homage to beer's dominance around 1950:

> From Milwaukee, Mr. Fritz, often moves me to the Ritz.
> Mr. Fritz is full of Schlitz, and full of play.

In the late 1970s, there were more than 1,600 taverns and 2,600 bowling alleys in the Milwaukee metro area. Peirce and Keefe wrote that first-shift workers in the machine shops often belted brandy and beer before punching in at 6 A.M., and added that "this fact explains in part why Wisconsin, with only 2 percent of the population, annually consumes more brandy than any other state. Wisconsinites down 20 percent of all brandy drunk in the United States." Consumers thrive, but the producers are fading away. The Miller, Pabst and Schlitz headquarters remain, but brewery automation and decentralized production in regional markets mean that only 2 percent of Milwaukee workers are in beer. One more tribute to diversity here.

A reformulation of the Schlitz brewing mix to speed up production drove customers away in the 1970s. From being a close second to Anheuser-Busch, Schlitz plunged to third behind Miller by 1976. The mix was reworked, but the defectors stayed away, many of them captured by light-beer forays from Miller and Anheuser-Busch. Nineteen eighty-one was a disaster for Schlitz. It closed its main Milwaukee plant; its merger with G.

---

* The slogan arose in 1871, when Schlitz tripled production to serve Chicago in the wake of its famous fire. As Joseph Schlitz's barrels rolled into Chicago, a local joke was about "the beer that made Milwaukee famous."

Heileman was stopped by the Justice Department; it lost $22 million during the first nine months.* Anheuser-Busch with 30 percent of the market and Miller with 22 percent left Schlitz far up the track at 8 percent. Preparing for price wars in 1982, Frank J. Sellinger, the portly brewmaster and CEO, predicted "blood years" ahead. Within the year, he was gone and Schlitz had been taken over by Stroh's. As for Pabst, America's oldest brewer after 142 years, it was down in fifth place by 1982, working on its fourth CEO in thirteen months.

The main industrial crisis for Milwaukee lies ahead, in the machine-tool sector that employs nearly 10 percent of the work force. As we saw in Chapter 7, 41 percent of the American market consisted of imported tools in 1982. In 1965, the U.S. exported five times the tools we imported. By 1981, we imported twice the tools we exported. More modern tool firms in Europe and Japan and the rising value of the dollar against foreign currencies meant imports quadrupled American market shares in five years. And, as the Makino official in Tokyo observed, our aging factories lacked "the flexibility to change manufacturing schedules" for rush orders. So when Detroit ordered new tools to make smaller cars in the late 1970s, a lot of orders went abroad. Future threats include numerically controlled tools and things like the "manless factory" of Yamazaki tools in Nagoya, where computers guide robots, and 12 men do the work of 220 in the new craft of "mechatronics." With one in ten Milwaukee workers in machine tools, the need for major job retraining and new high-tech industries is obvious.

This is the Milwaukee economy: diverse and strong in spite of tactical problems in beer and strategic threats to machine tools. On the social front, while the crime rate is very low, there have been racial tensions. Twenty-three percent of Milwaukee is black, the group expanding from 6,000 in 1940 to 147,000 today.

---

* The Heileman merger could have saved both Wisconsin firms. By rigidly enforcing antitrust laws, the Justice Department hurt both firms, thus helping the reigning "duopoly" of Anheuser-Busch and Miller. For without Schlitz, Heileman couldn't get into southern markets—while without Heileman, Schlitz was forced to merge with the weaker Detroit brewery at Stroh's. Noting how the "beer market today resembles a barroom brawl," Paul A. Gigot in *The Wall Street Journal* quoted an economist who observed how "the irony is that, in the name of protecting small brewers, Justice is going to lose them anyway," as the Big Two watched Schlitz and Heileman decline.

Hispanics add another 23,000 to the minority census. The blacks live in an area of sound and neat homes called the Inner City, divided from the Polish South Side by a viaduct. For more than 200 days in 1967, a Roman Catholic priest, James Groppi, led the blacks over the viaduct in open-housing marches that received national coverage. Late that year two people were killed in a brief riot.

A dozen years later, Peirce and Keefe found that groups formed after the riots, such as "We Milwaukeeans," had succeeded in reducing the tension, and producing agreements for minority jobs like one between Miller, Schlitz and Jesse Jackson's PUSH. The extremely low crime rate—unique for a big city with a large black population—suggests that factory jobs and fine city services have given minorities a stake in a stable city.

In 1981, tensions were revived by a familiar catalyst: charges of police brutality. After the death of a young black during a "wrong man" arrest, three policemen and two paramedics were indicted. The charges were later dismissed. A sizable Coalition for Justice for Ernie Lacy was formed. The group suggested that Lacy had died of a heart attack because the officers had failed to give lifesaving aid in an emergency, and a 1983 court decision agreed with the Coalition. The crisis reflected minority anger in Milwaukee over things such as only 128 black cops on a 2,000-member police force, despite a 1975 court decree against hiring bias. A 1981 Milwaukee *Sentinel* poll found that 67 percent of whites supported the police, while only 30 percent of blacks did so. The death of a white dancer who was in custody, and the alleged beating of a white businessman who was under arrest, began to erode even white support for the police.

Then on December 23, 1981, two policemen were killed. A young black was alleged to have gunned them down. A black alderman suggested outrageously that the alleged killer had shot the officers out of fear that they would kill him. The police, understandably furious at the alderman, struck for a day in protest. They demanded a police community relations program from City Hall. This demand was aimed mainly at the police chief, a petulant seventy-one-year-old with a lifetime appointment, who claimed that each policeman was a public-relations specialist by training. Calls for the chief's resignation by Mayor Maier and others were ignored.

Also troubling was the long recession of 1981–83 which hit

even diversified Milwaukee. Since domestic machine-tool orders fell 75 percent in two years, a city with almost 10 percent of its work force in the sector was vulnerable. By the fall of 1982, Milwaukee's 11.2 percent unemployment was two points over the national rate, in a city normally two points under America's average.*

Allis-Chalmers forecast $140 million in 1982 losses, with its stock dropping from over $30 to $6.25 at one point. Since machine tools are the last purchases in an economic recovery, some felt the sector would stagnate until 1984. On the bright side, Milwaukee's biggest employer, A. O. Smith, recalled all its workers when a big GM order came in for car and truck frames in early 1983. For two days, network news showed 20,000 Milwaukeeans lined up in an armory, trying for 200 extra jobs at Smith. Unemployment was now up to 11.6 percent, with 90,000 jobless in the area.

Also, family income has dropped sharply. It was 82 percent of nearby suburban median income in 1969, but only 67 percent by 1975. Otherwise, good services and a diverse economy earned the city fine ratings in urban surveys that year. It was twelfth among the fifty biggest cities in a comparative look in *Harper's*. In 1980, a HUD survey of urban needs rated Milwaukee the most stable of the Snowbelt cities with more than 600,000 residents.

Stability in skylines too. As of 1980, this city of 632,000 had only one 42-story skyscraper to ruin the view. This although the 1970s saw all Snowbelt downtowns sprout the boxes and filing cabinets that make Dayton and Boston indistinguishable from certain angles. Milwaukee is called "the smallest big city in the U.S.A." by Peirce and Keefe. It earned that title in part by not opening a culture center until 1979. Long before then, however, Pabst and Uihlein Halls had one of our Top Ten orchestras, the Milwaukee Symphony. Its appointment of Lukas Foss as conductor in 1981 was a fine coup, and his wife, Cornelia, a landscape painter, draws a charming portrait of the city. "In downtown Milwaukee, you *never* hear a car honk its horn," she recalls, "and I'm struck each time I go there from our home in

---

* The only cheer that fall was a World Series for the Brewers, their manager, Harvey Kuenn, one of Milwaukee's more than 1,600 tavern owners. This "Sudsway Series" with St. Louis was a lift, even if August Busch's Cardinals won the day.

New York at how *polite* people are." One drawback downtown is a growing universe of empty buildings. A huge, block-square department store across from the elegant Pfister Hotel has been an ominous sign. "When I first visited in 1980, it was open. The second time in 1981, it was boarded up. Then early in 1982, I was going down for dinner before a concert—and I smelled smoke. It had been set on fire." But elsewhere Mrs. Foss enjoys the small big city, with its miles of parks along Lake Michigan, and people strolling on summer nights among gazebos and pavilions. In 1981, the "winner" in an international competition to further develop the lakefront would have ultimately destroyed all this. Mrs. Foss recalled how "the winning design was commercial: a lot of shops, malls, hotels." The city fathers held an emergency meeting—and voted it down. Mrs. Foss suggests it was

> the smartest thing anyone could have done. They held on to several miles of grass along the lakefront for walkers, joggers and picnics. You know, even when it's cold and snowy, you *still* see people out there enjoying it. And even in summer, it's so big that it's never jammed like Coney Island. You also never see pieces of paper on the ground—there are a lot of picker-uppers in Milwaukee . . .

Boston's ambiance, manners and scale match that of Milwaukee, and as *The Boston Globe* said, the city is ". . . everything a Bostonian would expect, and less. But things get done. In fact, people expect their city to work. They have not yet developed the cynicism of the urban East. . . . Milwaukee is still—almost naively, it seems to an Easterner—American."

## Kansas City

"To anyone brought up there, as I was, Kansas City always meant the Missouri one. . . . The Union Depot, hotel life, banking, theaters, shopping—all the urbanities—were in Missouri."

So begins the autobiography of composer Virgil Thomson, born and raised in Kansas City before an adult life in Paris and New York. Some of his best music reflects the folk tunes, ditties, hymns and spirituals of a cosmopolitan cow town in 1910. The famous film scores for *The River, The Plow That Broke the Plains* and *Louisiana Story* recall formative years in a city that was small—but had "all the urbanities."

So it remained in the 1940s, when a French writer left Thomson's adopted home of Paris for an American tour. André Maurois later marveled, "Who in Europe, or in America for that matter, knows that Kansas City is one of the loveliest cities on earth?" For the town of Thomson's youth was still as pleasant as it had been when he enlisted in the 129th Field Artillery in which Harry Truman rose to early fame. And Maurois' pleasant hyperbole of the 1940s was based on solid evidence: 7,211 acres of parks, 118 miles of tree-lined freeways, and so many fountains that only Rome has more. Many of the fountains are in the Spanish-style Country Club Plaza, opened by J. C. Nicholas in 1922 as America's first shopping center. Its Toledo tiles and plashing fountains are a poignant reminder of What Might Have Been in the shopping-center line. Then there is the William Rockhill Nelson Gallery and Atkins Museum, built in the 1930s by the founder of the *Kansas City Star,* and easily the best small museum in America. This is a fine collection in both range and quality, with many familiar masterworks from the major schools, and the best Chinese collection outside of the Museum of Fine Arts in Boston and, inevitably, China itself.

But there was another Kansas City in the 1920s and 1930s. This was the open city run by Tom Pendergast, with his 60,000 "ghost votes," his $50,000 days at the track, his open tolerance of gambling, prostitution and narcotics. Only Chicago was more violent back then, and reform workers were actually killed at the polls on election day. In 1940, local housewives organized a crusade, and a Citizens Association elected a council and mayor. John Gunther recalled how Kansas City had quickly "jumped from being one of the worst cities in America to one of the best." It was this cleaned-up city with its parks, fountains and museums that had charmed André Maurois.

As the 1950s began, however, people were edging toward the suburban exits, and local taxes were rising to cover a shrinking revenue base. The downward spiral of revenue losses, service cuts and taxpayer flight was apparent in early eddies. A way to stop the tide was to annex the suburbs. Kansas City grew rapidly, from a city of 62 square miles in 1950 to one of 316 square miles today, the eighth largest in America. Within such vast and underpopulated borders, Kansas City could have expanded like New

York did in the early 1900s, after it had annexed the rural boroughs of the Bronx and Brooklyn. But the small scale of the city
of fountains and parks was maintained. Growth for growth's sake
is foreign to the Kansas City ethos.

The annexations brought in suburban taxes, and even some
farmland. To this expanded revenue base, Kansas City would
add a 1 percent tax on commuters. All this enabled it to cut
property taxes without first cutting services. But as the city aged
and service needs grew, the taxes remained too low. In 1976, for
example, there were these per capita comparisons for property
taxes: Boston, $503; San Francisco, $234; Kansas City, $44. The
city could have used its broader tax base to improve services,
but it didn't. So Kansas City suffered a 12 percent population
loss in the 1970s, which was striking for a city with so much
geography to flee from.

Kansas City got two major economic boosts in 1966, one public, one private. The public aid was a vote for a $150 million bond
to build a new Kansas City International Airport, with $200 mil-
lion more added by airlines and other firms. In *The Nine Nations
of North America,* Joel Garreau observes Kansas City's role as
the "crossroads of everything" in America, starting with the
Spanish trade along the Santa Fe Trail:

> Not far from the exact geographic center of the United States,
> it was where Easterners became Westerners. To this day, it is
> a great marketing-research location, because of its utter typi-
> cality. Even urban employers will tell you that its friendly,
> open, hardworking people are still a product of the prairie.

*Nation's Business* observed that at the time the bond had been
passed, "Kansas City was slipping behind cities of comparable
size in the quest for business investment. The airport's construction was perhaps the key move in the city's renaissance."

The crucial private boost for Kansas City in 1966 was the decision of Joyce C. Hall, founder of Hallmark Cards, to open an
eighty-five-acre city-within-a-city to be called Crown Center in
honor of his company's famous trademark. Garreau writes:

> This theme park to what might be called high-quality capitalism
> owes a large debt to Walt Disney, a Kansas City boy who was
> disappointed to see his Disneyland ringed by taco stands. He

told his friend Joyce C. Hall . . . to make sure not to make the same mistake—to make sure he bought enough land so that his monument, the Hallmark headquarters, wouldn't get overrun by blight, and Mr. Hall took the advice to heart.

So to J. C. Nichols' Spanish shopping center of 1922 and William Rockhill Nelson's striking museum of 1934 was added another man's vision in Kansas City. As early as 1955, Hall had begun buying up used-car lots, warehouses and run-down buildings in the Signboard Hill section. By 1966, Hall's eighty-five acres were ready. The man who brought good drama to television with the *Hallmark Playhouse* wanted good taste in the huge complex of offices, condos, hotels, malls and culture centers ahead. Eventually he would spend $500 million of his money, making Crown Center the biggest private family project since Rockefeller Center in New York. The Rockefellers had hired the best popular architect of the time, Raymond Hood. Hall hired an equivalent figure in 1966, Edward Larrabee Barnes.

When the city-within-a-city is finished in 1985, it will include 2 million square feet of office space, more than 2,200 rental and condominium apartments, the 730-room Hyatt Regency hotel, several culture centers, two retail areas and parking for 7,000 cars. By 1976, the half-finished Center was crown to $5.3 billion in building improvements since 1970. Among them were the airport, the Harry S Truman Sports Complex, and the Kemper Arena. All this bustle impressed the Republican Party. Kansas City got the 1976 convention for the Kemper Arena, the first of two Republican conventions held in Snowbelt states, their Sunbelt strategies notwithstanding. The previous convention to be held in Kansas City had been in 1900. It took place in a hall 364 feet wide with no interior columns, built in three months for the nomination of William Jennings Bryan. The media glowed about a revitalized Kansas City. The tragic collapse of the atrium skywalks at the Hyatt Regency hotel which caused 114 deaths in the summer of 1981 was a shocking exception.

Aside from the physical rebuilding of the 1970s, Kansas City has a diversified economy. Only small parts of the stockyards that built the old cow town remain, though the American Royal Livestock Exposition and Horse Show recently held its eighty-fifth renewal. The biggest single metro employer is TWA, with more than 10,000 workers out at the airport. Ford and GM auto and truck plants in the area are so big that only Detroit has more factory outlets for the industry. Hallmark and Fairfield Industries are the two *Fortune* 500 headquarters here. Three more on the second 500 list add more diversity: Morton Labs in drugs, Butler Manufacturing in metal products, and Russell Stover candies. And for those who pay taxes, Kansas City is also home to H. & R. Block, founded by the brothers Henry and Robert Bloch (who spell the company name with a *k* since the customers tend to do so). Henry Bloch, a past chairman of the local Chamber of Commerce, opposes "bigness for bigness's sake." He told *Time* that "no one is anxious to cover all this beautiful rolling countryside with concrete." This vigorous lack of push may be Reason #18 for using his firm.

The fight against concrete in the city of fountains and parks is seen in its literal underground economy, 20 million square feet of offices and warehouses in cool, underground caverns. Kansas City's base is a vast limestone bed, the twelve-foot-thick Bethany Falls Ledge. Two hundred and twenty million square feet of usable space could be hollowed out down there—equal to the office space in Manhattan. Kansas City has excavated and leased 10 percent of this phenomenal underground reserve, part of it as an international trade zone where imported parts arrive duty-free for assemblage with domestic parts. The duties are imposed as the finished product leaves the underground economy of Kansas City for taxable regions above. This saves higher duties for importing entire assembled products and adds more local jobs for those who produce the domestic parts or assemble the mix in Kansas City caverns. The limestone vaults have a uniform temperature of 55 degrees, and almost no dust or humidity. A developer tells *The New York Times* that, while a "surface building" costs $45 per square foot, K.C. underground goes for only $10 since "we don't have to build a roof or outside perimeter walls and there is virtually no heating cost because heat from the lighting and from people stabilizes temperature at about 70 degrees." The land above goes for a drive-in theater, a radio station, some homes and farmland. The host city of eighty-five Royal Livestock Expositions has just held the first Underground Space Exposition to discuss a growing national trend.

The diverse economy, the regional magnet of the Crown Center, the crossroads hub of KCI airport, the foreign trade zones and 220 million square feet of limestone to let—all that helped maintain a 3.9 percent unemployment rate in 1979 against 5.8 percent for America. Not good compared to Minneapolis and Wichita, but far better than most Snowbelt cities.

The bad news is the 12 percent population loss since 1970, and a rate of 1,420 violent crimes per 100,000. The crime compares well with Detroit or Houston, but poorly next to Milwaukee's 523 rate or Wichita's 650. Part of this may be a cultural legacy from the Pendergast era, but poor city services are also a factor. For all the money thrown at capital projects since 1970, Kansas City foolishly kept services on a leash. Until it raises taxes and improves essential services like fire and police, the downward spiral will continue. This could even turn into a polarized city. Kansas City is home of the Crown Center and of the Parade Homes for moderate-income blacks, a fifty-acre community of more than 500 town houses praised by Neal Peirce as "one of the nation's best housing offers." Yet Kansas City also has such terrible slums that during the heat wave of 1980 more than 100 elderly blacks died of dehydration.

Urban surveys rate Kansas City as average. It was nineteenth among fifty cities in the 1975 *Harper's* survey. A 1980 Princeton study rated it fifth among twenty-two Snowbelt cities for overall conditions, quite weak for manufacturing, but third for service receipts. A 1980 HUD study of urban needs put Kansas City just below the middle, thirtieth among fifty-eight cities. Kansas City can do better. For instance, there must be less of the penny-pinching that led to the firemen's strike that threatened public safety for several days in 1979. Firemen have the most dangerous work and are routinely courageous and civic-minded. When they strike, a city is usually at fault.

A paragon with problems. Otherwise a handsome hometown. Virgil Thomson. Harry S Truman. J. C. Nichols. Walt Disney. William Rockhill Nelson. Joyce C. Hall. And all the urbanities.

## Wichita

Food, oil, and planes make Wichita the boomtown of the Snowbelt. These three sectors inspire what *The Almanac of American Politics* calls "the Sun Belt city farthest north." Two rousing films with Gable and Tracy told the story: *Boom Town* was about the muck and money of oil in the 1920s, while *Test Pilot* told of the dashing aviators and small planes that made Wichita an adventure mecca in the 1930s—and today make it the current world capital of small-plane manufacturing. The three industries have made Wichita nearly recession-proof. Even in early 1982, as America suffered 8.8 percent unemployment, Wichita had a 3.7 rate. A unique mix of civic foresight and OPEC price shocks has produced the most stable Snowbelt city of all.

It began with food. Wichita was a major stop on the Chisholm Trail in the 1870s, processing more than a million cattle a year. Its dance halls and bars made it "the noisiest town on the American continent," and it remains a major slaughtering and packing center today. In the 1880s, it also became a major grain market and milling center. Nineteen fifteen saw the discovery of large oil reserves. Wichita still refines oil and sells equipment as the center of America's sixth biggest oil-producing state.

The third and most important leg of Wichita's economy began in 1919, when an oilman opened the first plane factory, and hired Walter Beech in 1921. Clyde Cessna and William Lear soon arrived, and the local Big Three of small planes were soon under way. During World War II, however, the big plane employer was Boeing, in a huge plant that built B-47s, B-52s and more B-29s than any other three similar plants in America.* After the war, Boeing mainly decamped to California and Washington, but remaining plants still make parts of planes. They were set to go on the B-1, when Jimmy Carter wisely canceled the project.

Small planes are the main industry here, and when *Nation's Business* profiled Wichita in 1975, the city was producing 65 percent of all light commercial planes on earth. Flying aces of the 1920s had given way to mere wealth. As the house organ of the Chamber of Commerce had gushed in its profile, "If you have the notion that Central City, U.S.A. (as some boosters call Wichita) is stultifying, forget it. There are few towns where you're as apt to rub elbows in a pub with people who've just flown in from such diverse places as Kuwait, Venezuela and Las Vegas."

---

* Neal Peirce recalls that many aircraft workers arrived in the 1940s and 1950s from the South, with Wichita "the scene of Kansas' worst race problems." Even in 1972, almost all of the city's 26,841 blacks lived in a well-defined 100-block ghetto, and "few American cities suffer from more rigid residential segregation." Wichita was also home to the Kansas Right to Work Committee, and several leading manufacturers were prominent Birchers. Peirce concluded that "most other Kansans think of it as a mediocre town with little class and a lot of right-wing extremist activity."

Wichita boomed during the 1950s and 1960s, a medium-sized city of 168,000 becoming a big one of 277,000 by 1970. But recessions and canceled plane orders often made for steep boom-bust cycles. By 1966, 26 percent of Wichita worked in airplanes, which was almost as bad as a 33 percent share of auto workers in Detroit. When the first of two Nixon recessions hit Wichita in 1970, unemployment soared to 11 percent and membership plunged in the International Machinists Union, from 19,000 to 5,000 in only a few months. Two big downtown hotels had closed by the time recovery began around 1972.

"You might say that 1970 really did it," recalled Wichita's mayor Garry Porter for *Nation's Business* in 1975. Porter, a psychiatrist and a native Californian, recalled how city leaders decided "they'd better really get cracking to diversify the economy." The city issued $60 million in industrial bonds as corporate lures, and soon added new offices or factories from Metropolitan Life, National Cash Register, J. I. Case and Safeway. The last opened a meat-processing center for the city's slaughter-and-pack sector, and by 1974, all packing plants had expansion plans under way. Cessna was the only *Fortune* 500 firm, but in the second 500 there were Gates Learjet, Coleman in metal products, and Energy Research Corporation. Wichita did an amazing turnabout in a decade. Airplanes had 26 percent of the jobs in 1966, but only 14 percent by 1975. This was the best example of "instant diversification" on record.

Luck helped too. OPEC price shocks after 1973 were a unique double boon for Wichita. As higher prices for home-heating and industrial fuel hurt Snowbelt states, they led to more drilling in a major oil state. As the oil center for Kansas, Wichita thrived. The second break from the OPEC hikes was an odd, countercyclical boost for small planes. At first, the 1973 oil embargo was a severe blow, since no oil meant no small planes. An industry analyst recalls how "they sent everyone home in the fall, then by March of 1974, demand was so strong, they brought them back —and then some." Once the Arabs settled for merely extorting money through price hikes, the OPEC crisis helped Wichita. As Cessna's chairman Russell W. Myers told *U.S. News & World Report* in 1976, "The 55-mile-per-hour speed limit and cutbacks in commercial aviation schedules have made business and private flying more acceptable to corporations and individuals who are too busy to cope with reduced airplane schedules and airport tie-ups." During the worst slump since the Depression, Cessna's work force grew by 4,000 between 1974 and 1976. Gates Learjet added 650 workers in 1974, then looked for 2,000 new employees. Boeing with its bigger planes laid off 1,000 workers in 1976, but a Chamber of Commerce official observed, "These people will be snapped up by other firms. In fact all three [Beech, Cessna and Gates Learjet] already have personnel officials interviewing at Boeing."

Another unique break for Wichita was the relocation of factories from Snowbelt cities to small towns. In a sidebar about three cities immune to the 1975 recession, *Newsweek* noted how high fuel costs meant airlines began to "cut back or abandon altogether service of many small cities and towns where corporations have built plants in recent years. Without commercial flights, executives have started buying more planes from Cessna, Gates Learjet and Beechcraft . . ."

Nineteen seventy-five was also a fine crop year. *U.S. News & World Report* noted "heavy purchases of farm equipment and . . . a brisk milling industry" for the Wichita area, with a record number of cattle leading to meat-packing growth. Rising oil prices, bumper crops and small-plane orders meant 4.3 percent unemployment against 9.0 percent for America. Wichita was so healthy in 1975 that a new shopping center opened, adding up to 2,000 new jobs. Two hotels had closed in the 1969–70 slump, but by 1975 a hotel-convention hall was opening. A major school-building program and a new City Hall were under way, as were a new zoo, art museum, agriculture coliseum, Indian culture center and planetarium—in the worst national slump since the 1930s. A history professor at Wichita State University claimed that "short of a first-rate meal, you can get just about anything in Wichita."

Since 1975, Wichita has had no equal among major Snowbelt cities for unemployment:

|  | 1975 | 1976 | 1977 | 1978 | 1979 | 1980 | 1981 |
|---|---|---|---|---|---|---|---|
| United States | 9.0 | 7.8 | 7.5 | 6.1 | 5.8 | 7.6 | 8.8 |
| Wichita | 4.3 | 5.4 | 5.5 | 4.1 | 3.2 | 4.1 | 3.7 |

The growing gap between the two rates after 1979 reflected at least four more breaks helping Wichita. The 1979 decontrol of domestic oil prices by Washington meant more drilling in Kansas fields. The second OPEC price shock in late 1979 crippled the Snowbelt even more, but again helped Wichita as an oil center, while making private jets even more popular among executives. These jets were now perceived as a business tool, so much so that when machine tools dropped 50 percent in 1982, private jet orders dropped 50 percent as well.

As higher fuel costs and decentralization of factories to small towns proceeded between 1976 and 1981, jet orders jumped from 183 to 389 a year, and turboprops went from 389 to 918. Another break was airline deregulation. This led to the fights between carriers like American and Braniff, and fewer airlines and scheduled stops. Executives had new reasons to buy private jets. Their growing demands meant huge windfalls for Don Love, a former Cessna salesman who speculated on unbuilt planes by buying "delivery positions" and then selling his place on the order line to corporations. Love made a small fortune by this trick on thirty-eight occasions, and early in 1982, *The Wall Street Journal* found him with "about $350,000 tied up so far in advance payments on a Citation III. He hopes to clear a personal record of $800,000 by selling his place on the waiting line to an impatient corporate buyer or actually take delivery and resell the plane at a profit."

Finally, the Reaganomic scourge for other Snowbelt cities helped Wichita. The speedup of domestic oil price decontrol by Reagan helped Wichita as a drilling center. The 1981 investment tax credits meant a year-end spree of private jet buys; December billings of $336 million set a new record. A final example of the "what's bad for America is great for Wichita" law was the PATCO air controllers' strike in 1981. As commercial flights were cut in half, even more CEOs looked to Wichita for relief. Oddly, PATCO's most militant defender, William Winpisinger of the International Machinists, would see his big Wichita local prosper off any new orders.*

Wichita couldn't lose. By 1980, the Princeton comparison of

---

* In 1975, Wichita's machinist union president Carl Courter told *Nation's Business* that "we haven't had but three strikes over the years . . . we try to work things out for everybody's good." Thus when the 1973 OPEC embargo threatened the local aircraft plants, he and the heads of the Big Three plane producers had hopped into one of their jets for a joint appearance in Washington, urging fair gas allocations for aviation.

fifty-eight big cities confirmed this fact. Among the twenty-two Snowbelt cities in the survey, Wichita was #1 for urban conditions and #1 for manufacturing value added. It was also #1 for retail sales growth and #1 for sales receipts. Only a #2 rank behind Columbus, Ohio, for wholesale sales prevented a sweep of all five categories among Snowbelt cities.

In 1982, reality came to Wichita. The worst slump since the Depression was too much even for a city that thrived off OPEC hikes, factory relocations, airline deregulation and PATCO strikes. The 3.5 percent unemployment of early 1982 suddenly tripled to 11 percent by the fall. Where Wichita had begun the year five points below America's jobless rate, it ended 1982 a point above it. The 11 percent rate matched Wichita's last previous slump in the 1969–70 recession.

Wichita's unusual crisis came from a sharp drop in plane orders, as 11,877 nationwide orders in 1980 fell to only 4,266 for 1982. The decline began in 1980, when fuel prices hit $2.00 a gallon, and small planes lost the weekend hobbyists. High interest rates in 1981 began thinning out corporate buyers as well. As the recession deepened in 1982, production went down sharply. By year's end, a national work force of 90,000 was cut by 40 percent. Sunbelt majors like Piper in Florida and Gulfstream in Savannah took losses, but the main problems were in Wichita:

• Learjet split into two parts long ago, with founder William Lear taking his Lear Fan group to Reno in the 1960s.* Gates Rubber bought the main Wichita firm, then relocated Gates Learjet to Tucson in 1981. Its main Model 55 is produced in Arizona, so Gates Learjet is less a Wichita factor. Unlike Cessna and Piper, who produce for annual quotas, Gates Learjet works to order. It was therefore stuck with less unsold inventory in 1982.

• Beech also builds to order, but the 1982 recession cut 11,000 workers to 7,500. Raytheon purchased Beech in 1981, and is investing heavily in R&D, with lighter planes of carbon fiber the goal. Early in 1983, a Beech salesman was optimistic. He noted that Beech was clearing a large site near its main Wichita plant, with a new training school and headquarters building set for 1984.

---

* Learjet's notable founder, the late William Lear, was one of our most versatile inventors since Edison. He patented the automatic pilot, car radio, 8-track stereo and the first private jet. His last breakthrough, a plane of carbon fiber capable of high fuel efficiency at 400 miles an hour, recently saw completion under the direction of his widow, Moya. Unfortunately, it was financed by England, and all 2,000 factory jobs went to a Belfast factory.

• Cessna was the big Wichita problem. Building 50 percent of the market, it was caught short by the 1982 slump. The Beech salesman recalls how Cessna's high production quotas meant that in 1983 "Cessna had so much iron standing in the fields out there that they've even parked some planes in airports 100 to 200 miles away to break up the concentration. They need a lift to get cash flow back and cover their debt service." A possible lift was Cessna's unorthodox "Company Line," a long-term lease offered in late 1982, as the "iron" piled up in Wichita. For a fixed fee immune to inflation, a five-year package covered a plane, hangar and maintenance, taking the risk out of ownership. Meanwhile, Cessna's nose dive was severe. Twenty-one thousand workers in 1980 were down by 7,700 by late 1982. Earnings plummeted by 70 percent in one year. Cessna even had the first losing quarter in its history.

Beyond the current slump, Wichita's main industry should survive. A *Wall Street Journal* survey in 1982 found 41 percent of more than 1,000 firms planning to buy a new aircraft by 1984. And technology breakthroughs by American firms should maintain our dominance of world markets. Small planes can now fly up to 2,500 miles nonstop. Cessna's Citation III can fly at 51,000 feet, where, with thinner air and less drag, fuel efficiency is increased. Even in the 1982 slump, Citation III orders were backlogged to 1985. While private planes were a corporate frill in 1969–70, they are now an accepted business tool in an era of high fuel costs, reduced commercial flights and decentralized factories. Only deep recessions like 1981–83 can upset Wichita's main industry again.

For once, optimism seems warranted for a Snowbelt city. Wichita's food and oil roles are vital to daily life, while small planes go beyond corporate use to a growing hobbyist market. These three legs of the Wichita economy plus the diversification drive of the early 1970s should soon revive the Snowbelt's premier boomtown.

Thus our four Snowbelt paragons. Plenty of jobs, not much crime. Diversity and stability. What can Minneapolis, Milwaukee, Kansas City and Wichita teach an ailing industrial region? Not much. Unlike Kansas City and Milwaukee annexing suburbs, dying cities like Cleveland or Baltimore can't grab Shaker Heights or Owings Mills. Unlike Minneapolis or Milwaukee, fading Snowbelt cities can't point to homogenous and stable populations or diversified economies. These Romes take decades to build. You can't graft diversity onto a run-down factory town overnight. And for all their brave talk, Snowbelt cities are mainly too late in attracting high-tech firms. There are few practical idealists like the founder of Control Data, who are willing to open smokeless factories in the South Bronx.

For example, look at Boston. This temporary home to 100,000 college students is also the permanent residence for 91,000 adults who never got beyond the eighth grade. Boston's great universities helped create the scientists and businessmen who opened America's first high-tech strip in the 1950s, but Route 128 and suburbia got the jobs, not a shrinking, less literate Hub. *The Boston Globe* want ads lead off each Sunday with several dozen pages from computer and electronic giants beyond the Boston city line: *Fortune* 500 members like Raytheon in Lexington, Digital Equipment in Maynard, Data General in Westboro, and Wang in Lowell. The Digital plant in Maynard is an old American Woolens factory, one of many such conversions in former textile mills. Those mills launched our industrial revolution a century ago; now high-tech phoenixes rise from their hulks in a postindustrial renaissance. Eight thousand work in the Maynard factory today—in a city where 8,000 recently lived. The huge infusion of jobs does wonders for this small town and the "rural revival," but nothing for Boston.

There is also Boston's dramatic, but misleading, revival downtown. First came the Back Bay redevelopment, anchored by the Prudential Center at one end and the Hancock Tower at the other. Then came the even bigger renewal of Government Center near the waterfront, with more than $600 million in urban renewal grants, and more than $1 billion in building a year. Government Center office space doubled, and landmarks arose: the innovative New England Aquarium of 1968; the dramatic City Hall of 1969; the old wharves converted to luxury housing in a landmark for the recycling movement. Finally there was the renovation of Quincy Market into an arcade of 120 boutiques and bistros, plus the decking out of nearby Faneuil Hall, noted by Herbert H. Denton in *The Washington Post:*

> Once the meeting place of Revolutionary patriots and the stage
> for serious and impassioned debate on liberty and the destiny
> of an emerging nation, it is now a fantasyland for grownups

. . . a bright warren of ice cream parlors, bakeries, a poster shop selling blowups of the early Beatles and a chi chi carryout featuring eggplant submarine sandwiches.

The recycled wharves with their $600-a-month rentals had once been workplaces for the unskilled. Until their redesign for living, the empty shells reflected more than 30,000 waterfront jobs lost since the heyday of the T Wharf in the 1950s. And the redevelopment of Government Center went beyond "cleaning up Scollay Square," once a charming congeries of cheap bars, burlesque houses and tattoo parlors—innocent compared to Boston's current "combat zone" with its open street prostitution. As T. D. Allman observed in *Harper's* in 1978, the Government Center redevelopment

> has saddled the business district with tax-exempt government offices, and most of the revenues the new restaurants and boutiques bring go into the state treasury. Meanwhile, more than *one thousand small-scale loft industries* [emphasis added] employing mostly low-wage workers who are now on the unemployment rolls were destroyed by the development process.

Not only were the unskilled wharf and loft jobs gone, but the new jobs in Government Center tended to be in specialized services like finance, insurance or real estate. Suburbanites got three of every five new jobs. More than 300,000 of Boston's daily work force commute—a staggering 55 percent share, compared to 18 percent in New York City.

In the middle of the high-tech circle of Route 128 and the booming revival downtown was one more dying Snowbelt city. This is the basic Snowbelt truth today.

CHAPTER 9

# THE FIVE DISASTERS

THE NEXT TWO chapters look at more typical big cities in the Northeast and Midwest. We start with the recent downtown revivals, and show how new office towers, shopping malls and sports arenas suggest a media myth of Snowbelt urban renaissance:

• Philadelphia has the town-house revivals of Society Hill and Queen Village, the vast Gallery shopping center of 1977, several new restaurant rows, and a recent string of world champion teams. It also has the second worst teen-age and black unemployment in urban America.

• Baltimore has the two recent media events of a new National Aquarium, opened in 1981, and a huge Harborplace arcade drawing more annual visitors than Disney World. But even in normal times, unemployment can go to 10 percent in this collapsing factory town.

Perhaps these two cities can be salvaged, but three others in this chapter are beyond the point of no return. Only major federal job creation and training programs can turn them around:

• St. Louis is the Carthage of America: most of its downtown was razed in the 1970s; most of its jobs have gone to surrounding county suburbs since 1960; 48 percent of its people have left since 1950.

• Detroit is cars, and the slump after 1979. Even as the Big Three auto giants recover today, future threats like declining domestic demand, robotization and outsourcing of auto parts abroad suggest that up to half of the current workers could lose their jobs by 1990.

• Newark is our worst city. This was a thriving factory town in 1950, bigger then than Dallas, Denver, Phoenix, San Antonio, San Diego or San Jose, to name six of the ten biggest Sunbelt cities today. Newark is dead last today in most city surveys. It lost 19 percent of its assessed value after 1969 and cut 33 percent of its police force after 1977—as violent crime soared 91 percent in three years.

• Our final chapter crosses the river from Newark to the greatest city on earth, the world's capital for commerce, communications and culture. But New York just took its first big census loss since 1790. Where New York's median family income was 3 percent above America's average in 1970, it was 17 percent below the national norm by 1978, as the middle class left. This will leave a polarized geography: the luxury lifeboat of Manhattan Island and the abandoned hulks of four Outer Boroughs elsewhere. We shall see the service crisis in five areas: crime, housing, health, mass transit and jobs.

As the 1975 recession came to an end, a rash of hotels, office towers, culture centers, malls and sports arenas broke out in downtown America. Most of these were Sunbelt blockbusters: the fifty-story Reunion Tower of Dallas, Pennzoil Place in Houston, John Portman's hotels in Atlanta. While the Snowbelt had fewer of these browbeaters, Chicago had the world's tallest building, the Sears Tower, and New York had the twin stilettos of the World Trade Center. Three blocks north of the Trade Center twins, the robust Gothic towers of the Woolworth Building recall the vigorous Snowbelt industry of 1914. The twins of 1970 seem merely sleek, postindustrial ciphers of decline.

Snowbelt cities at least have some humanly scaled arcades, malls and plazas. The Sunbelt began this trend in the 1960s, when an old chocolate factory in San Francisco's Ghirardelli Square was converted to an arcade of shops and restaurants, while carbarns in Salt Lake City became the mall of a new Trolley Square.* Recycling later moved east, to things like the landmark

---

* Recycling had many forms. A Cleveland power plant was turned into a theater. A torpedo factory in Virginia became an art center. An abandoned county jail in Wyoming became an art center, and as a radio spot said, tastelessly, "In Wyoming they're putting artists in jail . . ."

renovation of Quincy Market by Cambridge architect Ben Thompson and Maryland developer James Rouse. Rouse went on to open an even bigger mall of more than 120 shops at the Gallery in Philadelphia, and then the famous Harborplace arcade on the Baltimore waterfront.

The malls were an ambivalent symbol for old Snowbelt cities. They brought back suburbanites who had fled cities; half of Quincy Market shoppers were commuters. They brought back what Jane Jacobs had urged in 1959, a bit of retail pizzazz for downtowns that once died after 5 P.M. But recycled or new malls were mainly islands for the upscale, something for the media to confuse with the "comeback" of dying cities. It was easy to forget how the recycled lofts once held crucial factory jobs for the poor whose numbers steadily grow.

Another urban renaissance myth was the building of new sports stadiums. The Silverdome of Pontiac, host to Super Bowl XVI in 1982, was a fine distraction from the less photogenic fact of 16 percent unemployment in Detroit next door.

## Philadelphia

The Stanley Cup for 1974 and 1975, the World Series victory of 1980, the Super Bowl bridesmaid of 1981 and the NBA champions of 1983—these have lately soothed the famous Philly "boobirds." But Pete Rose and high-flying Eagles, Doctor J and eagle-eyed Flyers, are not enough. When the lights go down at the Spectrum or Veteran's Stadium, this is still the city that elected Frank Rizzo and, worse, re-elected him. Philadelphia is also:

• A city where 35 percent of the people lived below the poverty line in 1980, a middle-class exodus seeing 13 percent of the city leave in the 1970s.

• A city that in 1980 lost its longtime rank as the East Coast's busiest international port, and which also lost 43 percent of its factory jobs in the 1970s.

• A city with the second highest teen-age and black unemployment among big cities for 1980. A city where crime jumped 49 percent since 1977.

To continue our sports theme, look at the film *Rocky II*. This fable of a Philadelphia champion is also the story of the city's economic ruin. As the film opens, Rocky is happily married and reluctant to fight again so he looks for a job. His first stop is at the downtown offices that lined his jogging route on the way to the Art Museum steps. But like too many Philadelphia blacks and teen-agers, Rocky the white dropout can't get into a sector where 70 percent of office jobs are held by commuters. Service jobs were the only ones growing during the 1970s in Philadelphia, but Main Line commuters got most of the work. Rocky's problem was noted by the city's Tricentennial Commission in 1981: "Employers complain about the lack of basic skills—reading, writing and arithmetic, to be prosaic—far more than any lack of vocational training."

Rocky's next job stop is on the docks. Philadelphia's port has been in recent and rapid decline. In 1980, it lost its rank as the East Coast's busiest international port to Hampton Roads, losing 20 percent of its cargo volume that year—the worst such loss in the North Atlantic area. In 1981, its port authority chairman conceded to *The Wall Street Journal* that "all of a sudden, everybody's waking up to the fact that our ports aren't the greatest." Rocky cannot find work in the very harbor that attracted William Penn's landing party in 1682.

At last, Rocky finds work in the old meat-packing plant where he worked in *Rocky I*. But Philadelphia's factories lost 42 percent of their jobs in the 1970s—the worst share of factory losses for any big city. Rocky is soon laid off as the company cuts costs. In reality, the 14,000-member local of the United Food and Commercial Workers in Philadelphia only held on to some jobs by buying five A&Ps.

Philadelphia's economic decline over a decade has been dramatic:

#### UNEMPLOYMENT RATES

|  | 1970 | 1975 | 1980 |
|---|---|---|---|
| Philadelphia | 5.3 | 9.7 | 12.4 |
| U.S.A. | 5.0 | 8.5 | 7.1 |
| Philadelphia Jobless Rate as % U.S.A. | 6% | 14% | 75% |

Not only was Philadelphia losing jobs, but 80 percent of those losses were factory jobs—the only places left for its Rockys. For example, of 19,000 jobs lost, more than 15,000 were in factories.

All this led to 20 percent black unemployment and 32 percent teen-age joblessness in early 1981. As Professor George Sternlieb of Rutgers has observed, "Roughly 70 percent of the manufacturing jobs are held by people who live in the city, while only 30 percent of the office workers are city dwellers." This is a classic mismatch of available jobs and local skills, in a Snowbelt city shifting from a goods to a service economy. How did the city of William Penn, Benjamin Franklin, 1776 and the Philadelphia lawyer come to this?

Philadelphia's story to 1967 is well told by the late Jeanne R. Lowe in her superb book *Cities in a Race with Time*. After its founding on the banks of the Delaware and the Schuylkill rivers in 1682, this "Holy Experiment" of William Penn developed its ocean and inland ports into the biggest city of the colonies. Philadelphia was where the First Continental Congress met in 1774 and the Second in 1775, where the Declaration of Independence was signed in 1776; it was the seat of the Revolutionary government during the war, the Constitutional Convention of 1787 and, finally, the capital of a new nation in 1790.

A gradual decline began. The capital was transferred to Washington in 1800, the Erie Canal made New York the leading port for inland trade after 1825, and Lowe recalled how "the *coup de grâce* was administered in 1836, when President Andrew Jackson abolished the national bank." Elsewhere, Philadelphia was a civic pioneer on many fronts. The first volunteer fire brigade was organized by Franklin in 1736. The first free public health clinic in America was opened by Declaration signer Dr. Benjamin Rush in 1786—a forgotten landmark in 1979, when Philadelphia's only public hospital was closed. The Episcopal Church was founded here in 1789, and the first school lunch program was begun in the 1830s. The American Anti-Slavery Society was organized here in 1833, and the first Republican Convention was held in 1856.

To celebrate the nation's Centennial, Philadelphia held America's version of the Crystal Palace show in 1876. Richard Wagner was paid $5,000 for his potboiling "Centennial March," and 10 million visited the exposition. Five years later, the Pennsylvania Railroad opened up the Main Line commuter service to suburban living. From then on, Lowe noted, "Philadelphia's absentee aristocracy could commute easily to offices in the city whose politics they continued to control and whose real estate they held in trust."

John Gunther described the Main Line in 1947 as an area where "it doesn't matter on what side of the tracks you are. These are very superior tracks." He recalled George Sessions Perry describing the Main Line: "The people who own the city, have abandoned it." The suburban owners let a surrogate group of grafters run Philadelphia into the ground. Neal Peirce refers to this Republican machine of Boies Penrose as "one of the most corrupt and unsavory political machines the country has ever known." The result was a 1930s disaster that resembled the fiscal crisis of New York City after 1975. Jeanne Lowe recalls this earlier dress rehearsal in the City of Brotherly Love:

> When the city's assessments plummeted, making it impossible to continue adequate city services as well as payments on its huge municipal debt from the speculative 1920's, the city's bankers bailed Philadelphia out. But they agreed to do so only on the condition that the city maintain a balanced budget. As a result, city services slipped still further, and the bankers' do-nothing control tightened.

The results of this around 1945, as recalled by Lowe, included streets that were "the dirtiest in the country," flickering gaslights and garbage collected by horse-drawn carriages. There was so much disinfectant in the sewage-polluted water that a glass of it was dubbed a "chlorine cocktail." Gunther noted how

> One expert recently termed the Port of Philadelphia "the largest, vilest, and foulest fresh water port in the world"; its water is so tainted that, literally, it damages the steel walls of ships. Every day, some 350 million *gallons* of raw sewage pour into the rivers that are the city's only source of water supply.

Gunther recalled how property values had nose dived, from $5 billion in 1930 to about $3 billion by 1944. This amazing slump depressed revenues, and one, among many, results was that

> In 1930, twelve years after World War I, Philadelphia started a campaign to build a veterans' hospital. Today, two years after World War II, it still hasn't got one. Some 400,000 veterans of both wars live in the city; for them, 550 hospital beds are available. Conditions in Byberry, the hospital for mental diseases, make it a kind of Bedlam . . .

A new low occurred in 1946. Desperately trying to revive its role as the capital of something, Philadelphia went all out to land the United Nations, but as Gunther remarked, "though Philadelphia wanted the UN, the UN didn't want Philadelphia."

In 1947, however, things began to turn around. A Better Philadelphia Exhibition opened in Gimbel's, a handsome display of dioramas, scale models, winking lights and ringing bells. Four hundred thousand people paid $1 apiece to see this planner's vision of What Might Be. Around this time, the Young Turks came to ʻthe fore. This group of liberal Democrats had been inspired by the New Deal and Fiorello La Guardia's reformist rule in New York. In 1952, one of them was elected mayor. Under Joseph S. Clark and his ally and successor J. Richardson Dilworth, the finest urban renewal in America began.

It was directed by city planner Edmund Bacon, a disciple of Eliel Saarinen who believed that urban renewal and good design should be linked in what Lowe called a "contagion of excellence." This meant a decade of renewal downtown, with a rich series of variations on modern architecture that remain fresh and humanly scaled. Bacon wisely set the building height limit at 511 feet, the height of the base of William Penn's statue on top of City Hall. This pleasant bow to the founding father meant no skyscrapers to ruin vistas in America's fourth biggest city.

The handsome new downtown was complemented by the revival of the Society Hill neighborhood nearby. The area was rehabbed for upper-class "taste-setters" needed to revitalize a Market Street retail area that had seen sales drop 15 percent between 1949 and 1957. This was the first major town-house revival in an old Snowbelt city, a success that would later house 50,000 in meeting a goal noted by Lowe: ". . . how to preserve the historic values and enhance the intimate scale of the eighteenth-century brick row houses, the Colonial structures and narrow cobbled streets without transforming the whole area into a deadly museum." Mayor Dilworth admitted that Society Hill and some new, upper-class housing nearby were deliberate attempts to "get the white [leadership] back. We have to give the whites confidence that they can live in town without being flooded." Blacks backed this candid liberal with 80 percent of their vote, for they made major gains under Clark and Dilworth. Where few blacks had city jobs before 1952, almost 30 percent did within a decade. Where 29 percent of blacks owned homes in 1950, 44 percent did by 1966. There was also the first Civilian Police Review Board in America, and an aggressive Human Relations Commission that in 1961 launched a future buzz word by insisting city businesses show "affirmative steps" for equal employment opportunities.

Philadelphia lagged far behind New York City for public housing, but Mayors Clark and Dilworth made a strong drive to assure code standards in existing shelter. Where 66 percent of blacks lived in code shelter in 1950, 85 percent did by 1960. During a later, distinguished career in the U.S. Senate, Joseph Clark observed that "people take pride in the 'spectaculars'—the center city rebuilding projects like Penn Center. But the hard guts of it is finding poor families a decent place to live."

Without massive federal aid, however, there were larger forces beyond Clark's or Dilworth's control. In 1964, riots reflected job losses and fading hopes among the poor. Lowe's praise for the physical renewal is constantly qualified by her future warnings of disaster. Early in her narrative, she paraphrases urban analyst Raymond Vernon, who had turned from the glow of Penn Center and Society Hill to observe in 1959 that, for all the downtown revival, "Philadelphia would be left with vast 'gray areas' where the notion of a great resurgence in middle-income housing was 'chimerical,' and the long-run prospect was one of declining population and declining jobs." The only way to stop the decline, Vernon had added, would be "mass public intervention . . . on so large a scale as to constitute a basic departure in American public policy." That departure was promised by President Johnson in 1964, then abandoned in the wake of the war in Vietnam. With only Medicare and Medicaid surviving the ruins of the Great Society, big Snowbelt cities like Philadelphia collapsed in the 1970s, just as Vernon had warned in 1959.

Before this occurred, Jeanne R. Lowe had focused on the main problem for Philadelphia: sizable losses of factory jobs, even in the 1950s. Between 1952 and 1963, more than 63,000 manufacturing jobs were lost in the city with the biggest group of small factories in America. Eighty percent of its plants employed fewer than fifty workers. Many of these mini-plants were in ancient lofts, described by Lowe as " 'exhibits in an outdoor museum devoted to the birth of the industrial revolution,' clinging to streams that no longer power their machines and still huddled close to rail spurs in the age of truck transportation."

Although Philadelphia was the first big city to make a conscious effort to hang on to factories with a land bank for new factories to draw on, Lowe in 1967 noted a

> growing worry whether the city was producing the skilled workers necessary to attract and hold modern plants and growth industries. Skilled workers were in such short supply that the apparel industry was importing men from Italy but 9 percent of the labor force was unemployed.

The future looked worse. The baby boom saw workers growing faster than jobs. Factory closings meant even fewer first jobs for a growing census of unskilled workers. Forty-five percent of the younger workers in 1967 hadn't completed high school, and the dropout rate among fifteen-to-nineteen-year-olds was even higher.

Even the expansion of service jobs downtown was ominous for the unskilled. A $250 million Market Street East mall comprising a seven-block complex of shops, hotels and offices was a local version of Rockefeller Center. Lowe noted some University of Pennsylvania critics, who charged that the downtown "renaissance" ignored slums elsewhere. Unskilled workers could get jobs in hotels, restaurants and shops, if not in offices, but after fifteen years of handsome downtown renewal, poverty remained pervasive in Philadelphia. Lowe noted the "blue areas" of the city: areas circled in blue on planning maps for clearance and later reconstruction. Within the eleven square miles involved were 377,000 families, 80 percent of them nonwhite, of whom:

- 13 percent were unemployed in 1960.
- 54 percent lived in families earning $4,000 and under in 1960.
- 58 percent resided in sound housing, with all the facilities.
- 84 percent were unskilled or semiskilled workers in 1960.

Then the bottom fell out in the 1970s:
- Between 1969 and 1981, while losing 14 percent of its people, Philadelphia lost 20 percent of its jobs. The excess job losses reflected a massive shift from a goods to a service economy.
- The loss of 42 percent of all factory jobs in the 1970s was the worst among big cities. Of 138,000 jobs lost in the city during the decade, more than 100,000 were in factories. Services were the only area of job growth, with 35,000 new positions, but since

commuters held 70 percent of all downtown jobs, they dominated this one, minor, advance.

• The crucial factory losses should also be seen in comparison with the Philadelphia suburbs:

While the suburbs maintained a 1.5 percent share of America's factory jobs, Philadelphia went from a 1.9 percent share in 1958 to only 0.8 percent by 1977.

While suburbs were investing 12 percent more per factory worker than the national average for 1958–77, Philadelphia invested 36 percent *less*.

As a result, the period saw suburban factories go from being 8.3 percent more productive than the national average to 17 percent more so. Meanwhile, the aging Philadelphia plants went from being 2 percent more productive than America's to 8 percent less so.

As factory jobs for residents were lost and service jobs for commuters grew, the gap between Philadelphia and national unemployment rates grew. The mismatch of local skills and available jobs meant Philadelphia went from having 5 percent of its residents on welfare in 1960 to 14.2 percent by 1970, then 19.8 percent in 1980, which was one of America's higher urban rates. Only Detroit among big cities had higher jobless rates for blacks and teen-agers.

All the above led the Tricentennial Commission to conclude in 1982 that

> as the city's economic base moves from manufacturing to services, it should become less sensitive to cyclical fluctuations in unemployment. But given its large pool of low-skilled people, it is very likely that over the coming decade the average level of unemployment in the city will remain higher than in the nation.

Among the proposals of this unusually blunt, pessimistic report were a useful goal for today, and three tenuous hopes for tomorrow. The tactical goal would be more vocational training in public schools, the strategic hopes focused on a falling birth rate, more service jobs, and a role for Philadelphia as a Snowbelt energy center, given its famous port and its propinquity to natural-gas reserves of the Baltimore Canyon and anthracite fields of eastern Pennsylvania.

For vocational schools, the commission urged things like computer terminals in high schools to store metro job data, and a "job hotline" with daily updates on openings. Sometimes the Tricentennial group went too far, claiming that "career matters arise in every classroom from kindergarten up." This is a leaf from *Hard Times,* an insult to the fun and fantasy of childhood itself. More career orientation for older students was in order, however, and the report proposed to expand Philadelphia's specialty high schools beyond Engineering, Fine Arts and Fashion to similar magnet centers for Food Services, Health, Mechanical Trades and Sheet Metal, and Office Work.

As to hope gleaned from birthrates, the Tricentennial group noted a falling birthrate before 1972, after which the rate stabilized at some 25,000 births a year. This lower rate would mean fewer labor force entrants, compared to the past. It should also add, however, at least 15,000 new teen-age entrants to the work force, year after year, through the 1990s. Since Philadelphia lost 18,000 jobs in 1980 and 1981—with 15,000 of those jobs in factories—the teen-age jobless rate should grow off the new applicants. Further, where one in three births were nonwhite in 1960, one in two were by 1980. Given the problems minorities face in terms of low skills and job placement, this is another ominous trend.

The Tricentennial report's optimism about service growth in Philadelphia is also questionable. Not only do commuters hold most downtown jobs, but service growth sectors from the 1970s provide limited work for local residents. Hospital and health services both expanded more than 35 percent in the 1970s, but most of these jobs go to professionals, and one notes that Philadelphia's closing of its only public hospital in 1979 contrasts with expansion of private health services. As for a 72 percent expansion of college and university services in the 1970s, this growth by such as the University of Pennsylvania and Temple University is qualified by the waning baby boom, which will depress this growth sector in the 1980s. Finally, there was a 60 percent expansion of legal services in the 1970s, but since when have Philadelphia lawyers lived in Philadelphia?

Only two of eight service sectors shrank in the 1970s: hotels and personal services—both useful for unskilled workers. Personal services for daily living, like barbershops, beauty parlors and TV repair shops, are a good index of economic and social stability. They shrank 38 percent in the 1970s. Hotels are classic entry points for minority workers, and they shrank 35 percent in the 1970s. For all the talk about urban renewal in the 1950s and 1960s or the publicity in the 1970s about major new malls, town-house areas, and restaurant rows, the city's retail-wholesale job loss of 19 percent outpaced the 13 percent census loss for the decade. All this reflected the growing division of Philadelphia into the wealthy residents of downtown town house and high-rise areas and the poor of the West and North Philadelphia slums.

Philadelphia's town-house revivals began with Society Hill in the 1950s. The area now houses 50,000 residents in a handsome enclave of eighteenth-century homes on narrow cobblestoned streets. This revival expanded the city's central core census by 13 percent in the 1960s. Displaced from Society Hill, the poor moved on to Queen Village, where the gentrification wave hit in the 1970s. Housing values soared by 50 percent in a few years, and the poor moved on again, this time to slums in North and West Philadelphia. The middle class began to leave the city. Higher housing costs, fewer jobs and more crime led to Philadelphia's first big population loss since the original census of 1790, the year of Benjamin Franklin's death.

Meanwhile, there were new and misleading symbols of renaissance downtown. Gourmet dining, once confined to Bookbinders and Le Bec-Fin, had rapidly expanded into several new restaurant rows. Then there was the opening of The Gallery mall in 1977, a huge complex of more than 120 shops from James Rouse of Quincy Market fame. Late in 1980, Philadelphia announced plans for a Gallery II mall. Community groups protested City Hall's use of scarce federal Community Development funds to help build the mall, which could be privately financed. The new mall's service jobs would mainly go to commuters. With 22,000 abandoned apartments citywide and the poor continually displaced by gentrification, the precious federal housing funds were clearly needed for minimal code shelter. In a 1981 *New York Times* interview, George Sternlieb observed

> Philadelphia is a classic illustration of the "twin city" concept within an old industrial city, where you've got a relatively small, sophisticated high-income, post-industrial nucleus that's emerging. It's very charming, and when tourists come they

discover this and think "Gee whiz, I didn't know this was here." But it's surrounded by what increasingly is a very disturbing wasteland.

The final example of Philadelphia's decline is its port. The Tricentennial report sees the city as a Snowbelt energy center for the 1980s. It thinks high gas prices may drive commuters back to city life, while anthracite coal in Pennsylvania may prove a valuable export. The Return of the Commuter fantasy was long ago exploded by Snowbelt city census losses after the OPEC price shocks. The coal-export scenario is plausible, however; Philadelphia is still America's largest freshwater port, though its most troubled one.

Philadelphia has the deep Delaware for ocean commerce and the shallower Schuylkill for inland trade. Even though the Erie Canal made New York the main port for inland trade after 1825, Philadelphia area ports remained our busiest international harbors until Hampton Roads, Virginia, dethroned them in 1980.

The main reason was coal. Rising coal exports since 1979 were a growth sector for eastern ports able to handle the job. The Virginia harbor was ready, and by 1982 was handling 67 percent of all coal exports, with six new coal piers under construction. Since Sunbelt cities like Hampton Roads put more money into building piers than welfare payments, this gives them an edge over liberal northern cities. This said, the Philadelphia area was still caught unprepared by coal. It was like New York City in the 1960s, when that port stuck to bulk-cargo handling on aging docks as Port Newark across the Hudson modernized for containers. Port Newark is now the biggest container port on earth, while New York's wharves are mainly the vacant settings for pier fires or cute charity balls.

In 1980 alone, Philadelphia lost its top rank as international port, closed four more piers, had two container ports at half capacity, and lost 20 percent in cargo volume, the worst loss in America that year. A local civic group lamented a "slow but persistent spiral downward into economic stagnation."

On January 26, 1982, Mayor William Green III announced "the beginning of a waterfront renaissance that will continue for the next decade." Three hundred years after Penn's search for the "deepest draught of water," only twenty of forty-four piers remained downtown. The "renaissance" would be a billion-dollar development of condos, malls and office towers. The first stage would be a 278-unit condo, opposite the old Betsy Ross House. There would be 6,000 apartments by 1997, plus 900,000 square feet of retail and office space along the old "finger piers."

Given its economic decline, the city's soaring crime rate was inevitable. During the 1970s, as New York City's crime rate went up 55 percent, Philadelphia's skyrocketed by 180 percent, even though Mayor Rizzo bragged, "I will make Attila the Hun look like a faggot." However, Philadelphia's crime soared from a low rate base in 1970, so even by 1980, its 6,024 crimes per 100,000 compared well with 10,130 in New York. One reason for the wide gap may be a higher ratio of cops to citizens in Philadelphia: 4.5 per 1,000 against 3.3 in New York. The only city with comparable coverage was Chicago: its crime rate also in the 6,000 range. The two cities with more cops had far better arrest rates as well in 1980: Chicago police arrested one person for every three burglaries, Philadelphia one for every five and New York one for every eleven.

As the economy soured, crime rose 47 percent between 1977 and 1980 in Philadelphia. Service cuts also played a role. Mayor Rizzo had expanded patronage jobs, and issued a 13 percent raise for city workers in his 1975 re-election campaign. All this led inevitably to a "fiscal emergency" early in his new term, which meant a sharp hike in property taxes and overnight layoffs. With more taxes for fewer services, the middle class had even less reason to stay in Philadelphia.

The police were cut 8 percent after 1977, with over 1,000 of them cut by new mayor William Green III, long a liberal congressman. Green inherited a $167 million deficit from the Rizzo years. He cleaned out some patronage nests, hiked property taxes again and imposed a two-year freeze on municipal wages. Green told the unions to choose between layoffs or the freeze. He called their bluff and avoided more service cuts. At the same time, however, cutting over 1,000 cops as crime soared made no sense, and the city's only public hospital, closed by Rizzo in 1979, remained closed under Green. As a result, both public safety and health remained compromised.*

---

* One more service crisis for Philadelphia came when Republican governor Richard Thornburgh pushed through a law which made some welfare clients between

Threatening more disaster was a possible tax revolt by downtown commuters. Philadelphia was one of the first cities to tax commuters back in 1941. This 4 percent salary tax is crucial, since it forms half the local revenues. Commuters have pressed the state legislature for tax relief that would mean an annual loss of $100 million for Philadelphia. If that happens, the city would have to hike property taxes for the third time since 1975, or impose drastic new service cuts. A Philadelphia tax official observed that "giving a nonresident a lower tax than the city resident working in the same office would encourage people to leave Philadelphia and further deplete the city's tax base."

The city's severe problems are reflected in surveys since 1975:

• Philadelphia was fifty-seventh among sixty-five cities in a Midwest Research Institute survey of 1975.

• Philadelphia was forty-eighth among fifty-two big cities in a Princeton study of 1980, for manufacturing value added.

• Philadelphia was forty-ninth among fifty-eight cities in a HUD survey of 1980 comparing unemployment rates, income growth and poverty shares.

And then, Philadelphia lost 15,000 more factory jobs.


## Baltimore

The opening of the Harborplace arcade in 1980 and the National Aquarium in 1981 were major media events. By the summer of 1981, Baltimore had become a symbol of the Snowbelt revival for the national press. *Time* elaborated this notion with a cover story set in Baltimore titled "Cities Are Fun!" Recalling Mencken's fond gibe about his hometown resembling "the ruins of a once-great medieval city," *Time*'s Michael Demarest observed how

> Baltimore has gone from being a kind of national joke to a major tourist attraction, a city that can rightfully take pride in

---

ages 18 and 45 eligible for only three months of benefits a year. This threw 68,000 people off the rolls in 1982, about half of them in Philadelphia. As local "street people" expanded rapidly, a nun running a shelter told *The New York Times* in late 1983, "it's terrible to have to turn them away, especially the young women who are homeless and pregnant. It's horrible to wonder what will happen to them this winter. . . . . I'm afraid there won't be enough of those steam vents for everybody."

itself. The spirit of cooperation is almost unparalleled in America. Baltimore gives hope to all of us who believe that our destiny lies in our cities.

That "spirit of cooperation" was left undefined, but the cover story that followed was rich with dithyrambs on things like the "continuous celebration" along the Baltimore quays, with plenty of

milling on the promenades, perching on the bulkheads, dangling feet in the drink, flirting on the benches, lounging in the outdoor cafés, ogling, jogging, strolling, munching, sipping, savoring the sounds and sweet airs. In their midst, jugglers hurl batons, mimes mime, clowns pratfall and dancers soar.

This amalgam of Peter Brueghel, Ringling Brothers and Tivoli is the famous Harborplace arcade of James Rouse, also the developer of Quincy Market in Boston and The Gallery mall in Philadelphia. *Time* recalled how Rouse in 1955 had coauthored a treatise titled *No Slums in Ten Years*. He was still an urban optimist when the summer riots of 1967 broke out and inspired him to stop building suburban malls and start helping cities. The famous Boston, Philadelphia and Baltimore malls followed, as did the Snowbelt's only major "new town" of Columbia, Maryland, where Rouse and his wife live among 60,000 residents and 32,000 jobs.

In 1981, Rouse retired as head of his firm to devote himself full time to an Enterprise Foundation aimed at helping the "very poor." One method involved letting slum dwellers take title to buildings, thus halting evictions. Rouse started in the Adams-Morgan slum of Washington, using two run-down buildings with 747 code violations between them. Within two years, he had rehabbed 213 apartments, 200 more were planned and 20 percent of the units would go to the poor in a fast-gentrifying area. As 1982 began, Rouse was trying to raise $15 million to spread the Enterprise Foundation model to Denver, Louisville, Oakland and Pittsburgh.

Rouse has the clout to make rehab a household word in America, but only Washington can institute federal Section 8 rent subsidies or Community Development funds. Ever since Richard Nixon froze public housing funds in 1973, federal housing aid has slowly declined. Proposed Reagan cuts would start wrecking remnants like Section 8 or Community Development.

While handsome, Rouse's new town of Columbia is hardly an urban advance. Rouse told *Time* that Columbia is "living proof that the races can live together. What is really important about Columbia is the marvelous advance in race relations." But integration in cities is easy. Often, all you need is money. In New York, for example, the homeowner community of Laurelton, in Queens, has long shown how black and white families can live in harmony. These are all professionals, living in a handsome *"rus in urbe"* area. Mount Vernon, in nearby Westchester County, has also integrated the affluent for many years. The idea of upscale Columbia as an "advance in race relations" recalls how the Kerner Commission blamed "racism" for more complex class problems of urban poverty: lousy housing, poor health, inferior schools, low welfare payments, no jobs, no hope—the things that keep poor people of all races in their place.

The second point about Columbia is that it isn't a city. It's a nicely laid-out and carefully run enclave for the upper-middle class. With 800,000 trees and shrubs, it has more flora today than it had as unimproved countryside. It is closely monitored by housing covenants that, in theory, can even tell people when to paint their homes and with what colors. TV antennas are banned, chain-link fences barred, and boat trailers must never befoul a driveway. Even religion is carefully homogenized. Columbia has two Interfaith Religious Centers, neutral shells for Jew, Catholic, and Protestant alike. This saves Columbia money for maintenance, and supposedly encourages "fellowship." But as *The Wall Street Journal* observes,

> The arrangement leaves some parishoners cold, says the Rev. Richard Tillman, a Catholic priest at Wilde Lake Interfaith Center. "The trappings of Roman Catholicism aren't here," he says. "No stained glass, no pews, no steeples . . . You can't say, 'This is my parish.' "

Columbia, the *Journal* says, is a "suburb without surprises."

It is also a suburb without the poor. While 20 percent of Columbia is black, a survey of 500 households in 1981 found average family income was $37,880. Half of the adults were doctors, lawyers, engineers, managers or other professionals, 20 percent more were educators, a census found in Laurelton and Mount Vernon. As America suffered 10.4 percent unemployment in late 1982, Columbia bent under 1 percent. The rabbi of the local Jewish congregation noted that "my kids think even the nice parts of Baltimore are slums. They've had it a little too good here." Indeed the harsh class divisions, tax losses and service cuts of a real city are airbrushed from this three-color ad for integration. Columbia is a manicured escape from shaggy Baltimore nearby, where blacks became the majority in the 1970s, joining other troubled black majority cities like Atlanta, Birmingham, Cleveland, Detroit, Newark, New Orleans and St. Louis.* These grim realities east of Columbia undermine Rouse's view that "the rebirth of the cities really started during the past decade or so. Now we're right on the edge of a big transformation of the central city. Reports of the death of the American city were premature."

With similar optimism, Rouse suggests that, since most cities began as markets, the bistros and boutiques of a Harborplace arcade can regenerate dead urban tissue elsewhere. But when Belgian historian Henri Pirenne wrote about how markets became the medieval cities, he was describing a simpler agrarian era, and a slower, organic process. To graft on an array of cute shops to a troubled factory town like Baltimore is another affair. Harborplace in 1981 meant 2,300 service jobs, fun for tourists and, by *Time*'s accounting, only $1.1 million in new city revenues —and not much more. It draws more annual visitors than Disney World of Florida, but in its first year alone, the Orlando park created 7,500 new jobs and set off a local housing and office boom, in a city with 3 percent unemployment and far fewer needs than Baltimore.

On the evening of September 18, 1981, *ABC News: Nightline* gave a more realistic portrait of Baltimore. After having shown "the most dazzing downtown in America," Ted Koppel noted

---

* Again, poverty, not blackness, is the problem. The eight black-majority cities tend to draw the lowest ranks in urban surveys. In the *Harper's* survey of 1975, all eight of the cities were among the fifteen worst of the fifty big cities, and commanded five of the six lowest ranks. In the 1980 HUD survey of needs in fifty-eight cities, seven of the eight black-majority cities were among the eleven neediest cities. Birmingham only escaped this distinction by being too small for the survey.

things like 60,000 substandard apartments in a city of 400,000 homes, some of them only a few blocks from Harborplace. A Housing Authority official commented that locals "keep hearing in magazines and TV that they're living in a Renaissance City, and they don't see it." And while Baltimore's ebullient mayor William Schaefer glowed about a "remarkable recovery for a city that lost its pride," he also conceded that Baltimore had the highest property taxes in Maryland, and that the Harborplace drama was "*secondary* to what we're doing in the neighborhoods. Eighty-five percent of our budget and efforts go to the communities. It's not as *glamorous* as Harborplace—look, I've asked the press—I've practically *begged* them—come out and look."

Beyond this candid *Nightline* picture, there was a lot of press about Baltimore's homesteading program, where people buy vacant homes for $1, and revive them with pegged wood floors, Tiffany glass and ferns. After Richard Nixon froze the federal housing funds in 1973, Baltimore borrowed the homestead idea from neighboring Delaware, and now others were studying the Baltimore program.* There was also publicity about Baltimore's shopsteading program, where vacant mom-and-pop stores went for $100 apiece. Recycling even reached the Bromo-Seltzer Tower, long the local version of the Washington Monument. The four-faced clock whose twelve numbers spell the product name remains, but the big bottle of Bromo is gone from the top, and down within are art galleries and ateliers. Seven years of home- and shopsteading produced only 500 rehabbed homes and forty stores, adding a paltry $1 million to the tax rolls. Despite federal grants, city efforts and national press, there were still 15,000 hulks awaiting revival by 1982. As Joel Garreau observes, many Baltimore homestead neighborhoods "are tough. The edge of the rehabbed areas, where they fade off into hard-core slums, is commonly referred to as the 'frontier.' "

As for Harborplace and nearby redevelopment downtown, the best thing about it was said almost twenty-five years ago by Jane Jacobs when she accurately predicted that "Baltimore, after

---

* The *Los Angeles Times* recalled how, in a 1980 Baltimore television debate with John B. Anderson, future-President Reagan proposed a homestead program, "apparently unaware that one existed and that two blocks behind him stood a model rehabilitated neighborhood." This is Stirling Street, a heavily photographed cul-de-sac of forty-two brick homes from the 1830s with cobblestoned streets.

playing around for years with this plan and that for an abstracted and isolated civic-cultural center, has decided instead to build downtown, where these facilities can count most both as needed primary uses and as landmarks." The renewal decision came just in time. Companies were moving to suburbia. Even City Hall thought about leaving a downtown where the newest hotels and office buildings were thirty years old. This was such an aging city that, even in 1976, Neal Peirce and Michael Barone could truthfully note "the unspectacularity of Baltimore."

The plans for downtown spectaculars were in two stages. The first stage began in 1958, with a Mies van der Rohe building as anchor to a thirty-three-acre Charles Center complex of office towers and hotels. A planner recalls how "the first building in Charles Center wasn't even topped out yet, and [Mayor Theodore] McKeldin says, 'Charles Center is a great success. I propose we go to the Inner Harbor.' "

This second stage on the waterfront covers 207 acres, only two of which make up the famed Harborplace arcade. After twenty-five years, the Charles Center-Inner Harbor complex on 240 acres has fifty-one buildings and 18 million annual tourists in a very revived downtown. Jane Jacobs' call for multiuse downtowns works well here. In 1961, she had noted how the closing of the New York City aquarium had led to a dead downtown after 5 P.M. A decade later, a handsome new New England Aquarium in Boston was a keystone in the Government Center revival along the Hub waterfront. And in 1981, a new National Aquarium, also by architect Peter Chermayeff, crowned twenty-five years of redevelopment in downtown Baltimore. The national media suddenly discovered a "new" downtown, but a quarter century of patient evolution was involved. The miracle of Baltimore is hard to repeat in dying Snowbelt cities elsewhere.

Charles Center-Inner Harbor is also a minor part of Baltimore's drive to diversify. In sum, this is a dying Snowbelt factory town, still very susceptible to recessions. During two slumps between 1970 and 1974, for example, Baltimore lost 13 percent of all its jobs. Only St. Louis and Detroit lost more jobs in that time. Recessions in old factory towns are sudden flashes of lightning that reveal aging plants and dying city services. As a recession cuts factory orders and tax revenues, the plants defer modernization and the aging cities cut services even more. More citizens leave for the suburbs and more orders are lost to modern plants elsewhere. For example, GM's huge Borening Highway plant had been set for a $220 million overhaul to produce front-wheel-drive cars when the 1981 recession hit Baltimore. The factory, which had already laid off 3,700 workers since 1980, now furloughed the remaining 2,300 at Christmas. The modernization went on hold.

The leading example of this syndrome in Baltimore is steel, which employs 2 percent of all metro workers. Bethlehem's biggest mill in America is here at Sparrows Point, where Armco and Eastmet also have major plants. All of them failed to modernize until the late 1970s, so foreign firms and domestic aluminum plants picked up new steel or tin-plate orders. Once the world's largest steel mill, Bethlehem's Sparrows Point went from almost 30,000 workers in 1972 to only 17,500 by 1981. Then came the steel slump of 1982. Armco and Eastmet cut their payrolls in half in six months, but still lost money. Bethlehem's mill dropped from 17,500 to 13,000 workers by midyear.

All three were renovating. Eastmet had spent $50 million since 1975 on things like a new electric furnace, but, as Lydia Chavez reported in *The New York Times,* "as it was plugging in the furnace, electricity rates nearly doubled . . . The $1.3 million [monthly electric] bill is equal to the company's monthly loss." Armco's specialty was stainless-steel bars, but a four-year quota on these expired in 1980, as imports rose from 16 percent to 27 percent of our market. Bethlehem's Sparrows Point mill was caught halfway through its renovation by the 1981 recession. A new continuous-casting process will boost output by 10 percent and improve the quality of tin plates for the beverage container industry. In only five years, the aluminum industry has grabbed 85 percent of that market from Sparrows Point's aging mills. Bethlehem's overhaul will cost 2,500 more jobs. Even at full production, the mill will have gone from 30,000 to 15,000 workers in a dozen years. Local union president Edward Bartee reflects the rigid national union that rejected a three-year wage freeze in 1982: "Concessions do not create jobs. The company wants us to help finance the health plan that was one thing we got in a 115-day strike, and there is no way we are going to give it up."

Finally there is the port that has dominated Baltimore's economy for more than 200 years. Unlike Philadelphia and New York, Baltimore modernized in time for containerization. Peirce and Barone note how the port was "relatively free of graft and payoffs," which helped it land East Coast contracts for Volkswagen and Volvo. Its rank has slowly declined, from America's third busiest port in the 1940s to the sixth busiest in the 1970s and the eighth today. But it is still a major employer, with the Harborplace arcade a small segment in a huge waterfront. Just across the water from Harborplace, however, the 129-year-old Key Highway ship repair yard faced closing, after its orders fell 65 percent in nine years. By late 1982, nearly 80 percent of Baltimore's 6,100 shipyard workers were on layoff.*

As heavy industry shrinks in steel, autos and ship repair, Baltimore's director of economic development tells *The New York Times* that the city should capitalize on Johns Hopkins University, using it as a backup to biotechnology firms. This would pit Baltimore against San Antonio in a limited growth sector, in a minor offset to basic industry losses elsewhere. Since industry powers service growth, it's not surprising that the 1980 Princeton survey of fifty-two cities found Baltimore ranked forty-fifth for retail sales, forty-fifth for wholesale sales and forty-sixth for service receipts. The survey's authors, Professor Richard Nathan and James W. Fossett, had originally identified Baltimore and three other Snowbelt cities as "potential candidates for 'breaking out' of decline." But they found that even during the recession recovery between 1975–77, Baltimore population losses increased, while Social Security, unemployment and welfare payments grew substantially above total income during the decade. By 1981, 21 percent of Baltimore lived in poverty, and the city had the second highest unemployment among the major cities.

The slumping economy inevitably produced a rise in crime. The good news was that after 1977 Baltimore merely matched the national growth rate. Violent crime actually grew less rapidly, quite striking for a city prone to recessions, where one in five residents is poor. One reason may be that as other cities cut police sharply after 1977, Baltimore maintained a high ratio of 4.1 officers per 1,000 residents. However, Baltimore already had a high crime rate by 1977, double the national average. For the violent crimes of murder, rape, robbery and assault, Baltimore had 2,116 such crimes for every 586 in America in 1980.

---

* A closed Key Highway yard would leave a terrible, living legacy. Tests made by Dr. Irving J. Selikoff, chief of environmental medicine at Mount Sinai Hospital in New York, found that of 283 randomly selected workers, more than 86 percent of those Bethlehem employees had lung abnormalities associated with asbestos.

The high crime rate, three recessions and growing housing decay meant big census losses in the 1970s. During the colonial era, Baltimore, Boston, New York and Philadelphia were the only licensed ports of a mercantilist economy, and the first federal census found they had 67 percent of our city dwellers. A hundred and seventy years later, in 1960, Baltimore was still America's sixth biggest city. It took a minor census loss in the 1960s, but in the 1970s, 14 percent of its residents left, the exodus growing as the decade wore on. Baltimore was our ninth biggest city in 1980, dropping to eleventh rank about a month later.

Most of Baltimore's 123,000 emigrants after 1970 were white, and the city became our eighth big city with a black majority. Optimists might observe that 70,000 blacks in Baltimore suburbs grew to 126,000 during the 1970s. What occcurred, however, is what happened in the Washington, D.C., area, where 179,000 blacks in the suburbs in 1970 became 405,000 by 1980. As T. D. Allman observed in *Harper's,* a lot of slum misery was merely rearranged within large metro areas. The downtowns revived, but

> like the bombed-out European centers that were re-built following World War II [our cities] will be ringed by dingy working-class suburbs or, as one now frequently sees in Europe, *"bidonvilles,"* tin-can and clapboard shacks housing Europe's migrant workers, the counterparts of our own illegal aliens.

The Baltimore suburbs were partly resegregated in the 1970s as the central city went from 45 percent to 54 percent black. In 1969, city family income was only 74 percent of suburban income; by 1976, it was down to 63 percent.

As taxpayers fled, Baltimore grew more dependent on state and federal aid. The city, rated the sixth neediest of fifty-eight big cities by HUD in 1980, got 53 percent of its revenues in 1981 from state and federal sources: Annapolis sent Baltimore $503 million, Washington gave it $258 million apart from direct income transfers, mass transit and public housing funds. As Baltimore property values rose an anemic .5 percent a year, the city had to impose the highest tax rate in Maryland.

Luckily, the state of Maryland believes in cities. Two weeks after President Ford's "Drop Dead" sermon to New York City in 1975,* *U.S. News & World Report* noted that Baltimore had just finished fiscal 1975 with a $52 million surplus, the reason being simply that

> Maryland had relieved Baltimore of virtually all fiscal responsibility for mass transit, school construction, assessment of property for tax purposes, and the nonfederal share of welfare costs. The state is also paying a major portion of the city's health services and police protection costs . . .

This aid from Annapolis is virtually unmatched. The aid to Baltimore includes an active hand in the Charles Center-Inner Harbor redevelopment.

Nineteen eighty-one brought Reaganomics to Baltimore. A report to the Joint Economic Committee of Congress that summer noted that since the city "receives so much federal assistance, the proposed spending cuts will have a sharp impact . . . Baltimore anticipates losing an estimated $350 million in direct federal assistance."

The city rated sixth neediest by HUD in 1980 faced these federal cuts for 1981: 3,000 CETA trainees and 7,000 youth jobs gone, $34.4 million cut in health services and $24 million in social services, 12,000 kids removed from the school-lunch rolls, 34,500 families with welfare, food stamp and other federal income supports cut or reduced for a loss of possibly $60 million more. Baltimore estimated that cuts in federal economic development aid could cost another $60 million in private investment leveraged by the Washington grants.

This shock cut and the new recession were double blows for a dependent and cyclical city. Civic leaders went out beating voluntarism drums. Using the "Minnesota model," one group got two dozen firms to tithe 5 percent of pretax income. A "Blue Chip-In" campaign raised $500,000 more from local firms. That left only $349,500,000 to go in making up the Reagan cut.

## St. Louis

When the Pruitt-Igoe housing project opened with 2,600 apartments on forty acres in 1954, it was one of the largest projects on

---

* Actually, President Ford said, "I do not think it is a healthy thing for the Federal Government to bail out a city, and I mean any city, that has handled its fiscal affairs as irresponsibly over a long period of time as New York City has." The *Daily News* translated this into the famous headline: "Ford to City: Drop Dead."

earth, and St. Louis was our eighth biggest city. The project's designer, Minoru Yamasaki, went on to build the World Trade Center towers in New York. St. Louis lost 17 percent of its people in the 1960s, and the big project began to empty out. In 1973, Pruitt-Igoe was cleared, closed and then leveled by dynamite implosion in our eighteenth biggest city.

The project's collapse reflected a violent and shrinking city, deep in the downward spiral, with no state or federal life rings thrown its way. A city of 857,000 in 1950 had been nearly cut in half to one of 448,000 by 1980—the worst big-city loss in America. The forty-acre base of Pruitt-Igoe was now just the biggest of 5,000 weedy lots in the Carthage of the Middle West. In 1981, a *Washington Post* reporter visited the site to find "fire hydrants, spaced with geometric precision among the prairie grasses, and in one corner a barbecue pit. Skyscrapers, church spires and the landmark 630-foot [Gateway] arch encircle it like distant mountains."

The decline began in our Centennial year, when St. Louis fatefully seceded from its encircling county. Back in 1876, this rich river city of 335,000 didn't need the 40,000 rural residents of the county. So St. Louis voted to secede, becoming a half-moon-shaped enclave of sixty-one square miles. A century later, however, the cast-off county reversed the story. Between 1970 and 1978, as St. Louis lost 82,000 jobs, encircling St. Louis County gained 148,000 jobs.

In 1876, St. Louis had been the gateway to the West and the third biggest city in America. By 1904, St. Louis was so powerful that it did what no city on earth seems likely to do again: in one year, it was host to both the Olympic Games and the World's Fair. The latter was the Louisiana Purchase Exposition, which in seven months drew 20 million visitors from a nation of 82 million.

Back then St. Louis was also the biggest fur-trading center on earth and one of our biggest factory towns. It produced nearly 25 percent of our tobacco, and led the nation in everything from woodenware to vehicles. Thanks to the marriage of Adolphus Busch and brewer's daughter Lilly Anheuser, it also had the world's biggest brewery in 1904. Beer and shoes were the two big employers by World War II, with footwear employing 50,000. After the war, shoes shrank to 6,700 workers by 1970 and beer to only 8,000, as sectors like chemicals and transportation took off.

Even today, St. Louis is our sixth biggest headquarters city, with eleven *Fortune* 500 firms, ranging from Monsanto to Ralston Purina, from McDonnell Douglas to Emerson Electric.

The 1940s industry had meant some of the worst pollution in America. John Gunther claimed that St. Louis was a city where "you had to change your shirt three times a day, and where, literally, it was often impossible to see across the street." A fight led by local professor Raymond Tucker and the *Post-Dispatch* cleaned up the air quickly, and Tucker was later elected to three terms as mayor. The Tucker era left many civic improvements, but many citizens left as well. The *Fortune* 500 front offices were downtown window dressing for industrial flight elsewhere. As headquarters jobs stayed downtown for commuters, factory jobs for unskilled residents were going to St. Louis County. Between 1957 and 1973 county jobs grew more than 400 percent as city jobs declined by 20 percent.* The downward spiral was obvious even by the early 1950s, when a group of twenty-eight major corporation chiefs organized as a Civic Progress group to save the city.

A mix of downtown revival and neighborhood decay ensued. The media got their revival symbol from Eero Saarinen's 630-foot Gateway Arch, August Busch built a new ball park, and his team won the 1967 World Series. Two high-rise apartments were the first built downtown in decades. Even the notorious Mill Creek Valley slums were razed. This area of high disease and crime rates had featured squalid hovels with dirt floors, cold water and more than 5,000 outhouses. But once this filth was bulldozed, Neal Peirce recalled, a "generation of weeds" had followed in a "monument to Negro removal and mediocre planning." A federal study of 1971 rated 29 percent of St. Louis' remnant housing as "poor" with another 40 percent as "fair." Peirce observed that these slums were "of the grimmest kind: countless deserted and boarded-up buildings (the highest percentage of any American city) . . . The most frightening site of all, however, is less than 20 years old . . ."

This last was Pruitt-Igoe, where thirty-three high-rise towers

---

* As the city's black share went from 25 percent to 41 percent in this period, the encircling county was overwhelmingly white. Neal Peirce notes how, in one decade, 84,000 county homes received federal mortgage aid—just 1 percent of them bought by blacks. By 1973, only 2,500 of 33,000 McDonnell Douglas employees were black, the unavailable county housing a factor in their low share of jobs.

had replaced fifty-five acres of shotgun shacks. At first, the huge project was integrated, with only 10 percent of its tenants on welfare. But the city built no housing to replace the razed slums of Mill Creek Valley, and more poor blacks were arriving from the South. With less low-income housing and more demand for it in St. Louis, Pruitt-Igoe was soon all black, with a large welfare share. Designed for 10,000 but crammed with up to 20,000, it was also cheaply built and stingily maintained. St. Louis built no low-income housing after the 1950s, and when the Housing Authority ran out of operating funds in 1972, it actually voted to close all public housing. This was too much even for a Nixon Administration that elsewhere froze public housing funds. A federal subsidy was rushed to St. Louis, preventing the eviction of 25,000 tenants citywide.

Meanwhile, Pruitt-Igoe was emptying out. In the 1960s, the *Globe-Democrat* had described "a terrified city within a worried city, a matriarchal society of too many unwed or deserted mothers and uncontrollable children . . ." By 1971, a local Catholic priest was telling Peirce that "I can't really improve this place. My job is to help people to get out."

Back then, Peirce had written of "the gnawing fear that St. Louis might already have reached the point of no return," like Newark and Detroit. Indeed the Urban League had recently issued a survey suggesting that St. Louis might be the worst among the big cities studied. Even St. Louis' grasp on office jobs began slipping in the 1960s, as the encircling county's seat of Clayton outbuilt the dying enclave city during several years, calling itself "the new executive city" and "the second downtown." In 1971, General Dynamics said it would move its headquarters from New York City to St. Louis, since "St. Louis is well located, offers excellent facilities at reasonable cost and provides major living advantages for our people." But the company meant St. Louis County, not the shrinking central city, with a new front office in Clayton.

By 1971, even the gleaming Gateway Arch was beginning to pale. Peirce gamely tried to see how even rubble fields and tenements were "enhanced or in some measure redeemed by its lordly neighbor." Then he gave up, and noted architect Stuart Knoop's pithy insight about "an enormous *tour de force* leading to and from nothing."

In 1979, however, *U.S. News & World Report* ran a feature

titled "St. Louis: Dying City Bounces Back." The article claimed "progress was visible," and Mayor James J. Conway suggested that "professional, upwardly mobile people are returning. Hardly a day goes by without someone seeing me in the street and saying, 'Hey, Mr. Mayor, I've moved back to the city.' " The magazine stretched the thin case for revival with talk about proud ethnic neighborhoods, fancy condo rehabs and cultural events. It conceded, however, that "vexing problems remain." St. Louis County had circled the central city with ninety-one small cities, luring people and jobs away so that "downtown St. Louis often is dead. Observed a visitor who could see few signs of life from his hotel room, 'I can see from the phone book that many people live here. Where are they?' "

That question had already been asked in 1970, when census data showed a 35 percent population loss since 1950. St. Louis gambled on urban renewal and declared its entire downtown "blighted" in 1971. A state law gave private developers the right of eminent domain in such designated areas, and suddenly all of downtown was up for grabs. That led to Carthage. Robert Kuttner recalled in *The Revolt of the Haves* how the 1970s saw

> an orgy of bulldozing unparalleled in any other city. Entire sections of the city were razed, with little guarantee that anything would be built in their place. Today, no American city has a higher percentage of idle land, or a steeper decline in population.

The wholesale clearings included the demolition of sound buildings for a three-phase, $150 million project for Mercantile Trust. The Mercantile office tower went up, but phases two and three were shelved, leaving many weedy lots for sale. In another case cited by Kuttner, a May Company mall would have leveled what an F. W. Woolworth executive termed "the only remaining successful, diversified shopping area in St. Louis." The threatened Woolworth store there was the fifth busiest outlet in the national chain. One of its executives noted that many current area retailers "might not be able to obtain or afford the costly space in the mall. Most of the present businesses will be forced to relocate out of the city or cease operating altogether . . . The city has accelerated the decline of downtown."

Fallow land and tax abatements piled up. By 1981, there were the 5,000 weedy lots. By 1978, tax-abated or exempted value on St. Louis property totaled $2.8 billion, nearly equal to $3.2 billion in taxable values. All told, the city would lose $200 million to abatement over twenty-five years. These revenue losses on property were compounded by taxpayer exodus, as 47 percent of the city left after 1950. St. Louis was now a major federal ward. Before the Reagan shock cuts hit in 1981, federal aid was already 44 percent of the operating budget and 70 percent of the capital budget. The Reagan cuts fell heavily on a dependent city of the poor and the old:

- 16 percent of St. Louis was on welfare, against 5 percent nationally.
- 25 percent was over the age of sixty, against 15 percent nationally.
- 50 percent of all births were illegitimate, against 16 percent nationally.

Not surprisingly, St. Louis also had the highest big-city crime rate in America: 14,320 crimes per 100,000 citizens in 1980. Once again, this nearly tripled a national rate.

Nineteen eighty also saw GM phasing out a factory whose 10,000 jobs made it the second biggest employer in St. Louis. St. Louis had lost more than 300 factories with 58,000 jobs in the 1970s. It had started the decade with 15,000 business firms but had only 10,700 left by 1978, and was encircled by a county whose businesses grew from 12,000 in 1970 to 20,000 by 1978.*

In 1982, the Cardinals made the World Series again. Downtown was being renewed for $1 billion, and, as a housing consultant glowed to *The New York Times,* "the city is in the midst of

---

* A perverse consolation for St. Louis is the fact that East St. Louis, across the river in Illinois, is in even worse shape. Nearly half of its 55,000 residents are on welfare, from 25 percent to 30 percent are unemployed, and the "business district" consists of two blocks near City Hall. Washington funds more than half of East St. Louis' budget, so Reagan cuts were severe. Even before the cuts hit in 1982, more than 1,200 welfare clients were so poor that they couldn't afford heat that winter, one of the coldest winters in years. This was once the second biggest switching yard in America and the sixth biggest meat packer. But even by 1972, East St. Louis was so broke that when a railroad explosion destroyed 2,500 vacant homes, the mayor called it a "shot in the arm" since the demolition costs for the homes were spared.

a boom, just like the Cardinals. The Cardinals were lousy for years and now things have turned around, just like they have for the city.'' Just as Budweiser had beaten Schlitz, the Cardinals of August Busch beat the Brewers of Milwaukee. Meanwhile the *Times* noted the St. Louis census losses, and a Census Bureau projection that, if "the rate of exodus continued the city would be a ghost town by the year 2015." The newspaper also quoted a local industrialist, glowing about strong city "institutions." But rather than describing sound infrastructure, industry or services, this booster cited the Botanical Gardens, a dozen corporate head-quarters, a new opera company, the Symphony, the Art Museum and the university. Downtown revival and cultural amenities were once again dragged in to dress things up.

Meanwhile, the real St. Louis is where median family income in 1969 was 79 percent of suburban income before plummeting to only 57 percent by 1976. Only Newark was lower among America's twenty biggest metro areas. By 1975, the *Harper's* survey of the fifty biggest cities put Newark last and St. Louis next to last. St. Louis ranked fifty-first among fifty-two cities for urban conditions in the 1980 Princeton survey, and also fifty-first for service receipts, not surprising, given the bulldozed downtown.

The city was next to last in urban surveys, and had the highest crime rate in America for 1980. There was almost as much tax-abated or exempt property as there was taxable land. Forty-seven percent of its people had departed after 1950, a loss without equal in America. Left behind was a razed downtown, 5,000 vacant lots and a 630-foot steel arch spanning the ruins:

> . . . Two vast and trunkless legs of stone
> Stand in the desert. Near them, on the sand,
> Half sunk, a shattered visage lies, . . .
> And on the pedestal these words appear:
> "My name is Ozymandias, King of Kings:
> Look on my works, ye Mighty, and despair!''

## Detroit

The City of Champions in the 1930s, the Arsenal of Democracy during World War II, Renaissance City since 1977, but Motor City at all times.

The latter is the problem with the least diversified big city on earth, yoked to the auto slump after 1979. Almost 33 percent of Detroit's labor force is in auto-related work, with GM and Chrysler the two big employers. As a city of 1.8 million in 1950 shrank to one of 1.2 million by 1980, surviving auto plants and the unskilled minorities they employed dominated Motor City even more.

The 1975 slump saw 16 percent unemployed, second only to GM's company town of Flint at 20 percent. Then the Big Three auto firms had record years between 1976 and 1978, as people forgot about OPEC prices and foreign cars. When the second OPEC price shock nearly doubled fuel prices in 1979, however, the unprecedented four-year slump of the Big Three began. Since then there have been two recessions. There have been the high interest rates that, in Lee Iacocca's phrase, "put us up on blocks." There were the cheaper, fuel-efficient imports that went from 10 percent of our market in 1971 to almost 32 percent by late 1982.

Nineteen eighty saw Detroit make 30 percent fewer cars. Chrysler lost $1.7 billion and only survived through a $1.2 billion federal loan guarantee. Ford lost $1.5 billion—its first loss in thirty-five years. When it fell to an 18 percent market share, Ford announced it would close three plants, including a huge factory in Mahwah, New Jersey. Even GM barely made a profit. Imports had a 26 percent market share.

Nineteen eighty-one saw Ford lose $1 billion more. GM was so short of cash that it put its five-year, $40 billion retooling on hold. For every auto worker on layoff, there were two laid off by subcontractors in aluminum, glass, rubber or steel, perhaps 850,000 workers in all. Early in the recession, the auto town of Anderson, Indiana, had 17.5 percent unemployment. The phrase "sticker shock" entered the media lexicon, as did the buzz words "quality control." Imports now had a 28 percent market share.

Nineteen eighty-two began on a positive note, with a wage-concession pact between Ford and the UAW. Otherwise, the auto slump deepened. Sales were now at their lowest level in twenty-one years. GM cut the price of its 1983 models—the first such cut in its history. Sixty-eight years after Henry Ford's famous wage of $5 a day, his heirs needed $5 an *hour* in wage givebacks to stay open. In 1977, Henry Ford II had pledged to drive Japanese imports "back into the sea." In 1982, Ford tried to sell its Rouge Steel Company, the nation's eighth biggest, to Nippon Kokan, Japan's second largest steelmaker. Chrysler had a $266 million profit by late 1982, against a $408 million loss for the same time in 1981. But 133,811 Chrysler employees of 1979 were down to only 87,825 by the summer of 1982, and the firm had $2 billion in long-term debt and $1.5 billion in unfunded pension liabilities. Late in 1982, *U.S. News & World Report* noted how 450 auto plants had closed in seven years, with auto employment down 30 percent since 1978. Imports were now almost 33 percent of the market.

Beyond these recent problems and beyond even recovery from the slump since 1979, lies a minefield of strategic obstacles for the industry that drives Detroit. Cutbacks in reindustrialization, lack of faith by consumers in the quality and safety of American cars, the purchase and manufacture of auto parts abroad, reduced demand as the baby boom wanes, and increased use of robots are among the obstacles. Even in normal times, some think that many more of our auto workers may be out of the sector by 1990.

From now on, there will be few new openings in the auto plants. A familiar job path for unskilled Detroit youths will be virtually closed. Detroit usually has the worst unemployment rate for both youths and blacks, and now more disaster lies ahead for a city that lost 37 percent of its people after 1950, and half its white residents since 1970. Unless Washington revives programs for public works and job training on a large scale, more crime and taxpayer flight could empty Detroit at an even faster rate in the 1980s.

Adult workers on current layoffs will often not be rehired. They must be retrained or relocated to new jobs before they join Detroit youths in the ranks of the permanently unemployed. Workers buying 6,000 weekly copies of Texas Sunday papers in The Little Professor bookstore in Dearborn were not finding many jobs in Dallas, Houston or San Antonio.

Since 1950, Detroit has taken the third worst census loss among our major cities, as a city that was 23 percent black became one that is 64 percent black today. The tragic riot of 1967 was soon followed by the media image of "Murder City" in the early 1970s. A new black mayor in 1974 brought hope and some stability; although crime rates remained very high, murder dropped sharply after 1974. At the opening of the $337 million Renaissance Center along the waterfront in 1977, the press hailed a "Renaissance City," and three boom years for autos through 1978 seemed to confirm Detroit's new nickname. By 1981, unemployment was at 16 percent, the service crisis had erupted again, and Mayor Coleman Young estimated that 60 percent of Detroit was on some kind of public aid.

By the spring of 1981, too many service cuts and a $119 million deficit made new taxes essential. After several years of passive service cuts Mayor Young finally fought for and got new taxes. Things got worse in 1982, when even fewer auto jobs meant fewer local and state revenues. Recession compounded the impact of state tax caps passed by voters in better times. Huge fiscal shortages in 1982 forced Lansing to balance its budget with new tax hikes, and a phenomenal cut of $778 million from a $4.4 billion budget. The result was a threefold disaster for Detroit: state aid was cut drastically, the auto slump cut local city revenues, and the full force of the Reagan federal cuts hit Detroit in 1982.

Autos dominate our sixth biggest city. One symbol is the short list of *Fortune* 500 firms: Chrysler, GM, Burroughs, Fruehauf, McLouth Steel. These five front offices compare poorly with a dozen in far smaller Pittsburgh or St. Louis. As for the two major nonauto firms, McLouth Steel entered Chapter XI bankruptcy proceedings in 1981, and was kept alive in 1982 by benefit and wage concessions from its workers. Burroughs closed a Tierman Avenue factory with 660 workers in 1981, relocating it to the suburbs where many Detroit plants have lately decamped. These shrinking nonauto giants made Detroit all the more Motor City, with 33 percent of all workers in auto-related work.

As 1982 began, a tactical crisis for autos concerned wages. UAW workers got $20 an hour against $12 in Japan, and this added some $1,500 in costs to each car. Having lost $2 billion over the last two years, Ford asked the UAW to reopen the company contract. Hopefully, a renegotiation could match the $1 billion in wage concessions made by auto workers to save Chrysler in 1980. At first, the UAW resisted givebacks to Ford, even though auto workers earned 70 percent more than the average American worker. Shortsighted stances by the UAW in 1981 had already threatened plant closings that year.* On February 3, 1982, however, the UAW and Ford agreed on a package cutting $1 billion in wage and labor costs by 1985. Both sides also agreed on further talks about issues like profit sharing, control over plant closings, outsourcing of auto parts abroad and a version of Germany's "codetermination," where labor has some management roles. All this only resolved the tactical wage crisis at Ford. Ahead lay the five strategic obstacles to stability in the auto industry and, thus, Motor City itself:

• *Reindustrialization* was projected in 1979 as a five-year overhaul for the auto companies that could cost $80 billion. By early 1981, only GM was still proceeding on its own $40 billion schedule. That was cut back in 1982, as the industry's only profitable firm made just $333 million in the previous year. Back in 1978, when sales were good, the auto firms had $13 billion in working capital to gear up for the five-year retooling program. By the fall of 1981, industry losses of $5.5 billion in two years saw companies with only $300 million left in working capital.

• *Reduced demand* would be due to demographic trends and OPEC prices. The end of the baby boom meant the growth rate of the eighteen-to-twenty-four-year age group was half the rate between 1970 and 1975. First-time drivers were fewer in 1980, and by 1985, the age cohort would also decline in numbers. Meanwhile, higher fuel prices cut driving from 10,184 miles per car in 1972 to 9,400 by 1980. With fewer new drivers and less driving, the research firm of Sage Associates found the American market "just about saturated" in 1982. Sage projected that an annual market growth of 3 percent in the 1970s would be under 2 percent in the 1980s and about 1.3 percent in the 1990s. Recalling the booming 1970s, Lee Iacocca thinks "we will look back on that era as a

---

* One example concerned an aging Ford castings factory in Sheffield, Alabama. Ford claimed that the plant was losing $3 million a month, and proposed closing it, unless workers took a 50 percent wage cut and either bought the plant or entered a profit-sharing plan. The UAW refused the proposals, so 960 workers could lose their jobs. In contrast, workers at a GM bearings plant in Clark, New Jersey, had taken a 25 percent wage cut and bought their $53 million factory. The work force was cut in half, but 1,070 jobs were saved and GM placed orders of $100 million a year through 1984. The president of the UAW local observed, "I'd rather be an employed auto worker at $11 an hour than an unemployed auto worker at $13 an hour."

rather baroque period in our lives." Few in Detroit see a return to the mid-1970s, when America built 50 percent more cars than Japan. Many expect to see more of what happened in 1981, when Japan built 19 percent more cars than America.

• *Quality control* meant overcoming a legacy of consumer doubt about unsafe, gas-guzzling cars. The Big Three reaped their own harvest here: they had laughed at George Romney and the Rambler in 1954, and attacked Ralph Nader on auto safety in the 1960s. By 1982, however, Detroit was so mileage-conscious that —although Chrysler big-car sales were up 21 percent—Lee Iacocca proposed an excise tax of 25 cents per gallon of gas to "restore the trend toward fuel-efficient cars, and away from the gas guzzlers." But 1982 also found foreign cars sweeping the top ten spots in federal EPA fuel-efficiency tests. It was the fourth time in five years that imports had swept the field.

On safety, the Big Three still fight against installing air bags, although GM studies show the cost is less than prohibitive. Air bags in GM cars helped save 263 of 267 lives endangered in accidents, according to the Insurance Institute for Highway Safety, an insurance-industry research group. That Institute also released a 1981 study which claimed that American small cars were safer than Japan's (which also do not have air bags). Analyzing injury claims and fatal crashes between 1978 and 1980, the study found that twelve of the seventeen small cars with the worst safety records were Japanese, while similar American cars had the best records. Among comparable subcompacts, one had a 34 percent better chance of being killed in a Japanese car.

Also damaging in the next few years will be foreign advances in diesel cars. The Volkswagen Rabbit at fifty miles per gallon and the Nissan Sentra with forty-eight mpg led the 1982 EPA tests. Volkswagen is now testing a diesel car that gets ninety miles a gallon in EPA tests, and should be ready by 1985. The Battelle Memorial Institute in Columbus has shown that a $6,000 car with a median life of 100,000 miles could get even 100 miles a gallon on a diesel engine. But the Big Three failed to invest in a prototype and testing. Gas guzzlers outstayed their welcome for more than two decades after George Romney introduced the Rambler. The new generation of forty-miles-a-gallon cars from Detroit may soon be eating the diesel dust from Wolfsburg, West Germany.

• *Outsourcing* is becoming an ever greater menace to American auto workers. Every year the Big Three buy more auto parts abroad. Ford opened a $365 million factory in Mexico for a four-cylinder engine in 1980, and spent 40 percent of its capital budget outside America in 1982. GM builds its three-cylinder engine abroad, and its new subcompact in Spain. A federal report adds these annual purchases abroad: 1.7 million transaxles, 1.3 million aluminum cylinder heads, 500,000 rear disk brakes. Many auto-supply factories here lose jobs this way. Since more efficient plants, government subsidies and cheap labor abroad cut prices up to 30 percent, the Big Three increase such outsourcings each year. The "domestic content" requirement bill in Congress could stem this tide. This could help set off a trade war, and many think it would inspire Volkswagen, Honda and Nissan to close their new American factories.

• *Robotization* and reorganized factories will mean further job losses. More robots and more centralized production mean a Japanese subcompact is assembled in fourteen hours there against twenty-nine here. It takes 650,000 UAW members to produce 9 million cars, but only 430,000 Japanese workers to produce 11 million cars. Robots work three shifts a day without coffee breaks, cost half a worker's wages, and improve quality in precision work. Toyota and Datsun already use these "steel collar" workers to cast, forge, paint and weld. Only 1,800 robots work in U.S. auto plants today, but GM alone projects using 14,000 of them by 1990—meaning 40,000 less jobs for workers.*

Coleman Young took office during the long recession of 1974–75, which at one point meant 22 percent unemployment in Detroit, nearly *triple* the national rate. The severe slump was inevitably accompanied by a record murder rate in 1974. While Young helped stabilize the city and homicides dropped sharply in 1975, the city still had 18 percent unemployment, a $40 million budget

* One factory reform copied from Japan should benefit Midwest auto cities like Detroit, while damaging ones on the east and west coasts. The technique is "same-day parts delivery," whereby Japanese auto plants and suppliers are located near each other. Detroit concentrates more of its plants in the Midwest today. Of nine major assembly plants closed since 1979, four were in California and one in New Jersey, since both coasts are vulnerable. Since the Lake Superior region has 33 percent of the world's iron ore, even more centralization of auto plants seems likely in the Midwest.

deficit and more than 20,000 white-collar layoffs at Chrysler alone. One resident told *U.S. News & World Report* that "Winston Churchill would have trouble as mayor of Detroit." But rather than freeze municipal wages and hike taxes to balance the budget, Mayor Young took the easy path of most mayors in the 1970s, which in this case meant laying off almost 1,000 police for 1975 and 1976.

Early in August, Detroit narrowly avoided a riot after a white saloon owner killed a black youth who may have been tampering with his car. Crowds grew, and in one tragic incident, a white worker was dragged from his car and beaten to death by black kids. The man had survived a Nazi concentration camp. Coleman Young spent an evening cooling things off in a city with nearly 1,000 fewer cops on the streets.

The police cuts were felt again in 1976. While unemployment was "only" 12 percent and murders "less" than previous years, the problems of Detroit's jobless teen-agers were particularly severe. One estimate saw 75 percent of them jobless in the Bicentennial summer. Many roamed about in vicious packs, some boarding buses to calmly or violently rob customers. Others lurked near the Edsel Ford or Lodge freeways, *Time* noting how the packs fell "on stalled cars like army ants to rob, beat and rape terrorized motorists." The final blow came when 100 kids went wild at a Cobo Hall rock concert in August where they robbed, assaulted and raped. In his inaugural speech of 1974, Coleman Young had issued a warning to "all those pushers, all rip-off artists, to all muggers. I don't give a damn if they are black or white, or if they wear Superfly suits or blue uniforms with silver badges—hit Eight Mile road." The day after the Cobo Hall outrage, Young rushed home from a vacation, imposed a successful curfew, and rehired 450 police officers.

The Big Three auto companies had record sales years in 1976 and 1977 and Motor City's economy boomed. By the end of his first term, Young had produced apparent stability. The murder rate of 54 per 100,000 in 1974 was down to 36 by 1977. Census losses between 1975 and 1977 were half the record level of the previous five years. Best of all, Detroit's jobless rate was actually better than the national rate in 1977.

At center stage in 1977 was a giant symbol of urban revival: the $337 million Renaissance Center on the banks of the Detroit River. First proposed by Henry Ford II in 1971, and backed by his and fifty other companies, this had been the biggest private urban development in history. It consisted of four thirty-nine-story office towers grouped around a seventy-three-story hotel. Instantly, John Portman's structures were a new media logo for a Renaissance City. The outlandish scale and imposing site were soon controversial. Neal R. Peirce and John Keefe in *The Great Lakes States of America* recall how

> Ren Center was called a fortress by some critics—appropriately enough, given the massive blank walls it exhibited at street level, as if it keeps the surly mobs of the city at bay, far from visiting conventioneers in their encapsulated environment. (Someone sarcastically suggested that Detroit was founded as a fort . . . and might now die as one.)

Otherwise, Ren Cen seemed to be a development catalyst. Sixteen more buildings or renovations were planned in its wake, among them the Joe Louis Arena, which would hold the 1980 Republican Convention. More than 200 groups planned to join the GOP in holding Detroit conventions. The Ford and Rockefeller families announced a joint plan for two more office towers near the complex. Mayor Young claimed $603 million spent on fifty-three buildings was directly tied to Ren Cen alone. In 1977, Henry Ford II threw a $1,000-a-plate fund raiser for Young's re-election. The mayor toasted his host: "Hank the Deuce is my favorite industrialist."

Tom Wolfe commented that Portman's bulbous hotels succeeded "more than any other sort of architecture, in establishing the look of downtown, of urban glamour, in the 1970's and 1980's."

*The Wall Street Journal* noted that while Ren Cen lent "a sense of optimism" to Detroit, the downtown streets nearby, "considered dangerous, are mostly deserted at night. And less than a mile's drive from the hotel, dilapidated storefronts, weed-ridden lots and streets strewn with debris still prevail." By then, Ren Cen was $100 million in deficit, and losing retailers like Cartier and Courreges as suburban shoppers avoided downtown. The two new office towers from the Ford-Rockefeller pact opened, but had only 11 percent occupancy in late 1981. Wayne State anthropologist Leonard Moss observed that some now saw the Renaissance Center "as the dying gasp of the city, like the ancient Romans building their greatest monuments while their empire declined." Others clung to Ren Cen as a symbol of industrial power, like the Eiffel Tower had been for France at its Centennial Exposition of 1889. The great structure on the Seine had been a muscular, articulated iron and steel frame, announcing a new and vigorous era. But the sleek cylinders on the Detroit River were a muscle-bound bore, passive Stonehenge dolmens from a greater, mainly bygone, age.

As the stores began closing downtown, the Princeton survey of fifty-two American cities in 1980 found Detroit in last place for both retail sales and sales receipts. In 1976, Hudson's department store was already closing off floors within its 2.8-million-square-foot emporium. As the flagship store was slowly scuttled downtown, nine of its branches boomed in the suburbs. President Joseph L. Hudson, Jr., recalled how "a member of the City Council jumped on me not long ago for not trying to save our downtown store. A few days later, I ran into him at one of our beautiful new suburban stores, where he now does his shopping. He, too, had abandoned downtown." In 1980, Hudson's joined other department stores to loosely pledge new shops on Cadillac Square. Hudson also suggested demolishing its big store. A local journalist told Peirce and Keefe that

> Hudson's has slowly turned the tourniquet on that downtown store until it's now a pale shadow of its former self—so pale that everyone now agrees it's a reasonable thing for them to prepare to shut it down. You could see it coming five years ago. And Hudson's has continued to build suburban malls all around the city—a dozen in all now. Hudson's closed the big downtown store in 1983, and also dropped its sponsorship of the Thanksgiving Day Parade. The parade was saved, though, only after schoolchildren, private agencies and government workers coalesced to raise enough money for what Hollywood might title, "Miracle on Cadillac Square."

Neighborhoods were also pale shadows. No other big American city has as many private homes, but as commuters landed new office jobs in the Ren Cen enclave, local workers with mortgage money were so scarce that "the city of homes" issued only ten single-family home permits in 1979. Even before this, *U.S. News & World Report* had returned a decade after the 1967 riot to find that "Twelfth Street still appears to be little more than a mile-long scar cutting across the center of Detroit . . . Since the riot, about 12,000 people have left the strip . . ."

The street was later renamed Rosa Parks Boulevard, honoring the brave seamstress who launched the civil rights movement in 1955, and who now lives in Detroit, where she is active in civic affairs. In 1981, *The New York Times* reported that, after a decade of planning, a new supermarket and 350 row houses were under way in the old riot area. But the Virginia Park area had gone from 60,000 residents before the 1967 riot to only 25,000 by the fall of 1981.

As downtown declined, people left and unemployment returned to high levels, Detroit's crime rate soared again, yet Coleman Young cut 27 percent of his police in three years. No big city save Newark cut more police. Of the five other cities with more than a million people, Houston added 8 percent to its meager forces, while Chicago, Los Angeles, New York, and Philadelphia all cut between 7 percent and 10 percent of their forces. The Detroit cuts nearly tripled those of its peers, although Motor City had the highest crime rate of the six biggest cities. Young cut 700 of his 5,600 police in 1978, and another 700 cops in 1980, although murder and robbery rose more than 18 percent in the two years.

By early 1981, even Young was concerned about the growing service crisis. After three years of cuts, he finally looked for new revenues. He started off oddly, the *Washington Post* finding Young looking into casino gambling, saying,

> Let's be straight about this. There's already parimutuel gambling in this state. It's not like we're virgins . . . If the Atlantic City experience is any guide, legalizing gambling would raise property values and bring in $100 million more in taxes per year.

But property values are often depressed by casinos, and organized crime's link to casinos is well known. Also familiar is the fact that the second and third highest metro crime rates in 1980 were in Las Vegas and Atlantic City. Young finally dropped casinos for a sensible, long overdue package of higher taxes and wage freezes. He told the municipal unions to take the wage freeze or face layoffs. Having called their bluff, he then hiked taxes.

In promoting a referendum on the new income taxes in 1981, Young tarnished a good cause with racist appeals. He warned a black city that without the new revenues a white legislature in Lansing would run Detroit. Worse, he branded opponents of the new tax as "racists." *The Wall Street Journal* detailed how Young degraded his office and insulted the intelligence of his fellow blacks. At a white church, Young had said that "a tradition in this city is for every people of every ethnic background, of every color to come together in a time of crisis. We'll need that tradition to win on June 23rd." Later, however, he went before a group of black Democrats and claimed that whites opposing the tax "pretend that Detroit's problem is that black folks don't know how to manage government. They ain't after me, they're after us." * Young won his new taxes for 1981, racist appeals notwithstanding. These new revenues could only hold the line. Services remained poor in Detroit: the 27 percent cut in police since 1977 remained, and so did the crime wave. By the spring of 1981, *Time* turned from its American Renewal line to run a downbeat sidebar on Coleman Young. *Time* lamented that "the city's renaissance is on the verge of fading."

A year later, Detroit was in its third year of the auto slump. On June 5, it held its first Grand Prix, with world-class racers whipping around a track improvised from local freeways near the Ren Cen towers. Reporting for *CBS Evening News,* Roger O'Neill noted that "Detroit gambled that it would improve its image as a world-class city . . . But"—and here the camera zoomed back from a tight shot of Ren Cen to a wide-angle shot of a slum street with the huge towers deep in the background—"the city is broke . . ." †

---

* Similar black racism from Young occurred in a Democratic Party fight. Former state party chairman Morley Winograd attacked Young for deserting the party's gubernatorial candidate to back GOP incumbent William Milliken in 1978. Young didn't deny the charge, but counterattacked by claiming a "black-Jewish split here . . . [with] differences of philosophy of some Jews and some blacks." A UAW official bluntly noted this racist diversion as a "hustle," adding that Young and friends liked to "play on the guilt we're supposed to have."

† A year later, the auto industry had revived, but more automation meant high unemployment and crime in Detroit. The first half of 1983 saw murder up 16 percent and rape up 34 percent, and police down from 5,630 officers in 1978 to 4,051. The national press played up an effective, often middle-class "Neighborhood Watch" program here. But citywide crime was so alarming that Coleman Young imposed a summer curfew on youths for the first time since 1976.

A footnote on Detroit's fiscal and service crisis involves a state tax revolt. In the 1978 election, a state ballot proposal to cap state spending was passed. Normally, this Proposition E would have failed in a state that was thirty-ninth for the growth of state spending in the 1970s. But Proposition 13 fever was rampant in 1978, so Michigan voters passed Proposition E in the fall. New state outlays were now indexed to the annual growth of personal income, and this limit plus the 1980 recession led to huge state revenue losses. Suddenly Michigan had to cut the 1981 budget by a staggering 20 percent. Neal R. Peirce and John Keefe had hailed Governor William Milliken for his "unflagging commitment to the salvaging of Detroit" in the 1970s. Milliken had led an effort that tripled state revenue-sharing funds for cities, while also assuming more local school costs in Lansing. But the tax cap of 1978 and the auto slump since 1979 had been too much. Michigan wound up cutting welfare grants twice in two years. It had been among the top ten states for aid to colleges but now it was in the bottom ten. This was just like California, which had gone from being third for college spending to forty-fifth in the wake of the Proposition 13 tax cuts.

Among Michigan's many state cuts by 1981 had been aid to public schools. A cut of $233 million by Lansing in 1980 forced localities to quickly hike their property taxes. The cities and counties were already so burdened by school costs that they had borrowed $400 million in 1978–79 to keep the schools open. As state aid was cut after 1980, local school debts soared to $800 million by 1981, much of it borrowed at 12 percent interest. All this led to a sudden rash of public-school crises in the fall of 1981. Half a dozen districts threatened to be the first to close schools since the Depression. One Detroit suburb rejected tax hikes for schools four times in eleven months. Pontiac citizens voted down school tax hikes eight times in 1981.*

---

* The national press focused on the small city of Alpena, where 6,800 kids were locked out of schools prior to a November tax vote. The students held mass marches down Main Street, protesting their role as tax-revolt pawns. Part of the problem was the rural revival that saw Michigan metro areas grow only 1 percent as rural areas exploded by 20 percent in the 1970s. Alpena tax hikes to cover local aid for schools would have been only $87 more annually for a $20,000 home. But rural voters now dominated the Alpena school district, so the minor hikes were rejected four times. The fifth vote in November finally passed, and the schools were reopened.

The state fiscal crisis escalated in 1982. The auto industry was at 50 percent of its 1978 production levels, which meant $400 million less in state revenues. Governor Milliken faced two options: more federal aid or higher taxes. Since Ronald Reagan was cutting federal aid to states in the recession, Milliken was stuck with new state levies. Asking the legislature for a six-month hike of nearly 22 percent in state income taxes, he warned that "after all the cuts of the last two years, we are at a very dangerous point. We have to cut to the bone and beyond. We have reached a point where further cuts could have a disastrous effect on our future."

Milliken got the tax raise, but it wasn't enough. A mix of the spending cap, 14 percent unemployment and the Reagan cuts in federal aid soon produced a new state deficit of more than $778 million in a 1982 budget of only $4.4 billion. That meant a huge new slash of 18 percent in state aid. Once again, education took the major cuts. Welfare clients lost 11 percent of their benefits in two years, with thousands of recipients cut from the rolls through tighter eligibility. *The Washington Post* observed that Michigan had cut its budget by a sum proportional to cutting the Social Security system from the federal budget. When Michigan's credit rating was downgraded in 1982, five Japanese banks stepped forward to guarantee a $500 million loan to Lansing. The *Post* saw this as "ironic and unprecedented aid for the state hardest hit by Japanese economic competition."

## Ohio

Another Great Lakes state with a growing fiscal crisis since 1980 has been Ohio, which happens to be our second biggest auto state. A low state tax base also played a part here. Republicans have mainly run this tax-starved state over the years, Robert Kuttner recalling in *Revolt of the Haves* how

> once in a generation some cataclysmic event unexpectedly sweeps a liberal Democrat into office: he discovers how broke the state really is and cajoles the reluctant legislature to raise taxes. For this public service, he is thrown out of office after one term by the voters. Then the Republicans come back in and cut taxes, beginning the cycle again. That happened to

Governor Mike DiSalle in the sixties and John Gilligan in the seventies [and may now happen to Richard Celeste in the eighties].

On August 20, 1982, the last truck tire in Akron was "ripened" and "cured" in the red-brick plant that General Tires had opened back in 1915. Only 700 rubber workers were left in Akron, to make specialized tires for racing or experimental cars in the city that John Gunther had once dubbed "the rubber center of the universe." Before World War II, 90 percent of America's rubber came from Akron. During the war, Firestone at peak production had employed 16,000 workers. In the summer of 1982, only a few hundred hourly workers were left in the Firestone plant. The Generals' factory with its 1,265 workers had been the last major tire plant to close. Even these jobs were lost, although the union at General Tire had made wage concessions in 1979 and 1981, and kept the men working in 1976, when rubber workers struck for 141 days elsewhere. The concessions, the loyalty and more than 25,000 years of seniority were wiped out by the bottom line. Tires had left Akron at last.

Even during the nonrecession years between 1976 and 1979, the United Rubber Workers lost 20 percent of its membership at the Big Four tire companies. Tire firms folded their older Snowbelt factories, while a few new plants opened in nonunion Sunbelt states like Alabama, North Carolina, Oklahoma or Tennessee. Nineteen factories were closed in three years by the Big Four of Goodyear, Firestone, Goodrich and Uniroyal, the first three firms based in Akron.

OPEC prices and radial tires were the main problems. Petrochemicals are 85 percent of tire weight, so the two OPEC price shocks of 1973 and 1979 were severe blows for Akron. Higher gas prices meant less driving, and that deflated the tire replacement market, which is 70 percent of all tire sales. Car owners discovered what airlines and truckers had known for years: retreads need not be the tire of last resort. One of every five tires sold in 1981 was a retread. Lighter and more fuel efficient cars also put less strain on tires.

But the main blow for the replacement market was from radial tires, which wear twice as long as bias-ply tires before going bald. While the Big Four could do nothing about OPEC prices and their impact on tire use, they could have fended off the radial imports from Michelin of France and Bridgestone of Japan. But the Akron giants failed to retool for radials in time, so 12 million imported tires of 1978 became 18 million by 1981, as France and Japan rose from a 6 percent to a 10 percent market share in America.

Only Goodyear, still the world's leader, has truly reindustrialized in recent years. A $2 billion overhaul was launched in 1972, and several aging Snowbelt factories were closed. Some of the Goodyear retoolings were in Snowbelt plants, but many were in nonunion southern factories, among them the $300 million overhaul of Goodyear's automated showplace in Lawton, Oklahoma. Yet, Goodyear barely matched Michelin's bid to outfit the 1981 Escort and Lynx lines from Ford—Goodyear got 40 percent of the new radial orders, while Michelin got 60 percent.

As for the rest of the Big Four, Goodrich cut some losses by simply dropping out of the new-car-contract competition in 1981, switching to replacements alone. Uniroyal was saved mainly that year by wage concessions from the United Rubber Workers, with factory hands giving up cost-of-living allowances for three years as white-collar workers took "equality of sacrifice" cuts. As for Firestone, it talked with Bridgestone, the Japanese firm offering to buy the American company's radial truck-tire plant in Nashville. Bridgestone proposed to pay $89 million for the plant, with plans to modernize it for $47 million more. They then proposed to cover this huge investment by raising production 50 percent in five years.

The Big Four continue to decline. Between 1975 and 1980, as the *Fortune* 1000 earned 15.1 percent on equity each year, tire firms made only 7.4 percent. Some see Goodyear, Bridgestone and Michelin as the three main tire survivors up ahead. Goodyear as the lone American major might then join other surviving industrial giants: U.S. Steel and perhaps Bethlehem in steel; GM and probably Ford in autos; Boeing in passenger planes.

Among several Ohio cities affected by the tire slump was Dayton. This small city of 190,000 is striking for its inventions and normality. It was the first American city with a commissioner-manager government. Dayton is the home of the Wright brothers, the automobile starter, and the cash register. National Cash Register remains one of four *Fortune* 500 giants in this small city.

Dayton's normality was certified by Richard Scammon and Ben Wattenberg in 1970, when they suggested it was home to the typical voter of *The Real Majority*. Here dwelled their typical forty-seven-year-old housewife who was married to a factory worker, whose brother-in-law was a cop, and who was liberal on economic issues, but worried about social issues like busing, feminism and pot. A decade later, normality stood on its head. Too many Democrats bragged that they were liberal on social issues and conservative on economic ones, and Dayton was reeling from a massive loss of factory jobs. As Peirce and Keefe observed in *The Great Lakes States of America,* automation at National Cash Register and the closing of a huge Frigidaire plant led to the fact that "between 1969 and 1979 some 30,000 industrial jobs were lost in the city; whether the hemorrhaging could be averted before an irreversible downward spiral occurred remained an open question . . ."

In per capita terms, the 30,000 lost Dayton jobs were equal to 1.2 million factory jobs lost in New York City in one decade. The losses continued in 1980, when the Dayton Tire and Rubber factory closed, and Local 178 of the URW saw all its members thrown out of work. This new disaster meant that, despite a new downtown built in the 1970s, Dayton's downward spiral by 1981 included:

• Three school tax vote rejections since 1974. These local votes plus recent state cuts suggested even more deficits and crisis ahead.

• Dayton's 1.75 percent local income tax compares with a 4.3 percent rate in New York City. The property tax rate is even worse, with $0.35 per $100 in assessed value against $8.95 in New York. Referendums must be passed for each new tax, and a local law lets existing taxes expire every five years, absent votes to keep taxes alive.

• There was 14 percent unemployment early in the 1981 recession. The share of public school students on welfare rose from 39 percent to 57 percent in only five years. The city's crime rate of 13,777 crimes per 100,000 residents was the highest in Ohio for 1980, one of the highest in America, and almost triple the national rate of 5,899.

On December 27, 1982, Bethlehem Steel announced 10,000 layoffs in the worst such event in steel history. At the time, some 40 percent of all steelworkers were on layoff, most of them in Ohio Valley cities, and plant capacity was down to 29 percent.

Bethlehem's action would mainly affect its huge factory in Lackawanna, New York, in what was once America's fourth biggest mill. If the huge works south of downtown Buffalo closed at the end of 1983, 8,500 workers would lose jobs in a city of 23,000 and Lackawanna would lose Bethlehem's 66 percent share of local taxes. Before looking at similar disasters in several Ohio steel towns, let us briefly note highlights from a long-term steel slump:

• Imports had grown from 2 percent in 1959 to nearly 23 percent by the fall of 1982, as Japan, Canada, Germany and France led the charge, and nondemocratic nations like Romania, South Korea and Taiwan made inroads.

• Output had fallen from 91 million tons in 1970 to 60 million by 1980—and that was before the bottom fell out in 1981 and 1982.

• Jobs had dropped from 719,000 in 1957 to 306,000 in late 1982. Yet twice in 1982, the steelworkers had rejected wage givebacks. Only in 1983 were concessions finally made.

• Companies had lost more than $3.5 billion in 1982 alone. Some firms like U.S. Steel and Armco were diversifying into oil, chemicals or banking, rather than retooling old factories. More than 370 plants had been closed since 1959.

• Steel stocks had dropped 45 percent in value since 1975 as all stocks rose 49 percent in value. The day of the Lackawanna layoffs was also the day that the Dow-Jones Index set a new record of 1070.

In 1947, America was producing more than 50 percent of the world's steel as Europe and Japan rebuilt from the ruins of World War II. John Gunther observed in *Inside U.S.A.* that

> the basic power determinant of any country is its steel production, and what makes this a great nation above all is the fact that it can roll over 90 million tons of steel ingots a year, more than Great Britain, prewar Germany, Japan, France, and the Soviet Union *combined*.

Thirty-five years later, America was producing 14 percent of the world's steel in good times, and enduring a steel slump that saw capacity drop from 77 percent in 1981 to 33 percent for 1982. What had gone wrong?

Steel had failed to modernize. Describing our anemic retoolings in steel, *Business Week* noted in 1980 that "in the last five years, dividend payouts have averaged 72 percent of U.S. Steel's earnings and 83% of Bethlehem's earnings. That leaves little for modernization.''

Even when majors reindustrialized, the steel slump was too much. Inland Steel's No. 7 blast furnace is the largest in the Western Hemisphere and one of the most computerized on earth. But the steel slump occurred as No. 7 opened, leaving Inland with a lot of debt service and an underproducing mill. *The Washington Post* noted how this "hasn't been lost on Inland's rivals now facing investment decisions" in 1982. It was one more excuse not to retool.

U.S. Steel's purchase of Marathon Oil in early 1982 had sent a negative signal to steelworkers whose numbers shrank from 400,000 in 1980 to 250,000 by 1983. It reinforced their belief that Big Steel was putting profits above production. Workers recalled how U.S. Steel had closed sixteen plants with 13,000 workers in 1979 before the slump. They remembered how U.S. Steel led the majors in hiking prices 13 percent while cutting sales in 1981, making the big firm a $386 million profit—as it laid off 7,500 more workers. Now the Marathon sale suggested that even less modernization, and more plant closings, lay ahead.

So when Big Steel asked the United Steelworkers for a three-year wage freeze to save the troubled industry $6 billion for retooling, the USW local presidents rejected it in mid-1982. This happened although worker wages and benefits had been indexed to inflation under a no-strike pact of 1972, with USW-member wages and benefits zooming 195 percent since then, against 85 percent in real inflation. Average steelworkers cost their employers $19.42 an hour, against $10.15 in Japan or $11.46 in West Germany. The USW wage was the highest industrial salary on earth.

The union and the producers reached a tentative agreement cutting wages about 10 percent in the fall of 1982, but the local presidents again rejected the proposal. Since the industry was down to 30 percent capacity by November, the rejection and the possibility of a strike were incredible. Labor's attitude had gone beyond reasonable resentment over Big Steel's profit mania to an irrational animus against almost any concessions, despite the sizable wages. One month later, the 10,000 layoffs were announced by Bethlehem. Only in 1983 did the USW agree to a three-year wage freeze.

When not trying to get wage concessions, Big Steel was asking

Washington for relief similar to the voluntary import limits on autos worked out with Japan in 1981. An agreement was worked out with Europe in late 1982, but it affected only about 6 percent of the total imports, so the Big Eight were soon demanding quotas on Japanese steel as well. Since even Japan was down at 60 percent capacity as the world slump deepened in late 1982, the Japanese were predictably annoyed.*

Even assuming recovery in the Ohio Valley, steel faces major obstacles ahead. Workers will lose tens of thousands of jobs as continuous casters replace ingot production or the basic oxygen process retires the open hearth. Producers must somehow put $3 billion into annual retooling, or a 23 percent import share will rise in spite of quotas. And the Department of Transportation sounded an ominous note in a 1982 study which suggested that cars made of lighter steel, plastics and aluminum to improve fuel efficiency could cut Detroit's steel use 32 percent by 1985.

The Big Eight and the United Steelworkers must quickly agree on a sensible and lengthy wage freeze or reduction. That concession must be tied to job guarantees, controls on plant closings or more worker take-overs similar to the one proposed at Weirton. Only rapid and dramatic action by both sides can salvage what's left of our most troubled industry, whose weakness in 1982 is as revealing about America as its strength was to John Gunther in 1947.

• *Middletown* is the home of Armco, which employes a third of the local workers and tithes 2 percent of its pretax profits for local charities. Like a paternalistic Japanese firm, Armco resisted the wave of Ohio steel layoffs until late 1980 and then rehired its furloughed workers in 1981. By 1982, Armco was having what its CEO called "the most difficult period for Armco since the Great Depression." Carbon steel had earned $2.2 million in 1981, but then lost $82.3 million for the third quarter of 1982. Losses related to a nickel-mining operation in the Dominican Republic and

---

* Other foreign nations in the steel slump include England, where 178,000 workers became 96,000 in two years, and France, which lost 33 percent of its steelworkers in six years. France's Longwy section near Belgium is even more ravaged than the Ohio Valley, and was termed the nation's most devastated area by François Mitterrand. Thirty thousand steel jobs in Longwy in 1960 are down to 7,000 today. Even the firm that made the girders for the Eiffel Tower—the symbol of growing French industry in 1889—set layoffs for 66 percent of its workers in 1982.

shrinking profits in an oilfield-equipment line were also part of a nine-month loss of $162 million, against $224 million earned in 1981. Even the second most powerful steel giant could not ride out the 1982 slump.

• *Youngstown* saw the bottom fall out suddenly in the fall of 1977 as the huge Campbell Works closed at Youngstown Sheet & Tube. The big mill's previous fame had been as plaintiff in the Supreme Court case of 1952 testing Harry Truman's right to prevent steelworkers from striking during the Korean War. Now the works would be known as the place where the Lykes Corporation made the then-biggest industrial layoff in American history. Peirce and Keefe recall that the area had opened its first blast furnace back in 1803, "so that heavy metal manufacturing was woven into the very character of the area." Suddenly, however, 4,650 workers and up to 6,000 people in related services lost their jobs. Joel Garreau fits the Lykes closing into a regional disaster at the time:

> Shortly before Youngstown's Black Monday, September 17, 1977, when the first mill closed, throwing four thousand out of work, Bethlehem Steel laid off thirty-five hundred workers in Lackawanna, New York . . . and another thirty-five hundred in Johnstown, Pennsylvania. . . . Three thousand workers were out of a job in Conshohocken, New York, when another steel company declared bankruptcy.

Three years later, U.S. Steel demolished four mills in Youngstown by dynamite implosion. Although this was the visually dramatic method used in the instant leveling of the Pruitt-Igoe project in St. Louis, pictures of the smokestacks falling in a huge cloud of dust didn't get major media play. In 1980, people didn't want to admit that America had "reindustrialization problems." By 1982, however, the truth was out as pictures of the falling mill smokestacks became a new media cliché. By the fall of 1982, Youngstown had America's highest metro unemployment rate at 20.9 percent. Director Robert Aldrich while filming *All the Marbles* in Youngstown told *The New York Times* that "you don't have to be very smart to make a movie here—you put the camera down anyplace and it's just right. These streets have such a dejected, defeated, unused look."

• *Steubenville* is a small coal and steel town on the Ohio River. Its air has sometimes been called the dirtiest in America. That air has been cleaned lately—by massive layoffs. When candidate Ronald Reagan visited on October 7, 1980, to "listen to the heartland," 12.5 percent of the city was jobless. He made a fiery speech against unemployment, and the visit got major media play. For the first time in 1980, Reagan appeared as a friend of labor. While Middle America bought the image in November, Steubenville stayed loyal to its roots, voting for Jimmy Carter.

A year later, Steubenville had 15 percent unemployment and its Wheeling-Pittsburgh mill was at 50 percent capacity by early 1982. A group of local women organized The Concerned Wives of Laid-Off Workers, and Representative Douglas Applegate took them to see Vice President George Bush. The February 23 meeting was cordial, but recalling it later that evening on *The MacNeil-Lehrer Report,* Mrs. Donna Stuckey noted that Bush seemed poorly briefed. She added that 42 percent were on layoff at the Wheeling-Pittsburgh mill, and "anyone with ten years and under—that's it." Her husband was only five places away from a layoff on the seniority list. As for younger citizens in Steubenville, she noted that the Army "is some place to go . . ."

• *Weirton* is opposite Steubenville, across the Ohio River in West Virginia. The huge Weirton mill had been an original base for National Steel. For years, this factory of more than 12,500 workers had been a faithful earner, used by National to buy other mills and companies. By early 1982, the Weirton mill had aged, and was at 50 percent capacity in the recession, but still showed a profit off $1 billion in orders for 1981. Then on March 2, National announced from its Pittsburgh headquarters that it would "substantially limit its future capital investment" at Weirton. This was a virtual closing notice for one of West Virginia's biggest employers and its biggest taxpayer.

The Weirton workers decided to buy the mill through an Employees Stock Ownership Plan (ESOP) and keep it alive. With more than 10,000 jobs in a city of 26,000 the mill was even more than the city itself. Weirton borrowed $250 million for the biggest factory in the state. Walter "Butch" Bish, the head of the Weirton union local, reflected the positive community spirit when he told the *Washington Post:* "I said to my wife the other day, I always wanted to go into business for myself, but I never thought I'd start by buying a steel mill."

Ohio had been training for its 1980, 1981 and 1982 fiscal crises for years. Back in 1910, it had invented the 1 percent limit on property taxes, which was later rediscovered by California's Proposition 13. Decades of low taxes and poor state services had steadily ravaged Ohio's revenue base until it finished last among the fifty states for tax effort in the late 1970s.

Fiftieth place for tax effort was the powder keg for fiscal crisis —then the 1980 recession lit the fuse. In a dramatic turnaround, Governor James Rhodes wisely abandoned what *The New York Times* had called "Ohio's love affair with low taxes." He warned the legislature in December that unless it raised $395 million in new taxes to balance the state budget, he would release 6,000 convicts into the streets, cut the state payroll, and kick tens of thousands of welfare clients off the rolls. His threat galvanized the conservative body. The tax hikes passed. They were mainly regressive levies, like excise, sales or utility taxes, as opposed to raises in corporate or personal income taxes.

By late 1981, the auto, rubber and steel slumps had pushed Ohio unemployment over 10 percent. As the recession ravaged a weak revenue base, it also hiked state expenses for unemployment and welfare. Welfare costs jumped sharply from $1.4 billion in 1980 to $1.8 billion in 1981. And there was $184 million in Reagan federal cuts as well. Despite the big tax raise of 1980, the chronically undertaxed state was still $390 million short for the 1982 fiscal year.

Rather than stagger from deficit to deficit, Rhodes and the legislature decided to face both current and long-term fiscal problems by passing one huge tax hike to cover the next twenty months. This $1.3 billion measure was less regressive than the 1980 raise. While sales and utility taxes rose again, so did corporate franchise taxes.

Then came 1982. Only two months after the $1.3 billion tax bill, Ohio suddenly faced a new deficit for the biennial budget ending June 30, 1983. The state budget office now projected $768 million in new deficits ahead, and suggested that $250 million more might be needed to cover further school debts and growing welfare rolls in a state with 11 percent unemployment in February and headed for 12.5 percent by late 1982.

In short, Ohio was $1 billion short for the biennium, even though the legislature had just passed a $1.3 billion tax hike to cover earlier projected deficits. Once again, as in the California, Minnesota and Michigan examples noted earlier, too many tax cuts had combined with recession to wreck fiscal stability. A tax revolt begun when Taft was President was hard to reverse.*

## Newark

"There are good reasons why Newark should *not* be a dying city," wrote Neal R. Peirce in 1972. Those reasons remain.

As an insurance center, Newark is home to the #1 and #15 carriers on the *Fortune* list. It is second for insurance assets to New York City across the Hudson River. Prudential Insurance on Broad Street has more assets than any *Fortune* 500 industrial, or any firm save BankAmerica, Citicorp and Chase Manhattan.

As an office center, Newark's space expanded 64 percent between 1970 and 1978. From the foot of Manhattan, in Battery Park, to the west, six miles away, there is a dazzling skyline of office towers along Broad Street. "*Newark* is where you'll see *our* headquarters going up, reflecting our faith in the cities" goes a TV ad from Public Service Electric & Gas, America's tenth biggest utility, whose mirrored curtain walls glitter on Broad Street.

As a transit hub, Newark is well sited for river, rail, road and air. Newark Airport, fully modernized in the 1970s and with WPA murals by Arshile Gorky, is the eleventh busiest airport in America.† Port Newark has been the world's busiest container port, taking container traffic from an unprepared New York City long ago. The Penn Central tracks run right through the middle of town, and the Jersey Turnpike is nearby. All these factors combine in what Peirce has called "a natural transportation point unmatched in eastern America."

Newark has quite a past. Founded by Puritans in 1666, it is our oldest city after Boston and New York. As the seat of Princeton until 1756, it was home to college president Aaron Burr when his

---

* I am indebted to State Senator Donald E. Lukens (R–4th District), chairman of the Senate State Government and Federal Relations Committee, for some of the fiscal data above. The interpretation of it, however, is mine.

† In the 1930s, New York used foresight to break Newark's monopoly on air traffic. Mayor Fiorello La Guardia dramatized the fact that the world's biggest city had no airport by refusing to leave a TWA flight from Washington which had landed at Newark Airport "since my ticket says New York City, not Newark." He forced the flight to a military field in Brooklyn, the Alinsky-style ploy getting big media play. So as New York recovered from the Depression with the 1939 World's Fair, it also opened North Beach—now La Guardia—Airport.

famous son was born. Forty-eight years later, the son killed the founder of nearby Paterson in a famous duel on the Palisades. Newark would soon surpass Paterson as an industrial center. Thomas A. Edison lived in Newark until 1876, a year before he invented the phonograph and three years before the electric light. By 1910, Newark was producing 20 percent of all manufactured value in New Jersey, as the tenth biggest factory town in America. It was also our thirteenth biggest city that year, bigger even than Los Angeles or Washington, D.C. Almost half of Newark was foreign born; only 2 percent of it was black.

By 1950, 28 percent of Newark was black, many of them unskilled migrants attracted by a booming factory town. Only steel centers like Baltimore and Gary had a higher share of southern black migrants among Snowbelt cities back then. Newark as an opportunity magnet in 1950 was bigger than Dallas, Denver, Phoenix, San Antonio, San Diego or San Jose. But just as farm machines built in Illinois drove southern blacks off farms and into northern cities like Newark in the 1940s, Carrier air conditioners from Syracuse would now send northern middle-class whites off to help found a New South after 1950. The fateful regional transfer of people, jobs and wealth from the Snowbelt to the Sunbelt had begun.

Altogether, some 100,000 whites left Newark in the 1950s, and almost as many left in the 1960s. Even worse than the census losses, Newark lost 25 percent of its factory jobs, just as it became our second major city with a black majority. The city of promise in 1950 was a dying one by 1967, when chronic unemployment and poverty led to the infamous riot that summer. The trial of Mayor Hugh Addonizio in 1969 exposed the mess at City Hall. In 1970, Kenneth Gibson was elected to end corruption and stabilize a divided city.

Neal Peirce summarized the staggering problems Newark faced in 1971:

- Unemployment at 13 percent.
- The highest crime rate in America.
- The highest infant-mortality rate in America.
- 60 percent of the land tax exempt, half of it at Newark Airport.
- 33 percent of Newark on welfare, nearly triple New York City's share.

Republican Governor William Cahill was unable to move a legislature dominated by suburbs and small towns. He could not get a commuter tax for Mayor Gibson, so the growing office corridor on Broad Street downtown was like Newark Airport: rich, growing, mainly untaxed. No commuter tax meant higher local property taxes in Newark. In 1971, the tax rate of $9.21 per $100 in assessed values was double the $4.37 rate in New York. Newark's very high rate spurred even more taxpayer and industrial exodus. Gibson had no choice but to raise property taxes in order to maintain services for commuters and Newark residents. But the higher taxes drove out marginal factories, costing unskilled Newark residents even more industrial jobs.

By 1975, Gibson had restored outward calm to Newark. There were more black cops on the streets, and while the crime rate remained one of the highest in America, it rose only 11 percent in 1975 as America's grew 17 percent. Otherwise, the picture limned by Peirce in 1971 remained. A businessman told *U.S. News & World Report* that Gibson's first term was "supposed to be a holding action, and his second term was supposed to be the 'go years.' But, up until now, there's been no go."

Meanwhile, the untaxed downtown revival grew. Prominent was a new Gateway Complex of office towers on Broad Street, right above the Penn Central station. Untaxed commuters could now travel to work without having to touch Newark soil. Downtown office space grew 64 percent between 1970 and 1978, one of our highest urban growth rates. But like the Government Center expansion in downtown Boston, this mainly added commuter jobs, which were 63 percent of all Newark jobs, against an 18 percent commuter share of New York jobs. As Newark residents got poorer and untaxed commuters got jobs, there was a ghastly drop in the ratio of city-to-suburb family income. The five lowest performers among America's twenty biggest metro areas were:

### FAMILY INCOME AS SHARE OF SUBURBAN INCOME

|            | 1969 | 1976 |
|------------|------|------|
| Newark     | .60  | .42  |
| St. Louis  | .79  | .57  |
| Atlanta    | .72  | .62  |
| Baltimore  | .74  | .63  |
| Washington | .69  | .63  |

Newark was rated last among fifty cities in the *Harper's* survey of 1975. It was also last among fifty-eight cities in the 1980 HUD survey of urban need, based on unemployment, income growth and share of poor people. The Princeton survey of 1980 rated Newark forty-eighth among fifty-two cities for urban conditions, forty-seventh for manufacturing value added, forty-sixth for service receipts, and last for retail sales. Even the 64 percent office expansion downtown did little for shopping, since commuters took the Pennsy into town and back out, without lingering downtown. Newark took a sensational loss of 27 percent in retail sales between 1972 and 1977—the city with the next worst record in the Princeton survey, Rochester, had a 6 percent *gain* in sales.

Yet, despite all the evidence about America's worst big city, T. D. Allman concluded a 1978 essay on the urban crisis in *Harper's* with optimism from Mayor Gibson. Allman recalled how "one of the first times I heard the urban catastrophe thesis disputed," it had been Gibson, informing him that Newark was "the city of the future." Gibson had said, "Watch where Newark is now, and you will see where your city will be five or fifteen years from now." Allman noted that this "always seemed like a prophecy of doom. But then a year ago, Gibson was saying that the urban crisis had bottomed out, that cities were on the way up again."

Gibson cited the energy crisis, claiming that higher gas prices would drive back recent emigrants from Newark. But since most of them left before the OPEC shocks, this was nonsense.* As of 1980, there were many reasons why people would leave—not return to—America's worst city:
• Newark saw arson, arrears and abandonment reduce a tax roll of 48,487 property parcels in 1968 to one of 39,939 by 1980. This was a 17 percent loss of taxable parcels over a dozen years, against almost no loss in New York. Meanwhile, tax-exempt properties in Newark had grown from 2,731 to 8,387.
• Newark property worth $1.4 billion in 1968 fell to $1.1 billion by 1980. By comparison, New York's assessments rose from

---

* The opposite view is Alvin Toffler's "demassification" theme in *The Third Wave*. He sees OPEC prices keeping people in suburbia, as home computers start a new era of cottage industry. "Futurism" will not stop cities from being places for businessmen to meet and exchange ideas, or get services from ad agencies, bankers or insurers which require contact beyond computer terminals and Picturphones.

$32.5 billion in 1968 to $38.1 billion by 1980—only a 17 percent gain against 113 percent inflation nationally, but far better than Newark's loss of 21 percent in value.

• During Gibson's first term, crime rose only 3 percent, against 27 percent in America. As the 1970s wore on, though, Newark's high crime rate escalated 47 percent. Even worse, as the violent crimes of murder, rape, robbery and assault grew 25 percent across America, they skyrocketed 91 percent in Newark. Drastic cuts in cops probably played a key role:

|  | Census | Police per 1,000 | Crimes per 100,000 |
|---|---|---|---|
| 1977 | 336,000 | 4.3 | 9,022 |
| 1980 | 315,000 | 2.9 | 13,521 |
|  | − 6 percent | − 33 percent | + 47 percent |

Late in 1981, *The New York Times* ran a feature on its sister city. The headline typified the urban renaissance line: "Frustrated by Slow Renewal, Newark Looks for New Hope." The story noted a "decade of relative calm" in Newark, exemplifying the usual media confusion of stability with the absence of riots. The article skipped by problems like soaring crime or falling assessments to quote the chairman of Prudential: "I don't claim that the city is out of the woods . . . I think the people who live here can have hopes and dreams about the future of the city."

But when six Newark residents are murdered, raped, robbed or assaulted for every American so affected in 1980, just what hopes and dreams are there? Three hundred and fifteen thousand Newark residents below the Prudential tower hardly resemble the 50 million policyholders of a mutual pool that grossed almost $9 billion off 1980 investments. One hardly suggests that Prudential throw endless assets into reviving its hometown, and Prudential doubtless spends much time trying to recruit, train and retain as many Newark residents as possible. But when nearly two of three workers in Newark commute, the Prudential boss is hardly the only worker with hopes and dreams for Newark who takes the evening train out to Short Hills.

The best thing about America's worst city remains that handsome mirage seen from Battery Park in Manhattan. The big Prudential slab, the mirrored walls of the PSE&G and the two big Gateway towers make up a wall of solid illusion about local prosperity across the Hudson.

# CHAPTER 10

# NEW YORK CITY

IN THE WORLD's greatest city there is a needless downward spiral of service cuts and taxpayer losses, sustained by the mayor, the governor and the state legislature.

Manhattan has become a luxury lifeboat of office towers, hotels and lavish condos, while the four Outer Boroughs decline.

There is a middle-class exodus taking wealth creators from the city.

• *1. The Needless Spiral.* Governor Hugh Carey and the state legislature had a twofold role in the service crisis of New York City. As overseer of the Financial Control Board (FCB), which approves the city's budget, Carey indirectly forced deep service cuts after 1975. When New York's fiscal crisis erupted in 1975, Mayor Abe Beame could have imposed a wage freeze on city workers, while making token service cuts. The unions rejected the freeze, and Beame acquiesced. Massive layoffs were used to balance the budget, and Governor Carey and banker Felix Rohatyn devised the FCB to run a "profligate" city. The media hailed them for "saving" New York City, but in reality, the FCB mainly saved bankers and bondholders, while wrecking services with deep and incessant cuts.

Carey's second role in the New York City service crisis was shared with the state legislature. Together, they cut $2.3 billion in annual taxes after 1978, about 12 percent of the state revenue base. Here are three ways that the poor and the working poor have had to pay for the $2.3 billion in relief for the taxpayers of New York:

• Welfare. While Republican Governors Nelson Rockefeller and

Malcolm Wilson had offset two welfare grant cuts with two later grant hikes, Democrat Hugh Carey and the legislature froze the grant for six years. As OPEC inflation raged from 1974 to 1980, the grant remained at $258 a month for a family of four. Carey also froze the rent grant in 1975, which often forced tenants to choose between rent and food. They chose food, meaning less rent to maintain marginal slum buildings.

• Mental Health. Widespread releasing of patients from state mental hospitals has led to some 36,000 "street people" in New York City. If they were in state hospitals, Albany would have to pay all costs, but now it saves 75 percent of those costs under outpatient care. Albany doesn't throw psychotics out into the cold, but the releasing has gone too far. The helpless patients make up most of those who sleep in doorways and subways, freeze to death in winter, and even inhabit steam tunnels under Grand Central Station.

• Health. Harsh Medicaid cost controls have caused fiscal chaos in public and private hospitals. Albany has helped create an army of 1.4 million working poor who earn too much for Medicaid but too little for Blue Cross. Their costs, added to those of illegal aliens, lead to $250 million lost in annual free care at the city's sixteen public hospitals. Statewide, more than 220 hospitals had to cannibalize more than $1 billion in assets over five years to try to stay open. Twenty-seven private hospitals have closed since 1976 in New York City, mainly due to bankruptcy.

Avoiding the problems above would have meant deferring only 12 percent of the state tax cut. When the welfare grant was finally raised in 1981, it cost $120 million a year. If the state had spent $75 million on Medicaid care for the working poor and illegal aliens, it would have raised $225 million more as well in local and federal matching funds. If Albany had spent another $75 million for mental health, that could have meant decent aftercare and shelter for state patients released to communities. These added welfare, Medicaid and mental health outlays would have totaled $260 million in state funds, or 12 percent of the $2.3 billion in annual state tax cuts after 1978.

Mayor Ed Koch has deepened the downward spiral of service cuts and taxpayer loss in at least three ways. First, he sped up a seven-year plan to balance the city budget. Koch told bankers and federal overseers he could balance the books in three years. He did this with more service cuts.

Second, Koch followed former Mayor John Lindsay's mistakes with the city unions. Once again, a new mayor locked himself into a public fight with the unions, which led to huge settlements later on. Lindsay's posturings led to the transit strike of 1966 and the giveaway settlement that unlocked the candy store for later contracts. Koch began 1978 with a media campaign against the unions, so they threatened a strike. Inexplicably, Koch then handed unions $400 million a year more than they expected. All this meant even more service cuts to balance the budget under his three-year plan. In 1982, Koch ran for governor and another contract giveaway occurred. *The New York Times* denounced the inflated labor pact, and predicted the likely result that "anemic services will be further reduced." Indeed a new fiscal crisis erupted within three months, along with the threat of massive layoffs in 1983.

Third, Koch refused to tap major revenue reservoirs in New York. To avoid alienating bankers and bondholders, he often didn't stretch out payment on debt service. Worse, Koch gave endless tax breaks to powerful developers and realtors. A huge building boom of office towers in Manhattan reflected a healthy market, able to pass on higher property taxes to a long line of renters. But Koch kept commercial property taxes artificially low. Some project from $600 to $800 million lost a year off deflated assessments and tax abatements.

• *2. The Manhattan Lifeboat.* Jacob Riis photographs from 1900 show children, stacked like cordwood, asleep in alleys; grimy sweatshops; crowded firetraps. In 1982, there were some 36,000 street people; more than 500 sweatshops in the South Bronx, and hundreds more in Chinatown, Little Italy and northern Brooklyn; as for firetraps, some 14 percent of Bronx housing was foreclosed by 1980. In 1897, the year before the four Outer Boroughs were annexed to New York, Manhattan Island was New York City. Today it seems that way as well. There is a Renaissance for Manhattan, and the Dark Ages for the Outer Boroughs.
• Thirty-five million square feet of new office space was projected for Manhattan by 1985. A $500 million Convention Center from I. M. Pei should open by 1986. A $292 million hotel from John Portman crowns a major renewal in Times Square. A $250 million South Street Seaport mall from James Rouse opened in 1983 in Lower Manhattan. On a nearby landfill, a new Battery Park City

of 2,000 housing units and 5 million square feet of office space is under way. But stable Bronx and Brooklyn neighborhoods slowly turn into slums, as the poor move north in the Bronx and south in Brooklyn. In the 1970s, 870,000 New Yorkers left the city, for the first major census loss since 1790.

• Younger people have been revitalizing Manhattan neighborhoods like the Upper West Side, or slums like the Lower East Side and brownstone blocks in Harlem. Boutiques and bistros have been replacing mom-and-pop stores throughout Manhattan. Condo conversions and sky-high rents have been driving the middle class from Manhattan. Fourteen percent of the Bronx and 4 percent of Brooklyn is foreclosed and owned by City Hall. In both boroughs, for every property parcel to gain value in 1979, seven lost value.

• More than 100,000 new jobs were added to Manhattan's economy between 1978 and 1981, but there were 16,000 fewer New Yorkers with jobs. Almost all the job gains had been in specialized office work sectors like banking, communications, insurance and real estate. Commuters got the new jobs. Many of them were recent émigrés from New York's service crisis, having gone to Nassau or Westchester counties, or directly across the Hudson River to the high-rises of Fort Lee, New Jersey. Yet those same years saw the city lose 48,000 factory jobs. As Manhattan towers rise and specialized jobs open for commuters, Outer Borough factory areas like Hunts Point in the Bronx, Long Island City in Queens and Greenpoint in Brooklyn lose jobs for the increasingly unskilled residents of New York. Put another way, as Manhattan gained 150,700 private-sector jobs over four years, the four Outer Boroughs were losing 400 jobs. As property values fall and factories close, New York is heading for an intracity version of the "two Americas" seen by the Kerner Commission in 1968—Manhattan for the winners, and the Outer Boroughs for the rest.

• *3. The Middle-Class Exodus.* In 1981, Mayor Koch ran for re-election and claimed that the middle class sensed a new "spirit" in New York. But the service crisis produced by six years of cuts was getting worse, and the middle class was leaving en masse. Crime set new records in 1979, 1980 and 1981, even though the city was shrinking. Housing blight spread in the Bronx and Brooklyn, and even to stable homeowner areas in Queens. Subways were so chaotic that Moody Investors Service cited them in refusing a high bond rating in 1981. Virtually all New York emigrants in the 1970s were middle class or better. Eighty percent of them were from the Bronx and Brooklyn, both of them big homeowner boroughs.

Senior citizens took their pensions elsewhere. As the elderly grew only 8 percent in New York State, Sunbelt retirement states saw them grow 29 percent in California, 62 percent in Florida and 79 percent in Arizona. There are so many retired New Yorkers in Florida that twenty-nine New York law firms have branch offices in Florida, with more than 1,000 New York lawyers admitted to practice there. White students were 42 percent of the public schools in 1970, but only 28 percent by 1979. And where 2.7 million whites were in the local work force in 1970, only 2.1 million were by 1980. But the most vivid index of middle-class flight was a sharp drop in median family income. In 1970, New York City's median family income was 3 percent higher than the national average; eight years later, it was 17 percent below that norm.

The middle-class exodus means both fiscal and economic losses for the city. Income, sales and property tax bases shrink, the last dropping especially in the Outer Boroughs where the middle class lives. The exodus also drains wealth creators from New York, as skilled workers, managers and entrepreneurs depart. Often they are the ones who start or sustain the small firms that make up 90 percent of New York's businesses, employ 1.7 million workers and give first jobs to unskilled minorities.

As the middle-class wealth creators left in the 1970s, the gap between New York and national work-force participation rates grew. In 1968, the gap was narrow: 55 percent of all New Yorkers over sixteen had jobs, while 57 percent of all such Americans had jobs. Then the middle class left. Today, only 51 percent of these New Yorkers work, against 59 percent of America. Commissioner Samuel M. Ehrenhalt of the federal Bureau of Labor Statistics observed that this means New York City needs another 350,000 jobs simply to match national work-force participation rates.

Before detailing the service crisis, let me note those most affected by the rising crime, spreading slums, closed hospitals and run-down subways. For reasons of age, employment or dependency, they often cannot leave New York. In order of ascending numbers:

• There are *210,000 senior citizens* who live at or below the poverty line. Their numbers will grow in the 1980s, especially among those over the age of seventy-five. Health demands inevitably lead the growing needs, and the elderly poor are already the main force in New York's rising Medicaid costs.
• The common estimate for all Asian, Caribbean and Latin *illegal aliens is 750,000.* They cost nothing for welfare or Medicaid, but put strains on health and housing. Unable to protest sweatshops or overcrowded housing, they live and work in unsanitary, crowded conditions that lead to more fires and breed diseases like TB.
• There are *860,000 welfare clients* who went without a grant raise for six years. Their deflated income is a kind of "keystone" for the service crisis: rising crime, housing decay and declining health all spring from such increasingly hard, marginal lives. For several years, a broad coalition led by Mayor Koch, Cardinal Cooke and former governor Malcolm Wilson pleaded with Governor Carey and the legislature for a 10 percent grant raise.
• As for health care, *1,400,000 working poor* earn too much for Medicaid coverage under the state's low eligibility levels but too little for Blue Cross. In New York, a family of four earning more than $5,000 was deemed "too rich" for Medicaid coverage in 1980. The indigent debts of this group are staggering. For 1979 alone, they formed the vast majority of the "no pay" patients who cost private and public hospitals of New York about $340 million in free care.

These four groups comprise about 40 percent of New York City.

## CRIME: Slow-Motion Riot

Crime has escalated sharply in New York in the past few years.
• In 1980, seventy of seventy-three police precincts had rises in robbery, with sharp jumps in that violent crime in stable areas like Greenwich Village, Staten Island and the homeowner borough of Queens. New York had the highest robbery rate in America: 1,422 muggings for every 100,000 residents.
• Murder set new world records for a single city for three consecutive years. Though there were fewer citizens in New York each year, murder grew from 1,733 homicides in 1979 to 1,814 in 1980 and then 1,832 in 1981.

The city could not go from 31,106 police officers in 1975 to 22,170 by 1982 without problems. During those six years of relentless attrition, as the city census shrank 7 percent, police were cut 29 percent. As the cops on the beat or in cars faded from view, crime soared.

Fewer police meant fewer arrests. In 1980, as crime complaints rose 16 percent, arrests fell 5 percent. By the middle of 1981, Commissioner McGuire didn't bother asking about a "social experiment" to control crime with even fewer cops. Noting the pattern of rising crimes and falling arrests, he now told the *Times* that "our manpower losses finally caught up with us."

No precinct was safe. In 1979, major crimes rose in sixty of the seventy-three New York precincts. The thirteen exceptions tended to be high crime areas like Harlem or depopulated ones like the South Bronx. In 1980, normally safe areas reporting sharp rises in robbery included Greenwich Village up 36 percent, Staten Island up 26 percent and the North Bronx up 34 percent. Manhattan's fashionable Upper East Side went from 300 police in 1977 to 196 cops in 1981. Muggings there rose 17 percent for 1980 alone. And citywide, robberies were becoming more violent. In 1976, 19 percent of all murders involved robbery, but by 1980 some 26 percent did.*

Three more indices of the crime wave involve drugs, insurance losses and public-housing violence. Crime journalist Nicholas Pileggi suggests that drugs are now New York's third biggest employer, with from 100,000 to 300,000 working in that underground economy. Worse, he notes city estimates for the four leaders in annual gross revenues:

|  |  |
|---|---|
| Illegal Drugs | $45.0 billion |
| Retail Trade | 24.5 |
| Garment Trade | 17.0 |
| Manufacturing | 14.6 |

---

* In 1980, the most violent precinct was the 77th, in the Bedford-Stuyvesant section of Brooklyn. As successor for violence to the 42nd Precinct of "Fort Apache" in the South Bronx, the 77th was dubbed "The Alamo." Eighty-eight of its 108,000 residents were killed in 1980, with sixteen of the victims in one three-block area. Yet the 77th has some of the city's finest brownstones, well maintained by black homeowners on quiet side streets flanking Fulton Avenue, much of this revival aided by the Bedford-Stuyvesant Restoration Corporation begun by Senator Robert Kennedy.

As the federal South Florida Task Force drives smugglers to northern routes, New York's awesome drug trade should grow. Despite the phenomenal trade, however, the city narcotics squad was cut 57 percent after 1975, and drug felony arrests actually dropped from 697 in 1977 to only 565 by 1980. On another crime front, the Travelers Insurance Company paid full policy value for only 61 thefts in 1978—then for 800 in 1980. Finally, one notes how a 30 percent cut in housing-project cops since 1975 was accompanied by unusual violence in a relatively safe part of the slums. In 1980 alone, project crime soared 56 percent.

In early 1982, the *Times* did a series on the growing crime wave. A good example of how crime ruined the local economy was seen in a profile of Vic Barouh, founder of a $150 million office-equipment company based in the Greenpoint section of Brooklyn. This area is the city's major Polish enclave, a normally quiet area of charming small parks and asbestos-trimmed homes. As muggings of Barouh's 700 factory hands rose, he began wearing a .38 Colt to work, since "my people were getting hit all the time, beaten, harassed, what have you. How can I tell them to come to work? We could work three shifts, but we can't keep open at night. I'm even refusing orders because I know we can't fill them." He will cut workers from 700 to 200 by 1985, while enlarging factories in California, Canada, Ireland, Puerto Rico and Long Island.

Several odd proposals for fighting crime have arisen. One idea was advanced by Professors Raymond Horton and Charles Brecher in *Setting Municipal Priorities, 1981*. Giving the "lowest priority" to new police hires, they urged citizens to make fewer frivolous calls to the 911 system, and to "install police locks, window bars and antivehicular theft devices."

Representative Ed Koch campaigned for mayor in 1977 with a proposal for 50,000 adult auxiliary volunteers. Despite his call, only 7,000 had stepped forth by 1982. The patrolmen's union attacked them as a "misfit army of scabs."

The most famous volunteers, however, are not 7,000 adults in mock police blue, but some 700 teen-agers in red beret, the Guardian Angels of the New York subways. They began as thirteen boys patrolling Bronx subways, and within two years they were claiming twenty-one chapters across America. Some cities like New Orleans waved them in, others like Chicago or Atlanta bolted the door. In New York, a wave of publicity about the young volunteers overcame Mayor Koch's initial resistance. Their leader, Curtis Sliwa, got a lot of media play in 1981.*

The Angels are dedicated and their presence on subways is useful, but their claims are extravagant. They launched a drive to clean up graffiti in 1981, but the subways are as filthy as ever today. Sliwa claimed 144 arrests made by his troops, but the police couldn't confirm the number. The *Times* quoted an Angel in Philadelphia, bragging that "in three months, we will cut the crime rate on the transit system in half." Kids. And that is the problem. The media used these teens to mask the real issue of too few cops in the subways.

Subway police hires were frozen for five years after 1974. Three thousand two hundred officers shrank to 2,200 by early 1979, when the media reported a new wave of subway crime. After a month of this front-page news, Mayor Koch declared war on subway crime, backing his belated policy with overtime patrols. The patrols soon cut crime by more than 30 percent. Early in 1980, however, Koch cut back on the special patrols, and by the fall, the *Times* found subway crime up by some 70 percent.

With too few cops to draw on, even overtime patrols were not enough. William L. McKechnie, head of the transit patrolmen's union, recalls that when Koch created the special patrols, he ordered all cops back into uniform, ending all plainclothes details.

> This reassured customers—and the criminals. If a crook got on a train and *didn't* see a uniform, he didn't have to worry. He knew Mayor Koch wouldn't lie! It's like poker. We played an open hand—they played closed. Since 1975, we never had enough officers, but we could bluff a mix of uniforms and plainclothes police. Suddenly, we had to expose our hand.

The overtime patrols were rigidly deployed in evening hours, rather than during the peak crime hours from noon to 8 P.M., when school lets out and pickpockets work the rush hour. The late-night patrols soothed customers, but did little to fight crime.

---

* Sliwa and the Angels staged many stunts. They held a one-day "hunger strike," they wore cloth chains and insisted that arrested Angels were "political prisoners," and Sliwa claimed that he had been "kidnapped" twice, during difficult organizing drives in New York and Washington.

The criminals knew the rigid schedules, stopped working at night, and worked the more profitable, less protected, day shift. The cheapest weapon to fight subway crime was ignored: dogs. Canine patrols had long excelled in Philadelphia subways, where no officer with a dog has ever been seriously injured. New York's transit police have very high injury rates—812 injuries for only 2,200 cops in 1980. But with only a dozen dogs in 1982, New York again kept crime control, if not canines, on the leash.

Finally, City Hall began hiring transit police again. Pressure led by Councilman Edward Sadowsky and the Transit Authority led to a hiring binge. By late 1982, staff levels were almost equal to 1975, which was before the fiscal crisis and the rise of subway crime.

## HOUSING: The Foreclosure Flood

A housing crisis usually confined to the poor is also affecting the middle class. In the Outer Boroughs, the main problem is due to Mayor Koch's failure to foreclose and manage thousands of buildings in tax arrears. In Manhattan, too many households, many of them rich and single, drive up prices in a low-vacancy market, or convert rentals to luxury condos or co-ops (only the leper colony of Kalawao in Hawaii has fewer people per household than the average of 1.96 people per unit in Manhattan). The result is a rent war whose winners are rich singles or childless couples able to pay $1,200 a month for a studio apartment.

When the middle class has housing problems, one can imagine the hardship for the poor and the elderly. They live where most of the arson, arrears and abandonment occur. They suffer most when OPEC price fixing leads to heating-oil hikes that wipe out whatever profits remain for honest landlords in slums. Eight hundred and sixty thousand welfare clients also suffered a "maximum shelter ceiling" on rents, imposed by Governor Carey in 1975. This forced more than 33 percent of all clients to pay extra rent from a living grant that was frozen between 1974 and 1981.

Even back in 1970, it was not rent control that was creating slums, but lack of tenant income. Abandonment was under way long before OPEC fuel hikes delivered the *coup de grâce,* as oil prices rocketed from 11 cents a gallon in 1974 to $1.32 by 1982. The first net housing losses occurred in 1967, and a major arson outbreak in 1975 highlighted the ruins in Brownsville, Bushwick and the South Bronx. By late 1977, tens of thousands of buildings were in heavy tax arrears, and a foreclosure flood was set to inundate New York. A new law let City Hall take title to buildings after one year of tax arrears instead of three. This would short-circuit the abandonment cycle, with City Hall managing tenements in reasonable shape, inhabited by tenants still eager to save the buildings involved.

The new law took force in Koch's first year, the foreclosure universe doubling from 17,000 tenanted units to 33,000 in city management. A year later, City Hall owned 4 percent of Brooklyn's rental housing, 8 percent of Manhattan's and 14 percent of the Bronx's. Add units owing almost a year in taxes, and a city survey in late 1979 found that 25 percent of Manhattan, 27 percent of Brooklyn and 46 percent of Bronx rentals were either foreclosed or at the risk of being by 1980—668,000 of the city's 2.1 million units.

But after a fine start, Koch virtually scrapped the one-year foreclosure law. He began taking titles on a selective, limited basis. The better buildings were foreclosed in Manhattan, as Harlem hulks went without city maintenance for another freezing winter. In Brooklyn there were no foreclosures for three long years. Some landlords could skip taxes for five years, leaving behind burned-out and vacant shells.*

After a strong increase in city funds to manage the foreclosures in 1978, Koch let future abandonment run its course. As a result, some 44,000 property parcels rusted in the foreclosure pipeline by 1982.

Koch expanded rehab housing by 16,000 units a year, against 3,000 under Beame. He also properly focused most of this renovation in Outer Boroughs where 76 percent of the city lives. But housing rehab is very expensive, and done usually at the burned-out end of the abandonment cycle. It's much cheaper to simply foreclose and manage buildings that are a year in tax arrears and help thousands of tenants than revive a charred shell for a few lucky people at $60,000 per apartment.

Koch has also revived the Emergency Repair Program, the heating program of last resort for slum dwellers. Begun by Mayor

---

* Some charged the selective foreclosures favored white areas like Clinton over black or Hispanic ones like Harlem and the Lower East Side. The result of not foreclosing, however, is to let Harlem run down fast, thus opening it for redevelopment as a chic place to live.

Wagner after the 1964 Harlem rent strike led by Jesse Gray, ERP was a symbol of concern for the poor until Mayor Beame cut it back in 1974. Koch revived the program to full force, so literally hundreds of thousands of poor tenants are warmer and safer today. However, Koch's failure to manage and maintain the foreclosure flood means that ERP has to plug leaks from the needlessly raging flood. Until Koch starts managing foreclosures again, abandonment will keep spreading. The winding country lanes and Victorian river estates of Riverdale and the fine private homes of Sea Gate behind a high cyclone fence in Coney Island will hang on. But beyond the fence and rural roads, the foreclosure flood will sweep away much of middle-class New York, leaving the poor and elderly to inherit Outer Borough remains.

Arson was burning the South Bronx even before the fiscal crisis in 1975 cut 1,000 firemen and closed firehouses. The next year arson hit Central Brooklyn with full force, with 1,140 tenements torched in Bushwick alone. Then in 1977, a vacant block-square mill in Bushwick was set off by kids with matches. Before the five-alarm blaze was put out, it had spread over seven blocks, destroyed twenty-three buildings and left more than 250 people homeless. No one was killed, but this huge fire was the final blow. Mayor Beame hired more fire marshals for "red hat" patrols in the city's three high-risk arson areas. The deterrence strategy worked and arson dropped by 40 percent, and even by 70 percent in the South Bronx, Bushwick and East New York. Beame also proposed a bill that would have given City Hall first lien on fire-insurance payouts. Since most landlord arson is in buildings with major tax arrears, the bill would have effectively removed a main reason to burn.

The "red hat" patrols were scrapped by Koch, who later cut fire-marshal ranks as well. And the real-estate lobby in Albany amended the first-lien bill so that the mortgagee had first position on payouts. Since the mortgagee was often the landlord disguised as a dummy corporation, the first-lien bill was worthless in cutting insurance fraud. By 1979, arson was prevalent in a dozen neighborhoods. Arson had been 9 percent of city fires in 1975 but was 15 percent by 1980. When Koch impounded funds for forty-six new fire marshals in 1980, the Fire Department had so few firemen that it used 33 percent of all the overtime among city agencies, since firemen were often on double shifts. In 1980, a *Daily News* survey noted the results of deferred maintenance since 1975: rotting hose beds, broken respirators, and safety ropes that, in one infamous tragedy, broke as two firemen plunged to their deaths. A computerized dispatch system broke down frequently. Even before the fiscal crisis, the drop of fire inspections and rise in structural fires were striking in New York:

|      | Inspections | Structural Fires |
|------|-------------|------------------|
| 1968 | 264,000     | 27,000           |
| 1975 | 114,000     | 39,000           |

By late 1980, Mayor Koch realized that a famous Fire Department was in trouble. He appointed a new commissioner, who promptly hired more fire marshals and fire inspectors as a strong preventive force. But until City Hall gets first lien on insurance payouts, landlords can go on torching tenements in tax arrears with one hand and collecting claims with the other. Either that law must be passed, or one from Bronx DA Mario Merola, which would require landlords to use fire-insurance payouts for building repairs. Merola, long New York's premier arson fighter, has told the *Times* that politicians often "only appear in the neighborhood the day after a fire, announcing plans to apply for a multimillion federal grant to rebuild . . . It's better politics to rebuild a neighborhood than to preserve one that's there."

The two boroughs hardest hit by abandonment are the Bronx and Brooklyn. In 1979, both of them saw seven property parcels lose value for each parcel to gain value. In 1981, although 105,000 homes citywide got higher assessments from City Hall, more than 50,000 homes in the Bronx and Brooklyn saw their tax bills cut by an average of $190. This was one tax break that no homeowner wanted.

Parts of both boroughs are still splendid. There are the Fieldston and Riverdale enclaves in the Northwest Bronx, the latter with stunning views of the Palisades. There are stable and sizable homeowner areas in the Northeast Bronx with its great "greenway" on the Pelham Parkway. There are the fine Victorian homes of Brooklyn Heights and Cobble Hill, the tidy Polish and Italian sections of Greenpoint and northern Williamsburg. There are still about thirty square miles of stable middle- to upper-class homes in Brooklyn south of Prospect Park.

But how long will these last? For example, there is the South Bronx, advancing a few blocks north each year. In the 1960s, the South Bronx was down at 149th Street, where the vital "Hub" commercial strip still thrives, including the original Alexander's store. By 1970, the South Bronx was up to 161st Street and Yankee Stadium, spreading to the Grand Concourse as Jews fled to Co-op City. By 1975, the Concourse was so run-down that the block-square Roosevelt Gardens suddenly emptied out in a month. By 1977, the nearby Highbridge section saw big Noonan Plaza in similar trouble. This great Art Deco building was home to 280 families in its prime and a boroughwide tourist magnet, with swans gliding about a courtyard pool. Tens of millions of federal funds revived both Noonan Plaza and Roosevelt Gardens by 1982, but little else withstands the South Bronx tide.

Yet even the South Bronx has great homeowner blocks along Claremont Park, and a Historic Landmark area on Alexander Avenue where some homeowners have recently spent more than $200,000 reviving Late Victorian homes. Another sound home-owner area is even found near heavily burned-out Longwood Avenue. Other South Bronx landmarks include the marble factory where Daniel Chester French finished the statue for the Lincoln Memorial, the iron factory that cast the 8.9 million tons of the U.S. Capitol dome, and the graveyard of St. Ann's church, with the graves of both a signer of the Declaration of Independence, John Morris, and a signer of the Constitution, the latter being Gouverneur Morris.

The South Bronx is even slowly reviving as an economy. Well sited for river, rail, road and air, the huge peninsula has vast, cleared acreage in its Hunts Point and Port Morris sections. Textile mills have yielded to horrid sweatshops, and the machine-tool factories and forges are mainly gone, but signs of new life appeared in the 1982 recession. For the first time in years, electrical demand and commercial phone use rose in the South Bronx, and for every three businesses leaving the area, five moved in. Cheap rents, sizable yard space, and fine transport access were lures even in a recession, as 134 companies moved into or expanded in the area during a twelve-month period.

The 14.8 percent unemployment in the South Bronx in 1982 was almost six points above the city average. Crime was down a bit, but was still at a very high rate. Not all of the area is "Dresden," the appellation a flip media judgment. But the realities of extreme poverty and violence remain in a borough where 14 percent of all parcels are owned by City Hall.

Meanwhile, Manhattan gentrifies as even the worst slums are bid up in a 1 percent vacancy market. The Lower East Side, long the first stop for the poor of Europe and Latin America, is an example. Looking at the burnouts along Avenues B and C or the drug market on Avenue D, it's hard to see a comeback area. But one block was just rehabbed for the working poor, and the middle class is slowly filtering in. People pay six figures for tenements, and then convert them to studio cells renting for $600 a month. In Harlem, homeowner blocks are being revived near Marcus Garvey Park, as is a vast area north of this between 120th and 145th Streets. As the 1980s began, low-income blacks were slowly being driven across the Willis Avenue Bridge into the South Bronx.

Not even the middle class can hang on for long. Artists revived empty industrial lofts in SoHo and Tribeca in the early 1970s, but have been edged out by the rich. On the Upper West Side, big family apartments are being honeycombed into studios for singles, while useful mom-and-pop stores are replaced by trendy restaurants and shops. Useful service stores for shoe and TV repair, newspapers or dry cleaning have experienced rent hikes of 300 percent and even 500 percent in lease renewals (one camera shop was hiked from $9,000 a year to $48,000 in one blow). The only places that can cover such rents are expensive bistros and boutiques that cater to seekers of novelty rather than the new—cultivation as opposed to culture. Meanwhile, as neighborhood services decline, the *Daily News* observes "acres of onion quiches, cutesy postcards and strawberry daiquiris. But trying to get shoes reheeled or finding a decent hardware store is something else."

### HEALTH: Mecca in Ruins?

As crime and arson grow, trauma and burn cases rise in emergency rooms. As the foreclosure flood spreads abandonment, hospitals treat more tenants from unsanitary, overcrowded or unsafe housing. Yet in 1980, health lost its "essential service" rank in New York, as Mayor Koch gave this coveted status to highways and parks. He did this despite rising health demands and the fact that health was the city's leading industry, with $8 billion earned in 1979.

Ever since a Belle Vue clinic opened in 1784 on the current site of City Hall, public health has played a key role in New York. Starting with Irish and German refugees from the Great Hunger and the revolution of 1848, then growing with the onslaught from Central Europe and Italy between 1880 and 1920, the city welcomed 15 million immigrants as the "golden door" to America. These immigrants, and 6 million more after 1920, were often unhealthy, so the greatest health system in history was improvised to meet their needs. The early 1900s saw many public-health firsts: the free milk stations of Nathan Straus, and the first VD and well-baby clinics were among many landmarks. By the end of the La Guardia era in 1945, there were thirty-two comprehensive health clinics forming the biggest such urban network on earth.

The result today is a unique chain of sixteen public hospitals run by the city's Health and Hospitals Corporation (HHC) as the biggest nonfederal hospital system in the world. The sixteen HHC hospitals provide 4.7 million clinic visits and 3.1 million inpatient days a year to more than 3 million New Yorkers who, for reasons of age, income or geography, have nowhere else to go. Among these people are residents from five sizable middle-class areas in the Bronx, Brooklyn and Queens. Since the City Charter guarantees accessible, quality care to all New Yorkers regardless of their ability to pay, the HHC system gives some $250 million in free care annually to more than 2 million residents who earn too much to qualify for Medicaid and too little to buy Blue Cross.

Since Medicare and Medicaid let the poor and the elderly use private hospitals, they also play a major role in public health. The number of private doctors has shrunk by 45 percent since 1968, so clinic visits to both HHC and private hospitals have soared. New York City's 65 private hospitals include seven teaching centers and many world-famous specialty centers. They draw 12 percent of their patients from beyond the city, which adds more than $340 million a year to the local economy.

Yet the world's medical mecca may soon be in ruins. The 2 million medical indigents of New York cost the public and private hospitals roughly $340 million a year in free care. As a result, even Middle American communities have private hospitals with huge deficits. Wyckoff Heights Hospital serving the German and Italian neighborhood of Ridgewood, in Queens, lost $4.9 million in 1979, and has lived hand to mouth ever since. In the Jewish section of Borough Park, in Brooklyn, Maimonides Hospital lost $3.4 million for 1978, while Lutheran Medical Center in the Irish section of Bay Ridge lost $6.7 million in one year. All told, 31 of 113 hospitals in the city have closed since 1976, and another half-dozen could close inside a year.

In the public sector, while City Hall gives HHC a tax subsidy to cover things like the $250 million in annual free care, Mayor Koch has made unprecedented cuts in that support. By closing Sydenham Hospital in 1980, he closed down the only emergency room for the vast West Harlem area. By cutting the HHC subsidy, Koch deepened the problems for those "hospitals of last resort" for 3 million New Yorkers. These are also the busiest hospitals in New York. Nine of the city's ten busiest emergency rooms are in the HHC system. There is specialized trauma care at public hospitals like Jacobi in the Bronx, Kings County in Brooklyn or America's most famous ER at Bellevue, where a famed microsurgery team stitches back severed fingers, hands, arms and, in one famous case, two legs in an eighteen-hour operation.

The private hospitals lack even the shrinking subsidies from Mayor Koch. To make up for $90 million lost for free indigent care in 1980, they must rely on philanthropy, ingenuity or the charity of creditors. They cannibalize endowments, they sell equipment, they mortgage property, they borrow from banks, they fend off vendors, and they close. Even world-famous Mount Sinai and Columbia Presbyterian lost $5 million and $11 million respectively in 1978. As their clientele gets older, sicker and poorer in a waning city, so do the private hospitals of New York.

Most of the twenty-seven private hospitals closed after 1976 were in slums. In a domino effect, their patients moved on to nearby survivors. When six private hospitals closed in Central Brooklyn, a fiscal crisis erupted at the surviving Brooklyn Jewish Hospital nearby. In five years 5,200 beds were closed or decertified, so a rash of overcrowded hospitals occurred. An average occupancy of 84 percent in 1978 jumped to nearly 90 percent by 1979. The winter of 1980 found twenty-four hospitals at more than 100 percent occupancy, with ambulances shuttling patients in search of empty beds. Even during slow summer months, nine hospitals closed down their emergency rooms for a third of their shifts due to overcrowded wards. At one point in the fall of 1980, there wasn't an empty bed in the Bronx for two days.

A chronic shortage of nurses means a widening "white-cap gap" as the hospitals get overcrowded, supplies run out, and support personnel like messengers or nurse's aides are cut to save money. When St. Luke's Hospital runs out of toilet paper or another hospital uses sanitary napkins for surgical dressings, nurses leave. Too much forced overtime to cover the wards means even more exhausted RNs. Recent strikes by nurses at private hospitals have tended to be over working conditions as much as wages.

A statewide survey by the Hospital Association of New York State found that 222 hospitals had cannibalized $498 million in assets over five years. At that rate, the HANYS survey concluded, there would be no endowments left by January 1, 1995. Some suggest two main causes of the growing hospital debts: too many beds and inefficiency. The surplus-beds theory goes back to 1975, when there were 5,000 extra beds in New York City. But five years of hospital closings cut or decertified 5,200 beds, and the debts kept growing. The private hospitals alone lost $115 million in 1977 and then $124 million in 1979. Two years later, state planners still clung to the 5,000-extra-bed number, but overcrowded hospitals and ambulances shuttling patients about told a different story.

Extra beds and inefficiency were partly responsible for rising debts, but the two main scourges were too many indigents and restrictive state Medicaid controls. The indigents include 1.4 million working poor New Yorkers who earn too much for Medicaid coverage, and perhaps 750,000 illegal aliens who cannot qualify for public aid. Washington will not cover these 2 million, while Albany creates many of them through cost controls so tight that as Medicaid costs rose 48 percent across America, they inched up only 13 percent in New York. The three basic Albany controls may be called No Pay, Low Pay, Slow Pay.

• No Pay is restricted Medicaid eligibility. A family of four earning more than $5,000 in 1981 made too much for Medicaid coverage in New York, and some 900,000 residents lost coverage this way after 1969. They and 500,000 other working-poor indigents cause almost all of the $340 million lost by public and private hospitals to free care each year. Illegal aliens leave few unpaid bills. Ira Clark, director of Kings County Hospital Center, says that "when a guy goes out of his way to pay me, that's an illegal alien. He's scared stiff I'll turn him over to a collection agency, and they'll tip off Immigration. But some working poor guy with no Medicaid? Hell, you can repossess his *bathtub,* but he still doesn't pay!"

• Low Pay is the difference between what Medicaid pays and the actual costs for hospitals. A Medicaid "cap" on clinic payments allowed a maximum payment of $55 a visit in 1981, though hospitals averaged $70 in costs. The $15 lost for each Medicaid clinic visit, added to free indigent care, made for huge losses. Irwin Birnbaum, chief fiscal officer at Montefiore Hospital, in the stable North Bronx, observes that "our clinic losses are $4 million a year, and we're *not* a slum area. We have a lot of Medicare patients at Amalgamated Houses and Co-op City, but also a lot of working poor. We cover clinic losses through philanthropy, or things like private rooms and electives. But look, I'm not declaring dividends these days . . ."

• Slow Pay saw Albany keep Medicaid payments three months in arrears, about $200 million owed to the hospitals. The state lived off the borrowed cash, as hospitals fended off creditors, or borrowed at high interest rates. At one point, blood banks asked for $7 million owed them by hospitals owed $200 million by the state. Someone recalled "a real standoff, with neither side able to go on borrowing forever. But what can you do without blood?" Albany sustained the sluggish cash flow with endless changes in Medicaid rates and rules, with hospitals hopping to avoid new penalties or payment mazes. In 1979, hospitals were penalized for too many empty beds. In 1980, they were penalized for too many filled beds. Dr. S. David Pomrinse, the president of the Greater New York Hospital Association, notes that the endless Medicaid rate and rule changes "elevate hospital fiscal officers to godlike status, because those who can wend their way through the morass of fiscal rules and regulations and get their hospitals through another year are indeed worth their weight in gold."

These Medicaid cost controls save Albany a fortune, as hospitals founder or fold. The three controls saved the state at least $75 million a year. Had Governor Carey and the legislature deferred only 3 percent of the huge tax cut since 1978, and spent $75 million on Medicaid instead, this would have produced $225 million more in federal and local matching funds. This $300 million would have virtually wiped out deficits at all the private and public hospitals of New York State.

As the middle class continues to leave in the 1980s, New York will get poorer and older. Health demands will grow as health dollars shrink. There are five expanding health demands ahead.

• *1. More Poor People.* In 1969, the poor were 15 percent of New York City; by 1983, they had a 24 percent share. Add the estimated 750,000 illegal aliens, most of them working poor, and roughly one in four New Yorkers is either poor or near poor. Since the poor continue to have high birth rates, their share of the city would increase even without a middle-class exodus. Without adequate welfare payments, stable housing and a renewed federal jobs program, the health demands of these people can only grow.

• *2. More Elderly People.* The aged were 13 percent of New York in 1975 and are about 16 percent today. Their share should also grow in the 1980s, especially among those over seventy-five. Twenty-five percent of the elderly households are at or near the poverty line today, with many elderly whites living on fixed incomes as "holdouts" in minority slums like the West Bronx or the Lower East Side. There are also growing numbers of black senior citizens in Harlem and Bedford-Stuyvesant. Even today, New York's elderly use hospitals at a very high rate—only the aged of Boston use them more. While the aged, disabled and blind were only 25 percent of all Medicaid clients in 1979, they were 59 percent of all costs. Indeed, by 1983, City Hall has projected that Medicaid costs for the elderly alone will be two-thirds of all new program costs.

• *3. More Illegal Aliens.* While forming the industrious backbone of New York's cheap labor market, illegal aliens are a negative pressure for indigent debts and public health. While 1.4 million working poor cause most of the hospital debts, uninsured aliens figure as well. As for public health, there is the recent growth of sweatshops manned by illegal aliens.*

---

* New drugs like isoniazid cut 2,157 TB deaths in 1954 down to 283 by 1978. Then TB suddenly rose 17 percent in 1979, after thirty consecutive years of decline. Overcrowded aliens from countries with high TB rates helped revive this nineteenth-century disease, with cuts in Health Department control programs possibly

• *4. Less Public Health.* The Department of Health, built up over a century of immigration since 1880, is now The Sick Man of New York. For 1977 alone, the DOH lost 25 percent of its staff, against a citywide agency attrition of 1 percent. Altogether, the DOH has closed 8 of the city's 32 comprehensive clinics and more than 100 specialty clinics. All these cuts mean that the Department of Health has lost 400,000 annual visits. As cheap, preventive public health breaks down, this hurts the sixteen public hospitals in the HHC system in two ways. More people are added to the 4.7 million clinic visits in the system each year, and less preventive health care means more sick patients in HHC hospital beds.

• *5. More Mental Patients.* Perhaps the saddest symbols of New York's service crisis are patients released from state mental hospitals into the city's streets. A state hospital census of 85,000 patients in 1965 was down to 23,000 by 1983. City Council President Carol Bellamy noted that an average mental hospital stay of ten years in 1970 went down to one of twenty-four days by 1980. She pointed out how, despite a 70 percent drop in patients since 1965, only twenty-three underused mental hospitals consumed 85 percent of state mental health funds in 1982. These near-empty hospitals often were virtual jobs programs for upstate communities. Some $350 million was spent on caring for only 23,000 hospital patients, but only $170 million for community support or medical services for 80,000 chronic, mentally ill people in communities.

The tragic results of the state's "deinstitutionalization" policy are well known in New York City: filthy "street people" in subways or public libraries, "bag ladies" living in mounds of rags, or some who even live in dark steam tunnels far below Grand Central Station. An army of vagrants projected at 36,000 homeless citizens wanders the city's streets. In one tragedy, a derelict's body was found on a filthy mattress in a crypt under the sidewalk at 63 Wall Street. The man had been dead for five months.

During the 1970s, parts of the city like the Upper West Side

---

playing a part as well. Latins also bring tropical diseases. There were more than 6,000 active cases of parasitism and 300 of leprosy at last count in New York. Yet, although illegal aliens keep arriving from Latin America, Mayor Koch closed two of the city's three tropical-disease clinics in 1979.

had been swamped by state patients, many of them living in seedy "single room occupancy" hotels (SROs). After 1975, however, as rich Manhattan households grew and rents were bid up, even SROs were targets for rehab and resale as luxury condominiums. As the city gave handsome tax breaks for rehabbing, most SRO hotels were rapidly and brutally cleared. Fifty thousand SRO units in 1975 shrank to 19,000 units by 1980, at which point the phrase "street people" entered the media lexicon. The Bowery Men's Shelter and Catholic Worker outposts were overwhelmed. During the six days after Christmas in 1980, six men died of exposure on the streets.

The issue got so much coverage in early 1981 that Mayor Koch and Governor Carey began pointing fingers. Koch had the better claim. He could point to how Albany saved millions by dumping patients into the streets, since instead of paying 100 percent of state hospital costs, Albany paid only 25 percent for Medicaid outpatient costs. Defending Albany's outrageous policies, mental health "coordinator" Sara M. Connell informed the *Times* that "we don't admit people who are maybe a little strange and don't have a place to live. We are not a shelter. The city has not yet confronted the issue."

But the crisis was mainly caused by state dumping in the first place, rather than by city tax abatements encouraging rehab of SRO hotels later on. Another Albany diversion from this basic issue was to attack communities for not welcoming the unwanted state wards with open arms. As Ethel Sheffer and Raymond Schwartz of the West Side SRO Task Force wrote in a letter to the *Times,* Albany bureaucrats "had the effrontery to blame communities for not accepting this bewildering burden and at the same time implicitly blame their own clients for growing more disturbed, dependent and distressed." Albany's prime role in all this was transparent. The *Daily News* ran a blunt editorial, demanding an end to the state's miserly, passive and irresponsible role in emptying out hospitals.

Koch failed to handle the flood of street people. When social services commissioner Barbara Blum suggested city shelters in twenty-five neighborhoods, Koch called her a "crazy lady," adding that the new shelters would be "like spreading twenty-five cancers." At one point, he proposed rounding up all vagrants and holding them for seventy-two hours to give them food, a bath and medical care. The Civil Liberties Union attacked this idea, noting that removing vagrants "from the sight of other citizens is not going to improve their lot." By late 1981, Koch finally was supplying adequate shelter in armories, and 30 percent more vagrants had flooded in. In Albany, "coordinator" Connell attacked Koch's new shelters: "A society is really judged by how it takes care of its least desirable people and we are not doing a very good job of it." *

A stream of suits filed by lawyer Robert Hayes, a survey by the Community Service Society and activism from State Supreme Court Justice Richard Wallach helped focus public opinion on New York City's street people. In 1978, the year before Hayes began filing suits, the city had only 1,000 beds for the homeless in a program spending $8 million. By 1982 it was spending $32 million and had 4,350 beds. But the process remains grim. Winter months find thousands of vagrants housed in three armories, and shuttled by bus for gang showers and mass meals at the huge Men's Shelter on the Bowery. The solution is to open more permanent community homes for stable patients and keep the seriously disturbed patients in state hospitals for treatment. The funds for this job can come from a long-overdue closing and consolidation of the twenty-three underused state hospitals. This can provide a strong program of community shelters and aftercare, nearly twenty years after the wholesale releasing of patients began.

To conclude this section, let us look at some private hospitals that mirror the growing health crisis:

• **Bronx-Lebanon Hospital** is in two separate divisions, each anchoring solid parts of the South Bronx. A Gothic fortress serves housing projects and homeowner blocks near Claremont Park. The other wing serves residents of some fine Deco apartment buildings on the Grand Concourse. The odd problem here is that both areas serve viable slums and Medicaid covers only welfare

---

* One notes that Albany wasn't the only capital saving money by putting mental patients in communities with little aftercare. Legions of street people in most big cities are familiar sights today. In proposing the 1963 Community Mental Health Centers Act, President Kennedy predicted the centers could cut mental hospital populations in half. But the centers mainly went unbuilt, as state and county hospitals went from 505,000 patients in 1963 to 138,000 by early 1982. Even by 1975, public service workers' union president Jerry Wurf said "a lofty idea . . . has become something very ugly."

clients, not the working poor. For serving two areas of hardworking indigents, Bronx-Lebanon loses $4 million a year in free care.

Its fiscal crisis grew in three stages: the opening of Co-op City, the closing of two nearby public hospitals in 1976, and the Medicaid cost controls from Albany ever since. Co-op City's debut in the Northeast Bronx swept up the middle class and elderly from the Concourse with their Blue Cross and Medicare coverage. When Mayor Beame closed the two public hospitals in 1976, their indigents wound up at Bronx-Lebanon's two doors. Having lost Blue Cross and Medicare patients and gained indigents, Bronx-Lebanon now faced the state cost controls, which thinned the hospital's Medicaid census from 75 percent of its patients to just 50 percent by 1981. Hospital President Fred Silverman notes that

> even the poor get raises, so as families earned over $5,000, they lost Medicaid coverage. Only New York, Massachusetts and Michigan control Medicaid so closely. The other states give hospitals a pretty free hand in setting rates, and they don't have our burden of the working poor. And you know, if a patient isn't covered in *those* states—well the private hospital ships them to the County Hospital. We won't do that at Bronx-Lebanon.

The two units nearly closed in 1978. To Albany's credit, it improvised a special Medicaid advance payment to cover losses created by its own cost controls. Meanwhile, the big hospital has 90 percent occupancy, more than 200,000 clinic visits a year, and the second busiest private emergency room in New York. An active Ladies Auxiliary donates more than 70,000 hours a year. This hospital is loved, as well as needed. Yet both Mayor Koch and the federal Health Systems Agency have at various times proposed closing down one of its divisions.*

• *Wyckoff Heights Hospital* is one of several private hospitals with debts in middle-class areas. It serves the Germans and Italians of

---

* A fine example of working-poor voluntarism involves the Hunts Point Lions Club, which raised $24,000 in five months to buy Bronx-Lebanon a mobile health van. The van will focus on the high infant-mortality rate in the area, nearly double America's rate. Half the babies born at Bronx-Lebanon in 1981 were premature or low weight, so the van will educate expectant mothers, especially teen-agers prone to having low-weight babies. The van will also screen for hypertension, vision problems and the lead poisoning that affects all too many slum children.

Ridgewood, a homeowner area and one of the city's major Republican strongholds. This is still a stable base of cottage industry. There are more than 150 knitting mills in the area, many of them small operations in backyards. Yet this modern hospital lost $4.9 million in 1979 for serving this stable seat of the bourgeoisie.

Since its founding by the Deutsche Hospital Gesellschaft in 1894, this has been the only hospital for a huge area, with 380,000 people today. Albany realized how crucial the hospital was in 1975 by giving it a $24 million loan to build a new wing of 250 beds. The wing had a new emergency room, and those visits jumped from 22,000 to 50,000 a year. But clinics mean big losses under Albany's Medicaid cap on payments, so the busier the ER got, the more the debts grew.

The cap on clinic payments plus indigent losses meant $2.2 million lost in 1979. Then a federal Medicare rule deducted costs of nonelderly services like obstetrics. A big maternity service and a census that was 54 percent elderly saw Wyckoff Heights lose another $2 million off the deductions from Medicare payments. Late in 1979, the hospital was in trouble. A coalition led by Representative Shirley Chisholm and senior citizens led by Peter Orlando backed the trustees in keeping it open. They got a better Medicaid rate, settled some Medicare arrears, but cost controls kept piling up debts. Bankruptcy and even closing still threaten this busy modern hospital.

• *North General Hospital* in Harlem is on Marcus Garvey Park, once the solid Jewish neighborhood of Richard Rodgers' youth, now a Landmark District slowly coming back. Victorian brownstones and Romanesque churches in the area are handsome resources, and young professional couples are moving in. But the renaissance in Harlem may founder as health services fold. Back in 1977, HEW Secretary Joseph Califano called this "the worst served urban health area in America"—after which, Harlem lost three of its five hospitals as Flower & Fifth Avenue, Arthur Logan and Sydenham closed by 1980. Just as two closed public hospitals left indigent patients at Bronx-Lebanon's door, so did Sydenham impact North General, which lost $1 million for 1980. Late that year, North General's president wrote Governor Carey, warning that "the Harlem community is about to lose yet another hospital." In early 1981 the hospital had no assets. Even the building belonged to another hospital on the grounds of Beth Israel Hospital downtown.*

A 90 percent occupancy rate and 120,000 clinic visits a year made North General a vital Harlem resource. The spectacle of it closing only six months after Sydenham inspired Governor Carey to save North General.

The HHC system is often perceived as one big charity ward. But it's also a major service for the middle class in the Outer Boroughs, which have few hospitals compared to the famed specialty centers of Manhattan's East Side. Elmhurst and Queens Hospital Center are the two major hospitals in that huge homeowner borough. Woodhull Hospital serves a large section of northern Brooklyn plus Long Island City, in Queens, both middle-class ethnic areas. Coney Island Hospital is the major specialty center for more than 700,000 people in southern Brooklyn. This vast area in the HHC system ranges from the Jewish projects of Brighton Beach to the Italian homeowners of Bath Beach and the upper-middle-class residents of Mill Basin, many of them with marinas and yachts on Jamaica Bay.

One HHC hospital that is particularly crucial for the middle class is Jacobi Hospital in the North Bronx. With the sixth busiest emergency room in America, this is the main trauma center for the Bronx, and its 170,000 emergency room visits are twice the volume at the more famous Bellevue ER. A veritable country club, Jacobi is on sixty-two landscaped acres, with two hospitals, four staff residences, six tennis courts, and the Rose Kennedy Center for Mental Retardation. The complex is located on the verdant Pelham Parkway, in one of the most conservative homeowner areas in New York. These voters form the backbone of the tax revolt that would close down public hospitals like Jacobi.

Jacobi has been in constant turmoil since the fiscal crisis of 1975 erupted. Leonard Piccoli, its executive director since 1972, recalls the plague years:

---

* Health advocate Judy Wessler recalls Beth Israel's previous role in another case of health cuts for slums. "In 1974, Beth Israel was part of a group which said that the public Gouverneur Hospital should not open a surgical operating room, since the Lower East Side didn't 'need' it. They won. Without a surgery, Gouverneur could be closed as a hospital in 1976—and the Lower East Side no longer has an emergency room, despite all the young minority families and the elderly Jewish families."

> In the fall of 1974, we suddenly had to fire 200 people in 48 hours. So we put up charts of our personnel on the walls of a very big room. Then we marched our Chiefs around from chart to chart. It was "I'll give you a Senior Clerk and a couple of Messengers" stuff. We got 150 names—50 short. So we marched everyone around the room again . . .

After losing the 200 support personnel, an eighteen-month hiring freeze occurred as Jacobi's staff shrank from 3,500 to 2,800.

HHC President Joseph C. Hoffman imposed a second hiring freeze, on April Fool's Day of 1979. Beds had to be cut again, and Jacobi often went on "treat and release" status for the emergency room; ambulances could bring in only severe emergencies. Since ambulance drops form 80 percent of Jacobi's usual census, going on treat and release was a revenue disaster. As Jacobi reeled from City Hall cuts, the staff morale declined again as well. Regular nursing ranks shrank after 1978, as temporary "per diem" hires nearly tripled in two years. The per diems had only marginal value, since regular RNs had to constantly orient the interim nurses. HHC's vice president for nursing noted there was no guarantee that the per diem nurses were "safe nursing practitioners." Desperate for more staff nurses, Piccoli went beyond the usual sources in the Philippines for some reverse Lend-Lease, importing sixty-five nurses from England in the fall of 1980.

Albany's fiscal role in the crisis has been detailed, but what of Washington and City Hall? The federal role is easily summarized: there is no national health insurance system to pay for $250 million lost by HHC hospitals to free care each year, and the Reagan cuts for Medicaid may cost Albany $300 million a year.

As for City Hall, it often views the HHC system as a gold mine. Mayor Koch has focused on the tactical role of the sixteen public hospitals as revenue producers, rather than their strategic survival as hospitals for 3 million New Yorkers. HHC hospitals are fine investments. In 1979, for example, they spent $1.2 billion and earned back $795 million, or 65 cents for every dollar spent. No city agency remotely comes close to that rate of return.*

---

* Recall that HHC hospitals lose $250 million annually to free care, and $85 million more to Medicaid penalties, including the cap on clinic payments. Add that $335 million to the $795 million revenues, and HHC in 1979 actually lost only $80 million that year, most of that off poor billing/collection procedures reformed in the next year.

Off improved billing and collection, public hospitals made an extra $105 million in 1980. Instead of putting some of this back into the system for more staff and upgrading of physical plant, Koch used the full $105 million to close 22 percent of the city's budget gap for fiscal 1981. For another $30 or $40 million of the HHC gains, Koch could have "reindustrialized" his own public hospitals. More staff and more attractive wards would have led to more beds filled, even more revenues to cover fixed costs, just as Leonard Piccoli had done at Jacobi in 1977.

New York virtually invented public-health care during the last century. But since the fiscal crisis eruption in 1975, it has torn up the system.

## THE SUBWAYS: Chaos

On the morning of January 14, 1981, icy winds knocked out power to a third of New York's aging subway fleet, stranding 300,000 commuters for nearly an hour. After six years of deferred maintenance, the subways had inevitably collapsed. There were dark trains, freezing trains, stuck doors, short trains, a sea of graffiti, abandoned trains, and often simply no trains. Platforms filled up and stress rose like steam among the 2 million weekday commuters who form 30 percent of all mass-transit users in America. The head of a stress center at Presbyterian Hospital told the *Times* that harried commuters "have to go right in to work. It's stress piled on top of stress." One senior partner in a Wall Street law firm informed the *Times* that "vast numbers of persons are not at our early meetings. When you're a partner, you don't suddenly retire. How can you tell people who work for you to come in at 8 or 8:30, when you walk in at 9 or 9:30?"

"Travel time" for 2 million workers in Manhattan, and 1.2 million workers elsewhere, was growing. Even back in 1971, it was a factor in the relocation of a *Fortune* 500 firm to Denver, with the company president telling the *Times* a decade later how the company, in its New York days, got "no more than a 27-hour workweek by the time you take into account lunch hours and commuting problems. It's more like a 40-hour week out in Denver. People come to work daily and they tend to stay till they finish whatever they are doing, rather than rushing for a train."

After the fiscal crisis began in 1975, subway maintenance declined even more. Bankers like Felix Rohatyn compounded the problems by demanding fare hikes to placate the bond markets.

A raise from 35 to 50 cents per ride was passed in 1975 after thirty minutes of debate, but the bond market stayed closed for six more years. As Joe Conason wrote in *The Village Voice,* however, "it did help to close the market for the mass-transit system, causing a loss of millions of riders from which the system has never recovered."

Service cuts were piled on top of fare hikes as subway and bus miles were cut 20 percent between 1975 and 1978. Add flat capital spending and cuts in maintenance staff after 1975, and the subway spiral got deeper. Fare hikes, less maintenance and fewer daily runs meant far fewer riders and less revenue to cover fixed operating costs and, thus, higher fares to balance budgets, and even fewer riders. By 1981, George Sternlieb of Rutgers found enough subway chaos to threaten "an abrupt downturn" in New York's new office building boom. Frank G. Zarb, a Lehman Brothers partner and former federal energy czar under President Ford, warned that "the basic economic viability of our city is negatively affected."

Subways and business are a symbiosis in New York. Samuel M. Ehrenhalt, Regional Commissioner of the federal Bureau of Labor Statistics, observes the subway-work link in one striking fact: 42 percent of metro New York workers use mass transit with Chicago a distant second at an 18 percent share. Ehrenhalt points out "the great joker, the federal mass-transit aid formula. It's based on population, not ridership. So New York gets less than *half* per rider what all other cities get." With 30 percent of America's mass-transit riders, New York gets only 11 percent of federal funds. This share is even less than that for Nashville, Chattanooga, Fort Worth, Spokane and Tallahassee, cities that together average 15,400 riders a day, or one-third the daily average ridership of New York at 4:00 A.M. Ehrenhalt adds that "a lot of people take the subway into Manhattan, with two million riders a day. But with all those short trains and crowded platforms today, you have to be a broken-field runner to catch a train! You start to feel, 'I'm lucky I got to the office at all . . .' "

A *Daily News* series by Richard Edmunds saw 1977 as the year when capital plant cracks began to show. It was also the year when rush-hour service was cut to forty minutes. Subway trains that went 14,000 miles without a breakdown in 1977 broke down in 1980 after 6,000 miles. One hundred and nineteen trips were abandoned each weekday in 1977, but about 500 were by 1981, a rise of 308 percent for breakdowns in three years. Although the subway system has had a fine safety record, the National Transportation Safety Board in late 1981 accused the Transit Authority of a "haphazard approach to safety" that might lead to "the most tragic consequences." Nicholas Pileggi noted in *New York* magazine that major car overhauls were abandoned after 1974, with the Transit Authority "relying instead on periodic inspections of cars after they have gone 10,000 miles or more. In Boston, cars are inspected every 5,000 miles and in Washington, a relatively new system, inspections are made every 3,000 miles." Thirteen derailments in the first eight months of 1983 pointed to a system on the edge of a catastrophe.

With even a good safety record in jeopardy, the financial leaders of New York went on the attack. The Federal Reserve Bank of New York estimated that the subway chaos inflicted $165 million in annual lost business, with $328 million more lost in worktime and productivity. Moody Investors Service refused an investment grade rating on city bonds, citing the subway mess and its threat to the local economy. Standard & Poor's gave a low rating of BBB to city bonds, tempering the tepid endorsement by warning that "the transit dilemma is of critical concern to both commuters and the city's business community . . . If the appropriate steps are not taken to rectify these problems, deterioration of the city's economic base and central business district will result."

The bond agencies that had demanded incessant service cuts from Mayors Beame and Koch attacked the mess they had helped create. Even bond raters with no interest in services for ordinary New Yorkers knew what subway chaos did to the bottom line. Realtor Lewis Rudin, head of the business-oriented Association for a Better New York, had promoted service cuts for citizens and tax cuts for developers and realtors. But even he told the *Times* in 1981: "We've reached the point now that it's critical for department stores, for service industries, for the general business climate, to get this mass-transit system running properly—clean, safe, on time . . . [without fast relief] the companies will eventually say, 'That's enough,' and they'll move elsewhere."

The momentum for transit aid grew. In the summer of 1981, the state legislature passed a $5.6 billion subsidy, to be spread over a decade. This was still far short of the $14 billion capital plan of the Transit Authority. Only federal aid could cover the rest. But the federal transit aid formula remained based on population rather than ridership. As a congressman, Ed Koch had led forces that broke open the highway trust fund for mass-transit aid. As mayor, he pressed for revising the federal formula.

Despite cuts in food stamps, school lunches, CETA jobs and $400 million in annual aid to New York City, Reagan also proposes ending all federal operating subsidies for mass transit by 1984. All Reagan "offers" the city in the transit line is the West Side Highway, or Westway: a 4.2-mile highway that would cost $1.4 billion, or $8,600 an inch. After taking more stands on Westway than a cloverleaf intersection, Koch now supports the building of this lavish road for only 80,000 daily users, instead of trading in the Westway funds for transit aid to help 3.5 million daily users of buses and subways. Westway is to New York in the 1980s as the Moscow subway was to Russia in the 1930s, a costly diversion.

The aging subways await minor upgradings from the 1981 subsidies. Meanwhile, in a historic break with the capital of the publishing industry, William Jovanovich cited subway chaos as the main reason for Harcourt Brace Jovanovich moving most operations to Florida and California. Noting office space costs, energy costs and taxes as lesser reasons for relocation after 1982, he added that "the cost of space was not decisive in itself. As a national and international company, H.B.J. requires varied working hours. Such scheduling is not generally afforded in New York City. In my own view, the greatest social need of adults in New York City is a variable, reliable and safe transportation system."

A footnote on the subway chaos concerns its impact on street traffic. As subway fares rose and ridership fell, car use and congestion grew. In 1950, the fare was 10 cents, subways had 2 billion annual riders, and 700,000 cars entered and left Manhattan each day. Then fares rose sixfold, subway ridership was cut in half, and the number of cars doubled. By the 1982 fiscal year, the fare was 75 cents, subways had only 990 million riders, and 1.5 million cars visited Manhattan each day. By 1984 the fare had risen to 90 cents. Noting the fall of subways, rise of cars symbiosis, traffic chief Samuel I. Schwartz of the city's Transportation Department told the *Times* that "it means I have more customers, but I don't want any more customers. . . . We are not going to solve the traffic problem without solving the mass-transit problem." Once the world's busiest transit system, New York's was now fifth after those of Moscow, Tokyo, Paris and Mexico City.

As traffic crawled in Midtown, the word "gridlock" became a media cliché. Crosstown traffic dropped from an average of 6 miles an hour to 4.4 miles. The addition of more than 35 million square feet of office space in Midtown and Wall Street by 1985 suggested even worse congestion ahead. The opening of the huge IBM and AT&T buildings on Madison Avenue between 55th and 57th Streets made the crucial 57th Street corridor even more impassable. But even before their opening, Nicholas Pileggi wrote in *New York* magazine in 1981 that

> congestion is so heavy today that city ambulances (which have a 34 percent breakdown rate) take twice as long to respond to an emergency as do ambulances in any other city in the nation. According to the Regional Medical Services Council, 5,000 cardiac and trauma victims died last year on city streets because paramedics couldn't reach them in time.

As car traffic doubled, dangerous driving also occurred. In recent years, "traffic anarchy" grew as motorists ran red lights and ignored stop signs or speed limits. One city study showed that where one in fourteen drivers jumped red lights in 1980, one in eight did by 1982. The *Times* used radar to find seventy-two of seventy-eight cars exceeding the speed limit on Park Avenue.

Compounding the traffic chaos are new forms of transit. Express buses ship workers from Midtown to the North Bronx and to southern Brooklyn, and add to congestion by parking at angles to Midtown curbs while taking on long lines of subscribers. A new fleet of 6,000 powder-blue Peugeots from Fugazy Express competes with taxis for the more lucrative radio calls. Today, New York has five kinds of transit for five classes of people. Fugazy and taxis compete for radio calls from the very rich, taxis pick up pedestrians for prices only the upper middle class can afford, express buses are for the middle class, gypsy cabs help the working poor and poor in slums, and the aging subways and buses are for 2 million weekday workers. Eighty years after August Belmont opened the first Guastavino-tiled subway station near City Hall, the aging system is only the fifth best transit in town and the fifth most traveled on earth.

To be sure, the subways remain a cheap, efficient, rapid and generally safe system. It still takes only half an hour to go from Times Square to the country estates of Riverdale, or forty-five minutes from Greenwich Village to Aqueduct racetrack near the bay, and the subway still costs only 90 cents a ride, against $2 in London for often shorter distances.

The subways are often visible whipping boys for New Yorkers who want and deserve better services elsewhere: more cops, more firemen, more hospital nurses in wards. The subways are also the home for service-crisis victims. It is hard to find a subway car free of drug addicts, derelicts, or mental patients from state hospitals. The sight of them, the graffiti and the broken doors is translated by average straphangers into a "subway crisis." Thirteen derailments in 1983, however, were signs of a very real crisis.

## JOBS: Two Cities

The 1980s began with talk of an economic revival in New York, but behind the boom in Wall Street and Midtown was a second, dying city.

• *1. Office Boom . . . Local Jobs.* The Empire State Building has long been a barometer of New York's economic health. Containing many small firms from most sectors of the local economy, the Empire State's occupancy rate has reflected citywide boom or bust. Opened in the Depression, the landmark filled up only as World War II revived the economy. Its occupancy fell during three Eisenhower recessions, went back up in the booming 1960s, then down again to 89 percent occupancy during Nixon-Ford recessions. By late 1980, however, the Empire State Building was at 98 percent occupancy in the middle of a recession. All seemed well in New York.

A building spree in the 1980s saw New York expand its existing office space more than 25 percent in only five years. Around 1986, the headquarters capital of the world should finish its fourth skyline.

Skyline #1 began in Wall Street with the Singer Tower of 1908 and Woolworth Building of 1913. It ended in Midtown with two Deco landmarks, the Chrysler Building of 1930 and the Empire

State of 1931. By then there were about 35 million square feet of office space in Manhattan.

Skyline #2 was the result of a postwar splurge of tasteless modernist architecture, apart from the distinctive Chase Manhattan Bank, Lever and Seagram buildings. Park Avenue was flooded by high-rises with setbacks, and much of the distinctive Wall Street skyline was blurred by boxy forms. Fifty-eight million square feet of office space was added from 1954 through 1966.

Skyline #3 was even bigger. Sixty-one million square feet of new space was built between 1967 and 1972. This boom ended as the 1970 recession saw office jobs decline. The start of front-office relocation from New York began. By 1972, the office vacancy rate was up to 14.8 percent, with 31 million square feet of space to let. The World Trade Center alone added 9 million square feet to a glutted market. Only by 1978 did demand catch up with the supply of office space.

Skyline #4 began after 1978 and still grows today. In 1982 alone fifteen new office towers opened with 7.5 million square feet of space, the vacancy rate was down to 3 percent and rents sometimes quadrupled the levels of 1975. Through 1986, another thirty-five towers with 35 million square feet are planned beyond 183 million square feet today. Crowning Skyline #4 in 1986 will be a World Financial Center in Battery Park City, at the foot of Manhattan. Before then, however, there could be a repeat of the 1970s glut, leaving high vacancy rates and depressed rents in its wake.

Foreign business fueled part of the boom. There was heavy British investing behind four Wall Street towers. The Canadian firm of Olympia & York was building all over New York; among its projects was Battery Park City. Nearly 200 foreign bank branches operated in New York, and the city's banks financed over a third of America's foreign trade. International insurers also grew rapidly, with a new Insurance Exchange similar to Lloyd's opening among the many carriers along William Street downtown. Altogether, banks and insurers had almost 25 percent of the city's office space in 1982, and employed 250,000 workers. Much of their trade related to foreign business and, by 1981, nearly 15 percent of city office space was leased by foreign firms lured by longer leases and lower rents than those found in Hamburg, London or Paris.

The office boom did nothing for local workers. The new jobs

went mainly to commuters with specialized skills. Ad men, accountants, bankers, brokers, insurers, lawyers, publicists and realtors tended to live in the suburbs. Indeed, 600,000 daily workers commute to New York, a bigger work force than the local work forces of all but six American cities. Between 1978 and 1981, while New York gained 108,000 new jobs, its residents lost 16,000 jobs. The reason was the loss of 48,000 factory jobs at the same time, just the kind of work that the city's increasingly unskilled workers could do.

|  | 1950 | 1981 | |
|---|---|---|---|
| Factory Jobs | 1,040,000 | 480,000 | −54% |
| Finance and | | | |
| Service Jobs | 850,000 | 1,400,000 | +65 |

Almost all the recent job gains have been in Manhattan. From March of 1977 to March of 1981, for example, while the city added 150,300 new jobs, Manhattan added 150,700, as the four Outer Boroughs lost 400. Noting the growing gap between Manhattan and Outer Borough economies and the skilled and unskilled people they represent, economist Robert Lekachman wondered to the *Times* in 1982 about "what the consequences of this sort of two-world phenomenon will be for social stability."

Early in 1981, Desmond Smith wrote a *New York* cover story on what he dubbed "Info City," describing "the most massive restructuring of the city's economy since the Industrial Revolution. Just as Pittsburgh has meant steel, and Detroit has meant cars, New York is becoming the information capital—not just of the United States, but of the world." New elements like cable TV, credit cards, personal computers and electronic mail were being added to New York's longtime role as the world capital of banking and communications, as well as the capital of our networks, our advertising and publishing industries, and our stock market. Smith recalled how local clearinghouses had handled 38.2 trillion checks in 1980. The Stock Exchange handled 149 million shares on October 7, 1982, 46 million traded in the first hour. By 1981, some 46 percent of the city's jobs were related to information handling. The world's biggest factory town of 1950 was now capital to the Postindustrial Age.

But as Smith observed, "An information-based economy is labor-releasing, not labor-intensive." The city's second biggest private employer, New York Telephone, lost 30 percent of its jobs between 1970 and 1978, as automation helped cut 22,000 telephone and telegraph jobs citywide (in contrast, electric and gas utility jobs fell by only 100 in that period). As factories closed and services are automated, Smith's conclusion about Info City raised the specter of

> the rise of a super-rich mercantile class at the expense of the disadvantaged. New York, after a hundred or so years as the melting pot, has entered the age of the Uncommon Man. The common man has virtually no future in the brave new city. White-collar, high-technology jobs are no help to the unskilled poor.

At best, they might land jobs straining their eyes on a Vydec display screen, as a "machine tender" in an isolated office "data center." And even this was marginal, given the rapid strides in automation.

The gap has grown between New York and national work-force participation rates. In 1970, 58 percent of Americans over the age of sixteen had jobs, while 56 percent of New York's did. A decade of automation later, 59 percent of Americans over sixteen worked, against 51 percent in New York.

• **2.  Big Stuff . . . Small Firms.** In 1979, New York had 17.5 million visitors for a world's record. In 1980, a Wharton Econometric model projected a 7 percent rise in local retail sales, but city sales soared 18 percent, three times America's growth in a recession. Nineteen eighty also saw 6,000 hotel rooms open, and 90 percent occupancy rates in Midtown. In 1981, New York had 929 conventions or trade shows for 4.2 million people, against 1.8 million for runner-up Chicago. With more hotels than London and Paris combined, this is the top tourist and convention center in the world.

A $500 million Convention Center from I. M. Pei opening in 1986 will cover five blocks, and add 1,000 direct and up to 16,000 indirect jobs. An atrium hotel from John Portman will soon open near Times Square, with 2,600 rooms and an equal number of service jobs. A $250 million South Street Seaport from James

Rouse opened in the summer of 1983. The state and city have joint plans for a $1 billion redevelopment of the 42nd Street area, featuring four office towers with 4 million square feet of space, a 2.4-million-square-foot wholesale trade mart and a 500-room hotel.

But past the stores on Madison and Fifth Avenues, and beyond the luxury hotels and shopping malls, are the problems of more than 150,000 local firms with twenty-five employees or less, the small businesses that employ 1.7 million today. An example of their problems is how small service stores are driven from Manhattan by phenomenal rent hikes, as antique shops, bistros and luxury shops take their place. Mayor Koch won't back commercial rent control to save the barbers, bodegas, dry cleaners, hardware stores, mom-and-pops and the various kinds of repair shops crucial to daily city life. As useful services were driven from the West Side by wild rents, a resident told *The Wall Street Journal* that "now you go looking for shoes, and you're more likely to find a red-sequined jump suit in the window." Greenwich Village is also being overrun by bistros and boutiques, as small services are closed.

The same trend applies to hotels. Mayor Koch gives lavish tax breaks to luxury inns like the Helmsley Palace, where $140 a night is a cheap suite, while small hotels get no breaks. Family hotels in the $40- to $60-room range are good for tourists, but they went from 65 percent of all hotel rooms in 1975 to only 56 percent by 1981. Occupancy taxes are heavy burdens for these places, while they produce only trivial revenues for City Hall. Yet Mayor Koch refused to scrap the tax for rooms renting for under $50, while he handed out tax abatements to hoteliers with clout.

• **3. The Factory Losses.** The main disaster for New York's economy has been its industrial collapse since 1960. With 946,000 manufacturing jobs back then, this was the biggest factory town on earth. There are only 468,000 such jobs today. As New York lost only 7 percent of its overall jobs after 1960, it saw more than 50 percent of its manufacturing jobs disappear. This collapse has led to the grotesque good news that the city is fairly recession-proof. The loss of 290,000 factory jobs since 1970 alone has immunized New York against the boom-bust cycles that hit heavy-industry centers like Baltimore and Detroit. Boosters point to a city able to ride out hard times; realists note the hemorrhage of unskilled jobs.

The worst factory losses came between 1969 and 1976, when an average of 48,000 jobs were lost each year. Three years of stability followed, with only 500 factory jobs lost each year. Starting in 1979, factory losses resumed on an awesome scale, with 16,000 jobs lost annually through 1981.

Tax abatement was given by City Hall to those who converted factory lofts to luxury housing. A wave of factory evictions occurred, with light industry turned out of cast-iron buildings in new residential areas like SoHo or Tribeca. In one instance, a building was emptied of 17 small factories employing 700 workers, most of them unskilled minority workers in entry-level jobs. For three years, Mayor Koch sat on his hands as factories were cleared from lofts. "The gentrification of SoHo is a boon for us," gloated Jersey City's head of economic development, as an empty factory there was filled with small firms fleeing New York. In 1970, SoHo was a center of light industry, where some 30,000 factory jobs surrounded some 1,000 artists who revived vacant factory lofts. Factory workers and artists coexisted in the harmony of industry and creation. Then SoHo became posh. The brick walls were exposed and wood floors were stripped, as galleries, boutiques and fancy restaurants arrived. A lot of rich nonartists wanted to live in the old cast-iron hulks. So artists were evicted, as were small firms making Christmas novelties, hats, paper boxes, handbags and umbrella frames.

Or there is the West Village, long a home for factories as well as bohemians. On Charles Street near the Hudson River is a former Romanesque warehouse, which now has 120 apartments. Three blocks south on Greenwich Street is a block-square National Landmark warehouse, where 280 housing units open in 1984. Across the street from this is an old Vita Herring factory, where 120 more units opened in 1982. And two blocks south on Hudson Street is "Printing House," with more than 150 small apartments in an old graphic arts plant covering half a block. Four industrial buildings that once employed nearly 1,000 unskilled workers now house about 650 upscale tenants instead.

The pressure of the rich to stay in Manhattan sees even former maid's quarters selling for over $400,000 on Central Park West. This redoubles pressures on industrial lofts in Manhattan, where most of the city's factory jobs remain. Councilwoman Ruth Messinger, long the chief critic of the Koch failure to stem loft conversions, observed in 1980 that there were

> 500,000 manufacturing jobs left in New York, 65% of them in Manhattan, and most of them low-income. I can easily foresee a situation in which the garment and printing industries quit the city . . . [leaving] a transient population that moves every time their $500 studios get leaky windows.

In 1981, Koch finally slapped a land tax on loft converters in Lower Manhattan and the garment center. He also declared four "forever factory" areas. Unless natural causes like business failure cleared a loft, these areas were barred to residential conversions: the garment center, the meat markets near 14th Street, the fur district of the West 20s and the graphic arts district of the West Village. Councilwoman Messinger promptly dismissed the land tax as a tool against factory evictions, since "land is notoriously undertaxed in this city." The tax is indeed a token in a city where, Desmond Smith observes, factory tenants pay only $3.75 a foot in annual rent, while residences pay $12 and co-ops go up to $100 per square foot, meaning that "an army of lawyers, computer programmers, and promoters have marched in to convert the lofts and factories into living and work space . . . more than half the 4,600 loft buildings in New York now house people —the workers in the information hive."

More than 300,000 factory jobs remain in Manhattan today, and the press of both household and worker bees is intense on the 2,300 lofts in industrial use. A recent example arose on West 39th Street—"milliner's row." In late 1981, a dozen hatmakers with 250 workers among them faced eviction at one building. The ubiquitous Councilwoman Messinger noted at a press conference that offices could pay twice the factory rents and "I warned the city officials of this impending problem early last year, but they refused to deal with it . . . as the Convention Center goes up, as lower Manhattan is being developed, the squeeze on nearby factory lofts is going to be on." Mayor Koch's four "forever factory" zones applied only to residential conversion, not white collars replacing blue ones. Nat Griszeck, owner of Arista Hats with twenty workers at the West 39th Street building, now faced his fourth move in five years. City Hall pointed out merely that Midtown was already a huge office center. It suggested that the dozen hat makers buy a building or find cheaper space in the Outer Boroughs, but this would cut them off from the essential daily exchange in the Manhattan garment center.

Indeed, garment jobs, which once supplied 350,000 of the city's million industrial slots, were down to 150,000. To earlier inroads from nonunion plants down south, cheap imports from the Far East, and the growth of sweatshops in the Southwest and New York City itself, City Hall was now adding the pressure of office-space seekers.

Four business sectors expanding offices beyond the high rents of Midtown and Wall Street are back offices from banks or corporations, ad agencies, law firms and publishing houses. Banks now command 15 percent of all city office space, and recent expansion by national and foreign branches has meant back offices must find cheaper space. Corporate back offices go even beyond Manhattan to bring pressure on factory space along the big Atlantic Avenue strip in Brooklyn, which is also being gentrified by loft-livers. Such Outer Borough areas also need to be designated "forever factory" zones from City Hall.

The law firms' drive for more space saw seven of the bigger firms consider erecting four new co-op towers around Times Square. This is a welcome idea for a 42nd Street revitalization that, after many decades of talk, may occur. At the same time, however, it reflects the growing needs of even established firms for cheaper space.

As for advertising, the phrase "Madison Avenue" has long been elastic: Grey has been on Third Avenue since the "El" came down in 1952; J. Walter Thompson is on Lexington; Wells, Rich is on Fifth; and Ted Bates is on Broadway. Now ad firms look for cheaper space on "Madison Avenue South" in the East 30s and 20s. Much of this will be in existing offices, but some of it will mean more pressure for hatters, furriers and garment makers in the area.

Finally, there are the publishers. The Harcourt Brace move to the Sunbelt was partly due to transit problems. Other firms now are looking south of 34th Street, to areas like Lower Fifth Avenue. Many existing offices and former department stores along the old "Ladies' Mile" may be involved, but publishers may also be one more office pressure on old loft factories in that "forever factory" zone. After twenty-five years in no-man's-land on Union Square, Farrar, Straus & Giroux is back in the publisher's mainstream. The Viking Press has just moved to the old Stern's Department store on 23rd Street, Abrams is now at 17th and 5th Avenue, and Scholastic Press has moved to the NYU campus on Washington Square. Meanwhile, how do major printing firms in the area hang on to factory lofts? *

• Computers were mainly developed in the New York area, but from 1958 through 1979, computer, communication and electronic factory jobs in New York dropped from 86,000 to 40,000. IBM today has more executives and workers in its new building on 57th Street than it did when its world headquarters was in New York.

• The Brooklyn Naval Yard has been a major industrial site since 1801. The first steam warship, *The Robert Fulton,* was built there in 1814, the *Monitor* was ironclad there for the Civil War, and during World War II, this was the world's largest naval yard, with 69,000 workers. Then shipbuilding went south or to Japan. The huge drydocks are empty, and most of the forges are banked. In early 1979, the Nepco Forge met a rush order for special parts to contain the accident at Three Mile Island, but the huge yard has only 2,300 workers today. It is slowly reviving and has tremendous space at hand with fine expressways nearby, but it has gone from 69,000 to 2,300 workers, which is exactly a thirtyfold loss of industrial jobs over four decades.

• Piano making has long been a New York specialty, with the famous company town of Steinway still found in the northeast corner of Queens. Back in 1872, when the famous upright maker Sohmer & Company opened, there were 171 piano manufacturers in New York. One hundred and ten years later, Sohmer was producing 3,000 of America's 200,000 annual pianos when new owners decided to relocate to Connecticut. That left Steinway as the best and last of the New York breed. As the industry of piano making fades, the service of music making in New York has grown from 2,000 musical events in 1950 to about 6,000 today in the world capital for concerts, if not concert grands. President Harry Sohmer told the *Times* that "it's an odd analogy, but I think of Sohmer the way I think of some of those old New York

---

* In addition to the old lofts and department stores in the area from 14th to 34th Street, there are many residential hotels, put up after 1910. They provide reasonably priced shelter for pensioners and, in some cases, patients dumped from state mental hospitals. Office-space demands ahead, like housing demands on the West Side after 1975, may lead to more forced residential evictions in this area.

beers—Piels, Rheingold, Trommer's. These were strictly New York products and in a way so were we." Once there were 130 breweries, now there are none. Once there were 171 piano factories, now there is one.

Two factory footnotes involve cleared industrial sites owned by the city and the city's poor vocational programs. New York has thousands of acres of cleared, city-owned industrial land in the Outer Boroughs. But industrial parks in the College Point area east of La Guardia Airport or the Flatlands section of southern Brooklyn have been mainly fallow since the Lindsay era. As already seen, the South Bronx has the huge Port Morris and Hunts Point factory areas, and even more empty land nearby in burned-out residential areas. With superb rail, river, road and air access, the South Bronx is a fine site for the sprawling, single-story plants of high tech. A Bathgate Industrial Park nearby has had two factories move in recently, but the big sites are in Hunts Point-Port Morris. And these won't come back without far less crime, far more code housing, and a well-trained work force.

As to training workers, while New York's elite high schools lead America, its vocational output is poor. With 7 percent of America's public schools, New York State schools led by its biggest city get 15 percent of all National Merit Scholarships and 35 percent of all Westinghouse Scholarships. Indeed, the city's Stuyvesant and Bronx Science high schools were two of the three 1982 leaders among all American schools for National Merit scholars (the third was Phillips Exeter Academy). But in training factory or service workers, New York City's public schools have far to go.

When machinery and metal factory jobs in New York go from 108,000 in 1960 to just 52,000 in 1979—this may partly reflect outdated equipment used in "training" public school students. When the public hospitals of the HHC system recruit 35 percent of their nurses from the Philippines, one wonders why the Clara Barton High School for Nurses isn't expanded. When trade schools teach typesetting, is one surprised that printers flee to New Jersey in an automated age? When schools teach manual typewriting in the late 1970s, is it amazing that even secretaries are shipped in from suburbia? Outdated materials and production modes have long been the rule in New York's vocational schools. Since 40 percent of high-school students don't graduate, where can this generation find work without better training?

### Ending the Service Crisis

In New York there are sizable and untapped revenue resources at hand. Albany's role in limiting resources for services has been detailed. City Hall has also kept the service crisis alive. Mayor Koch has refused to fight the real-estate lobby and raise more taxes from the booming commercial property of Midtown and Wall Street. State Comptroller Edward Regan has projected that more than $150 million is lost annually to tax abatement in New York City. Special Deputy Comptroller for New York City Sidney Schwartz has estimated that up to $650 million more is lost in annual taxes due to deflated city assessments on existing property.

In 1978, Koch began his first year as mayor with a crusade against the city unions. This produced a needless standoff at the bargaining table, only resolved when Koch added an extra $400 million a year to soothe the rank and file. Even Koch's court journalist Ken Auletta abandoned his usual obeisances to observe how, in the 1978 spitting match with the unions,

> Koch, sharing [former mayor John V.] Lindsay's penchant for theatrical poses, said their demands were "outrageous." In truth, the unions knew the mayor was posing; the new mayor did not know he was. In December 1977, a major city leader told this reporter, "Don't quote me, but I would be glad to settle for a straight 6 percent." . . . But Koch's public bluster, like Lindsay's, hardened their demands, bringing greater membership pressure on union leaders to humiliate their City Hall foe.

Instead of 6 percent, the unions got an 8 percent raise over two years, or what amounted to $400 million extra for an already wide budget gap. The same needless giveaway happened in 1982, when Koch, running for governor, gave the unions raises of 8 percent and 7 percent through 1984.

Koch's second mistake was balancing the budget too quickly. Abe Beame, his predecessor, had worked out a gradual, seven-year plan to phase out expense budget items from the capital budget to reach a truly balanced city budget. But Koch wanted to please powers like Felix Rohatyn, Governor Carey, the bond-rating services and the city's federal overseer, Senator William Proxmire. Early in 1978, he rashly pledged to balance the city books in only four years. Later he topped himself, promising a balanced budget in three years. Services already reeling from Beame cuts since 1975 now faced new cuts to cover wider budget gaps produced by inflated union wages and the headlong drive to balance the books.

To make things worse, Koch ruled out even the merest hint of municipal bankruptcy. This threw away a useful club to pressure bankers and unions.

A final example of Koch's needless escalation of the fiscal-service crisis was his relationship with Washington. Since the Lindsay era, the mayor of New York had led the nation's mayors in lobbying on Capitol Hill or at the White House. Koch shunned that traditional role. He boycotted meetings of the militant U.S. Conference of Mayors. When confronting Jimmy Carter or Ronald Reagan, Koch was obsequious. Although Reagan cut $400 million in federal aid to New York in 1981, Koch didn't fight it at all. Only after winning the Republican nomination for mayor in late 1981 did Koch attack Reaganomics as a "sham and a shame."

To meet his self-imposed goal of balancing the budget in three years, Koch had only three options: raise local taxes, impose more service cuts, or rely on luck. The wisest choice would have been tapping into an $800 million revenue reservoir of tax-abated or underassessed properties, almost all of them in Manhattan. But Koch was eager to please developers and realtors, so that obvious revenue path was ignored.

A mix of cuts and luck was left. The service cuts came on top of 60,000 employees cut by Mayor Beame. Beame had rendered a lot of civil service fat, but was down to the bone before leaving City Hall. Now Koch cut through the bone, and into the marrow of city services. For example, he cut 20 percent more from already thin police ranks, which were now at their lowest manning level since 1954. Koch did this as crime rose 27 percent in his first three years, with robbery and murder setting new records for both 1980 and 1981.

As for luck, this was brief. It held in 1980, when Koch's budget office informed the Treasury Department of "higher than expected revenue" from external forces, noting how

inflation, good retail sales, and a 50 percent increase in petroleum-related prices drove sales tax revenue up. . . . High cor-

porate profits raised revenues from business taxes. Stock
volume, rising to unprecedented levels, produced unexpectedly
large gains in the stock transfer tax.

Record volume on the Stock Exchange, the OPEC price hike of
late 1979 and remarkable retail sales in 1980 had been major
windfalls. A devalued dollar also made New York a better buy
for foreign tourists, meaning extra sales taxes off $3.1 billion
spent by them in 1980 alone.

Most of the luck was gone by 1981. Recalling how Special
Deputy Comptroller for New York City Sidney Schwartz had
warned of a return to normalcy, Wayne Barrett summarized that
auditor's findings in *The Village Voice:* "Employment and retail
sales have slowed, hotel occupancy and tourism are down, the
stock transfer tax is almost phased out, and the strength of the
dollar is deadening the city economy." A stronger dollar meant
tourism was down for the first time in five years. The stock transfer tax was all but gone—just before the record trading days in
the summer rally of 1982.* The energy sales tax windfall of 1980
was gone, replaced by the oil glut of 1981 and the falling prices
that cut sales taxes.

The bottom fell out in 1982. Mayor Koch opened the recession
year claiming "the worst pain is behind us," but the first three
months saw corporate tax revenues fall by 3 percent. Koch ordered a minor agency cut in the summer and then compounded
growing revenue losses with another inflated labor pact. Two
weeks before his Democratic primary for governor against Mario
Cuomo, Koch gave municipal workers a 15 percent raise over
two years. Inflation was projected at a much lower rate than the
wage hike, and the giveaway of $1.4 billion was politically bi-
zarre; the unions were heavily backing Cuomo.† Even Koch supporters on the *Times* editorial page attacked the wage pact, pre-
dicting that only higher taxes and/or service cuts could cover the
costs. A week later, Koch claimed in a debate with Cuomo that
"it's my expectation that there will not be any new taxes."

---

* There is also talk of reviving the stock transfer tax. With many trading days
above 100 million shares in 1982, this tax at its maximum rate could have generated $531 million that year. Koch began hinting that brokers whose trade soared
25 percent in 1982 should "bear part of the pain" in closing the gap.
† Cuomo was predictably quiet about the 1982 labor giveaway, with *Times* columnist Sydney Schanberg observing how "he too chose the diplomacy of politics
over the straight talk of fiscal hard facts."

Three weeks later, Koch imposed a hiring freeze on top of a new cut of 2.25 percent in agency budgets. Within two months, two more cuts had been ordered and Koch was threatening to let attrition take its toll or lay off from 6,600 to 14,400 workers in closing a budget gap now projected at $1.5 billion through July 1, 1984.

Part of the gap was caused by bad luck. Recession, a strong dollar and deflation cut revenues badly; an average revenue gain of 14 percent in sales and income taxes plunged to 2.6 percent for fiscal 1983. Other bad breaks were Reagan cuts in federal aid and a looming state deficit of $600 million, the latter inevitable, given the recession and all the state tax cuts since 1978. But much of the new fiscal crisis was made by City Hall, through things like the 1982 labor pact.

There are various ways to raise new revenues in New York. One untapped revenue reservoir involves more stretching out of the city's sizable debt. Such restructuring is already done by the Municipal Assistance Corporation of Felix Rohatyn, which pays off short-term notes over a longer period. Much of New York's debt lies outside this mode, which in 1977 had saved the city $160 million. Since debt consumes more than 12 percent of the city's expense budget, more such restructuring can occur.

Other revenue measures like higher parking fees or steeper commuter taxes have been proposed by Professors Raymond Horton of Columbia and Charles Brecher of NYU, coauthors of *Setting Municipal Priorities*. But, notes Horton to *New York* magazine, "property tax reform is the key. The rest is pretty much nickel-and-dime stuff, and it's probably not worth the animosity it creates. You can string nuisance taxes together for years and never get big money." He added that, while city property values had grown $30 billion in recent years, city assessments had fallen by half a billion. By simply raising assessments to match new value, he saw the city raising an extra $600 million a year by 1985.

The main revenue reservoir is all that undervalued commercial property in Manhattan. Despite all the new office space opened after 1980 and a tripling of rents in Wall Street since 1979, the city's market was so strong that it had a 3 percent vacancy rate in late 1982. With heavy demands for space in a strong seller's market, higher property taxes could be easily passed along. Tax hikes don't kill building booms, only space gluts do.

• *Tax Abatement.* New York lost $156 million in potential revenues to tax abatement in 1981. Part of these breaks went to projects like factories, office buildings and hotels in a program abating some $100 million that year. The remaining $56 million in abatements went to a J-51 program for housing rehabilitation. J-51 began as a useful incentive to upgrade cold-water flats. But Koch was soon extending J-51 tax breaks to those converting empty industrial lofts into luxury housing.

The abatement program was so controversial that even conservative State Comptroller Edward Regan attacked it. His audits focused on windfalls for developers and corporations that didn't need tax breaks to build. Regan noted how "millions of dollars in forgone tax revenues can essentially be seen as funds that have to be compensated for by other taxpayers, or as services that the city does not render to its citizens." Even more blunt was Regan's assessment of the abatements in the fall of 1980, when he remarked in a campaign year that "they create campaign contributions, yes. They create Chamber of Commerce and media approval, yes, but there is no hard evidence that these actions create new jobs."

Regan was the most prominent among many critics of the abatement program. The attacks mainly focused on tax breaks for luxury hotels or office towers built by rich firms like IBM or AT&T. Within eighteen heady months, Mayors Beame and Koch had approved 131 of 145 applicants for tax relief, even though, as Robert Kuttner writes in *Revolt of the Haves,* the city's real-estate market "was clearly rebounding on its own. Ninety percent of the dollar value of exemptions went to Manhattan, and although the rationale of the program was the creation of permanent jobs only 2 percent of the tax savings went to industrial projects."

Midtown led the way. Kuttner recalls that while IBM had been assembling its huge site at 57th and Madison since 1936, the city was willing to abate $7.2 million in taxes to America's fourth most profitable corporation in 1980. AT&T had earned $6.9 billion in 1981, but Koch still gave it $20 million in tax abatement as an "incentive" to build its new headquarters on 56th and Madison. Six blocks south of these two was the new Helmsley Palace Hotel. With 6,000 hotel rooms, 10 million square feet of factory space and dozens of major office towers in his empire, owner Harry Helmsley hardly needed tax relief for his new inn.

But Koch gave him a $6 million abatement to build, as Council-woman Ruth Messinger complained that "I have trouble believing that a hotel that charges $140 a night for a room on 50th and Madison wasn't a good economic venture for its owner . . . I mean, what would [Harry Helmsley] have done if we hadn't given him the $6 million—built it in Newark?"

Running against Koch in the 1981 Democratic mayoral primary, Assemblyman Frank Barbaro recalled how realtors had been the biggest bloc of donors to Koch's 1977 campaign, giving it some $350,000. Ten of New York's biggest landlords and developers alone had given $175,850 to the Koch campaign in 1977 —and later received $60 million in tax abatements. As Barbaro also pointed out, even private clubs got this public subsidy by 1981, with the City Racquet Club getting a $385,000 tax abatement and the New York Health and Racquet Club a $285,000 break. As Barbaro asked in 1981: "Are city taxes for subways or squash?" *

• *Tax Assessments.* As abatements cost the city $156 million annually in potential revenues, underassessed property losses amounted to perhaps $650 million more. Mayor Koch had simply kept taxes too low on the booming commercial property in Midtown and Wall Street. Both State Comptroller Regan and Special Deputy Comptroller for New York City Sidney Schwartz found a huge gap between soaring property values and city assessments of value. Regan found that between 1976 and 1980, as local inflation rose 27 percent, the assessments inched up only 7 percent on office buildings. Off this gap alone, he projected an annual revenue loss of $800 million.

Schwartz observed that as the market value of New York's property rose $30 billion after 1976, assessments from City Hall dropped half a billion. As market values rose 48 percent, assessments dropped 2 percent. Projecting a fiscal 1982 loss of $687 million in property tax revenues off these deflated assessments,

---

* While Mayors Beame and Koch handed out too many tax breaks to unworthy firms in eighteen hectic months, some abatements helped launch and sustain Skyline #4 after 1980. Also, abatement produces net revenue gains. For example, an undeveloped site on Lexington Avenue was paying only $250,000 in taxes when its owners got a $6 million abatement spur to build, the tax break spread over ten years. Since the new office building should produce $24 million in new taxes during those ten years, the city would net $1.8 million a year during that decade, against $250,000 for a fallow site.

Schwartz concluded that "the failure of the City's real estate tax revenues to share in the substantial growth in property values is a major factor in the City's recurring fiscal problems."

Koch replied that he had raised the assessed value of city properties from $38.6 billion to $42.6 billion, with Schwartz approving that 1981 raise. The $119 million in new property taxes in 1981 was welcome, but far short of the revenue potentials projected by both Schwartz and Comptroller Regan. Under state law, Koch could raise assessments only 10 percent in 1981, but nothing had prevented him from raising them in previous years, when the office boom had taken off. As values soared and vacancy rates dropped, this seller's market could have easily passed on higher taxes to a long line of renters in Manhattan. Indeed, many firms were signing rent escalator clauses tied to future tax hikes as the price of a prestigious Midtown or Wall Street address.

Two examples of the deflated assessments in Midtown are the Pan Am Building and Rockefeller Center. Had these two household names been assessed at market value, they alone could have added more than $40 million in annual new taxes, enough to offset thin police ranks or understaffed hospital nurses. Upon its sale in 1980, the Pan Am Building became an overnight and notorious example of the city's deflated assessments. On the yellowing ledgers at the city's Finance Department, this prime Midtown block had been "valued" in 1980 at only $93 million but was sold for $400 million to Metropolitan Life. Finance Commissioner Philip R. Michael has noted that usual assessments value commercial property at 60 percent of real market value. By that standard, a building sold for $400 million should have an assessed value (AV) of $240 million, not $93 million. Multiplying the $147 million in lost assessed value by the city tax rate of $8.95 per $100 in AV yields $13.1 million in annual lost taxes.

These losses pale next to the revenue reservoir at Rockefeller Center. Putting a price on this landmark is like valuing the *Mona Lisa*. One billion dollars for the three square blocks of prime Midtown is a conservative value, and that would mean an assessed value of $600 million. But in 1981, Koch assessed the Center at only $221 million, meaning $379 million in lost assessed values. Multiplying this by the city tax rate, the city loses $33.9 million in annual property taxes.

A year after the Pan Am sale, the nearby Manufacturers Hanover Trust building was sold. The price was $161 million, the city assessment was only $31 million. At proper 60 percent valuation, the city would have made $6 million a year in extra taxes. This and the Pan Am sale were part of a tripling of values in Midtown:

| Sales Date | Building Sold | Price per Square Foot |
| --- | --- | --- |
| 2/80 | Celanese | $ 85 |
| | Seagram | 140 |
| 7/80 | Pan Am | 178 |
| 9/81 | CIT | 300 |
| | Manufacturers Hanover | 334 |

Despite these tripled values, a 2 percent vacancy rate in 1981, and tenants signing leases with rent-escalator clauses for higher taxes, a new state law meant Mayor Koch could hike assessments only 5.5 percent in 1982. That meant only $190 million more in new property taxes citywide, with the hot Manhattan office market producing $143 million of the new gain. The big revenue reservoir lay mainly untapped.

So New York kept losing the $600 to $800 million in annual property taxes projected by State Comptroller Regan and Special Deputy Comptroller for New York City Schwartz. Assume the city could raise half its deflated assessments on commercial property without sending shock waves through Midtown and Wall Street. This could raise up to $400 million in new annual revenues, restoring major services to adequate force:

| | |
| --- | --- |
| 6,000 police officers at $30,000 | $180 million |
| 4,000 nurses and support workers at $20,000 | 80 million |
| 2,000 firemen at $30,000 | 60 million |
| 1,000 sanitation men at $30,000 | 30 million |
| Management of more foreclosed buildings | 50 million |
| | $400 million |

There are a few more ways to draw funds from untapped revenue sources in New York. For example, there are assessment appeals. In *Revolt of the Haves,* Robert Kuttner recalls how shrewd lawyers and a chaotic appeals process helped civic booster Lewis Rudin—who gave Koch $18,400 in 1981 campaign gifts—win 32 percent of his assessment appeals in 1978. These assessment lawyers swamp the undermanned Tax Commission in an appeals process which, Kuttner observes, had "all the careful deliberation of a tobacco auction . . . Each case takes less time than a traffic ticket." He recalls how all this rush meant that of $297 million in lower assessments for 1979

> the lion's share went to big downtown commercial properties. Most of the *Fortune* 500 headquarters buildings won big reductions, as did the New York Stock Exchange. Topping the list was Mobil Oil's headquarters on Forty-second Street. Mobil, hardly a candidate for public alms in 1979, got its assessment reduced by $7 million [an annual loss in city taxes of $626,500].

More Tax Commission staff could reduce such giveaways.

Another $600 million may be lost annually to local tax evasion. This loss projected by City Hall in 1981 is based mainly on sales tax skimming in the local underground economy. Collections can be improved by hiring more state and city auditors, who, until recently, monitored only 2 percent of all registered sales vendors in New York City. Despite evidence that each new auditor brought in from five to fifteen times his salary in new collections, Koch waited until 1981 to double auditor ranks. Around that time, he also appointed a new finance commissioner, Philip R. Michael, a former federal prosecutor of organized-crime tax cases. Michael appointed a computer expert as his first deputy, and computer matches of various city tax rolls began. One match found that 115,000 companies had paid city corporation taxes without paying city commercial rent taxes. Data files on more than twenty taxes supervised by the Finance Department should uncover more of the same. More auditors and computers should also mean more prosecutions. Michael was even planning to indict realtors who filed false claims of income and costs in appealing for lower assessments. Even Councilwoman Messinger allowed that "I think they're starting to do some good things now. The only question is why they didn't do all this sooner."

Governing a big city is done by sober and slow strategies. Koch's stunning defeat in the 1982 Democratic primary for governor showed the limits of his often undignified and footloose style. In campaigning, he outspent Mario Cuomo by 4 to 1, yet the better-known Koch was badly beaten statewide, and barely carried New York City by 51 percent.

Koch's commitment to civil rights was proved long ago as a lawyer for Freedom Riders in the early 1960s. His leadership on liberal issues in Congress after 1968 is a proud record, highlighted by the landmark use of the highway trust fund for mass-transit aid. For all his public boorishness, Koch is a bright and sensitive man who quickly grasps complex issues and programs. He is often ready to put programs to best use for neglected citizens, as in the time he has spent in working out a faster city program for emergency heat repairs for tenants. Mayor Koch is not a racist or a man who hates the poor.

But all this hardly excuses his performance as a mayor who fails to fight bankers and realtors, and winds up wrecking services instead. A mayor of New York must defend the interests of the poor and the elderly, maintain the loyalty of the middle class, and be able to always lead all other mayors in Washington.

Ed Koch likes to compare himself to Fiorello La Guardia, and the media likes to honor his claim. This is an age where personalities outweigh policies as the glitter of style replaces the gold of content. Mass opinion is formed by television news stressing visual symbols and quips over complex issues. Koch is La Guardia in the TV image. But where Koch soothes bankers and realtors while cutting city services, La Guardia had this to say when bankers came to Washington seeking federal aid: "The bastards broke the People's back with their usury, and now they want to unload on the Government. No, no. Let them die: the People will survive."

This may be unfair, even to bankers, but it is certainly light-years away from Ed Koch. Koch, for all his wit and fulminations, is simply no match for the memorable portrait of La Guardia in Arthur M. Schlesinger, Jr.,'s *The Politics of Upheaval*.

La Guardia stood with passion for honesty and progressivism in government. More than that, he charged these sometimes dreary positions with a free-swinging Latin exuberance which made reform as exciting as corruption . . .

[Admiring the organist at Radio City Music Hall, La Guardia exulted] "That's how our city must be run. Like the organist, you must keep both hands on the keyboard and both feet on the pedals—*and never let go.*'' It was personal government, yet government continuously dedicated to civic ideals.

Someday it may return to New York City and the other dying cities of the Snowbelt and Sunbelt states.

# CONCLUSION

WHAT ARE THE CAUSES of America's urban problems? Reasons are advanced from gentrification to clearances for urban renewal, from growth in the number of welfare families to slumlords' greed. But these are all effects of larger causes that have to do with instability and irresolution.

Beyond our picture of America's dying cities is a larger frame of social decay. There is the plague of drugs and guns seen in Chapter 6 and the fact that only the Soviets drink more. Some 162,000 Americans died of trauma in 1982 and 300,000 were permanently disabled. In this culture of waste, 19 percent of our adults are illiterate and 18 percent of our babies illegitimate.

It has happened before. We remember Rome. By the fourth century, as historian Michael Grant writes, Roman cities were "thoroughly dilapidated," as "the whole of the old middle-class civilization fell rapidly apart." The infrastructure was crumbling and the middle class was shrinking, mainly as a result of huge and inequitable tax demands to support a mercenary army. Salvian of Marseilles described Romans' tax evasion and their society's social ruin.

> Taxation, however harsh and brutal, would still be less severe and brutal if all shared equally in the common lot. But the situation is made more shameful and disastrous by the fact that all do not bear the burden together. The tributes due from the rich are extorted from the poor.

Expensive mercenaries, unfair tax burdens, infrastructure rot, middle-class shrinkage and tax evasion are all familiar. Augustus boasted, "I found Rome built of bricks; I leave her clothed in marble." Indeed, he built libraries and temples on the Palatine Hill overlooking the vast slums of the Suburra.

Still closer in time to America's urban renewal is the Paris of Napoleon III in the 1850s. The dictator told Baron Haussmann, his Robert Moses, that he wanted to be a second Augustus, with a "second city of marble." So the poor were chased from the center of town to mean obscurity in Montmartre, as "haussmannization" built the famous boulevards and downtown parks. An admiring Lord Palmerston wrote that Napoleon III, "following the career of Augustus," had done more for the prosperity of France than Augustus had done for Rome. In 1871, the poor of Paris seized a "revived" city in a rage, and in the anarchy of the Paris Commune hostages including the archbishop of Paris were killed. Then the troops of Thiers came in from Versailles and in one week that horrified France for decades, more than 17,000 Communards were executed.

No such wholesale battles await our cities, but their slow death will proceed unless there is major social change. Unless equity and stability can be revived in America, its cities will become as polarized as Rome under the Caesars or Paris under Napoleon III. Here are four ways we might begin to restore fairness and purpose. The first two proposals should appeal to conservatives, the latter two to liberals; all aim at a moderate result.

One path to equity would be to revive the military draft. When blacks are 11 percent of America but 33 percent of its army, one has what Senator Ernest Hollings calls "an employer of last resort" for the poor, not a levy drawn from all classes. Requiring some kind of national service from all young citizens would also save tens of billions in annual costs for mercenaries, create a huge reserve to bolster a conventional—rather than a nuclear— defense of NATO, and add several million volunteers to our unique and huge system of church and civic groups.

A second means to stability would be an all-out attack on drugs, going beyond the Reagan initiatives to a thorough drive against organized crime. Not since Thomas Dewey busted the rackets in the 1930s has there been such a need to break the mob.

A third road to a more even distribution of resources would be real tax reform. This would mean closing unproductive loopholes, reviving a strong inheritance tax and generally restoring fairness and progressivity to the IRS code. There should also be limits to certain entitlements: double-dipped federal pensions, Social Security indexing, or college loans for families earning $75,000.

A fourth route toward stability was discussed in Chapter 6. It involves a thorough public works program, complemented by a federal guarantee to train, retrain or relocate workers who need such aid. Full employment remains the crucial and unmet goal supported by Dewey in the 1944 campaign, and signed into law by Truman in the Employment Act of 1946.

The draft, drug control, tax reform and full employment— these federal programs and a revival of civic interest, in voting or voluntarism, can help restore equity and stability to America and save its cities. We can have more jobs and less crime, fewer drugs and more hope, and a nation recovering a will to live. Today, apathetic Americans reflect Livy's warning to Rome that "we can bear neither our diseases nor their cures." Hope for America and its cities can and must be revived. A proud ancient city of marble with two million people became a crumbling forum where cows grazed in medieval times. It need not happen here.

> Come, my friends,
> 'Tis not too late to seek a newer world. . . .
> Though much is taken, much abides; and though
> We are not now that strength which in old days
> Moved earth and heaven, that which we are, we are,—
> One equal temper of heroic hearts,
> Made weak by time and fate, but strong in will
> To strive, to seek, to find, and not to yield.

# ENDNOTES

In addition to the following documented sources, I used, throughout the book, information gleaned from the ongoing reporting of such national dailies and weeklies as *The New York Times; The Wall Street Journal; U.S. News and World Report; Newsweek; Time.* With regard to individual cities, I made frequent use of their regional/local newspapers, among them, *The Boston Globe; The Los Angeles Times; The Washington Post; The New York Daily News.*

## PART I: THE SUNBELT

### Chapter 1: SUNBELT IN SUNSET

*p. 22*   New Orleans, poorest of fifty big cities: *New York Times,* Sept. 8, 1980.
Texas gave welfare to one in three poor children: *Final Report, 1980 Commission on the Future of the South,* Southern Growth Policies Board, table on p. 18.

*p. 23*   Net migration figures: *Statistical Abstract of the United States: 1980,* Table 11, p. 13. U.S. Bureau of the Census. (Table's data go to Apr. 1, 1979; author adjusts date for Apr. 1, 1980.)

*p. 23*   Crime data here, as elsewhere, from annual Uniform Crime Reports of the FBI. Crime rates adjusted by author to match census gain or loss on year-specific basis in 1970s.

*p. 23*   *Yakuza* move on Honolulu: *New York Times,* Jan. 2, 1981.

*p. 24*   Princeton study: Ibid., Mar. 30, 1980.
Pentagon payroll and prime contracts: *The Unprotected Flank,* Northeast-Midwest Congressional Coalition, 1980, Tables 8 and 14.
Imbalance of payments figure: *The State of the Region 1981,* Northeast-Midwest Congressional Coalition, p. 37.

*p. 25*   *The Unprotected Flank's* relevant tables here are Tables 4 on 1950–80 job trends, 8 (payrolls), 3 (construction), 14 (contracts).
Combat divisions and tactical preparedness: Ibid., pp. 23–24.

*p. 25*   Neal R. Peirce article: *Washington Post,* Jan. 18, 1981.
"tidewater strategy": *The Unprotected Flank,* p. 27.

*p. 25*   "Current Pentagon spending patterns": Ibid., p. 29.

*p. 26*   "not especially good for General Motors . . .": *American Regionalism,* Editorial Research Reports, *Congressional Quarterly,* 1980, p. 82.
Pentagon payroll figures: *The Unprotected Flank,* Table 8.

*p. 26*   Special welfare aid for the Sunbelt: *The State of the Region 1981,* p. 44.

*p. 27*   Some of the western coal and oil-shale data: Joel Garreau, *The Nine Nations of North America,* Houghton Mifflin, 1981, pp. 287–327.

*p. 27*   Eight of ten states with highest jobs growth: Bureau of Labor Statistics, Department of Labor, has data on nonfarm job growth.

*p. 28*    State treasury windfalls through 1990: *New York Daily News*, Mar. 28, 1980.

*p. 28*    Fuel consumption data in Snowbelt: *The State of the Region 1981*, p. 32.

*p. 28*    Half their export earnings for oil by 1980: *Washington Post*, Dec. 20, 1980.

*p. 28*    Data on cold-related deaths: Ibid., Nov. 28, 1981.

*p. 29*    Canadian oil data: *New York Times*, Sept. 2, 1981.

*p. 29*    Tulsa data: *Wall Street Journal*, Oct. 5, 1982.

*p. 29*    Denver oilman quote: Ibid., Apr. 8, 1982.

*p. 29*    Idaho oil drillings: Ibid., Dec. 14, 1981.

*p. 30*    Reagan quote and RAND study: *New York Times*, Apr. 12, 1981.

*p. 30*    Four times the wells of non-Communist world: *The New York Times Magazine*, Aug. 30, 1981.

*p. 30*    "fuel of last resort" quote: *New York Times*, Mar. 28, 1981.

*p. 30*    Wyoming coal output: Ibid., June 4, 1982.

*p. 30*    "the Saudi Arabia of coal" quote: Ibid., Nov. 19, 1980.
Metric tons projections: Ibid.

*p. 31*    "Trains, Trains and more Trains": Ibid., May 27, 1981.

*p. 31*    Wyoming-Arkansas slurry: *U.S. News & World Report*, March 29, 1976.

*p. 31*    Garreau article was in *Washington Post*, May 17, 1981.

*p. 31*    Pollution in Stroudsburg creek: Ibid., May 20, 1981.

*p. 32*    Exxon projections for year 2015: Garreau, *The Nine Nations of North America*, p. 300.

*p. 32*    "These are not nice plants. . . .": *U.S. News & World Report*, Dec. 7, 1981.

*p. 32*    More carbon dioxide from synfuel: *U.S. News & World Report*, Dec. 7, 1981.

*p. 33*    Edward Noble quote: *Wall Street Journal*, Dec. 28, 1981.

*p. 33*    *Washington Post* citation: Feb. 7, 1982, issue.

*p. 33*    Canceled Morgantown project: *New York Times*, June 25, 1981.

*p. 33*    Jennings Randolph's synfuel flight: *Washington Post*, May 17, 1981.

*p. 33–34*   Oil expert on Feisal "sting": *Wall Street Journal*, Dec. 28, 1981.

*p. 34*    Colony project in Colorado: *New York Times*, Nov. 6, 1981.

*p. 34*    Footnote on Occidental and Tenneco project: *Wall Street Journal*, Aug. 31, 1981.

*p. 35*    Hawaii alternative energies: *New York Times*, Mar. 29, 1981.

*p. 35*    Boiling solar ponds: Ibid., Aug. 3, 1981.

*p. 35*    Ormat Turbines and Great Salt Lake: Ibid., Mar. 6, 1981.

*p. 35*    ARCO invests in PVCs: From *Business Week*, special issue on "The Reindustrialization of America," June 30, 1980.

*p. 36*    Daniel Yergin quote: *The New York Times Magazine*, July 11, 1982.

*p. 37*    Daniel Webster quote: Neal R. Peirce, *The Mountain States of America*, W. W. Norton, 1972, p. 18.

*p. 37*    California Aqueduct quote: Neal R. Peirce, *The Megastates of America*, W. W. Norton, 1972, p. 658.

*p. 37*    Colorado Compact "signed in an unusually wet year": *Science 81*, June issue.

*p. 38*    Footnote description of 500-mile reservoir project: From James Wright, *The Coming Water Famine*, Coward-McCann, 1966.

*p. 38*    Carson City manager quote: *New York Times*, Jan. 25, 1981.

*p. 38*    Paiute Indian leader quote: Peirce, *The Mountain States of America*, p. 175.

*p. 39*    Sinking of Venice: *U.S. News & World Report*, May 31, 1982.

*p. 39*    Ogallala aquifer data: From *Science 81*, June issue; *New York Times*, Aug. 11, 1981; and *U.S. News & World Report*, June 29, 1981.

*p. 39*   Food grown on High Plains: *U.S. News & World Report*, June 29, 1981.
*p. 39*   John Boslough quote: *Science 81*, June issue.
*p. 39–40*   Kansas, Nebraska and Texas data: *New York Times*, Aug. 11, 1981.
*p. 40*   Congressional proposal to import water from Missouri River: Ibid.
*p. 40*   Colorado study: *U.S. News & World Report*, June 29, 1981.
*p. 40*   Joanne Omang quote: *Washington Post*, May 30, 1981.
*p. 40*   Jonathan Lash quote: *Washington Post*, May 30, 1981.
*p. 40*   Colorado water-rights prices: *New York Times*, Aug. 9, 1981.

## Chapter 2: THE MYTH OF THE NEW SOUTH

*p. 42*   John Gunther phrase is heading for Chapter 40, "The South: Problem Child of the Nation," from *Inside U.S.A.*, Harper & Bros., 1947.
*p. 42*   Runner-up for *Time* cover in 1971: Michael Barone, Grant Ujifusa and Douglas Matthews, *The Almanac of American Politics 1980*, E. P. Dutton, 1979, p. 170.
*p. 42*   George Wallace quote: Sandra Stencel, "The South: Continuity and Change" in *American Regionalism*, Editorial Research Reports, *Congressional Quarterly*, 1980, p. 44.
*p. 42–43*   *Congressional Quarterly* drive down IS 85: Ibid., pp. 34–35.
  Many details of Southern economic growth: Ibid., p. 36–7.
*p. 44*   Growth of Southern black elected officials: Ibid., p. 44.
*p. 44*   Gene Burd on the Bliss Blitz: "The Selling of the Sunbelt: Civic Boosterism in the Media" in *The Rise of the Sunbelt Cities*, edited by David C. Perry and Alfred J. Watkins, Sage Publications, 1977.
  *Wall Street Journal* article summary: Ibid., p. 136.
*p. 44*   Gene Burd quote: Ibid., p. 142.
*p. 44*   C. Vann Woodward essay: Ibid., p. 138.
  The Poor as a Share of All People table: Based on table on p. 40 of *American Regionalism*, 1980.
*p. 46–47*   Footnote on Indians and Puerto Rico: Navajo data from *New York Times*, Dec. 12, 1981; Puerto Rican data from *New York Times*, Oct. 28, 1982, and *Washington Post*, Aug. 3, 1982.
*p. 47*   "There was the promising beginning of growth . . .": *Final Report of the 1980 Commission on the Future of the South*, Southern Growth Policies Board, 1981, p. 11.
*p. 47–48*   1981 Bureau of Labor Statistics survey: *New York Times*, Dec. 21, 1981.
  Urban Institute study: Ibid., Nov. 5, 1981.
  Commission on Future of South on energy: *Final Report*, p. 11.
*p. 48*   "sophisticated migrants to the region . . .": Ibid.
*p. 49*   "low levels of educational achievement . . .": Ibid., p. 29.
*p. 49*   "More of the children of the South . . .": Ibid., p. 11.
*p. 49*   Slight decline in southern births, 1970s: Ibid., p. 15.
*p. 50*   Share of southern children getting welfare: Ibid., p. 18 table.
  Welfare payment contrast, South and non-South: Ibid., p. 17.
  Children excluded from welfare, table: Ibid., p. 18 table.
*p. 50*   Children excluded from Medicaid: Ibid., p. 17.
  Infant mortality rates: Ibid.
  Education per pupil outlays: Ibid., p. 16.
  40% of America's poorest children in South: Ibid., p. 17.
  Footnote: Ibid., data on p. 17.

## Chapter 3: SOUTHERN CITIES

### FLORIDA

p. 52    Jacksonville nuclear power: *U.S. News & World Report,* Sept. 1, 1975. Jacksonville tax load, cited in study from the Department of Finance, the District of Columbia, 1975.

p. 53    Cape Canaveral job losses in 1970s: *New York Times,* Nov. 23, 1980.

p. 53    Cape Canaveral data: *U.S. News & World Report,* Dec. 24, 1979. High tech in central Florida: From ad in *Fortune* magazine, 1981, titled "Florida: A New Economic Force."

p. 53    1976 real-estate crash: *U.S. News & World Report,* Aug. 23, 1976. 1981 condo problems: *Wall Street Journal,* Nov. 25, 1981.

p. 54    Epcot quote from Disney spokesman: *U.S. News & World Report,* Dec. 24, 1979. Florida as "southern California" of late 1990s: *U.S. News & World Report,* Dec. 24, 1979.

p. 54    Cecil Andrus quote: *Wall Street Journal,* June 23, 1981. *Times* quote: From Jan. 22, 1982, issue.

p. 55    Sinkhole story: *Washington Post,* May 11, 1981.

p. 56    Quote from engineer: *New York Times,* July 23, 1981.

p. 56    1906 draining of South Florida: Ibid., Dec. 17, 1981. Footnote on phosphate: *U.S. News & World Report,* May 23, 1977.

p. 57    Lobbyist quote: *New York Times,* Nov. 27, 1981. Tax cuts cited by ad from Florida Department of Commerce, 1981.

p. 57    Seminole County official quote: *Washington Post,* Aug. 19, 1981.

p. 57–58    Neonatal intensive care story: *New York Times,* July 11, 1981.

p. 58    Blind and crippled fight for free transit: Ibid., Dec. 20, 1981. CETA cuts and budget data: *Washington Post,* Sept. 19, 1981.


### MIAMI

p. 59    "Baghdad of Biscayne Bay" quote: From *Arthur Frommer's Dollarwise Guide to the Southeast,* 1980, by Susan Poole, p. 254.

p. 59    Mrs. Tuttle and blossoms: Neal R. Peirce, *The Megastates of America,* W. W. Norton, 1972, pp. 457–58.

p. 59    Key West–Havana bridge footnote: Joel Garreau, *The Nine Nations of North America,* Houghton Mifflin, 1981, p. 181. Florida land rush quote: Peirce, op. cit., pp. 457–58.

p. 60    Atlanta banker quote: *New York Times,* June 29, 1981. p. 60–61 "cream of Cuban society": Peirce, op. cit., p. 485.

p. 61    Belen Prep story: *Washington Post,* Aug. 4, 1981. The *Fortune* ad was "Florida: A New Economic Force," from 1981.

p. 62    DuPont story: Garreau, op. cit., p. 201. "economy . . . facing due south": Ibid., p. 172.

p. 62    Fur coats sold in August: Ibid., p. 177.

p. 63    Insurance exchange: *Washington Post,* Mar. 29, 1981.

p. 63    Drug smuggling estimate: *Time,* Nov. 23, 1981. "shedding the institutions . . .": Garreau, op. cit., p. 195. Kimball estimate of real estate: Ibid., p. 190. *Washington Post* quotes: From Aug. 6, 1981, issue.

p. 63–64    Banks fail to report deposits: *Time,* Nov. 23, 1981. "outlaws used to rob banks": Garreau, op. cit., p. 192.

p. 64    Customs Service quote: *New York Times,* Aug. 12, 1981.

p. 65    "Smuggling dope into the region . . .": *Time,* Nov. 23, 1981.

p. 65    Red column jumps off graph: *New York Times,* Mar. 4, 1981.

*p. 66* TV cameras on Collins Avenue: Ibid., Nov. 16, 1981.
Miami hotel owner's quote: Ibid., Jan. 31, 1982.
*p. 66* Legal researcher quote: *Time*, Nov. 23, 1981.
Police response times: *New York Times*, Dec. 23, 1980
*p. 67* Footnote on Palm Beach: *U.S. News & World Report*, Mar. 1, 1982.
*p. 67* "Tax us" plea: *New York Times*, Jan. 31, 1982.
*p. 67* "Thirty-six of the first": *New York Times*, June 1, 1981.
*p. 68* Governor Gilligan quote: Peirce, op. cit., p. 485.
*p. 68* Professor Perez' comments in Letter to *The New York Times*, May 18, 1981.
*p. 69* Kolberg's remarks: On *The MacNeil-Lehrer Report*, summer of 1981.
*p. 69* "Am I supposed": *The Wall Street Journal*, Mar. 30, 1981.
*p. 70* School principal quote: *New York Times*, Aug. 10, 1981.
*p. 71* "not refugees . . .": Garreau op. cit., p. 173.
*p. 71* *Washington Post*, Oct. 25, 1981.
*p. 71* Mayor Ferre quote: *Time*, Nov. 23, 1981.

ATLANTA

*p. 72* Clark Gable quote: Lyn Tornabene, *Long Live the King*, Putnam, 1977.
*p. 72* "tax base . . . shrinking . . .": *New York Times*, Oct. 29, 1981.
*p. 73* John Portman's forte: *Time*, July 5, 1976.
*p. 73–74* Horace Sutton describes Portman hotel: *Saturday Review*, Sept. 4, 1976.
*p. 74* Jonathan Schlefer and the Omni: *The Progressive*, July 1981.
*p. 74* Portman quote in footnote: *Nation's Business*, August 1976.
*p. 74* Portman quote: *Wall Street Journal*, Oct. 19, 1981.
Profile of Atlanta: *Nation's Business*, April 1976.
*p. 75* Chamber of Commerce study: *New York Times*, Oct. 29, 1981.
*p. 75* Atlanta's research director on jobs: *Los Angeles Times*, May 17, 1981.
*p. 75* Jackson's first fifteen months: *Time*, Apr. 21, 1975.
*p. 75* "the mayor's mind . . .": *U.S. News & World Report*, Apr. 7, 1975.
*p. 76* Quotes from Jackson's attack: *Time*, Apr. 21, 1975.
*p. 76* Jackson on annexation: Ibid., Apr. 21, 1975.
*p. 76* Crouch article: *The Village Voice*, Apr. 29, 1981.
*p. 76–77* "we've been successful . . .": *Los Angeles Times*, May 17, 1981.
*p. 77* "we are ideologically liberal . . .": *Nation's Business*, April 1976.
*p. 78* Crouch article: *The Village Voice*, Apr. 29, 1981.
*p. 78* Jordan interview: *60 Minutes*, June 6, 1981.
*p. 78* Crouch article: *The Village Voice*, Apr. 29, 1981.
*p. 79* Dwight Thomas quote: *The Washington Post*, Apr. 20, 1981.
*p. 80* Brown quote: *ABC News: Nightline*, Mar. 1, 1981.
*p. 80–81* Jackson luncheon remarks: *Washington Post*, Oct. 25, 1981.
*p. 81* Dean and Young remarks: Ibid.
*p. 81* Andrew Young interview: *New York Times*, Jan. 3, 1982.
*p. 82* Peachtree Street businessman quote: Ibid., Feb. 12, 1982.
*p. 82* Footnote: Jean-Jacques Servan-Schreiber, *The World Challenge*, Simon & Schuster, 1981, p. 267.
*p. 82* Andrew Young on Atlanta's racial calm: *New York Times*, Jan. 3, 1982.
*p. 82–83* John Lewis quote: Ibid., Oct. 26, 1981.

BIRMINGHAM

*p. 83* Birmingham: "A City Reborn,' in *Time*, Sept. 27, 1976.
*p. 84* Mayor Arrington on transit shutdown: *New York Times*, Mar. 1, 1981.
*p. 85* Historical background: *The Encyclopaedia Britannica*, 11th edition, 1911, Vol. 3, p. 983.

*p. 85*   Lack of growth: Michael Barone, Grant Ujifusa and Douglas Matthews, *The Almanac of American Politics 1980,* E. P. Dutton, 1979, p. 14.

*p. 85*   Lost steel jobs: From *Nation's Business* profile of Birmingham, November 1975 issue.

*p. 86*   Arrington quote: *New York Times,* Mar. 7, 1981.

*p. 86*   1980 urban fares equal fare hikes all previous six years: From study of U.S. Conference of Mayors, quoted in *New York Times,* July 2, 1981. Quote is also from *Times* piece.

*p. 87*   Arthur Shores story: *Nation's Business,* November 1975 profile.

*p. 87*   Nathan remark: *New York Times,* Mar. 15, 1981.

NEW ORLEANS

*p. 88*   Judd Rose quote: *ABC News: Nightline,* Feb. 1, 1983.

*p. 88*   Jorge Luis Borges as jazz patron: *Washington Post,* May 18, 1982.

*p. 88*   Walker Percy quote: Neal R. Peirce, *The Deep South States of America,* W. W. Norton, 1974, p. 96.

*p. 88*   "You can make it illegal, but you can't make it unpopular!": John Gunther, *Inside U.S.A.,* Harper & Bros., 1947, p. 805.

*p. 89*   Isamu Noguchi quote: *Saturday Review,* Sept. 4, 1976.

*p. 89*   Louisiana State University study: *New York Times,* Sept. 8. 1980. Deputy police chief quote: Ibid., Nov. 20, 1981.

*p. 89*   "Blacks and whites live": *Washington Post,* June 11, 1981.

*p. 90*   Data on Superdeductible: Ibid., Sept. 8, 1980.

## Chapter 4: TEXAS CITIES

HOUSTON

*p. 92*   Early history of Houston: Neal R. Peirce, *The Megastates of America,* W. W. Norton, 1972, p. 530; also from article by William D. Angel, "To Make a City: Entrepreneurship on the Sunbelt Frontier" in *The Rise of the Sunbelt Cities,* edited by David C. Perry and Alfred J. Watkins, Sage Publications, 1977, pp. 117–18.

*p. 92–93*   Galveston and Houston early histories: *Encyclopaedia Britannica,* 11th edition, 1911, Vol. 11, pp. 430–31 (Galveston) and Vol. 13, pp. 828–29 (Houston). Details of Channel dredging: Angel, op. cit., pp. 118–19.

*p. 93–94*   Shell Oil and air conditioning: Joel Garreau, *The Nine Nations of North America,* Houghton Mifflin, 1981, p. 6.

*p. 94*   "the blob that ate East Texas" remark and annexation data: From report on annexation, Southern Growth Policies Board, 1980, pp. 100–107. Jesse Jones quote: Peirce, op. cit., p. 530.

*p. 94*   Impact of Spacecraft Center: Angel, op. cit., pp. 123–26.

*p. 95*   Link of pols and plutocrats: Ibid., pp. 123–26.

*p. 95*   "kind of economic stimulus . . .": Peirce, op. cit., pp. 534–35.

*p. 95*   Footnote: Based on material in Theodore C. Sorensen, *Kennedy,* Bantam Books, 1966, pp. 213–17.

*p. 96*   Hofheinz quote: *U.S. News & World Report,* Apr. 5, 1976.

*p. 96*   Footnote: From *New York Times,* Oct. 24, 1982.

*p. 96*   "Many Houston brokers . . .": *Wall Street Journal,* Apr. 6, 1982. Footnote: From *New York Times,* Oct. 25, 1981.

*p. 97*   "City of the Future": Ad in *Forbes,* Oct. 12, 1981. "the biggest draw for opportunity-seekers . . .": Garreau, op. cit., p. 138.

*p. 97*   Michigan book store, Texas papers: *New York Times,* Apr. 16, 1981.

*p. 98*   Houston shrugs off Sun Belt boom report: *New York Times,* Jan. 9. 1981.

*p. 98*  Saudis in Houston: *Washington Post,* Apr. 19, 1981.
Gunther on Houston: John Gunther, *Inside U.S.A.,* Harper & Bros., 1947, p. 827.

*p. 99*  Banker's quote: *U.S. News & World Report,* Apr. 5, 1976.

*p. 99–100*  Brown & Root story: *New York Times,* Sept. 19, 1981.

*p. 100*  Wealth and poverty in Houston: Michael Barone, Grant Ujifusa and Douglas Matthews, *The Almanac of American Politics 1980,* E. P. Dutton, 1979, p. 865.

*p. 100–101*  Black and white voting power: Ibid.

*p. 101*  Footnote: Based on *Washington Post,* Apr. 20, 1982.

*p. 101–102*  Poor water system: *New York Times,* May 28, 1981.

*p. 102*  Houston resembles Los Angeles: Garreau, op. cit., pp. 218–19.

*p. 103*  Las Vegas gambling: *New York Times,* Oct. 21, 1981.

*p. 103*  New breed in Houston: Ibid., Nov. 27, 1981.

*p. 104*  Material unless otherwise noted is from "GROWTH and Our Threatened Way of Life," a special issue of *The Texas Magazine* in the *Houston Chronicle,* Dec. 6, 1981.

*p. 107*  Demographic comparison: *New York Times,* Dec. 16, 1981.


## DALLAS

*p. 109*  Quote on Braniff failure: *Wall Street Journal,* May 14, 1982.

*p. 110*  ". . . isn't any reason for Dallas" and "skyscrapers soaring . . .": Warren Leslie, *Dallas Public and Private,* Grossman Publishers, 1964, pp. 22–24.

*p. 110*  Dallas drawbacks: Peirce, op. cit., *The Megastates,* pp. 544–45.
Dallas and railroad: Leslie, op. cit., pp. 24–25.

*p. 111*  "My banker friend . . .": John Gunther, op. cit., p. 830.
"Hundreds of Dallasites became millionaires . . .": Peirce, op. cit., p. 545.

*p. 111*  Sakowitz on fashion: *New York Times,* Aug. 6, 1981.
Dallas profile: *Nation's Business,* January 1975.

*p. 112*  Billy Rose story: Gunther, op. cit., p. 830

*p. 112–113*  Some of the data on trade, aerospace, electronics and office space are from *Nation's Business* profile, January 1975.

*p. 113*  "a low-flying horse . . .": Leslie, op. cit., p. 22.

*p. 114*  Mary Kay story: *60 Minutes* in 1981.
"Born Again Balm": Michael M. Thomas, *Someone Else's Money,* Simon and Schuster, 1982, p. 136.

*p. 114*  Religious milieu: Peirce, op. cit., p. 540.

*p. 114*  "There was no organization." Leslie, op. cit., pp. 68–69.

*p. 115*  "the Assembly was beginning to age . . .": Peirce, op. cit., p. 542.

*p. 115*  J. Erik Jonsson appointed mayor: Leslie, op. cit., p. 67

*p. 115*  Vought gets landing strip: Ibid., p. 70.

*p. 115*  Racial integration story: Ibid., p. 72.

*p. 116*  Civic apathy quote: Ibid., pp. 84–85.

*p. 116*  West Dallas material: Ibid., p. 33.

*p. 117*  Public housing story: Ibid., pp. 36–37.

*p. 117*  J. Erik Jonsson and "Goals for Dallas": Peirce, op. cit., p. 543.

*p. 118*  Peter Applebome feature: *New York Times,* May 10, 1981.

*p. 119*  Quality of life study: Ben-chieh Liu, *Quality of Life Indicators in U.S. Metropolitan Areas,* Praeger, 1976.

*p. 119*  1981 congressional study: From the Joint Economic Committee of Congress, July 31, 1981, pp. 32–33.

*p. 122*  Las Colinas story: *New York Times,* Sept. 15, 1981.

SAN ANTONIO

*p. 124* "veritable cattle capital . . .": Peirce, op. cit., p. 549.

*p. 124* San Antonio's annexation problems: Arnold Fleischmann, "Sunbelt Boosterism: The Politics of Postwar Growth and Annexation in San Antonio" in *The Rise of the Sunbelt Cities,* edited by Perry and Watkins, 1977.

*p. 124* Mexican wages: Gunther, op. cit., p. 833.

*p. 125* GGL goals: Fleischmann, op. cit., p. 165.

*p. 125* Population growth: Ibid., p. 168.

*p. 125* Archbishop Lucey's leadership: Gunther, op. cit., p. 834.

*p. 126* Cisneros a media star: *Life,* July 1981.

*p. 129* Military data: *New York Times,* Dec. 28, 1981.

RIO GRANDE CITIES

*p. 130* Rio Grande and Third World: Ibid., July 18, 1981.

*p. 131* El Paso water supply: *Washington Post,* Feb. 13, 1981.

*p. 131* McAllen police tapes: *Washington Post,* June 2, 1981.

*p. 131* Mayoral candidate quotes in McAllen: *New York Times,* May 11, 1981.

*p. 132* George Parr suicide: *Time,* Apr. 14, 1975.

*p. 132* Migrant system: Peirce, op. cit., p. 554.

*p. 134* "Mexico . . . a country of large landowners.": *The New Republic,* Sept. 25, 1971.

*p. 134* Mexico's food self-sufficiency drive: *New York Times,* Nov. 6, 1981.

*p. 134* Clements quote and Raspberry column: *Washington Post,* Apr. 8, 1981.

*p. 135* Texas Prison data: *New York Times,* Dec. 19, 1981.

## Chapter 5: ROCKY MOUNTAIN CITIES

DENVER

*p. 136* Greeley letter, and Villard's comment in footnote: William Harlan Hale, *Horace Greeley, Voice of the People,* Collier Books, 1961, pp. 207–08.

*p. 136* "quite possibly the best hotel . . .": John Gunther, *Inside U.S.A.,* Harper & Bros., p. 223.

*p. 137* Denver in a rut: Ibid., p. 224.

*p. 137* ". . . the most lunatic paper . . .": Ibid., p. 225.

*p. 138* Job data: Ibid.

*p. 138* *Congressional Quarterly* quotes: *American Regionalism,* Editorial Research Reports, *Congressional Quarterly,* 1980; "Rocky Mountain West" chapter by Tom Arrandale, p. 67.

*p. 138–39* Building boom data: *Wall Street Journal,* Apr. 6, 1982.

*p. 139* Joseph Coors article: Ibid., June 4, 1981.

*p. 139–40* Office space glut: *New York Times,* May 11, 1981.

*p. 140* Richard Lamm article: *The New Republic,* May 5, 1971.

*p. 140–41* Natives versus migrants: Gunther, op. cit., p. 216.

*p. 141* Lamm quote: *Congressional Quarterly,* op. cit., p. 64.

*p. 141–42* Denver blacks: Neal R. Peirce, *The Mountain States of America,* W. W. Norton, 1972, pp. 38–39.

*p. 142* Air pollution indices: From report of U.S. Council on Environmental Quality, printed in *Statistical Abstract of the United States: 1980,* table 368 (total of days in table found by combining "unhealthful" and "very unhealthful" days for cities involved).

*p. 143* 3 million acres of cropland lost a year: From the National Agricultural Lands Study, U.S. Department of Agriculture, 1980, discussed in *New York Times,* June 16, 1981.

*p. 143*  5 billion tons topsoil lost a year: One more USDA study, cited in *Washington Post*, July 25, 1981.

*p. 143–44*  Greeley quotes: Hale, op. cit., p. 317

*p. 144*  Major farm state with major water problem: Gunther, op. cit., pp. 214–15.

*p. 144*  Weld County data: *New York Times*, June 16, 1981.

*p. 145*  Prairie sphinx moth returns: Ibid., Sept. 5, 1981.

PHOENIX

*p. 145–46*  Barbour and Peirce quotes: Peirce, op. cit., *States of America*, pp. 236–37.

*p. 146*  Copper data: From *Nation's Business* profile of Phoenix in its May 1976 issue.

*p. 146*  Cotton data: Ibid.

*p. 147–48*  Computers and industry: Ibid.

*p. 148*  "one of the best examples . . .": Peirce, op. cit., p. 239.

*p. 149*  Princeton study: Cited in *New York Times*, Mar. 30, 1980.

*p. 150*  No building code in 1972: Peirce, op. cit., p. 237.

*p. 150*  Medicaid footnote: *Washington Post*, Oct. 26, 1981.

*p. 151*  Casa Grande and NFL football: *New York Times*, Feb. 3, 1982.

*p. 151*  Sky glow in Arizona footnote: *CBS Evening News*, 1982.

*p. 152*  Salt River Irrigation project: John Gunther, op. cit., p. 902.

*p. 153*  "give Arizona . . . irrigated land . . .": Ibid., pp. 902–03.

*p. 153*  Aquifer "overdraft": Peirce, op. cit., p. 234.

*p. 153–54*  Details on Arizona aquifer law and water conservation in Lubbock: From *New York Times* series on water, August 1981.

*p. 154*  "as strict as Arizona's new law is . . .": *Life*, July 1981.

*p. 154*  Opie article: *The Progressive*, July 1981.

LAS VEGAS

*p. 155*  1982 slump: *New York Times*, Dec. 15, 1982.

*p. 155*  "casino gambling . . .": Peirce, op. cit., p. 158.

*p. 155*  "to clean up gambling . . .": Gunther, op. cit., pp. 78–79.

*p. 156*  The mob and The Strip: Peirce, op. cit., p. 162

*p. 156–57*  Hughes in Las Vegas: Ibid., pp. 164–65.

*p. 157*  Williams quote: *New York Times*, June 6, 1981.

*p. 158*  Jefferson quote and revenue estimates: *Time*, Dec. 6, 1976.

*p. 159*  Reopening of MGM Grand Hotel: *New York Times*, July 31, 1981.

*p. 159*  West side slum in Vegas: Peirce, op. cit., p. 168.

## Chapter 6: CALIFORNIA CITIES

CRIME AND TAXES

*p. 160*  Theodore Roosevelt quote: In article by John Gregory Dunne on California in *New West*, 1979.

*p. 160*  "theology *in extremis*": John Gunther, *Inside U.S.A.*, Harper & Bros., 1947, p. 52.

*p. 160*  Bertrand Russell quote: *American Regionalism*, Editorial Research Reports, *Congressional Quarterly*, 1980; "California: Living Out the Golden Dream" chapter by Richard Kipling and William V. Thomas, p. 131.

*p. 161*  Tear-gas grenade growth: *New York Times*, Feb. 7, 1981.

*p. 161*  Armed cults: Ibid., Dec. 17, 1980.

*p. 161*  *Soldier of Fortune* magazine: *Wall Street Journal*, Sept. 15, 1981.

*p. 161*  Survivalist condo in desert: *New York Times*, Jan. 15, 1981.

*p. 162*   "the authorities will try to take our weapons . . .": *Los Angeles Times,* May 6, 1981.

*p. 162*   Richard Johnson family: Ibid., May 6, 1981.

*p. 163*   ACLU attack on "garbage" law: *New York Times,* May 23, 1982.

*p. 163*   Earl Huntting material: *New York Times,* Mar. 28, 1981.

*p. 164*   Field Poll on California taxes in 1980: *Washington Post,* May 29, 1981.

*p. 165*   Table and accompanying analysis: Harold Meyerson, "Prop 13: Nightmare Takes Form as Surplus Dries Up" in *Democratic Left,* October 1981.

*p. 165*   "One third of our 100 engineering faculty . . .": *Wall Street Journal,* Feb. 12, 1982.

*p. 165*   *Time* quote on Upton Sinclair: Gunther, op. cit., p. 53.

*p. 166*   Gunther and Lippmann quotes: Ibid., p. 54.

*p. 166*   Kaiser's 300,000 riveters: Ibid., p. 71.

*p. 166*   Aerospace grows 228 percent as California economy grows 81 percent: Robert Deutsch, "Aerospace in Crisis" in *The Nation,* Feb. 22, 1971.

*p. 166*   California gets 24 percent all prime defense contracts, 40 percent all R&D: Neal R. Peirce, *The Megastates of America,* W. W. Norton, 1972, p. 679.

*p. 166*   California had 69 percent all net migration in 1960s: *Statistical Abstract of the United States: 1980,* U.S. Bureau of the Census, 1981, table 11.

*p. 166*   616,000 aerospace workers down to 450,000: Robert Deutsch, op. cit. Slowed growth by mid-1970s: *U.S. News, & World Report,* Dec. 29, 1975.

*p. 166*   California's gross national product: Ibid.

*p. 167*   Job growth 1976–79: Bureau of Labor Statistics, Department of Labor.

*p. 167*   "thinks Jerry Brown has gone too far . . .": *Time:* Apr. 14, 1975.

*p. 167*   "Reagan, as a conservative . . .": Robert Kuttner, *Revolt of the Haves,* Simon and Schuster, 1980, p. 60.

*p. 167–68*   Los Angeles housing prices rise 1974–78: Ibid., p. 51.

*p. 168*   Orange County lotteries, *U.S. New & World Report,* July 11, 1977.

*p. 168*   Kuttner points out: Kuttner, op. cit., p. 50.

*p. 168*   Big tax winners from Proposition 13: Ibid., pp. 69, 83.

*p. 168*   "fiscally irresponsible . . .": Ibid., p. 69.

*p. 169*   "The moment of truth . . .": *New York Times,* Jan. 10, 1981.

*p. 169*   Senator Boatwright data: *Los Angeles Times,* May 21, 1981.

*p. 169*   Assembly and Senate cuts: Ibid., May 22 and June 5, 1981.

*p. 169*   Health services cuts: Harold Meyerson, op. cit.

*p. 170*   San Francisco voluntarism: *Washington Post,* May 29, 1981.

*p. 170*   "public officials say that California . . .": Ibid., Apr. 12, 1982. California fiscal crisis in fall of 1981: *New York Times,* Oct. 27, 1981.

*p. 170*   New round of 1982 cuts: Ibid., Nov. 9, 1982.

*p. 170–71*   Huge new deficit by July 1983: Ibid., Nov. 7, 1982.

*p. 171*   Brown's economic policy director quote: *The Wall Street Journal,* Nov. 21, 1981.

*p. 171*   Silicon Valley as "Detroit of the next generation": *Wall Street Journal,* Feb. 16, 1982.

*p. 171*   40 percent of America's engineers and computer professionals in California: *U.S. News & World Report,* Aug. 23, 1982.

*p. 171*   Old factories closing: *New York Times,* Oct. 26, 1981, and Oct. 27, 1982.

*p. 172*   Bank of America projection: Ibid., Oct. 26, 1981.

*p. 172*   Security Pacific National Bank projection: Ibid., Oct. 27, 1982.

*p. 172*   Japanese cars on West Coast: Joel Garreau, *The Nine Nations of North America,* Houghton Mifflin, 1981, pp. 280–81.

*p. 172*   Japanese firms in Silicon Valley: *New York Times,* Nov. 1, 1981.

*p. 172*   Silicon Valley II in Roseville?: Ibid., June 11, 1981.

*p. 172*   Japanese firms in California: *Los Angeles Times,* May 17, 1981.

*p. 172–73*   California a part of Japan: Joel Garreau, op. cit., p. 279.

*p. 173*   Japanese "bullet train": *New York Times,* Apr. 1, 1982.

SAN FRANCISCO

*p. 173*   Unemployment rate comparisons: From October 1980 report of "Employment and Earnings," Bureau of Labor Statistics, U.S. Department of Labor, December 1980.

*p. 173*   1980 tourist slump: *New York Times,* May 10, 1981.

*p. 173–74*   Violence in 1850s mining camps: James L. Spates and John J. Macionis, *The Sociology of Cities,* St. Martin's Press, 1981, pp. 509–10.

*p. 174*   Barbary Coast closed: Ibid., p. 514, quoting from Herbert Asbury, *The Barbary Coast,* Doubleday, 1933.

*p. 174*   Office towers go up 1960–75: Peirce, op. cit., pp. 629–30.

*p. 174*   "highest crime rate . . . bar none . . .": Ibid., p. 632.

*p. 174*   Highest median housing cost: *New York Times,* June 9, 1981, citing a federal study.

*p. 174*   Household size drops in 1970s: Ibid.

*p. 175*   RAND Corporation demographer quote: Ibid., Aug. 21, 1981.

*p. 175*   Chinatown data in 1972: Peirce, op. cit., pp. 639–40.

*p. 175*   Reagan and Proposition 13 cuts impact on health: *New York Times,* Oct. 27, 1981.

*p. 175*   High suicide rate: *Washington Post,* Dec. 26, 1981.

*p. 176*   New tourist maps and drive on muggers: *New York Times,* July 30, 1981.

*p. 176*   Cable car system closed for repair: *New York Times,* Aug. 4, 1982.

*p. 176–77*   Selling "Disneyland without Mickey Mouse": From report by Barry Peterson on *CBS Evening News* in fall 1982.

*p. 177*   Oakland service cuts: Harold Meyerson, op. cit., *Wall Street Journal,* Feb. 16, 1982.

*p. 177–78*   Oakland vote and quote: *New York Times,* May 3, 1981.

*p. 178*   BART subway and Oakland: Peirce, op. cit., p. 646.

LOS ANGELES

*p. 178*   Metro area factory comparisons: From September 1980, in "Employment and Earnings," December 1980, Bureau of Labor Statistics, U.S. Department of Labor.

*p. 178*   Los Angeles and New York job comparisons and quote: Joel Kotkin's article, *Washington Post,* Nov. 3, 1980.

*p. 180*   Early railroad rate war: John Gregory Dunne article in *New West,* 1979.

*p. 180*   Early oil discoveries: Richard Kipling and William V. Thomas, op. cit., p. 144.

*p. 180*   "No Dogs or Actors Allowed": Ibid.

*p. 180–81*   L.A. mass transit in 1930s: Peirce, op. cit., p. 654.

*p. 181*   "nineteen suburbs in search . . .": Gunther, op. cit., p. 43.
       "40 suburbs in search . . .": Peirce, op. cit., p. 650.
       "100 suburbs in search of . . .": Richard Kipling and William V. Thomas, op. cit., p. 145.

*p. 182*   Data through 1970: Peirce, op. cit., pp. 676–77.

*p. 182*   Aerospace, the most dynamic element: Ibid., pp. 678–79.

*p. 183*   "aerospace remains the largest cog . . .": Joel Kotkin quote from *Washington Post,* Nov. 30, 1980.

*p. 183*   Wall Street aerospace expert quote: *New York Times,* Oct. 9, 1981.

*p. 183*   Footnote on possible Stealth bomber battle: Ibid., Oct. 5, 1982.

*p. 183*   Palmdale as new defense town: *Washington Post,* Apr. 23, 1982.

*p. 184*   "a veritable chemical factory . . .": Peirce, op. cit., p. 655.

*p. 184*   206 days a year "unhealthy": Data for 1978 from U.S. Council on Environmental Quality, printed in *Statistical Abstract of the United States: 1980,* table 368.

*p. 184*   Los Angeles smog plan: *New York Times,* Sept. 2, 1982.

*p. 184*   Los Angeles exports some pollution: Garreau, op. cit., p. 4.

*p. 184*   Downtown People Mover: Eric Mankin, "The Little Train That Shouldn't" in *New West,* 1979.

*p. 185*   San Andreas fault: Peirce, op. cit., p. 614.

*p. 186*   Earthquake unpreparedness: *Time,* Sept. 1, 1975.

*p. 186*   Worst earthquake scenarios for Los Angeles and San Francisco: *New York Times,* Feb. 9, 1981.
           Footnote on earthquake predicting: *New York Times,* Nov. 2, 1981.

*p. 186*   Red Cross spokesman quote: *New York Times,* Feb. 9, 1981.

*p. 187*   Diablo Canyon footnote: *Time,* Feb. 9, 1975.

*p. 187*   East Los Angeles gangs: An article by Tracey Johnston in *New West,* 1979.

*p. 188*   CRASH program: *Los Angeles Times,* May 20, 1981 (also on new youth gang program).

*p. 189*   Minor inequities in 8500 Plan: Ibid., May 6, 1981.

*p. 189*   Day after the 8500 defeat: Ibid., June 4, 1981; includes Braude and Gates quotes.

*p. 189*   Runaway pension plan costs: Ibid., Apr. 26, 1981.

*p. 190*   Bill Moyers' report: On *CBS Evening News* in 1982.

*p. 190*   Legal Aid cuts: *TheWall Street Journal,* Jan. 28, 1982.

*p. 190*   "War room" to manage Los Angeles' problems: *Los Angeles Times,* May 10, 1981.

# PART II: THE SNOWBELT

## Chapter 7: THE THREE MYTHS

### THE MYTH OF LIMITED RESOURCES

*p. 198*   13.3 percent cut in federal aid to cities 1981: *New York Times,* summarizing survey of Joint Economic Committee of Congress, Oct. 17, 1982.

*p. 198*   "ironically, the erosion of the tax base . . .": Robert Kuttner, *Revolt of the Haves,* Simon and Schuster, 1980, p. 169.

*p. 199*   New York City loses 270,000 manufacturing jobs from 1970 to 1976: Bureau of Labor Statistics, Department of Labor, 1980.

*p. 200*   $292 million surplus becomes $195 million deficit: *Wall Street Journal,* Aug. 31, 1981.

*p. 200*   Felix Rohatyn on "taxurbs": *New York Daily News,* Apr. 7, 1981.

*p. 201*   Professor Richard Wade quote: Long Island *Newsday,* Sept. 13, 1981.

*p. 201*   Arthur D. Little executive quote: "The Reindustrialization of America," a special issue of *Business Week,* June 30, 1980.

### THE MYTH OF UNCONTROLLABLE CRIME

*p. 204*   The Gallup Poll referred to was made in late 1980, and was released by National League of Cities in 1981: *New York Times,* May 15, 1981.

*p. 204*   Professor Nathan Glazer quote: *New York Times Book Review,* Jan. 31, 1982.

*p. 204*   President Reagan quote: *Wall Street Journal,* Sept. 29, 1981.

*p. 205*   Mayor John V. Lindsay quote: On a summer broadcast in 1981 of *ABC News: Nightline,* at time of Brixton, England, riots.

*p. 205*   The New York City murder data, like all crime data unless otherwise noted, are from Uniform Crime Reports of the FBI for the years 1977, 1979 and 1980.

*p. 205*   Professor Harvey Brenner study in footnote: *Washington Post,* Aug. 7, 1982.

*p. 206*   Baby boom and crime rate: Landon Y. Jones, *Great Expectations,* Coward, McCann & Geoghegan, 1980, Chap. 11, especially pp. 148–49.

*p. 206–7*   Foreign gun comparisons: Partly from *Washington Post,* Dec. 21, 1980.

*p. 208*   lack of money: *Washington Post,* Nov. 20, 1981.

*p. 208*   "drug for producers": *U.S. News & World Report,* Mar. 22, 1982.

*p. 208*   Rapid rise in price of cocaine: *Washington Post,* Nov. 11, 1982.

*p. 208*   Cocaine traffic up 50 percent between 1980 and 1981: Ibid., Oct. 24, 1982. Alleged DeLorean cache of $6.5 million: Ibid.

*p. 208*   Marijuana sales; our third biggest crop?: *Newsweek,* Oct. 25, 1982.

*p. 208–9*   Michigan study on declining student marijuana use: Ibid.

*p. 209*   74 percent of Americans against legalizing marijuana: *Newsweek,* Oct. 25, 1982.

*p. 209*   Temple University heroin study: *New York Times,* Mar. 22, 1981.

*p. 209*   Summary of proposed Reagan crime cuts in footnote: *Washington Post,* Nov. 20, 1981.

*p. 210*   Bangkok DEA office cuts: *Washington Post,* June 24, 1981.

*p. 211*   Mario Cuomo quote: *New York Daily News,* Feb. 3, 1981.

*p. 212*   The Tom Wicker TV program on crime appeared on Channel 5, WNEW, in New York City in winter of 1982.

*p. 212*   Suburban crime up only 7 percent since 1975: *Wall Street Journal,* Sept. 2, 1981.

*p. 212*   *U.S. News & World Report* cover story in its July 13, 1981, issue.

*p. 213*   Footnote on Boston arson: Ibid., Feb. 7, 1983.


THE MYTH OF REINDUSTRIALIZATION

*p. 214*   Sunbelt-Snowbelt capital spending: "The State of the Region 1981," Northeast-Midwest Congressional Coalition, 1981, p. 21.

*p. 213*   Joseph Engelberger quote: On *ABC News: Nightline,* spring of 1982. Auto and steel worker losses over years: *U.S. News & World Report,* Sept. 13, 1982.

*p. 214*   "the rubber center of the universe": John Gunther, *Inside U.S.A.,* Harper & Bros., 1947, p. 443.

*p. 214*   Carl Sagan quote: On *The MacNeil/Lehrer Report,* fall of 1982.

*p. 214*   Engineer college grads: *New York Times* supplement on "High Tech Careers," Oct. 17, 1982.

*p. 214*   Footnote on illiteracy: From testimony of Education Secretary Terrel Bell in late 1982 to House subcommittee.

*p. 214–15*   Labor Department projections: *U.S. News & World Report,* Feb. 21, 1983.

*p. 215*   Robert B. Reich quote: *New York Times,* Nov. 26, 1981.

*p. 216–17*   Capital spending 1960s, 1970s: *U.S. News & World Report,* Dec. 13, 1982.

*p. 217*   Commerce Department projections: *New York Times,* Dec. 14, 1982.

*p. 217*   Continuous-caster comparisons: Ibid., June 20, 1982.

*p. 217*   Thomas A. Murphy quote: *New York Times Magazine,* Jan. 4, 1981.

*p. 217*   Akio Morita quote: *U.S. News & World Report,* Oct. 12, 1981.
Machines make machine tools: W. E. Lunt, *History of England,* Harper & Bros., 1951, p. 582.

*p. 218*   Solar cells research: *Washington Post,* Dec. 12, 1982.

*p. 218*   Japan's rapid microchip gains: *New York Times,* Feb. 28, 1982.

*p. 218*   Stephen Lohr quote: *New York Times Magazine,* Jan. 4, 1981.
Gutenberg Bible comparison: *Wall Street Journal,* July 23, 1982.

*p. 218*   First computer of 1946: *60 Minutes,* CBS, summer of 1982.

*p. 218*   Japanese personal computers: *New York Times,* Aug. 1, 1982.

*p. 218–19*   Fujitsu Computer School and Japan capital outlays: Jean-Jacques Servan-Schreiber, *The World Challenge,* Simon and Schuster, 1981, pp. 191–95.

*p. 219*   Supercomputers: *New York Times,* Oct. 28, 1982.
Yamazaki mechatronic factory: Ibid., Dec. 13, 1981.
Footnote: *Newsweek,* Aug. 9, 1982.

*p. 220*   Trade with Japan and Common Market: *New York Times,* Jan. 17, 1982.

*p. 219*   Working capital for auto retooling: Ibid., Dec. 6, 1981, summarizing a Commerce Department report on industry given to U.S. Senate.

*p. 220*   Declining auto demand in 1990s: *U.S. News & World Report,* Mar. 8, 1982.

*p. 220*   Productivity 450,000 Japanese workers: *New York Times,* Dec. 13, 1981.

*p. 220*   Insurance study of U.S. and Japanese small cars: Insurance
Commerce Department study: *New York Times,* Dec. 6, 1981.

*p. 221*   Steel diversification late 1970s: *New York Times,* Nov. 23, 1981.

*p. 221*   Steel plant using steam engines: From special *Business Week* issue on reindustrialization, June 1980, as is the quote.

*p. 221*   Detroit rush orders to retool: Ibid.
Textile rush orders to retool: *Business Week,* June 1980.

*p. 222*   Footnote on textile retooling: *Wall Street Journal,* Dec. 21, 1981.

*p. 222*   Tool imports rise as exports decline: Ibid.
*Business Week* quote from June 1980 issue.

*p. 222*   Aging of American machine tools: *New York Times,* Aug. 15, 1982.

*p. 223*   Chicago tool fair: *New York Times,* Sept. 16, 1982.

*p. 223*   French auto slump: Ibid., Oct. 6, 1982.

*p. 223*   Swiss watch slump: *New York Times,* Nov. 29, 1982.

*p. 223*   The Four "New Japans": Ibid., Aug. 24, 1982.

*p. 224*   An aging Japan: *New York Times,* June 13, 1982.

*p. 224*   Neglect of Japanese aging: Ibid., and *Wall Street Journal,* Nov. 8, 1982.

*p. 225*   The *Milwaukee* magazine reference is made in text.
*U.S. News & World Report* reference is from Sept. 21, 1982, issue.

*p. 225*   Carnegie-Mellon study: Ibid.

*p. 225–26*   Lord Byron attacks capital-crime law: *The Encyclopaedia Britannica,* 11th edition, 1911, Vol. 4, pp. 897–905.

*p. 226*   Robots could replace 40 percent of factory workers by 1990: *Washington Post,* Oct. 27, 1982.

*p. 226*   14,000 advanced Japanese robots: *New York Times,* Dec. 27, 1981.

*p. 227*   Three Japanese mechatronic factories: *Newsweek,* Aug. 9, 1982.

*p. 227*   Robot sushi chef: Ibid.

*p. 227*   Japanese Industrial Robot Association survey quote: *New York Times,* Dec. 27, 1981.

*p. 227*   Footnote on worker health advances in robotics: Ibid.

*p. 227*   GM robots: Ibid., Oct. 17, 1982.

*p. 227*   GE automation: *Wall Street Journal,* Oct. 21, 1982.

*p. 227*   Joseph Engelberger quote: *ABC News: Nightline,* spring of 1982.

*p. 228*   Poll of Japanese workers and managers: *Newsweek,* Aug. 9, 1982.

*p. 228*   *Business Week* projects 38 million white-collar jobs affected by automation: *Washington Post,* Aug. 7, 1981.

*p. 228*   MIT analyst quote: *New York Times,* Oct. 17, 1982.

*p. 228*   Key-punch operators replaced by computers: Ibid.

*p. 228*   Footnote on export of key-punch jobs: *NBC Nightly News,* late 1982.

*p. 229*   Computer graphic data: *New York Times,* Oct. 17, 1982.

*p. 229*   "Info City" quotes from Feb. 9, 1981, issue of *New York.*

*p. 229*   U.S. Postal Service material: *U.S. News & World Report,* Mar. 1, 1982.

*p. 229*   Office productivity survey: Made by the International Data Corporation and cited by Randy J. Goldfeld in *Office Today,* ad supplement to *New York Times* in summer 1982.

*p. 230*   New Ronald Reagan cuts in late 1982: *Washington Post,* Dec. 4, 1982.

*p. 231*   Charles Schultze quote: Ibid., Jan. 24, 1982.

*p. 231*   Studs Terkel paraphrase: Made on *ABC News: Nightline* in 1982.
"Atari Democrats" program: In article for *Wall Street Journal* in late 1982 by Representative Timothy E. Wirth.

*p. 232*   Aaron S. Gurwitz article: *Wall Street Journal,* Oct. 27, 1982.
*U.S. News & World Report* survey of infrastructure in Sept. 27, 1982, issue.

*p. 234*   Sar A. Levitan quote: Ibid., Feb. 21, 1983.
AT&T, IBM and Xerox training programs: *Education in America,* Editorial Research Reports, *Congressional Quarterly,* 1981, pp. 63–75.

*p. 234*   PIC jobs in New York City: *U.S. News & World Report,* Feb. 21, 1983.
America's poverty share cut from 22 percent to 11 percent: Ibid., Aug. 16, 1982.

*p. 234*   355,000 families in Michigan lose health insurance: *Wall Street Journal,* Apr. 6, 1982.

*p. 235*   Johns Hopkins study: *U.S. News & World Report,* June 14, 1982.
Footnote on unemployment benefits: *Newsweek,* Oct. 18, 1982.

*p. 235*   Germany's training program for adults: *The MacNeil-Lehrer Report,* fall of 1982.

## Chapter 8: THE FOUR PARAGONS

*p. 238*   Buffalo background: *New York Times,* Nov. 29, 1982.
Gary fed loans and income: *U.S. News & World Report,* Nov. 22, 1982.
Fort Wayne-Springfield fight for Harvester plant: From *The MacNeil-Lehrer Report,* Aug. 20, 1982.

*p. 239*   Footnote on Indiana automobiles: Neal R. Peirce and John Keefe, *The Great Lakes States of America,* W. W. Norton, 1980, p. 293.

*p. 239*   Flint, Michigan background: *U.S. News & World Report,* Mar. 1, 1982.
Stamford footnote: *New York Times,* Oct. 8, 1982.

*p. 240*   Gunther, quote: From *Inside U.S.A.,* Harper & Bros., 1947, p. 401.
Lowell background: *Washington Post,* Oct. 31, 1982.

*p. 241*   Footnote New Bedford: *Encyclopedia Britannica,* 11th edition, 1911, Vol. 19.

### MINNEAPOLIS

*p. 241*   Urban Institute and Irving Wallace prediction: *Boston Globe,* June 3, 1982.

*p. 242*   Third biggest loser of branch factories: HUD study of cities, 1980.
Princeton study cited: James W. Fossett and Richard P. Nathan, "The Prospects for Urban Revival," 1980.

*p. 243*   5 Percent Club and Donald Fraser quote: *New York Times,* July 27, 1981.
Dayton-Hudson Corporation material: Ibid., Feb. 28, 1982.

*p. 243* $10 billion more could be raised by corporations: Figure derived by multiplying the $2.3 billion in corporate gifts for 1979 by factor of five. Those gifts in Table 589 of *Statistical Abstract of the United States: 1980,* U.S. Bureau of the Census, 1981.

*p. 243–44* William C. Norris quotes: *New York Times,* Feb. 28, 1982, and July 27, 1981.

*p. 244* *Business Week* salute to Norris: From its special issue on reindustrialization in June 1980.

*p. 244* City Venture Corporation background here and below: From "Job Creation Through Private Sector Leadership," a brochure from CVC, spring of 1981.

*p. 244* Northside factory material: From Control Data brochure of 1980 titled "Technology for the Inner City—Experience and Promise," an address by William C. Norris in 1978.

*p. 245* Selby factory material: Ibid.

*p. 245* Baltimore and Philadelphia plans: CVC brochure, op. cit.

*p. 245* South Bronx as "the highest mountain": *New York Times,* July 27, 1981.

*p. 245–46* "a plan advocating relocation . . .": CVC brochure, op. cit.

*p. 246* Education in Minnesota: Neal R. Peirce, *The Great Plains States of America,* W. W. Norton, 1973, pp. 143–45.

*p. 247* Voter backing of Quie: *The Almanac of American Politics 1980,* by Michael Barone, Grant Ujifusa and Douglas Matthews, E. P. Dutton, 1979, p. 458.

*p. 248* Quie cuts taxes, gets big deficits: *Wall Street Journal,* Aug. 31, 1981.
New deficit $768 million: *New York Times,* Nov. 6, 1981.
Fraser-Latimer quote: *Washington Post,* Oct. 26, 1981.

MILWAUKEE

*p. 249* Henry Maier's preinaugural remarks: Ibid., Jan. 21, 1981.

*p. 250* Maier remarks on press: From original transcript, Office of the Mayor, Milwaukee.

*p. 250–51* Maier's comments: *New York Times,* Feb. 14, 1981.

*p. 251* Material on early Socialism in Milwaukee and America is from Sidney Lens, *Radicalism in America,* 1969, Thomas Y. Crowell, pp. 210–11.

*p. 252* Footnote: Gunther, op. cit., p. 325.

*p. 252* Paul Hassett quote: Peirce and Keefe, op. cit., pp. 145–46.
"Workfare" program: *U.S. News & World Report,* Apr. 4, 1977.

*p. 253* "the outlook is brighter in Milwaukee . . .": Ibid., May 15, 1978.

*p. 253* Footnote on factory relocations: From HUD study of cities, 1980.

*p. 254* 1,600 taverns and 2,600 bowling alleys: Peirce and Keefe, op. cit., pp. 144–45.

*p. 254–55* Part of Schlitz story from ibid.; part from *New York Times,* Jan. 24, 1982; and part from *Wall Street Journal,* Jan. 5, 1982.

*p. 255* Pabst story: *New York Times,* Jan. 24, 1982.

*p. 255* Footnote on mergers: *Wall Street Journal,* Sept. 7, 1982.

*p. 256* "We Milwaukeeans": Peirce and Keefe, op. cit., pp. 148–49.

*p. 256* Coalition for Justice for Ernie Lacy background: *New York Times,* Apr. 18, 1982.

*p. 257* Machine-tool orders down 75 percent in two years: *New York Times,* Aug. 15, 1982.

*p. 257* The *Harper's* survey: Arthur M. Louis, "The Worst American City," January 1975 issue.

*p. 257* Most stable of Snowbelt cities: HUD study of cities, 1980.

*p. 257–58* Cornelia Foss on Milwaukee: Interview with author.

*p. 258* *Boston Globe* quote: In Peirce and Keefe, op. cit., p. 144.

KANSAS CITY

*p. 258*   Opening quote: Virgil Thomson, *Virgil Thomson,* Da Capo Press, 1977, p. 3.

*p. 259*   André Maurois quote: *Time,* Aug. 16, 1976.

*p. 259*   Only Rome has more fountains: From *Nation's Business* profile of Kansas City in its March 1976 issue.

*p. 259*   Kansas City in Pendergast era: Peirce, *The Great Plains States of America,* pp. 69–71; and also Gunther, op. cit., pp. 344–48.

*p. 260*   Property tax per capita comparisons: *U.S. News & World Report,* Apr. 5, 1976.

*p. 260*   "crossroads of everything": Joel Garreau, *The Nine Nations of North America,* Houghton Mifflin, 1981, p. 358.

*p. 260*   "Not far from the exact geographic center . . .": Ibid., p. 331.

*p. 260*   "Kansas City was slipping behind . . .": *Nation's Business,* March 1976 issue.

*p. 260–61*   Crown Center: Garreau, op. cit., p. 329.

*p. 261*   $5.3 billion in improvements: *U.S. News & World Report,* Apr. 5, 1976.

*p. 261*   Some of the economic highlights: *Nation's Business* profile, March 1976.

*p. 262*   Henry Bloch quotes: First is from ibid.; the *Time* quote is from its Aug. 16, 1976, issue.

*p. 262*   Underground caverns' office space: *Nation's Business* profile, March 1976; and also *New York Times,* June 12, 1981.

*p. 263*   Parade Homes community: Peirce, *The Great Plains States of America,* p. 74.


WICHITA

*p. 263*   "the Sun Belt city farthest north": Barone, Ujifusa and Matthews, op. cit., p. 326.

*p. 264*   Early days of small planes: From *Nation's Business* profile of Wichita in February 1975 issue.

*p. 264*   Boeing production in World War II: Gunther, op. cit., p. 263.

*p. 264n.*   Footnote: Peirce, *The Great Plains States of America,* p. 239.

*p. 265*   Drop in union membership: *Nation's Business* profile, February 1975.

*p. 265*   Small planes industry analyst: Author's interview with Drew Stekette, of General Aviation Manufacturers Association.

*p. 266*   "heavy purchases of farm equipment . . .": Ibid., Mar. 31, 1975.

*p. 266*   "short of a first-rate meal . . .": Ibid.

*p. 267*   Machine tools drop 50 percent, so do small planes: Interview with Drew Stekette.

*p. 267*   December 1981 billings of $336 million: Ibid.

*p. 268*   Analysis of 1980–82 slump: Ibid.

*p. 268*   Beech salesman quote: Interview with author.

*p. 268*   Footnote on William Lear inventions: Neal R. Peirce, *The Mountain States of America,* W. W. Norton, 1972, p. 172.

*p. 268*   The carbon-fiber plane: Mike Wallace on *60 Minutes,* 1981.

*p. 269*   Cessna losses in 1982: *Wall Street Journal,* Oct. 21, 1982.
            Brighter future for small planes: Interview with Drew Stekette.

*p. 270*   Boston background: *Washington Post,* Dec. 7, 1980.
            Maynard, Massachusetts factory: *Ben Wattenberg's Journal,* PBS, 1981.

*p. 271*   Government Center redevelopment: T. D. Allman, "The Urban Crisis Leaves Town" in *Harper's,* December 1978.

*p. 271*   Suburbanite share of Boston jobs: *Washington Post,* Dec. 7, 1980.

## Chapter 9: THE FIVE DISASTERS

PHILADELPHIA

*p. 274*   35 percent of city under poverty line: Michael Petrovsky, ed., "Race, Poverty & Unemployment," an interim report for the Century IV Project, Center for Philadelphia Studies at the University of Pennsylvania (referred to in text as the Tricentennial Commission), 1981.

*p. 274*   43 percent of factory jobs lost in 1970s: John M. L. Greenstein, ed., "Economic Development," another interim report of Century IV Project.

*p. 274*   Second highest teen-age and black unemployment: Bureau of Labor Statistics survey of eleven large cities, 1980, U.S. Department of Labor.

*p. 275*   70 percent of office jobs held by commuters: Survey by Professor George Sternlieb of Rutgers University, referred to in *New York Times,* Aug. 15, 1981.

*p. 275*   Tricentennial Commission quote: From Greenstein, op. cit.

*p. 275*   Decline of Philadelphia port: *Wall Street Journal,* June 30, 1981.

*p. 275*   Table derived from the Tricentennial Commission's Greenstein report, op. cit., Figure 13.

*p. 275*   Factory job losses and unemployment rates: *New York Times,* Jan. 31, 1982.

*p. 276*   George Sternlieb quote: Ibid., Aug. 15, 1981.

*p. 276*   Philadelphia's early history: *The Encyclopaedia Britannica,* 11th edition, 1911, Vol. 21, pp. 367–73; and also from Jeanne R. Lowe, *Cities in a Race with Time,* Vintage Press edition, 1968, pp. 316–18.

*p. 276*   Absentee aristocrat owners: Lowe, op. cit., p. 318.

*p. 277*   The Main Line: John Gunther: *Inside U.S.A.,* Harper & Bros., 1947, p. 604.

*p. 277*   "one of the most corrupt and unsavory . . .": Neal R. Peirce, *The Megastates of America,* W. W. Norton, 1972, p. 263.

*p. 277*   "When the city's assessments plummeted . . .": Lowe, op. cit., p. 319.

*p. 277*   Gunther quotes, op. cit., pp. 606–07.

*p. 278*   Better Philadelphia Exhibition and Young Turks: Lowe, op. cit., pp. 320–25.

*p. 278*   ". . . how to preserve . . .": Ibid., p. 347.

*p. 278*   Dilworth quote: Ibid., p. 352.

*p. 279*   Progress for blacks under Clark and Dilworth: Ibid., pp. 353–56.

*p. 279*   Joseph Clark quote: Ibid., p. 332.

*p. 279*   Paraphrase and quote from Raymond Vernon: Both ibid., p. 315.

*p. 279*   Aging factories: Ibid., p. 361.

*p. 280*   Decline of labor skills: Ibid., p. 366.

*p. 280*   "blue areas" of poverty: Ibid., p. 398.

*p. 280*   Job loss figures: Mainly from Greenstein, op. cit.

*p. 280–81*   Factory loss comparisons with suburbs: Ibid.

*p. 281*   Welfare growth since 1960: Petrovsky, op. cit., Figure 9.

*p. 281*   Tricentennial Commission report quote: From Greenstein, op. cit.

*p. 282*   Tricentennial Commission recommendations on vocational schools: From Petrovsky, op. cit.

*p. 282*   Births data through 1990s: Ibid., Table 8.

*p. 282*   Service data from 1970s: Greenstein, op. cit., Figure 11.

*p. 283*   Society Hill revival expands central core: *U.S. News & World Report,* Aug. 8, 1977.

*p. 283*   Queen Village gentrification pushes out poor: Ibid.

*p. 283*   Gallery II mall proposal: *New York Times,* Nov. 22, 1980.

*p. 283–84*   Professor George Sternlieb quote: *New York Times Magazine,* May 10, 1981.

*p. 284*   Philadelphia as energy center: From Petrovsky, op. cit.

*p. 284*   Background on port problems: *Wall Street Journal,* June 30, 1981. 1982 "waterfront renaissance" plan: *New York Times,* Jan. 27, 1982.

*p. 284*   William Penn quote: *Encyclopaedia Britannica,* loc. cit., p. 372.

*p. 285*   Frank Rizzo quote: *Time,* May 3, 1976.

*p. 285*   William Green III cuts police and freezes wages as mayor: *New York Times Magazine,* May 10, 1981.

*p. 286*   Commuter tax story and tax official quote: *New York Times,* Nov. 15, 1981.

*p. 286–87*   "Baltimore . . . a major tourist attraction . . .": *Time,* Aug. 24, 1981.

*p. 287*   Rouse's rehab housing in Washington: *Washington Post,* Jan. 17, 1982.

*p. 287*   Columbia, Maryland, material: *Wall Street Journal,* Nov. 29, 1982.

*p. 290*   Footnote on homesteading: *Los Angeles Times,* June 21, 1981.

*p. 290*   Baltimore homestead neighborhoods: Joel Garreau, *The Nine Nations of North America,* Houghton Mifflin, 1981, p. 52.

*p. 290–91*   Jane Jacobs quote: From her *The Death and Life of Great American Cities,* Vintage edition. 1961, p. 404.

*p. 291*   "the unspectacularity of Baltimore": Neal R. Peirce and Michael Barone, *The Mid-Atlantic States of America,* W. W. Norton, 1977, p. 82.

*p. 291*   Baltimore planner's quote: *Wall Street Journal,* Sept. 22, 1981.

*p. 291*   Baltimore loses 13 percent all jobs in 1970–75 period: *U.S. News & World Report,* Apr. 5, 1976.

*p. 292*   Borening Highway auto plant: *Washington Post,* Feb. 7, 1982.

*p. 292*   Baltimore's steel background: *New York Times,* June 20, 1982.

*p. 292–93*   Port "relatively free of graft and payoffs": Peirce and Barone, op. cit., p. 77.

*p. 293*   80 percent shipyard workers laid off by late 1982: *Washington Post,* Oct. 11, 1982.

*p. 293*   86 percent shipyard workers with abnormal lungs: *New York Times,* Sept. 3, 1982.

*p. 293*   Biotechnology urged for Baltimore: Ibid., June 20, 1982.

*p. 294*   Rearrangement of slums: Allman, op. cit.

*p. 294*   City-to-suburb income: From HUD studies of cities in 1980.

*p. 294*   Baltimore's high dependence on state and federal aid: From "The Regional and Urban Impacts of the Administration's Budget and Tax Proposals," a study on impact of Reagan cuts, done for the Joint Economic Committee of Congress: Government Printing Office, July 31, 1981, pp. 26–28.

*p. 295*   Baltimore with $52 million surplus: *U.S. News & World Report,* Oct. 20, 1975.

*p. 295*   Study for Joint Economic Committee, op. cit., for quote and also data on the proposed federal cuts affecting Baltimore in 1981 and later years, pp. 26–28.

*p. 295*   "Blue Chip-In" campaign: *Time,* Aug. 21, 1981.

St. Louis

*p. 296*   The cleared site of Pruitt-Igoe: *Washington Post,* Mar. 13, 1981.

*p. 296*   St. Louis in the early 1900s: *The Encyclopaedia Britannica,* 11th edition, 1911, Vol. 24, pp. 24–27.

*p. 296*   Later economic history St. Louis: Neal R. Peirce, *The Great Plains States of America,* W. W. Norton, 1973, pp. 59–61.

*p. 297*   Air pollution: Gunther, op. cit., p. 357.

*p. 297*  County jobs grow 400 percent as city's shrink 20 percent: Peirce, *The Great Plains States of America*, p. 66.

*p. 297*  Mill Creek Valley slums, also housing data: Ibid., pp. 52–54.

*p. 297*  Few blacks in county suburbs: Ibid., p. 68.

*p. 297–98*  Pruitt-Igoe story: Ibid., pp. 54–57.

*p. 298*  "gnawing fear . . . the point of no return": Ibid., p. 57.

*p. 298*  Growth of county and Clayton: Ibid., p. 66.

*p. 298*  Peirce quote on Gateway Arch in ibid., p. 49.

*p. 299*  "St. Louis: Dying City Bounces Back": *U.S. News & World Report* feature in its July 23, 1974, issue.

*p. 299*  Entire sections razed: Robert Kuttner, *Revolt of the Haves*, Simon and Schuster, 1980, p. 182.

*p. 299*  Mercantile Center story and Woolworth official quote: Ibid., p. 185.

*p. 300*  Property tax losses: Ibid., p. 184.

*p. 300*  Major ward of federal government: From a Brookings Institute study, quoted in *New York Times* of Oct. 20, 1981.

*p. 300*  City's dependent population: *Washington Post*, Mar. 13, 1981, and *New York Times*, Jan. 5, 1981.

*p. 300*  GM plant phases out 10,000 jobs: *New York Times*, Jan. 5, 1981.

*p. 300*  300 factories lost with 58,000 jobs: *Washington Post*, Mar. 13, 1981. Business firms, city-county comparisons: *New York Times*, Jan. 5, 1981.

*p. 300*  Footnote on East St. Louis: *New York Times*, Jan. 6, 1982.

*p. 300–301*  Cardinals and St. Louis comebacks together?: Ibid., Oct. 17, 1982.

*p. 301*  Median family income plummets relative to suburbs: The HUD report on cities in 1980.

*p. 301*  The poem is "Ozymandias," by Percy Bysshe Shelley.

DETROIT

*p. 302*  Some of material on auto slump: *U.S. News & World Report*, Mar. 8, 1982.

*p. 302*  Data on suppliers and Anderson, Indiana: Jean-Jacques Servan-Schreiber, *The World Challenge*, Simon and Schuster, 1981, pp. 93 and 95.

*p. 303*  Ford tries to sell steel plant to Japan: *New York Times*, July 23, 1982. Chrysler makes profits, cuts workers: Ibid., Aug. 29, 1982.

*p. 303*  *U.S. News & World Report* summary of job losses: Sept. 13, 1982, issue.

*p. 304*  60 percent of Detroit receives public aid: *New York Times*, Apr. 27, 1981.

*p. 305*  Footnote on Clark, New Jersey, factory: Ibid., Oct. 26, 1981, and *U.S. News & World Report*, Sept. 13, 1982.

*p. 305*  Drop in capital funds for auto industry 1978–81: *New York Times*, Dec. 6, 1981.

*p. 305*  Drop in new drivers and miles driven: Ibid., summarizing Department of Commerce study submitted to Congress on Dec. 1, 1981.

*p. 305*  Sage Associates projection through 1990s: *U.S. News & World Report*, Mar. 8, 1982.

*p. 305–306*  Lee Iacocca quote: *Wall Street Journal*, Aug. 16, 1982.

*p. 306*  Iacocca urges gas excise tax: *ABC World News Tonight*, fall 1982.

*p. 306*  Insurance Institute study of low cost and high safety rate of air bags: *New York Times*, Oct. 18, 1981.

*p. 307*  Fourteen hours to assemble Japanese subcompact versus twenty-nine hours here: *U.S. News & World Report*, Mar. 8, 1982.

*p. 307*  Footnote on "same-day parts delivery": *Wall Street Journal*, Nov. 24, 1982.

*p. 307–308*  Detroit's problems in 1975: *Time*, Feb. 10, 1975.

*p. 308*  "Winston Churchill . . . trouble as mayor of Detroit": *U.S. News & World Report*, Apr. 7, 1975.

*p. 308*   1,000 fewer police in 1975 and 1976: *Nation's Business* profile of Detroit in its October 1976 issue.

*p. 308*   Youth gangs in summer of 1976: *Time*, Sept. 6, 1976.

*p. 308*   Coleman Young's inaugural warning: Neal R. Peirce and John Keefe, *The Great Lakes States of America*, W. W. Norton, 1980, p. 210.

*p. 309*   Quote on Ren Center: Ibid., p. 214.

*p. 309*   Sixteen buildings planned in wake of Ren Cen: *U.S. News & World Report*, Mar. 28, 1977.

*p. 309*   Coleman Young claims $603 million construction tied to Ren Cen: Peirce and Keefe, op. cit., p. 215.

*p. 309*   "Hank the Deuce . . .": Ibid., p. 221.

*p. 309*   Tom Wolfe on John Portman: *Wall Street Journal*, Oct. 19, 1981.

*p. 309*   *Wall Street Journal* on downtown Detroit: Ibid.

*p. 310*   Ren Cen and Eiffel Tower: *New York Times*, Nov. 1, 1981.

*p. 310*   Joseph L. Hudson quote: *Nation's Business* October 1976 Detroit profile.

*p. 310*   "Hudson's has slowly turned the tourniquet . . .": Peirce and Keefe, op. cit., p. 215.

*p. 310*   Detroit issues only ten home permits in 1979: Ibid., p. 219.

*p. 310–11*   Twelfth Street decade after 1967 riot: *U.S. News & World Report*, Aug. 29, 1977.

*p. 311*   Twelfth Street in 1981: *New York Times*, May 21, 1981.

*p. 312*   Coleman Young's racist appeal to black Democrats: *Wall Street Journal*, June 24, 1981.

*p. 312*   Young's racist rhetoric about "black-Jewish split": *New York Times*, Mar. 30, 1981.

*p. 312*   "the city's renaissance . . . fading": *Time*, June 15, 1981.

*p. 313*   Michigan thirty-ninth for growth of state spending: Kuttner, op. cit., p. 294.

*p. 313*   Michigan cuts budget 20 percent in 1981: *New York Times*, Nov. 29, 1981.

*p. 313*   "unflagging commitment to the salvaging of Detroit": Peirce and Keefe, op. cit., p. 191.

*p. 313*   Localities borrow $400 million for schools: *New York Times*, Oct. 31, 1981.

*p. 313*   Footnote on Alpena and rural growth: Ibid., July 8 and Oct. 21, 1981.

OHIO

*p. 314–15*   Democrat-Republican cycle: Kuttner, op. cit., p. 319.

*p. 315*   The last truck tire in Akron: Mainly from *New York Times*, Aug. 21, 1982.

*p. 315*   "rubber center of the universe" and prewar dominance of Akron: Gunther, op. cit., p. 443.

*p. 315*   United Rubber Workers job losses: *U.S. News & World Report*, May 21, 1979.

*p. 315*   General rubber industry background: *New York Times*, March 17, 1981.

*p. 316*   Uniroyal wage concessions: Ibid., Feb. 14, 1982.

*p. 316*   Tire firms' equity return 1975–80: Mar. 17, 1981.

*p. 317*   Hemorrhaging of Dayton: Peirce and Keefe, op. cit., p. 356.

*p. 317*   Data on Dayton in 1981: *New York Times*, Jan. 10, 1981.

*p. 317*   The 10,000 layoffs announced for Lackawanna plant: *ABC World News Tonight*, Dec. 27, 1982.

*p. 318*   Summary of steel problems, from 1947 to 1982: *U.S. News & World Report*, Sept. 13, 1982; and Gunther's quote is from op. cit., p. 615.

*p. 319*   Inland No. 7 furnace: *Washington Post*, Jan. 31, 1982.

*p. 319*   Steel firms diversify: Ibid., Nov. 23, 1981.

*p. 319*   U.S. Steel closes sixteen plants in 1979: Ibid., Aug. 2, 1982.

*p. 319*   Comparing national steel wages: *New York Times,* Nov. 28, 1982.

*p. 320*   Japan at 60 percent steel capacity: *Wall Street Journal,* Oct. 11, 1982.

*p. 320*   Footnote on British steel losses: *New York Times,* Sept. 6, 1982; French losses; Ibid., Oct. 8, 1982.

*p. 320*   Department of Transportation study: *Washington Post,* Oct. 24, 1982.

*p. 320*   Armco as paternalistic firm: *New York Times,* Dec. 12, 1981.
Armco slump in 1982: *Wall Street Journal,* Oct. 19, 1982.

*p. 321*   Long history of steelmaking in Youngstown: Peirce and Keefe, op. cit., p. 357.
Youngstown layoffs fit industry pattern: Garreau, op. cit., p. 80.

*p. 321*   Robert Aldrich quote: *New York Times,* Nov. 23, 1980.

*p. 322*   Steubenville's dirty air: Peirce, *The Megastates of America,* p. 336.

*p. 322*   Background on Steubenville: *The MacNeil-Lehrer Report,* Feb. 23, 1982.

*p. 322*   Weirton mill: *Parade* magazine, Dec. 12, 1982.

NEWARK

*p. 324*   Peirce quotes: From his *The Megastates of America,* p. 218.

*p. 324–25*   Newark's early history: *The Encyclopaedia Britannica,* 11th edition, 1911, Vol. 19, pp. 460–61.

*p. 325*   Newark problems in 1971: Peirce, *The Megastates of America,* p. 219.

*p. 326*   Governor Cahill tries to help: Ibid., p. 222.

*p. 326*   Newark in 1975: *U.S. News & World Report,* Apr. 7, 1975.

*p. 326*   Family income comparisons table: From HUD study of cities 1980.

*p. 327*   T. D. Allman observations: Allman, op. cit.

*p. 328*   Feature article on Newark: *New York Times,* Oct. 31, 1981.

*p. 328*   Background on Prudential: Ibid., Apr. 5, 1981.

**Chapter 10: NEW YORK CITY**

*p. 333*   Manhattan gains 150,700 jobs as Outer Boroughs lose 400 jobs: *New York Times,* Oct. 17, 1982.

*p. 334*   Work-force participation rates: Bureau of Labor Statistics study in 1981, U.S. Department of Labor, New York Regional Office.

CRIME: SLOW-MOTION RIOT

*p. 335*   Seventy-one of seventy-three police precincts show gain in robberies: Jack Newfield, "The Service Crisis" in *The Village Voice,* Apr. 15, 1981.

*p. 336*   Robert McGuire quote: *New York Times,* Nov. 18, 1980.
Crime complaints rise, arrests fall: Ibid., July 5, 1981.
"our manpower losses . . . caught up with us": Ibid.

*p. 336*   Middle-class neighborhoods and robbery: Newfield, op. cit.
Upper East Side cut in police: *New York Daily News,* Sept. 6, 1981.
Footnote on 77th Precinct in Brooklyn: *New York Times,* July 22, 1981.

*p. 337*   Insurance claims escalate in two years: *New York Times,* Jan. 31, 1982.

*p. 338*   Philadelphia Guardian Angel quote: Ibid., Aug. 7, 1981.
William L. McKechnie quote: From interview with author.

HOUSING: THE FORECLOSURE FLOOD

*p. 343*   South Bronx revival as industrial site: *Wall Street Journal,* Sept. 16, 1982.

*p. 344*   Decline of neighborhood services: *New York Daily News,* July 27, 1981.

HEALTH: MECCA IN RUINS?

*p. 348*   Ira Clark quote: From interview with author in 1979.
Irwin Birnbaum quote: From interview with author in 1981.

*p. 348*   "But what can you do without blood?": From interview with author in 1981.

*p. 349*   Aged, disabled and blind have high share local Medicaid costs: From report on city hospitals to Mayor Koch in June 1979.

*p. 350*   Carol Bellamy data on deinstitutionalization: From her 1979 report "From County Asylums to City Streets" as quoted in a letter from her in *New York Times*, dated Oct. 18, 1982.

*p. 351*   Koch attacks social services commissioner as "crazy lady": Wayne Barrett and Andrew W. Cooper, "Koch's 99 Attacks Against the Other New York" in *The Village Voice*, Apr. 15, 1981.

*p. 352*   Sara Connell quote: *New York Times*, in 1981.

*p. 352*   Jerry Wurf quote in footnote: *U.S. News & World Report*, Feb. 24, 1975.

*p. 353*   Fred Silverman quote: From interview with author in 1981.

*p. 353*   Footnote on mobile health van of South Bronx Lions Club: *New York Times*, Aug. 22, 1982.

*p. 355*   Judy Wessler quote in footnote: From interview with author in 1981.

*p. 355*   Leonard Piccoli quote: From interview with author in 1980.

THE SUBWAYS: CHAOS

*p. 358*   1975 fare hike: Joseph Conason, "10 Decisions That Wrecked the Transit System" in *The Village Voice*, Apr. 15, 1981.

*p. 358*   Samuel M. Ehrenhalt quotes: From interview with author in 1981.

*p. 358*   Richard Edmunds series on subways in spring of 1981 for *New York Daily News*.

*p. 359*   National Transportation Safety Board quote: Nicholas Pileggi, "Wounded City" in *New York*, Nov. 2, 1981.

*p. 359*   Comparison of subway car inspections: Ibid.

*p. 359*   Standard & Poor's quote: *New York Times*, Apr. 5, 1981.

*p. 359*   Lewis Rudin quote: Ibid.

*p. 360*   William Jovanovich quote: Ibid., Feb. 11, 1982.

*p. 360*   Data on number of cars entering city and the Samuel I. Schwartz quote are from NYC Transportation Department study: Ibid., Oct. 23, 1982.

*p. 361*   Data on congestion in city streets: Pileggi, "Wounded City." "traffic anarchy": *New York Times*, Dec. 5, 1982.

JOBS: TWO CITIES

*p. 362–63*   Office space figures through the years: Ibid., Jan. 31, 1982.

*p. 363*   Foreign banks expand branches: From advertising supplement to *New York Times*, Oct. 31, 1982, from The Real Estate Board of New York article by Martin Mayer.

*p. 363*   British mining and aerospace investments in Wall Street property: *New York Times*, Aug. 8, 1982.

*p. 363*   Much of foreign business material from Real Estate Board article by Martin Mayer.

*p. 364*   Table based on material from *New York Times*, Sept. 6, 1982. Manhattan job gains, March 1977 to March 1981: Ibid., Oct. 17, 1982. Professor Robert Lekachman quote: Ibid., Sept. 19, 1982.

*p. 364*   Desmond Smith, "Info City": *New York*, Feb. 9, 1981.

*p. 365*   Telephone, telegraph and utility job comparisons: Derived from New York Regional Office Bureau of Labor Statistics, U.S. Department of Labor.

*p. 365*   Wharton Econometric projection: *New York Times*, Jan. 21, 1980.

*p. 366*   Small stores' problems: *New York Daily News*, July 27, 1981.

*p. 367*   Factory losses from 1969 through 1981: New York Regional Office, Bureau of Labor Statistics, U.S. Department of Labor, 1981.

*p. 369*   Ad firms look at "Madison Avenue South": Ibid., Nov. 5, 1981.

*p. 370*   Computer job losses 1958 through 1979: Derived from New York Regional Office, Bureau of Labor Statistics, U.S. Department of Labor data.

*p. 370*   Brooklyn Naval Yard material: *New York Times*, Sept. 6, 1982.

*p. 370*   Sohmer pianos and New York piano making: Ibid., Aug. 13, 1982.

*p. 371*   Typesetting and manual typewriters: *New York Daily News*, Sept. 1, 1980.

*p. 372*   "Koch . . . said their demands were 'outrageous' . . .": Ken Auletta, *The Streets Were Paved with Gold*, Vintage Books, 1980, pp. 309–10.

*p. 373–74*   "inflation, good retail sales . . .": Report of NYC Office of Management and Budget to U.S. Treasury Department in 1980, quoted by Wayne Barrett, "Koch's Mythical Budget Miracle" in *The Village Voice*, Aug. 26, 1981.

*p. 374*   "Employment and retail sales have slowed . . .": Ibid.

*p. 375*   Some of the fiscal-crisis data from *New York Times*, Nov. 21, 1982.
Koch talks of reviving stock transfer tax: Ibid., Nov. 30, 1982.

*p. 375*   Professor Raymond Horton quote: *New York*, Dec. 13, 1982.

*p. 376*   The $156 million projection made in report by State Comptroller Edward Regan, released in summer 1981.

*p. 376*   Both Edward Regan quotes: Wayne Barrett, "Ned Regan's Double Standard" in *The Village Voice*, Mar. 16, 1982.

*p. 376*   New York's real-estate market: Robert Kuttner, *Revolt of the Haves*, Simon and Schuster, 1980, p. 170.

*p. 377*   Assemblyman Barbaro's real-estate charges made Aug. 27, 1981.

*p. 377*   Special Deputy Comptroller for New York City Sidney Schwartz data: Barrett, "Koch's Mythical Budget Miracle."

*p. 378–79*   Manufacturers Hanover sale: *New York Times*, Aug. 26, 1981.

*p. 379*   Undermanned Tax Commission: Kuttner, op. cit., pp. 190–92.

*p. 380*   $600 million a year in unpaid taxes: *New York Times*, Oct. 18, 1981.

*p. 380*   Councilwoman Ruth Messinger praises new City Hall reform, with qualification: Ibid.

*p. 381–82*   Schlesinger on La Guardia: Arthur M. Schlesinger, Jr., *The Politics of Upheaval*, Houghton Mifflin, 1960, pp. 130–33.

*p. 383*   Decline of Rome in 4th century: Michael Grant, *The Fall of the Roman Empire*, The Annenberg School Press, 1976, p. 138.
Salvain of Marseilles quote: Ibid., pp. 109–10.

*p. 384*   Palmerston quote on Paris in the 1850s: J.P.T. Bury, *Napoleon III and the Second Empire*, Harper & Row, 1968, p. 60.

*p. 385*   The excerpt at the end is from *Ulysses*, by Alfred, Lord Tennyson.

# BIBLIOGRAPHY

Michael Barone, Grant Ujifusa and Douglas Matthews. *The Almanac of American Politics 1980*. New York: E. P. Dutton, 1979.

*Business Week*. "The Reindustrialization of America." New York: McGraw-Hill Publications, 1980.

Editorial Research Reports. *American Regionalism*. Washington, D.C.: Congressional Quarterly, Inc., 1980.

Editorial Research Reports. *Education in America*. Washington, D.C.: Congressional Quarterly, Inc., 1981.

*The Encyclopedia Britannica: 11th edition*. New York: The Encyclopedia Britannica Company, 1911.

Joel Garreau. *The Nine Nations of North America*. Boston: Houghton Mifflin Company, 1981.

John Gunther. *Inside U.S.A.*. New York: Harper & Brothers, 1947.

William Harlan Hale. *Horace Greeley, Voice of the People*. New York: The Crowell-Collier Publishing Company, 1950.

Jane Jacobs. *The Death and Life of Great American Cities*. New York: Random House, 1961.

Joint Economic Committee of Congress. *The Regional and Urban Impacts of the Administration's Budget and Tax Proposals*. Report released on July 31, 1981. Washington, D.C. U.S. Government Printing Office, 1981.

Robert Kuttner. *Revolt of the Haves*. New York: Simon and Schuster, 1980.

Sidney Lens. *Radicalism in America*. New York: Thomas Y. Crowell, 1966.

Warren Leslie. *Dallas Public and Private*. New York: Grossman Publishers, 1964.

Jeanne R. Lowe. *Cities in a Race with Time*. New York: Random House, 1967.

W. E. Lunt. *History of England*. New York: Harper & Brothers, 1951.

Richard P. Nathan and James W. Fossett. *The Prospects for Urban Revival*. Princeton University draft, 1980.

Nation's Business. *Bicentennial Salute to America's Cities*. A 20-part series in 1975 and 1976. Washington, D.C.: U.S. Chamber of Commerce, 1975 and 1976.

Northeast-Midwest Congressional Coalition. *The State of the Region 1981: Economic Trends in the Northeast and Midwest*. Edited by Jacqueline Mazza and Bill Hogan. Washington, D.C., 1982.

Northeast-Midwest Congressional Coalition. *The Unprotected Flank: Regional and Strategic Imbalances in Defense Spending Patterns*. Edited by Jacqueline Mazza and Dale E. Wilkinson. Washington, D.C., 1980.

Neal R. Peirce. *The Deep South States of America*. New York: W. W. Norton & Company, 1974.

———. *The Great Plains States of America*. New York: W. W. Norton & Company, 1973.

———. *The Megastates of America*. New York: W. W. Norton & Company, 1972.

———. *The Mountain States of America*. New York: W. W. Norton & Company, 1972.

Neal R. Peirce and Michael J. Barone. *The Mid-Atlantic States of America*. New York: W. W. Norton & Company, 1976.

Neal R. Peirce and John Keefe. *The Great Lakes States of America*. New York: W. W. Norton & Company, 1980.

David C. Perry and Alfred J. Watkins, editors. *The Rise of the Sunbelt Cities*. Beverly Hills: Sage Publications, 1977.

Arthur M. Schlesinger, Jr. *The Politics of Upheaval*. Boston: Houghton Mifflin Company, 1960.

Jean-Jacques Servan-Schreiber. *The World Challenge*. New York: Simon and Schuster, 1981.

Southern Growth Policies Board. *Final Report 1980 Commission on the Future of the South*. Edited by Pat Watters. 1981.

James L. Spates and John J. Macionis. *The Sociology of Cities*. New York: St. Martin's Press, 1981.

Tricentennial Commission of Philadelphia. *Economic Development*. Edited by John M. L. Greenstein. Interim report for the Century IV Project, Center for Philadelphia Studies at the University of Pennsylvania, 1981.

Tricentennial Commission of Philadelphia. *Race, Poverty and*

*Unemployment.* Edited by Michael Petrovsky. Interim report for the Century IV Project, Center for Philadelphia Studies at the University of Pennsylvania, 1981.

U.S. Bureau of the Census. *Statistical Abstract of the United States: 1980* (101st edition). Washington, D.C.: Government Printing Office, 1980.

U.S. Bureau of Labor Statistics. *Employment and Earnings* report for December, 1980. Washington: General Printing Office, 1980.

U.S. Bureau of Labor Statistics, New York regional office, Various work force studies, 1981.

U.S. Department of Housing and Urban Development. *The President's National Urban Policy Report 1980.* Washington, D.C.: General Printing Office, 1980.

U.S. Federal Bureau of Investigation. *Uniform Crime Reports* for 1977 and for 1980. Washington, D.C.: Government Printing Office, 1978 and 1981.

James Wright. *The Coming Water Famine.* New York: Coward, 1966.

# INDEX

# INDEX